ALSO BY NEIL SIMON

Rewrites: A Memoir

THE COLLECTED PLAYS OF NEIL SIMON

VOLUME IV

BY NEIL SIMON

A TOUCHSTONE BOOK
PUBLISHED BY
SIMON & SCHUSTER

TOUCHSTONE
Rockefeller Center
1230 Avenue of the Americas
New York, NY 10020

First Touchstone Edition 1998

TOUCHSTONE and colophon are registered trademarks
of Simon & Schuster Inc.

Designed by Barbara M. Bachman

Manufactured in the United States of America

10   9   8   7   6   5

Library of Congress Cataloging-in-Publication Data
Simon, Neil.
    The collected plays of Neil Simon.
    Vol. 1 originally published under title:
The comedy of Neil Simon.
    Vols. 1–2 contain 15 plays originally published 1971–1979.
    Contents: v. 1. Come blow your horn—Barefoot in the park—The odd couple—[etc.]
    I. Title.
PS3537.I663   1986   812'.54   86-12639   CIP

ISBN 0-684-84785-X

HOW TO STOP WRITING
AND OTHER IMPOSSIBILITIES

*P*roposals, a play that was written and produced prior to this volume going to press, is to be my last play . . . maybe.

I presently have no thoughts for a new play, but that hasn't stopped me before. To quote Walter Kerr, a former reviewer for *The New York Times* and my favorite critic ever, from his opening night review of my December 1966 play, *The Star-Spangled Girl*, "Neil Simon didn't have an idea for a new play this year, but he wrote it anyway." It was the best bad review I ever received. From it I learned that if you do not have a burning passion to write a particular story, if you are not so eager to get to the typewriter in the morning and so reluctant to leave it when the sun begins to set, so driven that you're willing to forgo family, friends, food and sex, so preoccupied that you have trouble remembering your daughter's first name or that you've forgotten to remove your socks when taking a shower (if indeed you found time to take the shower), then don't write the play. It takes all that motivation just to make it a passable work. To make it something wonderful, to quote Hemingway, or to quote the biographer who quoted Hemingway, "The writing of a book [for me a play] should destroy the writer. If there is anything left, he has not worked hard enough. The writer himself does not matter, the book is everything."*

He said this when he was in his mid-thirties. I've just turned seventy, and I'd settle for getting out of bed in the morning without hurting and to hell with the play. At sixty-five, Hemingway ended his life with a double-barreled blast in Idaho, while at seventy, I'm still churning out three pages a day and more than likely planning an opening date for next year's opus. Hemingway's work finally

---

* From *Hemingway, the 1930s* by Michael Reynolds.

destroyed the writer, while I'm still bent over the typewriter, pounding the keys. . . . Papa Hemingway, am I not trying hard enough?

There is a vast difference between Hemingway and me, which any voting member of the Nobel Prize for Literature committee could tell you. He had a life. I had a career. I envied his life, but I would have been ill-suited to live it. I would never shoot a lion. I'd get no kick out of bringing down a tiger; an antelope's head on my wall wouldn't thrill me at all; and I'm sure I'd get sick at a bullfight as well.

I read three biographies of Hemingway and still haven't reached a conclusion as to whether he was courageous, daring and fearless or a bully. Coming to blows with a lightweight (in boxing-division terms) such as F. Scott Fitzgerald at a party in France did not endear him to me. But *The Old Man and the Sea* is a masterpiece, and with it came the world's acclaim (the fourth or fifth time over) and my awesome respect for his talent.

The closest I ever came to derring-do was killing a few small spiders in our kitchen to quiet the screams of my teenage daughter. I had put on the boxing gloves when I was a twelve-year-old schoolboy, taking on an opponent who was twice my weight, which might account for his decking me thirty-one seconds into the first round. I picked myself up, punched him in the glove instead of his face and I went down again. I told him I couldn't come out for the second round because I was late for supper. As a young boy I had no problem stepping on ants or an occasional snail. Growing boys need to show their power to nature once in a while, because they can't show it around the house. But now that I'm into my seventh decade, I walk carefully around all insects, giving them a wide berth. At my age, I deem their lives as precious as my own. If they add up good deeds and bad at the gates of Heaven, I want to knock quietly with a record on the right side of the ledger.

So why even bring up any comparisons of Hemingway to myself? No two writers could be more dissimilar in every aspect of their lives and their work. He is arguably one of the greatest writers in American letters, and I'm not one of those who would argue against it. I have my following, if longevity scores you points in the writers' weight room, but I have to fight off those detractors who attack me for committing the heinous crime of being "popular." To my credit, I will say, throwing humility to the winds, that being "popular" is a much greater attribute than being *"un*popular." Unless you're *very* unpopular, which might get you into a select group called "cult favorites." Being *"too* popular," however, is an unpardonable sin, at least if you had any thoughts of trying to be accepted by that lofty circle of writers who decide who does and who does not get into the Pantheon. I'm not sure where the Pantheon is. I think it used to be at 48th Street off Madison Avenue, but since Thai restaurants became the in thing, the Pantheon has relocated.

Actually, I'm not trying to get into anything. You reach a certain age in your life when you feel fortunate just to be able to ply your trade. I don't care how great a baseball player you are, you get between twelve and fifteen years to swing your bat (barring injuries) and then you get a loud salute from the fans on Old Timers Day even if you're only forty-two. But as a writer, even well past seventy and upward, no one can come and take your pen away. You can push it up and down on the pages you work on, stopping only when it becomes too heavy to lift, and today's ballpoints are a good deal lighter than those bulky, leaky ink holders that stained your fingers and blotched your script when you were a boy, no matter how beautiful they look today in the window of your better antique stores.

No, what I want is exactly what Hemingway wanted, and in this one area, we have something in common. To conclude the quote attributed to him at the beginning of this introduction, he said, "What you pray for after all the praise for your last one is a good, solid idea for your next project." That pursuit can turn even energetic and talented young writers into doddering old fools and can have some two-time National Book Award winner moaning to himself, "I'm through. That's it. I'll tell my agent to get me a movie."

Perhaps Hemingway spent months each year chasing marlins off the Florida Keys or even risking death as a rhino picked up his scent in the bush, kicking up the dust around him, ready to charge, just so the great novelist could avoid starting that next book. A bad review in *The New York Times* or *Saturday Review of Literature* could cause him greater calamity than if the rhino hit him at full speed, sending him flying into a Nairobi hospital, where a seven-month recuperation was far more pleasant than a failed work. The one phone call a writer never wants to get is the one from his publisher asking, "How's the new book going?"

I am never short of ideas. What I *am* short of is *good* ideas, and knowing what's good and what's *not* good is a dicier business than you suppose.

There is no point going to my office if I have nothing that I care enough about to commit to for the next year or two of my life. My hobbies or avocations take up so little time that I cannot use them as an excuse for not writing. An hour and a half of tennis, two, sometimes three days a week, gives you no realistic alibi for not working. However, once I'm a quarter or a third of the way into a new play, I can feel the excitement flowing through my bloodstream. You're so anxious to get the words down, your mind is rushing faster than your fingers can write. You're in the zone, as the athletes call it. Those rich ideas, however, do not come along that often. Since I've written thirty plays in thirty-six years, you would call that being extremely prolific. But if you cross out the six or seven ideas I committed to paper and then to production that should have been committed to the back of a filing cabinet, a fairer estimate would be that I had one good idea every two years, and coming up with that good idea does not automatically mean that you will do it justice. So let's say that I had one good idea every three years, and if I had known that beforehand, I might have gone on those safaris with Hemingway (although I don't think I'd have gotten through the tetanus shots).

Where does an idea for a play come from, anyway? And once started, how do you know it's any good? The answers to those questions are so flimsy (speaking to fledgling writers now) that you can release your bated breath because you'll learn very little from my next sentence . . . I'm not sure where they come from, and knowing it's a good idea, when you get one, can dissipate after a week or two of enthusiastic writing as quickly as snow melting in Jacksonville, Florida.

Even when an idea flashes across my brain like a comet in the sky, I have to quickly jot down a sentence or two before the comet diminishes into oblivion. I never try to think past the first two minutes of a play on that first day. Better to put your toe in the water before plunging into an icy pool, because chances are the latter approach will cool off your ardor before its time. I'll try to think of a title as soon as I can, to use as a road map that will keep me from wandering off onto some country road that leads nowhere. *The*

Sunshine Boys came in an instant because they were what the play was all about. It gave me both the story and the conflict. The story was about two ex-vaudevillians who come out of retirement to do one last show. The "sunshine" in the title was the irony because there was nothing but bickering between these two old war horses. Just a few short thoughts like that begin to shape the play for me. Having gotten that far in the thinking process, the water now seems safe enough to get in as far as your ankles.

At this point, probably the second day of work, I start doodling the names of the lead characters on my pad. Vaudevillians usually had catchy names just in case their act wasn't all that good. I called them Lewis and Clark, appropriating the names of the two great explorers, then filled in the rest, to wit Al Lewis and Willie Clark. Since Clark had the more dominant role, I thought Willie was a stronger name than Al. It's a writer's prerogative. You don't have to agree. By the third day, I knew how they dressed, where they lived, how many children they had. (Willie had none, just a nephew to rely on; I figured the lonelier he was, the more exasperating he was.) I knew that Al's wife had died and that it was a loss to him but that Willie's wife probably divorced him years before and married a piano player. It helped the audience understand why he was so difficult to get along with.

There is a stimulating sense of joy when you create characters who never existed before in anyone's mind but your own, when you give them a history, a philosophy and a destiny. In due time, you take two steps to the side and let them live out their lives either as they'd want to do or as they couldn't help avoiding, since character, the Greeks tell us, is fate. As on the cover of the famous album of *My Fair Lady*, there was George Bernard Shaw, somewhere up in the heavens, with strings on his fingers manipulating the lives and movements of Professor Higgins and Eliza Doolittle. Shaw was no fool, of course, and he knew, as all good writers know, that if you pull the strings too tightly, they will snap and your characters will fall out of your reach, floundering about helplessly, losing their most important attribute—their own truth. Instead of controlling your characters, you must collaborate with them and, in time, become a witness to their behavior. In the end, you may think you have written it, but if you do your work well, you find you were merely there to put to paper everything they said and lived through.

If you wrote a false line, they simply wouldn't say it. (Well, they *would* say it because you're forcing them to, but no one hearing it would accept it.) You finally know you've succeeded when the curtain goes up on opening night, and you feel as though you went to the box office and bought a ticket and gazed with childlike surprise at the developments going on in that world beyond the footlights. You sense that you had as little to do with it as the couple sitting next to you in the theater. Not too long after that, you make the ultimate sacrifice. You give them up, just as you give up your children when they enter adulthood.

Alas, unlike your children, who may only call you once in a while, your created children *never* phone you. It does give you a thrill, however, to know that they are well and you hear that they are traveling now, to London, Paris, Australia and South Africa, or even that they're spending time as close as the Paper Mill Playhouse in New Jersey.

The five plays in this volume are all examples of this process, with varying degrees of success, depending on your point of view. It's not necessary for you to like them all, but if you do get involved with their lives, their troubles, their joys, their humor and their fallibilities, then you and I haven't completely wasted our time. In looking at how I pulled the strings, once in a while you'll find I got them hopelessly entangled, and at other times, I completely disappeared and became a voyeur—a voyeur to a few characters on these pages who, to this day, still haunt me.

Neil Simon

Los Angeles, CA

September 23, 1997

RUMORS

A FARCE

NEIL SIMON

ACT I

Scene: A large, tastefully renovated, Victorian house in Sneden's Landing, New York, about forty minutes from the city. Despite its age and gingerbread exterior, the interior is modern, mono-chromatic and sparkling clean. A nice combination.

An entrance doorway at Upstage Right leads onto an open vestibule. To the right of the door is a powder room. One step down is the large and comfortable living room. The color is predominately white.

There are two furniture groupings in the living room. Stage Right are a love seat and two chairs. Upstage of the love seat and near the powder room door is a table and a telephone with a long cord. Center Stage is a large sofa and coffee table. Two chairs Stage Left are part of a grouping with the sofa. On the Stage Left wall is a mirror in an ornate frame. Against the Upstage wall are a well-stocked bar and a stereo system enclosed in a gorgeous cabinet. Between these two pieces is a closed door leading to the cellar.

From the living room, a curved staircase leads to a landing and two doors; each to a bedroom. On the landing is a railed ban-nister. At the Stage Left end of the second-floor landing is an archway leading to a hallway and more bedrooms. Downstage of this archway is an extension of the balcony which can be used as a playing area.

Through the living room, at Left, double doors lead into a dining room and then, the kitchen. A huge window above the front door looks out onto a wooded backyard. A large window in the Stage Right wall overlooks a yard and the driveway beyond. Headlights of approaching cars may be seen through this window.

At Rise: It is about eight-thirty at night on a pleasant evening in May.

CHRIS GORMAN, *an attractive woman, mid-thirties, paces anxiously back and forth, looking at her watch, biting her nails. SHE is elegantly dressed in a designer gown. SHE looks at the phone, then at her watch again. SHE seems to make a decision and crosses to the cigarette box on the coffee table. SHE takes out a cigarette, then puts it back.*

CHRIS. Oh, my God!

(*Suddenly, Charley's bedroom door opens on the second landing and KEN GORMAN, about forty, dressed smartly in a tuxedo but looking flushed and excited, comes out to the rail. THEY BOTH speak rapidly.*)

KEN. Did he call yet?
CHRIS. Wouldn't I have yelled up?
KEN. Call him again.
CHRIS. I called him twice. They're looking for him . . . How is he?
KEN. I'm not sure. He's bleeding like crazy.
CHRIS. Oh, my God!
KEN. It's all over the room. I don't know why people decorate in white . . . If he doesn't call in two minutes, call the hospital.
CHRIS. I'm going to have to have a cigarette, Ken.
KEN. After eighteen months, the hell you are. Hold on to yourself, will you?

(*HE rushes back in, closes the door behind him. SHE returns to pacing.*)

CHRIS. I can't believe this is happening. (*SHE crosses to the cigarette box. The PHONE rings.*) Oh, God! (*SHE calls out.*) Ken, the phone is ringing. (*But HE's gone. SHE crosses to phone and picks it up.*) Hello? Dr. Dudley? . . . Oh, Dr. Dudley, I'm so glad it's you. Your service said you were at the theater.

(*Charley's bedroom door opens, KEN looks out.*)

KEN. Is that the doctor?

CHRIS. *(Into phone.)* I never would have bothered you, but this is an emergency.

KEN. Is that the doctor?

CHRIS. *(Into the phone.)* I'm Chris Gorman. My husband Ken and I are good friends of Charley Brock's.

KEN. Is that the doctor?

CHRIS. *(Turns, holds phone, yells at Ken.)* It's the doctor! It's the doctor!

KEN. *(Angrily.)* Why didn't you say so? *(HE goes back in, closes the door.)*

CHRIS. *(Into the phone.)* Dr. Dudley, I'm afraid there's been an accident . . . I would have called my own doctor, but my husband is a lawyer and under the circumstances, he thought it better to have Charley's own physician . . . Well, we just arrived here at Charley's house about ten minutes ago, and as we were getting out of our car, we suddenly heard this enormous—

(KEN suddenly comes out of the bedroom)

KEN. Don't say anything!

CHRIS. *(To Ken.)* What?

KEN. Don't tell him what happened!

CHRIS. Don't tell him?

KEN. Just do what I say.

CHRIS. What about Charley?

KEN. He's all right. It's just a powder burn. Don't tell him about the gunshot.

CHRIS. But they got the doctor out of the theater.

KEN. Tell him he tripped down the stairs and banged his head. He's all right.

CHRIS. But what about the blood?

KEN. The bullet went through his earlobe. It's nothing. I don't want him to know.

CHRIS. But I already said we were getting out of the car and we suddenly heard an enormous—what? What did we hear?

KEN. *(Coming downstairs.)* We heard . . .

CHRIS. *(Into phone.)* Just a minute, doctor.

KEN. *(Thinks, coming downstairs.)* We heard . . . we heard . . . we heard . . . an enormous—*thud!*

CHRIS. Thud?

KEN. When he tripped down the stairs.

CHRIS. Good. Good. That's good. *(Into phone.)* Dr. Dudley? I'm sorry. I was talking to my husband. Well, we heard this enormous *thud!* It seemed Charley tripped going up the stairs.

KEN. *Down!* Down the stairs.

CHRIS. *Down* the stairs. But he's all right.

KEN. He's sitting up in bed. He'll call him in the morning.

CHRIS. He's sitting up in bed. He'll call him in the morning.

KEN. *You!*

CHRIS. *You!* He'll call *you* in the morning.

KEN. You're very sorry you disturbed him.

CHRIS. I'm very sorry I disturbed you.

KEN. But he's really fine.

CHRIS. But he's really fine.

KEN. Thank you. Goodbye.

CHRIS. *(To Ken.)* Where are you going?

KEN. *Him! Him!* Thank *him* and say goodbye.

CHRIS. Oh. *(Into phone.)* Thank you and goodbye, Doctor . . . What? . . . Just a minute. *(To Ken as HE goes upstairs.)* Any dizziness?

KEN. No. No dizziness.

CHRIS. *(Into phone.)* No. No dizziness . . . What? *(To Ken.)* Can he move his limbs?

KEN. *(Irritated.)* Yes! He can move everything. Get off the phone.

CHRIS. *(Yells at Ken.)* They got him out of *Phantom of the Opera.* *(Into phone.)* Yes, he can move everything . . . What? *(To Ken.)* Any slurring of the speech?

KEN. NO! NO SLURRING OF THE SPEECH.

CHRIS. *(To Ken.)* Don't yell at me. He'll hear it. *(Into phone.)* No. No slurring of the speech.

KEN. I've got to get back to Charley. *(KEN starts to back into Charley's room.)*

CHRIS. *(Into phone.)* Any what? *(To Ken.)* Any ringing of the ears?

KEN. I can't believe this . . . No. Tell him no.

CHRIS. *(Into phone.)* Yes! A little ringing in the ears.

KEN. I told you to say no.

CHRIS. It sounds more believable to have ringing.

KEN. Jesus!

CHRIS. (*Into phone.*) Who? His wife? Myra? . . . Yes. Myra's here.

KEN. (*Rushing downstairs.*) She's *not* here. Don't tell him she's here. He'll want to speak to her.

CHRIS. (*Into phone.*) Dr. Dudley? My mistake. She's not here. I thought she was but she wasn't.

KEN. She just stepped out. She'll be back in a minute.

CHRIS. (*Into phone.*) She just stepped back. She'll be out in a minute. Yes. I'll tell her to call.

(*KEN goes back upstairs.*)

CHRIS. . . . Okay, thank you, Dr. Diddley . . . Dudley. Enjoy the show. Ken and I saw it, we loved it . . . Especially the second act. Who's playing the Phantom tonight?

KEN. Are you going to review the whole Goddamn show? (*KEN goes back into Charley's room.*)

CHRIS. Oh, Charley's calling me. (*Calls out.*) Just a minute, Charley. (*Into phone.*) He sounds a lot better. I have to go. Yes, Doctor, I will. (*SHE hangs up, furious at Ken.*) Don't you *ever* do that to me again. He must suspect something. I didn't get his name right once.

KEN. (*Coming out of the bedroom.*) If anyone calls again, don't answer it. (*HE starts to go into the bedroom.*)

CHRIS. Then why did you tell me to answer that one?

KEN. Because I thought the bullet went through his head, not his earlobe. Fix me a double vodka, I left Charley standing in the shower.

CHRIS. If he drowns, you're making that call.

(*KEN goes into the bedroom.*)

CHRIS. I don't know why we're always the first ones here. (*SHE fixes the vodka.*) Never came late once in our lives. Someone else could have dealt with all this. (*SHE goes to the cigarette box once more. The DOORBELL rings. SHE jumps.*) Oh, SHIT! Shit shit shit shit!

(*The upstairs door opens, KEN comes out.*)

KEN. Who's that? Who is that?

CHRIS. Am I near the door? Do you see people in here? You think I'm on roller skates?

KEN. Let me think a minute.

CHRIS. Take your time because I don't answer doors. I only speak to Dr. Dudley.

KEN. All right. It's got to be Lenny or Ernie, one of the others. We've got to open the door.

CHRIS. You've got arms, reach down.

KEN. I've got to dry Charley off and bandage his ear. Don't tell them what happened. I need a few minutes to figure this out. Can't you stall them?

CHRIS. His best friends are coming to his tenth anniversary, his wife isn't here, he shoots himself in the earlobe and I'm supposed to make small talk when they come in?

KEN. Attempted suicide is a criminal offense, not to mention a pretty ugly scandal. Charley's deputy mayor of New York. He's my client and my best friend, I've got to protect him, don't I? Just play the hostess for a few minutes until I figure out how to handle this.

(The DOORBELL rings again.)

CHRIS. Play the hostess? There's no food out, there's no ice in the bucket. Where's the help? Where's the cheese dip? Where's Myra? What am I supposed to do till you get back, play charades? I'm lucky I can still speak English.

KEN. You're a lawyer yourself, can't you figure out something to say?

CHRIS. Contracts! I draw up legal publishing contracts. If someone walks in the door and wants to make a deal, I CAN HANDLE THAT!!

KEN. Take it easy. Calm down. I'll be right back.

(The DOORBELL rings again.)

CHRIS. Put some slippers on Charley and tell him to answer it.

KEN. *(Yells.)* Would you relax? Drink my vodka.

CHRIS. Why is a vodka better than two puffs of a cigarette?

KEN. Because they know you quit and if they see smoke in here, they'll know something is wrong.

CHRIS. You mean falling at their feet is going to look better?

(The DOORBELL rings impatiently.
KEN runs into the bedroom and closes the door. CHRIS crosses to the front door. SHE opens it.
CLAIRE rushes into the living room. SHE's an attractive woman in an evening gown. SHE holds a handkerchief to the side of her mouth, a purse in the other hand.)

CHRIS. Claire, darling, you look beautiful. Where's Lenny?

CLAIRE. *(Coming in.)* In the car. We had an accident. Brand new BMW, two days old, the side door is smashed in. Don't tell Charley and Myra, I don't want to ruin tonight for them. *(SHE crosses to mirror and looks at her face.)*

CHRIS. Oh, my God! Are you hurt?

CLAIRE. My lip is swelling up. *(Looks in the wall mirror.)* Oh, Jesus, I look like a trumpet player.

CHRIS. Where's Lenny?

CLAIRE. He's coming. He's walking slowly, he's got whiplash. His seat belt went right around his neck, and pulled him straight up. I left him dangling.

CHRIS. Oh, sweetheart, I'm sorry. Is there anything I can do?

CLAIRE. Just don't tell Myra. This party means so much to her.

LENNY comes in through the front door. He's wearing a tuxedo, one hand holds the back of his neck, in the other arm HE has a gift box from Steuben's.)

LENNY. *(In pain, but smiles. His neck is stiff.)* Hi, Charley! Hi, Myra! We're here, kids.

CHRIS. They're upstairs, Lenny.

LENNY. *(To Chris.)* Did she tell you what happened? Some stupid bastard shoots out of his garage like a Polaris rocket. I've got four doors on one side of the car now.

CHRIS. How does your neck feel?

LENNY. Stretched out, over to one side. I look like a Modigliani painting. *(HE crosses to the phone.)*

CHRIS. Do you want a drink?

LENNY. I don't think I could swallow past my shoulders.

CLAIRE. Of all nights to happen.

LENNY. Here's their gift. Steuben glass. *(HE shakes box. We hear broken glass RATTLE.)* If someone brings them a bottle of glue, they'll have a nice gift. *(HE starts to dial, carefully.)*

CLAIRE. *(Looks at her mouth in a hand mirror.)* I could have lost the tip of my tongue. I'd be speaking Gaelic the rest of my life.

LENNY. *(Waiting for his call.)* A brand new, spotless car, never touched by human hands. Buffed and polished by German women in Munich and now it looks like a war memorial. *(Into phone.)* Hello? This is Leonard Ganz. Is Dr. Dudley there, please?

CHRIS. Dr. Dudley?

LENNY. *(Into phone.)* Yes, it is. I have a whiplash injury . . . I see . . . Do you know what theater he's in?

CHRIS. Oh, God, I need a cigarette so badly.

LENNY. Could you? It's important. I'm at—*(HE looks at phone.)* 914-473-2261 . . . Thank you very much. *(HE hangs up.)*

CLAIRE. I've got to settle my stomach. Is there anything to eat? Some canapes or something?

CHRIS. Gee, I don't see anything.

CLAIRE. No canapes? Where's the cook, Mai Li? She makes great canapes.

CHRIS. Mai Li? I didn't see her. I think she's off this week.

CLAIRE. The week of their anniversary party?

CHRIS. I think she had to go back to Japan. Her mother was sick.

CLAIRE. Mai Li is Chinese.

CHRIS. I know. Her mother was visiting Japan.

LENNY. *(Still bracing his neck.)* I can only look up. I hope tall people are coming to this party . . . Where's Ken?

CHRIS. Ken? He went to the bathroom.

LENNY. And where's Charley and Myra?

CHRIS. They're still getting dressed.

LENNY. They're not ready? We had a *car* accident and we're on time.

CLAIRE. *(Looks in hand mirror again.)* My lip is getting gigantic. I don't think I have enough lipstick to cover it.

LENNY. No nuts or pretzels? I didn't even have lunch today. Three goddamn audits with the IRS on an empty stomach. *(HE gets up.*) Claire, get me a Diet Coke, please, and something to munch on. (*HE starts for the stairs.*)

CHRIS. Where are you going?

LENNY. To the john. I haven't had a chance to do that either.

CHRIS. There's a guest powder room down here.

LENNY. Isn't Ken using that?

CHRIS. No, he's using the one in the guest bedroom upstairs.

LENNY. (*Pointing to the powder room.*) Why didn't he use this one?

CHRIS. I don't know. He said he had to go badly and he ran upstairs.

LENNY. If he had to go so bad, the one downstairs is closer.

CHRIS. You know how it is when you have to go badly. You don't want to stop running.

LENNY. But this is a shorter run.

CLAIRE. Lenny, it's not an Olympic event. Why don't you just go?

LENNY. That's why they build guest bathrooms. (*Starts for powder room.*) If Dr. Dudley calls, I'll be right out. (*HE goes into powder room and closes door.*)

CHRIS. Claire, we have to talk.

CLAIRE. (*Goes to sit near Chris.*) What is it?

CHRIS. I'm coming apart at the seams.

CLAIRE. Your dress?

CHRIS. No, my nerves. I think I'm going to crack.

CLAIRE. I can see. (*Taking Chris's hand.*) Your hands are like ice. Something is going on here, isn't it?

CHRIS. Oh, God, you're so smart. You're so quick to see things.

CLAIRE. You're scaring me, Chris. Tell me what's happening.

CHRIS. Well, all right. Ken and I arrived here about ten minutes ago, when suddenly we heard this enormous . . .

(*Charley's bedroom door opens. KEN steps out.*)

KEN. Hey, Claire! You look lovely.

CHRIS. Yes! I was just telling her that. She looks enormously well, doesn't she? (*To Claire.*) Isn't that the dress you wore for Cerebral Palsy?

CLAIRE. No. I got this for Sickle Cell. Hi, Ken.

KEN. Where's Lenny?

CLAIRE. He's in the john. Where's Charley and Myra?

CHRIS. (*To Ken.*) Still getting dressed?

KEN. Yes. Still getting dressed . . . How's the new BMW? Is Len happy with it?

CLAIRE. Delirious.

KEN. Did he get the new features he asked for?

CLAIRE. More than he asked for.

KEN. Great.

CLAIRE. Are you through in the bathroom, Ken? I have to go myself. (*SHE starts for the stairs.*)

KEN. I think Myra's in there.

CLAIRE. Then I'll use Mai Li's bathroom. Call me if she gets back from Japan. (*SHE goes into the kitchen.*)

KEN. (*Waves his arms at Chris.*) Up here! Quick!

(*CHRIS rushes up the stairs.*)

KEN. Hurry up!

(*Breathlessly, SHE gets there.*)

KEN. What did you tell her?

CHRIS. I can't remember.

KEN. You can't remember?

CHRIS. I couldn't follow it, I was talking so fast. Why can't we tell them the truth? They're going to find out anyway.

KEN. I don't *know* the truth yet. Charley is still mumbling. Now go inside. He wants to see you.

CHRIS. See *me*? Why does he want to see me?

KEN. He's crying like a baby. I can't stop him. He needs a woman.

CHRIS. . . . To do what?

KEN. To cry on. I can reason with him but I can't comfort him. Let him cry on your shoulder for two minutes, for crise sakes.

CHRIS. (*Starting into Charley's room.*) Is he still bleeding? I paid twelve hundred dollars for this dress.

(*SHE goes in and closes the door just as LENNY comes out of the powder room.*)

KEN. Oh, hi, Len!

LENNY. (*Looks up, winces.*) Oh, Jesus. (*HE grabs his neck.*) Hi, Ken. Did you hear about the BMW?

KEN. Yeah. Congratulations. Excuse me. (*HE turns to go.*)

LENNY. Where are you going?

KEN. To the john.

LENNY. Didn't you just go?

KEN. . . . Yes. But not enough. Be right with you.

(*HE goes into the guest room, just as CLAIRE comes out of the kitchen with a bag of pretzels, unopened.*)

CLAIRE. This is very weird.

LENNY. Give me the pretzels. (*HE grabs the bag.*)

CLAIRE. (*Pours two Cokes.*) There's plenty of food in the kitchen, but nothing's cooked.

LENNY. Why didn't you open this first? (*HE struggles with the bag.*)

CLAIRE. There's a duck, roast ham, smoked turkey, all defrosting on the table. There's pasta sitting in a pot with no water.

(*LENNY can't open the bag. HE bites into it.*)

CLAIRE. Everything's ready to go, but no one's there to start it. Doesn't that seem strange to you?

LENNY. Not as strange as him peeing twice in a row . . . Have you got something sharp, a nail file or something?

CLAIRE. Chris started to tell me something and then she clammed up.

LENNY. The door on my BMW opened like tissue paper but this thing is like steel.

CLAIRE. Her hands were as cold as ice. She couldn't look me straight in the eye.

LENNY. This would be a safe place to keep your jewelry!! (*HE tries one last time to open it, then throws it away.*) Goddammit!!

CLAIRE. And why are they taking so long to get dressed? What is that about, heh?

LENNY. What are you so damn suspicious for? Give the people a chance to come down.

CLAIRE. Oh, you don't notice anything is wrong?

LENNY. Yes, I noticed. I noticed the towels in the bathroom were piled up on the sink and not on the rack. I noticed there's only a sheet-and-a-half left on the toilet paper. I think it's sloppy, but not a scandal.

CLAIRE. Really? Well, I'm not so sure I'd rule out a scandal. (*SHE walks away from him.*)

LENNY. You think I don't know what you're talking about? I hear what's going on. I hear gossip, I hear rumors and I won't listen to that crap, you understand. He is my friend, she is the wife of my friend.

CLAIRE. Fine! Okay, then forget it.

LENNY. I don't listen to filth and garbage about my friends.

CLAIRE. I said forget it.

LENNY. (*Looks at her.*) . . . All right. Come here. (*HE walks to the extreme Downstage Right corner of the living room.*)

CLAIRE. What's wrong with here?

LENNY. They could hear us there. Here is better. Will you come here!

(*SHE crosses to him. HE looks around, then to her.*)

LENNY. It's not good.

CLAIRE. What's not good?

LENNY. What I heard.

CLAIRE. What did you hear?

LENNY. Will you lower your voice?

CLAIRE. Why? We haven't said anything yet.

LENNY. All right. There's talk going around about Myra and— This hurts me. Stand on my other side. I can't turn.

(*SHE turns with her back to him. HE moves to her other side.*)

LENNY. There's talk going around about Myra and Charley. Only no one will tell it to my face because they know I won't listen.

CLAIRE. I'll listen. Tell it to my face.

LENNY. Why would you want to hear things about our best friends? He's my best client. He trusts me. Not just about investments and taxes, but personal things.

CLAIRE. I don't do his taxes, what's the rumors?

LENNY. Jesus, you won't be satisfied till you hear, will you?

CLAIRE. I won't even *sleep* with you until I hear. What's the rumors?

LENNY. . . . All right. Your friend Myra upstairs is having herself a little thing, okay?

CLAIRE. What kind of thing?

LENNY. Do I have to spell it out? A thing. A guy. A man. A fella. A kid. An affair. She's doing something with someone on the sly somewhere and it's not with Charley. Okay?

CLAIRE. You don't know that. You only heard it. You haven't seen it.

LENNY. Of course I haven't seen it. You think they invite me to come along? What's wrong with you?

CLAIRE. You are so naive, it's incredible. Get real, Lenny. Myra's not having anything with anybody. Your friend, Charley, however, is running up a hell of a motel bill.

LENNY. Charley? My friend, Charley? No way. Not a chance. He wouldn't even look at another woman.

CLAIRE. He may not be looking at her, but he's screwing her.

LENNY. Will you lower your voice! . . . Where did you hear this?

CLAIRE. Someone at the tennis club told me.

LENNY. *Our* tennis club?

CLAIRE. What is it, a sacred temple? People gossip there.

LENNY. Christ! Bunch of hypocrites. Sit around in their brand-new Nikes and Reeboks destroying people's lives . . . Who told you this?

CLAIRE. I'm not going to tell you because you don't like this person anyway.

LENNY. What's the difference if I like them or not? Who told you?

CLAIRE. Carole Newman.

LENNY. CAROLE NEWMAN?? I knew it, I knew it. I *hate* that Goddamn woman. She's got a mouth big enough to swallow a can of tennis balls.

(The guest room door opens and KEN steps out onto the landing.)

KEN. *(Affably.)* How you two doing?

LENNY. Hey! Just fine, Ken.

KEN. Had anything to eat yet?

LENNY. Just a plastic bag.

KEN. Great! Be right back.

(KEN goes into Charley's bedroom and closes the door.)

LENNY. Wasn't it Carole Newman who spread the other rumor?

CLAIRE. What other rumor?

LENNY. The rumor that you and I were breaking up.

CLAIRE. No. It wasn't Carole Newman.

LENNY. It wasn't? Then who was it?

CLAIRE. It was me.

LENNY. *You* started the rumor?

CLAIRE. Me, you, the both of us. When we were thinking about separating, didn't we go around telling everyone?

LENNY. We told friends. That bitch told strangers.

CLAIRE. Hey! Hey! Do *not* call Carole Newman a bitch to my face. Besides, Carole Newman didn't start the rumor about Charley. Someone else at the club told her. (SHE *walks to the bar.*)

LENNY. Who was the one who told her?

CLAIRE. Harold Green.

LENNY. Harold Green? Who the hell is Harold Green?

CLAIRE. He's a new member. He was just voted in last week.

LENNY. I never voted for him.

CLAIRE. Yes, you did. By proxy. We were in Bermuda.

LENNY. I don't believe it. A goddam proxy new member spreads rumors about my best friend? Who does he play tennis with?

CLAIRE. He doesn't play tennis. He's a social member. He just eats lunches there.

LENNY. . . . This son of a bitch is a non-playing proxy social new member who just eats lunches and spreads rumors? What does he do for a living?

CLAIRE. He sells BMWs.

(Charley's bedroom door opens and KEN steps out.)

KEN. Did anyone else get here yet?

CLAIRE. Not to speak of, no.

LENNY. Is anything wrong?

KEN. (*Coming downstairs.*) Why? Does anything seem wrong to you?

LENNY. You mean aside from the fact there's no food, no guests, no host, no hostess, and that you and Chris only appear one-at-a-time and never together. Yes, I'd say something was wrong.

KEN. Okay. (*HE's looking at the floor, thinking.*) Okay, sit down, Len, Claire.

(*LENNY and CLAIRE sit. HE sits in the chair opposite.*)

KEN. All right, I can't keep this quiet anymore . . . We've got a big problem on our hands.

LENNY. (*To Claire.*) Aha! What did I just say, Claire?

CLAIRE. You just said, "Aha!" What is it, Ken? Tell us.

KEN. Charley . . . Charley, er . . . Charley's been shot.

CLAIRE. *WHAT???*

LENNY. *SHOT???*

CLAIRE. Oh, my God!

LENNY. Jesus Christ!

CLAIRE. Don't tell me this!

LENNY. I can't catch my breath.

CLAIRE. Please don't let it be true.

LENNY. (*Wailing.*) *Charley, Charley, no! No, Charley, no!!!*

KEN. Take it easy, he's not dead. He's all right.

CLAIRE. He's not dead?

LENNY. He's all right?

KEN. He's alive. He's okay.

LENNY. Thank God, he's alive!

CLAIRE. Where was he shot?

KEN. In the head.

CLAIRE. In the *head*? The *head*? Oh, my, God, he was shot in the *head*!!!

KEN. It's all right. It's not bad. It's a superficial wound.

LENNY. Where did the bullet go?

KEN. Through his left ear lobe.

CLAIRE. The ear lobe? That's not too bad. I have holes in my ear lobes, it doesn't hurt.

LENNY. I saw this coming, I swear. The truth, Ken, did *she* do it?

KEN. Who?

LENNY. Myra, for crise sakes. Who else would it be?

KEN. Why would Myra shoot Charley?

CLAIRE. You don't know what's going on?

LENNY. You haven't heard?

KEN. No. What's going on?

CLAIRE. Charley's been having a hot affair with someone.

LENNY. It's not hot. You don't know if it's hot. Nobody said it was hot. *(To Ken.)* It's an affair. A plain affair.

KEN. *(To Lenny.)* Who told you this?

LENNY. Nobody told me *that*. What I heard was that *Myra* was having a thing.

KEN. A thing with who?

LENNY. A man. A guy. A fellow. A kid. Who knows?

CLAIRE. Someone else told me it was *Charley* who was having the affair.

KEN. What someone else?

LENNY. Some bitch at the club named Carole Newman.

CLAIRE. She is *not* a bitch. And she only told me what Harold Green told her.

KEN. Who's Harold Green?

LENNY. *(Quickly.)* Some goddamn proxy new social member who doesn't even play tennis. Comes to the club to eat lunches and spread rumors.

CLAIRE. Well, it seems to me Charley's the one who's having the affair if Myra was hysterical enough to shoot him.

KEN. Listen to me, will you, please? Myra didn't shoot him. *Charley* fired the gun. He tried to kill himself. It was attempted suicide.

CLAIRE. *SUICIDE???*

LENNY. Jesus Christ!

CLAIRE. Oh, my God!

LENNY. Don't tell me that.

CLAIRE. I don't believe it.

LENNY. *(Wailing.) No, Charley, no! Charley, Charley, no!*

KEN. Will you stop it! It's enough grieving. He's all right.

CLAIRE. Oh, Charley.

LENNY. It's all because of that no-good fucking Harold Green. That guy's out of the club. I can get the votes.

KEN. Can we stick to the main topic here? Nobody knows if anybody had an affair. I don't *know* why Charley shot himself.

LENNY. *(To Ken.)* So how is Myra taking this? My God, she must be a wreck.

CLAIRE. *(Rising.)* I should go up to her. Let me go up to her.

KEN. *(Stopping Claire.)* Don't go up to her. There's no point in going up to her. She's not here. She's gone.

CLAIRE. She's gone? Charley shoots himself in the head and Myra leaves the house?

LENNY. She walks out on him *now*? *Now* when he's laying up there with a bullet in his ear?

KEN. It's not in his ear. It went *through* his ear. WILL YOU LISTEN TO ME? PLEASE!!! . . . Maybe she wasn't even here when it happened. Chris and I were driving up when we heard the shot. The front door was locked. I ran around the back and broke in the kitchen window.

CLAIRE. I saw that. I thought maybe Mai Li did it and maybe Myra fired her. But I didn't know then that Mai Li's mother was sick in Japan.

LENNY. *(To Claire.)* Don't talk for a while. Let me and Ken talk. You just listen. *(To Ken.)* So you broke in and rushed upstairs. Was he on the floor?

KEN. No. He was sitting in bed. The television was on. One of those evangelist shows. A bottle of Valium was on the night table. He was half-conscious. I figured maybe he took a couple of pills to make himself drowsy, put the gun to his head, started to fall asleep and shot himself through the ear.

CLAIRE. Is that blood on your shirt, Ken?

KEN. *(Looking down at his shirt.)* Where?

CLAIRE. Below the second stud.

KEN. Oh, shit, I didn't see that. That won't come out, will it?

LENNY. That's what you're worried about? A stain on your dress shirt?

KEN. I don't give a damn about my shirt. I'm trying to prevent Charley from getting a suicide rap. When the others walk in here, I don't want to explain to them how I got blood on my good silk shirt.

CLAIRE. You could borrow one of Charley's.

KEN. He's two sizes too big for me.

CLAIRE. I don't think they'd notice your cuffs if Charley has a big bandage on his ear and Myra's not even at the party.

LENNY. Let the man finish the story, will you, please? *(To Ken.)* Did he tell you anything? Did he say why he did it?

KEN. Not a word. He was barely conscious.

LENNY. Did he leave a note or anything?

KEN. He had a piece of paper in his hand. I tried to take it from him, but he tore it up and threw it into the john. He flushed before I could get to it.

CLAIRE. This is not happening. I'm not hearing this.

LENNY. *(To Ken.)* Did you call the police?

KEN. No. Just the doctor. We told him he fell down the stairs. As long as he wasn't hurt, I didn't want to make this thing public.

LENNY. We've *got* to call the police. This man is the Deputy Mayor of New York. We're talking front page on the *New York Times*. Pictures of Charley with his suit jacket over his head.

KEN. Exactly. That's what I'm trying to avoid till we find out what happened.

LENNY. If we keep this quiet, we're all accessories. I deal with the IRS boys. I'd be the first one they'd go after.

KEN. Why would they go after you?

LENNY. With attempted suicides, they open up everything. They'd want to see his books, his portfolio, his entire financial picture. They'd want to know how a Deputy Mayor could afford a big house like this.

KEN. That's no secret. Myra's a wealthy woman. She bought the house.

CLAIRE. She did? I didn't know that.

LENNY. *(To Ken.)* You hear that? Now tomorrow it'll be all over the tennis club.

KEN. I'm not bringing in the police until I have to. I don't know what *you're* nervous about. Unless you have something to hide you don't want the IRS to know.

LENNY. Are you accusing me of hiding something? I'm the one who wants to bring in the police. Maybe *you're* the one who has something to hide. You make out his contracts. You made out his will.

KEN. Are you accusing me and Charley of conspiracy to defraud the city?

(*CAR LIGHTS flash on the window.*)

CLAIRE. I hear a car pulling up.

LENNY. (*To Ken, starting for the phone.*) If you're not calling the police, I am.

KEN. Oh, no you're not.

LENNY. You're telling me what I'm not going to do?

CLAIRE. (*At the window.*) It's pulling up the driveway.

LENNY. Suppose the neighbors heard the gunshot and have already called the police?

KEN. I'll deal with that problem when it arises.

LENNY. Maybe the car is the police. Then the problem has arosen.

CLAIRE. (*Looking out the window.*) It's a Volvo station wagon.

LENNY. A Volvo??!

KEN. Now I suppose you're worried it's the Swedish police.

CLAIRE. It's Ernie and Cookie.

LENNY. Ernie and Cookie?

KEN. (*To Claire.*) Why didn't you tell us?

CLAIRE. Why didn't you listen?

(*LENNY and KEN join Claire at the window. Charley's bedroom door opens and CHRIS steps out.*)

CHRIS. Ken, Myra and I are having trouble with her zipper.

KEN. No, you're not.

CHRIS. I'm not?

KEN. They know about it.

CHRIS. About Myra's zipper?

LENNY. We know that Myra's not here. Ken told us.

CHRIS. Oh.

CLAIRE. (*At the window.*) They're stopping to look at our BMW.

CHRIS. Did you tell them about Charley cutting his ear shaving?

KEN. They know *everything*. The gunshot, the ear lobe, the flushed note down the toilet, everything.

CHRIS. (*Angrily to Ken, coming downstairs.*) *Why didn't you tell me you told them?* . . . They must think I'm an idiot.

LENNY. How is Charley?

CHRIS. He fell asleep. He's hugging the pillow with his thumb in his mouth.

CLAIRE. They're coming up to the house. I can't believe she's wearing a dress like that to a party like this.

KEN. All right, what do we do? Do we tell them or not?

CLAIRE. Why not? Ernie is Charley's analyst. Everything you tell your analyst remains confidential.

LENNY. What his *patients* tell him. We're not his patients. His patient is asleep sucking his thumb.

CHRIS. I can't believe I'm paying a baby sitter for this night.

(*The DOORBELL RINGS. THEY ALL freeze.*)

LENNY. So what did we decide? Do we call the police or not?

CHRIS. I say no. Cookie has her cooking show on television. Suppose she accidentally says something on the air?

LENNY. On a cooking show? Do you think she gives out suicide recipes?

KEN. I still think we say nothing till I find out what's happened. Better safe than sorry. Claire, open the door.

LENNY. Chris, get us some drinks. Let's look like we're having fun.

(*CHRIS rushes to the bar, gets drinks and sits beside Lenny on the sofa.*)

CLAIRE. So what is it? We're telling Ernie but we're not telling Cookie?

LENNY. *We're not telling either one of them!* I'm sorry we told you!

(*The DOORBELL RINGS.*)

LENNY. Just open the door!

KEN. Claire, don't open it until I get upstairs. If Charley wakes up, maybe I can get the story from him. (*Dashes upstairs to Charley's bedroom.*)

CHRIS. (*To Ken.*) I took the Valium away from him. I hid them in the medicine cabinet.

KEN. Gee, what a good hiding place. (*Exits into Charley's room.*)

(*CLAIRE crosses to the front door. LENNY and CHRIS quickly sit on the sofa with their drinks as if THEY're having an amusing chat.*)

LENNY. (*To Chris.*) So, Mrs. Thatcher replies, "I don't know, perhaps it's in my umbrella stand."
CLAIRE. (*At the front door.*) Are we ready?
LENNY. Yes! We're ready, we're ready!

(*CLAIRE smiles and opens the front door. CHRIS and LENNY break into loud LAUGHTER.*
ERNIE and COOKIE are at the door. ERNIE is in his early fifties, in a tux and carrying a gift box. COOKIE is in her forties, wears a god-awful evening gown. SHE carries a sausage-like cushion under her arm.)

CLAIRE. Cookie! Ernie! It's so good to see you. (*Hugs them both.*)
CHRIS. Oh, God, that is so funny, Lenny. You should have been an actor, I swear.
CLAIRE. Everybody, it's Ernie and Cookie.
LENNY. (*Still laughing.*) Hi, Ernie. Hi, Cookie.
CHRIS. (*Waves, laughing.*) Hi, Cookie. Hi, Ernie.
ERNIE. Hello, Chris. Hello, Lenny.
CHRIS. (*To Lenny.*) So go on with the story. What did Mr. Gorbachev say?
LENNY. (*After an awkward silence.*) Mr. Gorbachev? . . . He said, "I don't know. I never ate cat food before."

(*There is much forced LAUGHTER.*)

ERNIE. Sorry we're late. Did we miss much?
CHRIS. You have *got* to get Lenny to tell you the story about Mrs. Thatcher and the cat food.

(*LENNY shoots Chris a dirty look.*)

ERNIE. (*Laughs.*) It sounds funny already. Heh heh heh.
COOKIE. Everyone looks so beautiful.

CLAIRE. Cookie, I am cr-azy about the dress. You always dig up the most original things. Where do you find them?

COOKIE. Oh, God, this is sixty years old. It was my grandmother's. She brought it from Russia.

CLAIRE. Didn't you wear that for Muscular Dystrophy in June?

COOKIE. No. Emphysema in August.

CLAIRE. (*Looking at the cushion.*) Oh, what a pretty cushion. Is that for Charley and Myra?

COOKIE. No, it's for my back. It went out again while I was dressing. (*SHE opens the pretzels, easily.*)

ERNIE. You all right, honey?

COOKIE. I'm fine, babe.

CHRIS. You and your back problems. It must be awful.

COOKIE. It's nothing. I can do everything but sit down and get up.

ERNIE. Hey, Lenny, is that your BMW? (*HE laughs.*) Looks like you put a lot of miles on in two days.

LENNY. A guy shoots out of a garage and blind-sides me. The car's got twelve miles on it. I've got a case of whiplash you wouldn't believe.

COOKIE. (*Crossing to other side of the room.*) Oh, I've had whiplash. Excruciating. My best friend had it for six years.

(*LENNY nods sardonically. SHE picks up the Steuben gift box.*)

COOKIE. Oh, this looks nice. Who brought this? (*SHE turns it to see the label but loses control and drops it.*) Oh, my God . . . Did I break anything? (*SHE shakes the box. It RATTLES.*) What was it?

LENNY. Steuben glass.

COOKIE. Oh, don't tell me! Lenny! Claire! . . . I'm so sorry.

ERNIE. It was an accident, honey. (*To Lenny and Claire.*) We'll replace it, of course.

LENNY. Sure, if you want. I don't care.

CHRIS. What about a drink, everyone?

ERNIE. I'll have something.

CHRIS. What do you want?

CLAIRE. I'll get it.

LENNY. (*Getting up.*) I'm right near the bar.

ERNIE. You're all going to get me a drink? Such friendly people. I'd love a bourbon, please.

(CHRIS crosses to the bar.)

COOKIE. I should have let what's-her-name pick it up. Moo Loo.

CHRIS. Mai Li . . . Here you go, Ern. *(Gives Ernie his drink.)*

COOKIE. Where's Ken?

CLAIRE. Ken? Ken's with Charley.

COOKIE. And Myra?

CLAIRE. Myra's with Ken . . . They're waiting for Myra to get dressed.

COOKIE. *(Grabbing the back of a chair and screaming.)* Ooooh! Ooooh! Ooooh!

CLAIRE. What is it?

COOKIE. A spasm. It's gone. It's all right. It just shoots up my back and goes.

ERNIE. You all right, poops?

COOKIE. I'm fine, puppy.

LENNY. Listen, maybe we should all sit outside. It's such a beautiful evening.

ERNIE. *(Smiles.)* Okay. Okay, you kids, what's going on here?

CLAIRE. What do you mean?

ERNIE. You think I don't notice everyone's acting funny? Three people want to get me drinks. Chris wants me to hear this funny story. Lenny wants to get us all outside. Everyone creating a diversion. Why? I don't know. Am I right?

CHRIS. No wonder you're such a high-priced doctor. OK . . . Someone's going to have to tell them.

LENNY. Tell them what?

CHRIS. About the surprise.

LENNY. What surprise?

CHRIS. The surprise about the party.

COOKIE. What surprise about the party?

CHRIS. Well, I think it's the cutest thing, isn't it, Claire?

CLAIRE. Oh, God, yes.

CHRIS. Tell them about it.

CLAIRE. No, you tell it better than I do.

COOKIE. I'm sorry. I think I'm going to have to sit down.

CHRIS. I'll help you.

LENNY. I'll do it.

CLAIRE. I've got her.

(*THEY all help lower Cookie onto the sofa, beside Ernie.*)

COOKIE. The cushion. I need the cushion.

LENNY. Here it is. (*HE puts the cushion behind her back.*)

ERNIE. You all right, chicken?

COOKIE. I'm fine, Pops . . . So what's the big surprise about?

CHRIS. Well . . . Charley and Myra decided . . . because they were going to have their closest friends over to celebrate their tenth anniversary . . . they weren't going to have any . . . servants.

COOKIE. (*Nods.*) Uh huh.

CHRIS. No Mai Li, no anybody.

COOKIE. (*Nods.*) Uh huh.

CHRIS. Isn't that terrific. No help. Just us.

COOKIE. Why is that terrific?

CHRIS. Because!! We're all going to pitch in. Like in the old days. Before money. Before success. Like when we were all just starting out. Those were the best times in our lives, don't you think?

COOKIE. No, I hated those times. I love success.

CHRIS. But don't you find these are greedier times. Lazier, more selfish. Nobody wants to work anymore.

COOKIE. I work fourteen hours a day. I cook thirty-seven meals a week. I cook on my television show. I cook for my family. I cook for my neighbors. I cook for my dogs. I was looking forward to a relaxed evening. (*SHE reconsiders.*) But I don't want to spoil the fun. What do we have to do?

CLAIRE. We have to cook.

COOKIE. You mean all of us cooking in the kitchen together?

CHRIS. Everyone except Charley and Myra. Claire and I told them to stay up there and relax. We'll call them when we're ready.

COOKIE. What are we going to make?

CLAIRE. It's all laid out. Roast ham, smoked turkey, duck and pasta?

ERNIE. Roast ham? Duck? . . . That's too much cholesterol for me.

LENNY. Ernie, we didn't come here to live longer. Just to have a good time.

COOKIE. I just don't understand why we're all wearing our best clothes to cook a dinner.

CLAIRE. That's not your best clothes. It's a fifty-year-old Polish dress.

COOKIE. A sixty-year-old Russian dress.

ERNIE. The dress is hardly an issue worth arguing about.

COOKIE. I didn't say we wouldn't cook it.

ERNIE. She didn't say we wouldn't cook it. Why is everyone getting so worked up about this?

CLAIRE. All right, Ernie, let's not turn this into group therapy, please.

ERNIE. This is nothing like group therapy, Claire. You, of all people, should know that.

LENNY. Oh, terrific. Let's just name all the people in your Thursday night group, Ernie, heh?

COOKIE. Why are Ernie and I being attacked? We just walked in the door.

CHRIS. Please lower your voices. We're going to spoil the surprise for Charley and Myra.

ERNIE. What surprise? It was their idea.

COOKIE. Listen, I don't want to take the blame for ruining this party. *(To the Group.)* I'll do all the cooking myself and Ernie'll do the serving.

ERNIE. Honey, no one's asking you to do that.

CHRIS & CLAIRE. If she wants to do it, let her. Sure. Why not? Fine with us.

LENNY. If it makes her happy, she can clean up, too.

COOKIE. *(Struggling to her feet.)* Okay, then it's settled. Just give me forty-five minutes. I promise you this is going to be the best dinner party we ever had.

(Suddenly, we hear a GUNSHOT from Charley's room.)

COOKIE. Oh, my God!

(EVERYONE freezes. COOKIE falls back onto the sofa.)

CLAIRE. Oh, give me a break.

ERNIE. What the hell was that?

(Charley's bedroom door opens and KEN, looking harassed, comes out, looks over the railing and tries to appear calm.)

KEN. It's fine. It's okay. It's all under control. Hi, Ernie. Hi, Cookie . . . Oh, Chris, honey, could I see you up here for a minute . . . (*HE smiles at them and returns to Charley's bedroom.*)

CHRIS. (*Politely.*) Would you all excuse me for a minute? I hate when this happens. (*SHE goes calmly up the stairs and into Charley's room.*)

ERNIE. Am I crazy or was that a gunshot?

LENNY. A gunshot? Nooo. I think it was a car backfiring.

ERNIE. In Charley's bedroom?

COOKIE. Ernie, maybe you should go up and see.

LENNY. Why? Chris and Ken and Charley and Myra are up there. There's more of them than us.

COOKIE. You just can't ignore a gunshot. Ernie, please go up and see.

LENNY. Oh, I know. I know. I know exactly what it was . . . It was a balloon. They've been blowing up party balloons up there all day.

ERNIE. What kind of a balloon was that, the Goodyear blimp? . . . I'm going up.

LENNY. Then how are we going to get the dinner ready? Charley and Myra must be starved. You and Cookie get started. I'll have a white wine spritzer, Ern. Claire, why don't you put on some music? (*Rushing upstairs.*) I'll be right down. Let me know if Dr. Doolittle calls. (*HE disappears into Charley's bedroom. The TELEPHONE rings.*)

CLAIRE. I'll get it. (*SHE crosses to the phone.*)

ERNIE. I still think it sounded like a gunshot.

COOKIE. Let's get dinner started, Ern. Help me up. (*Tries to get up out of the sofa.*)

CLAIRE. (*Into the phone.*) Hello? . . . Who? Dr. Cusack? Yes, he is. Who is it, please?

ERNIE. (*To Claire.*) Is that for me?

CLAIRE. (*Into phone.*) Uh huh. Uh huh. (*To Ernie.*) It's a conference call. Mr. and Mrs. Klein, Mr. and Mrs. Platt, Mr. and Mrs. Fishman.

ERNIE. Oh, it's my Friday night group. I have a telephone session with them.

COOKIE. Go on, honey. I can get up myself.

(*ERNIE runs into the kitchen.*)

CLAIRE. (*Into phone.*) He's coming, folks. (*The other line on PHONE RINGS. SHE switches buttons.*) Hello? . . . Yes it is. No, my husband just called.

(*COOKIE gets down on the floor and crawls on her hands and knees.*)

CLAIRE. Yes, I'll tell him. (*SHE holds the phone.*)

LENNY. (*Comes out of Charley's room.*) Who's on the phone?

CLAIRE. Dr. Dudley's service.

LENNY. (*Nods and comes downstairs. HE sees Cookie crawling on the floor.*) Oh, my God. What's that?

CLAIRE. It's Cookie.

COOKIE. It's all right. I do this all the time. It takes the pressure off my back.

LENNY. Where's Ernie?

CLAIRE. (*Pointing toward the kitchen.*) In there. He's got a session with his Friday night group.

LENNY. They're all in the kitchen?

CLAIRE. No. On the telephone.

COOKIE. (*Crawling toward the dining room.*) Ah! Ah! Ah!

LENNY. Your back again?

COOKIE. No. Little shirt pins on the floor. (*SHE crawls off into the kitchen.*) Ah! Ah! Ah!

LENNY. (*To Claire.*) She must be such fun to live with.

CLAIRE. What happened upstairs? Is Charley all right?

LENNY. He was sleeping. Ken wanted to hide the gun in the closet so Charley wouldn't find it. He tripped on Charley's slippers and the gun went off next to his head. He can't hear a thing in both ears.

CLAIRE. Ken or Charley?

LENNY. Ken. Charley was out cold from the Valium. (*Sees the phone is hung up.*)

CLAIRE. They hung up. I already took the message.

LENNY. You couldn't tell me that while I was on the balcony? What'd they say?

CLAIRE. They said Dr. Dudley already called this number. He doesn't want to be called out of the theater again.

LENNY. (*Angrily redials the phone.*) I'm getting a new doctor. I'm not putting my life in the hands of the drama critic for Mount Sinai

Hospital. (*Into phone.*) Hello? This is Leonard Ganz again. Dr. Dudley did *not* call this number. Please have him call me back. It's important. (*HE hangs up the phone.*)

CLAIRE. So what did Ken want Chris upstairs for?

LENNY. To call Ken's doctor to ask him what to do for his ears. He wouldn't be able to hear what the doctor was saying on the phone. I've got to get back upstairs. (*HE starts back upstairs.*)

CLAIRE. You mean she told the doctor a gun went off? Then she'll have to explain about Charley.

LENNY. No. She was going to say Ken was outside and a man-hole cover blew up next to him.

CLAIRE. That's a good idea.

LENNY. Except the doctor wasn't in. His service said he was still at the theater. There must be some kind of flu going around on Broadway. (*HE runs upstairs. When HE hits the top step, the PHONE rings.*) They purposely wait till I get on top of the stairs. Answer that, will you?

CLAIRE. (*Crossing to the phone.*) This is all too hard to follow. I need a bookmark in my head or something. (*SHE picks up the phone.*) Hello? Oh, Dr. Dudley, thanks for calling back. (*To Lenny.*) You want to speak to him?

LENNY. (*Running down the stairs.*) No. I'm taking a stress test.

CLAIRE. You know, if Ernie can't figure out something's wrong here, I'm not going to his group anymore.

LENNY. (*Picking up the phone.*) Hello, Dr. Dudley? . . . Thanks for calling back . . . Well, some idiot nailed me in my BMW about twenty minutes ago. I've got a little whiplash here . . . Charley? Charley Brock? . . . No, I wasn't calling about Charley. Why? (*Covering the phone, to Claire.*) Jesus! Dr. Dudley is Charley's doctor, too. (*Into the phone.*) No, Charley's a lot better. He's resting now . . . Chris Gorman? You know Ken and Chris? Yes, I think she did call. (*Covering the phone, to Claire.*) He's Ken's doctor, too.

CLAIRE. Maybe he has a franchise.

LENNY. Will you make yourself busy. Put on some music. (*Into phone.*) Dr. Dudley? I'm sorry. A cold compress? . . . Good idea. Let me connect you to Chris. Hold on. (*HE presses "Hold" button, then looks at extension numbers.*) Which button rings in Charley's room?

CLAIRE. Why? Who's going to hear it up there?

LENNY. (*Not covering phone.*) Jesus, you are a pain in the ass. I'd better run up and get Chris. (*Taking the phone off "Hold."*) Dr. Dudley? . . . What? . . . Oh, yes, my wife has a pain, too. It's no bother. Can you hold for Chris, please? (*Putting the phone on "Hold," then dashing upstairs.*) We owe this guy a gift. Let's give him Cookie as a patient. See where Ernie is with my drink, will you? (*HE goes into Charley's bedroom.*)

(*The dining room door opens and ERNIE comes out with a drink.*)

ERNIE. I thought I heard Lenny in here. I have his spritzer.

CLAIRE. I'll hold it for him. How's Cookie? (*SHE takes the drink.*)

ERNIE. Not well. I gave her some aspirins for her back, but she dropped them in the sauce.

CLAIRE. Good. Then we'll all get rid of *our* headaches.

ERNIE. Did Lenny say what that sound was?

CLAIRE. The gunshot?

ERNIE. It *was* a gunshot?

CLAIRE. No, I was referring to the sound you *thought* was a gunshot.

ERNIE. It wasn't a balloon, I know that.

CLAIRE. No. It was a can of shaving cream. It exploded.

ERNIE. Shaving cream exploded?

CLAIRE. It's all right. It washes off.

ERNIE. Incredible.

COOKIE. (*Sticking her head out the dining room door.*) Ernie? I need you to put out some garbage.

ERNIE. I'm not through talking to my group yet.

COOKIE. They're fighting with each other. I put them on hold.

(*COOKIE and ERNIE exit into the kitchen.
Charley's bedroom door opens and LENNY and KEN come out.
KEN holds a towel over his ears.*)

LENNY. It'll clear up in a minute. These things don't last long.

KEN. You think this'll last long?

LENNY. (*Opening the guest room door.*) Lie down in the guest room for a while, Ken. You'll feel better.

KEN. (*Looking into the guest room.*) Maybe if I lie down in the guest room for a while . . .

LENNY. Right.

CLAIRE. (*To Lenny.*) What did the doctor say to Chris?

LENNY. He referred her to another doctor. He's not feeling well himself . . . My neck is killing me again. Where's my spritzer?

KEN. (*Coming out of the guest room; to Lenny.*) Is your sister here?

LENNY. No, my *spritzer*!! Come on, Ken. I'll heat that towel up again.

KEN. Don't tell your sister about Charley. Not till we hear the whole story.

(*THEY go into the guest room.*
The kitchen door opens and COOKIE comes out. SHE holds a ladle in one hand and her other hand supports a bag of ice on her hip.)

COOKIE. I've got a problem, Claire, can you help me? Ernie went out the kitchen door to put out some garbage bags and the door locked. My hands are full of grease. Could you let him back in?

CLAIRE. Of course. We would all miss him terribly. (*SHE exits to the kitchen.*)

ERNIE. (*Enters through the front door on his own.*) I purposely went around so you wouldn't have to go to the door.

(*Charley's bedroom door opens and CHRIS steps out.*)

CHRIS. Oh, hi! . . . Where's Claire?

COOKIE. She went out to the kitchen to let Ernie in.

CHRIS. (*Looking at Ernie.*) Oh. Okay. (*SHE smiles and goes back into Charley's bedroom, closing the door.*)

(*The dining room door opens and CLAIRE comes out.*)

CLAIRE. Oh, there you are . . . Cookie, the water's boiling over on the pasta.

COOKIE. Why didn't you turn it down?

CLAIRE. I don't know. I don't watch your show.

COOKIE. I'll get it. Ernie, get another bag of ice. I'm melting. (*SHE exits into the kitchen.*)

ERNIE. (*Following Cookie, to Claire.*) I'm beginning to feel like one of my patients. (*HE laughs and goes to the kitchen.*)

(*Charley's door opens and CHRIS comes out.*)

CHRIS. (*Big smile.*) Well, everything is just fine.

CLAIRE. It's all right. They're in the kitchen.

CHRIS. God, I'd smoke a Havana cigar if I had one. (*Coming downstairs, scratching under her arms.*) I'm getting hives under my arms. (*Going to bar to make herself a vodka.*) Did you hear about Ken? He's deaf.

CLAIRE. He's better off. He's out of this thing now.

CHRIS. Why are we protecting Charley this way? Ken is deaf, Lenny can't turn his neck, Cookie's walking like a giraffe, I'm getting a blood condition. (*SHE scratches.*) For what? One more gunshot, the whole world will know anyway.

CLAIRE. The whole world isn't interested. Paraguay and Bolivia don't give a rat's ass.

(*We hear another CAR coming up the driveway.*)

LENNY. (*Coming out of the guest room.*) There's another car coming up.

(*We see the HEADLIGHTS flash on the window.*)

LENNY. Was anyone else invited?

CHRIS. Harry and Joan, but they canceled. They went to Venezuela. But they said they'd call tonight.

LENNY. From Venezuela?

CLAIRE. Jeez, maybe they *will* hear about it in Bolivia.

LENNY. So who's coming up the driveway?

CHRIS. Maybe it's Myra. Maybe she's come back.

LENNY. Myra drives a Porsche. This is an Audi. (*HE comes halfway down the stairs.*)

CLAIRE. Ask Ken. He might know.

LENNY. Ken is reading lips right now. I don't think he can pick up on "Audi."

(We hear a loud CRASH from the kitchen.)

LENNY. Jesus, what the hell was that?

CHRIS. Cookie just blew up the micro-wave, what else?

LENNY. Chris, go inside and see what happened. Claire, go to the window and see who's coming. I'll go up and see how Ken and Charley are doing . . . *(HE has been gesturing with a white towel.)* I feel like I'm at the fucking Alamo. *(HE rushes upstairs, just as:)*

(The dining room door flies open and ERNIE comes out, flicking his fingers in pain.)

ERNIE. Damn, I burned my fingers! Hot hot hot, oh, *God,* It's hot!

CHRIS. Oh, dear.

ERNIE. Sonofagun, that hurts. Oh, fuckerini!

CLAIRE. What happened?

ERNIE. *(Quickly.)* Cookie dropped her ice bag and slipped against the stove. The hot platter was about to fall on her, so I lifted it up. Then I dropped it on the table and it broke the water pitcher and the glass shattered on her arm and she's bleeding like hell. I got a dish towel on her wrist and I propped her up against a cabinet. But I need some bandages for her arm and some ointment for my fingers. I never saw anything happen so fast.

LENNY. I can't believe he's in pain and said all that without missing a word.

CLAIRE. *(To Lenny.)* Get the bandages. Why are you standing there?

LENNY. I was hoping there was more to the story. *(HE rushes into Charley's room and closes the door.)*

ERNIE. I'm sorry, Claire. Did you ask for a drink?

CLAIRE. Listen, you have other things to think about.

ERNIE. Right. *(HE exits.)*

(CHRIS and CLAIRE stare at each other.)

CLAIRE. You know what this night is beginning to remind me of? . . . *Platoon.*

(A car DOOR slams outside.)

CHRIS. There's the car. I don't even want to know who it is. Why don't you go and look?

CLAIRE. Like it's going to be good news, right? *(SHE crosses to the window and looks out.)* It's Glenn and Cassie.

CHRIS. Glenn and Cassie Cooper? Together?

CLAIRE. That's how they're walking.

CHRIS. I heard they were having trouble.

CLAIRE. Not walking. *(SHE comes away from the window.)*

CHRIS. Jesus! Do you know that Glenn is running for the State Senate in Poughkeepsie?

CLAIRE. So?

CHRIS. That's all he needs is to walk in here and be part of a hushed-up suicide attempt. He can kiss his career goodbye.

CLAIRE. Maybe Ken'll figure this all out before they ring the doorbell.

(The DOORBELL rings.)

CLAIRE. Well, it's going to be a tough campaign.

CHRIS. Listen, I have to go to the bathroom. You get the door, I'll be right out. *(SHE starts for the powder room.)*

CLAIRE. Wait a minute! I haven't gone since I got here.

CHRIS. Yes you did. In Mai Li's room.

CLAIRE. Yes, but no one was at the door then.

CHRIS. The hell with it. Someone else'll get the door. Come on.

(THEY BOTH go into the powder room and close the door behind them.
The DOORBELL rings again. LENNY comes out of the guest room.)

LENNY. Isn't anybody going to get the door? . . . Chris? . . . Claire? . . .

KEN. *(Peering out from the guest room.)* Are you talking to me?

LENNY. No, Ken. Put the towels back on your ears. (*Yelling down.*) Claire? . . . Chris? . . . Where are you? . . . Ah, screw it. I'm beginning to feel like my car. (*HE goes back into the guest room and closes the door.*)

(*The dining room door opens and ERNIE comes out with paper towels wrapped around the fingers on both hands. HE is wearing an apron. HE shouts up.*)

ERNIE. Lenny? You got those bandages?

(*The DOORBELL rings again.*)

ERNIE. Nobody getting that door? . . . These kids are up to something, I know it. (*HE crosses to the front door and tries to open it with burned fingers. HE is finally successful.*)

(*GLENN and CASSIE COOPER, a handsome couple, stand there in evening clothes. GLENN holds a gift from Ralph Lauren's. THEY seem very much on edge with each other.*)
ERNIE. (*Smiles.*) Hello.
GLENN. Good evening.

(*THEY walk in, look around. ERNIE closes the door with his foot.*)

ERNIE. Good evening. I don't know where everyone is.
CASSIE. You mean we're the first?
ERNIE. No. Everyone's here. They're just—spread out a little.
GLENN. Could I have a drink, please? Double Scotch, straight up.
CASSIE. (*Not looking at Ernie.*) Perrier with lime, no ice.
ERNIE. Sure. Fine. I don't believe we've met. I'm Ernie Cusack.
GLENN. (*Coolly, nods.*) Hello, Ernie.
ERNIE. Excuse my hands. Little accident in the kitchen.
GLENN. Sorry to hear it.
ERNIE. I would stay and chat but my wife is bleeding in the kitchen.
GLENN. Your wife?

ERNIE. Cookie. A water pitcher broke, cut her arm. I burned my fingers.

GLENN. That's a shame.

ERNIE. Nothing to worry about. We'll have dinner ready soon. Nice meeting you both. (*HE returns to the kitchen.*)

GLENN. I wonder why they're not using the Chinese girl?

CASSIE. Do I look all right?

GLENN. Yes. Fine.

CASSIE. I feel so frumpy.

GLENN. God, no. You look beautiful.

CASSIE. My hair isn't right, is it? I saw you looking at it in the car.

GLENN. No, I wasn't.

CASSIE. What were you looking at then?

GLENN. The road, I suppose.

CASSIE. I can always tell when you hate what I'm wearing.

GLENN. I love that dress. I always have.

CASSIE. This is the first time I've worn it.

GLENN. I always have admired your taste is what I meant.

CASSIE. It's so hard to please you sometimes.

GLENN. What did I say?

CASSIE. It's what you *don't* say that really drives me crazy.

GLENN. What I *don't* say? . . . How can it drive you crazy if I don't say it?

CASSIE. I don't know. It's the looks that you give me.

GLENN. I wasn't giving you any looks.

CASSIE. You look at me all the time.

GLENN. Because you're always asking me to look at you.

CASSIE. It would be nice if I didn't have to ask you, wouldn't it?

GLENN. It would be nice if you didn't need me to look, which would make it unnecessary to ask.

CASSIE. I can't ever get any support from you. You've got all the time in the world for everything and everyone else, but I've got to draw blood to get your attention when I walk in a room.

GLENN. We walked in the room together. It was already done. Cassie, please don't start. We're forty-five minutes late as it is. I don't want to ruin this night for Charley and Myra.

CASSIE. We're forty-five minutes late because you scowled at every dress I tried on.

GLENN. I didn't scowl, I smiled. You always think my smile looks like a scowl. You think my grin looks like a frown, and my frown looks like a yawn.

CASSIE. Don't sneer at me.

GLENN. It wasn't a sneer. It was a peeve.

CASSIE. God, this conversation is so banal. I can't believe any of the things I'm saying. We sound like some fucking TV couple.

GLENN. Oh, now we're going to get into language, right?

CASSIE. No, Mr. Perfect. I will not get into any language. I don't want to risk a scowl, a frown, a yawn, a peeve or a sneer. God forbid I should show a human imperfection, I'd wake up with the divorce papers in my hand.

GLENN. What is this thing lately with divorce? Where does that come from? I don't look at you sometimes because I'm afraid you're thinking you don't like the way I'm looking at you.

CASSIE. I don't know what the hell you want from me, Glenn. I really don't.

GLENN. I don't want *any*thing from you. I mean I would like it to be the way we were before we got to be the way we are.

CASSIE. God, you suffocate me sometimes . . . I want to go home.

GLENN. Go home? We just got here. We haven't even seen any-one yet.

CASSIE. I don't know how I'm going to get through this night. They all know what's going on. They're your friends. Jesus, and you expect me to behave like nothing's happening.

GLENN. Nothing is happening. What are you talking about?

CASSIE. Don't you fucking lie to me. The whole goddamn city knows about you and that cheap little chippy bimbo.

GLENN. Will you keep it down? Nothing is going on. You're blowing this up out of all proportions. I hardly know the woman. She's on the Democratic Fund Raising Committee. I met her and her husband at two cocktail parties, for God sakes.

CASSIE. Two cocktail parties, heh?

GLENN. Yes! Two cocktail parties.

CASSIE. You think I'm stupid?

GLENN. No.

CASSIE. You think I'm blind?

GLENN. No.

CASSIE. You think I don't know what's been going on.

GLENN. Yes, because you don't.

CASSIE. I'm going to tell you something, Glenn. Are you listening?

GLENN. Don't you see my ears perking up?

CASSIE. I've known about you and Carole Newman for a year now.

GLENN. Amazing, since I only met her four months ago. Now I'm asking you to please lower your voice. That butler must be listening to everything.

CASSIE. You think I care about a butler and a bleeding cook? My friends know about your bimbo, what do I care about domestic help?

GLENN. I don't know what's gotten into you, Cassie. Do my political ambitions bother you? Are you threatened somehow because I'm running for the Senate?

CASSIE. *State* Senate! *State* Senate! Don't make it sound like we're going to Washington. We're going to Albany. Twenty-three degrees below zero in the middle of winter Albany. You're not *Time*'s Man of the Year yet, you understand, honey?

GLENN. (*Turning away.*) Oh, boy, oh, boy, oh boy!

CASSIE. What was that?

GLENN. (*Deliberately.*) Oh-boy, oh-boy, oh-boy!

CASSIE. Oh, like I'm behaving badly, right? I'm the shrew witch wife who's giving you such a hard time. I'll tell you something, Mr. *State* Senator. I'm not the only one who knows what's going on. People are talking, kiddo. Trust me.

GLENN. What do you mean? You haven't said anything to anyone, have you?

CASSIE. Oh, is that what you're worried about? Your reputation? Your career? Your place in American history? You know what your place in American history will be? . . . A commemorative stamp of you and the bimbo in a motel together.

GLENN. You are so hyper tonight, Cassie. You're out of control. You've been rubbing your quartz crystal again, haven't you? I told you to throw those damn crystals away. They're dangerous. They're like petrified cocaine.

(CASSIE *is looking through her purse.*)

GLENN. . . . Don't take it out, Cassie. Don't rub your crystal at the party. It makes you crazy.

(*SHE takes out her crystal. HE grabs for it.*)

GLENN. Put it away. Don't let my friends see what you're doing.
CASSIE. Fine. Don't let *my* friends see what *you're* doing.

(*The guest room door opens. LENNY comes out onto the balcony.*)

LENNY. Glenn! Cassie! I thought it was you. How you doing?
KEN. (*From inside the guest room.*) I'm feeling better, thanks.
LENNY. Not you, Ken. It's Glenn and Cassie.
GLENN. (*Big smile.*) We're fine. Just great. Hi, Len . . . Cassie, it's Len . . . Cassie.
CASSIE. (*A quick nod.*) Leonard.
LENNY. Did it suddenly freeze up out there?
GLENN. Freeze up?
LENNY. Isn't that an icicle Cassie has there?
GLENN. No. It's a quartz crystal.
LENNY. Oh. Where's Chris and Claire?
KEN. (*From the guest room.*) Did somebody come in?
LENNY. (*Angrily, to Ken.*) GLENN AND CASSIE!! I *TOLD* YOU!! (*To Glenn.*) It's Ken. His ears are stuffed up. Bad cold . . . Who let you in?
GLENN. The butler.
LENNY. The butler? The butler's here?
GLENN. He's getting us drinks.
LENNY. Is he alone?
GLENN. No, the cook's with him.
LENNY. Mai Li? God, what a relief. They came back. We didn't have any help here for a while.
GLENN. Really? Where's Charley and Myra?
LENNY. Charley and Myra? I guess they're in their room.
KEN. (*From the guest room.*) My towel fell off, Lenny.
LENNY. (*Angrily, to Ken.*) I'LL GET YOU A TOWEL. I'VE GOT TO GET THE BANDAGES FIRST. (*To Glenn.*) Excuse me, kids. I've got to get some bandages. (*HE knocks on Charley's door.*)

Charley? Myra? Is it all right if I come in? *(In Myra's voice.)* Sure, come on in. *(HE goes into Charley's room and closes the door.)*

(The guest room door opens and KEN comes out.)

KEN. Lenny? . . . Lenny, where'd you go?

(GLENN and CASSIE look up.)

GLENN. Ken? Hi. It's Glenn and Cassie.
KEN. Lenny? Is that you? *(HE looks down.)* Who's that? Glenn? Is that Glenn?
GLENN. Yes. And Cassie. I hear you have a cold.
KEN. You think I look old? I haven't been sleeping well lately . . . Hi, Cassie. Do the others know you're here?
GLENN. Yes. We just saw Lenny.
KEN. Have you seen Lenny?
GLENN. Yes. He went into Charley's room.
KEN. I'm sorry. I can't hear anything. A manhole cover just blew up next to my ear.
GLENN. That's terrible.
KEN. I said, "A manhole cover just blew up next to my ear."
GLENN. Yes. I hear you.
KEN. I'm sorry. I can't hear you. Anyone getting you a drink?
GLENN. Yes, the butler.
KEN. Sorry, there's no help here. They're in the Orient somewhere.
CASSIE. *(To Glenn.)* I think he's gone dotty.
KEN. Yes, a hot toddy would be nice. I'm going to see if Lenny's in Charley's room. We're all coming down soon. *(HE knocks on Charley's door.)* Myra? Mind if I come in?
LENNY. *(As Myra, from inside.)* Sure, honey. Come on in.

(KEN goes into Charley's room.)

CASSIE. I'll be right back.
GLENN. Where are you going?
CASSIE. To rinse off my crystal. *(Starting to the powder room.)* . . . I suppose you'd like to make a quick phone call while

I'm gone, heh? (*SHE tries to open the powder room door, but it's locked.*) Anyone in there?

CHRIS. (*From inside.*) Who is it?

CASSIE. Cassie. Who's that?

CHRIS. (*From inside.*) It's Chris . . . Just a minute, Cass. (*We hear a FLUSH. CHRIS comes out and closes the door.*) I didn't hear you ring, Cassie. I would have opened the door. Hi, Glenn. (*SHE crosses to him and gives him a kiss. By now she's getting pretty crocked from her vodkas.*)

GLENN. Hi. Listen, is anything going on here?

CHRIS. I don't know . . . Who have you seen?

GLENN. Well, Lenny and Ken for just a second. And the butler and Mai Li.

CHRIS. You saw Mai Li and the butler? My God, I must have been in there for a long time.

CASSIE. Are you through in the bathroom?

CHRIS. Me? Yes. Sure.

CASSIE. (*Tries the door again, but it's locked.*) You left it locked.

CLAIRE. (*From inside.*) Who is it?

CASSIE. Cassie. Who's that?

CLAIRE. (*From inside.*) It's Claire. Just a minute, Cass. (*We hear a FLUSH. The door opens and CLAIRE comes out.*) Hi, Cass. Hi, Glenn. Don't you look beautiful . . . Where are the boys?

GLENN. Well, Lenny and Ken are up with Charley and Myra. Myra sounded very excited.

CLAIRE. You spoke to Myra?

GLENN. No. I heard her talk to Ken and Len.

CLAIRE. I'd love to have a copy of that conversation.

CASSIE. Is anyone else in the bathroom, because I have to go. (*SHE looks inside, then goes in and locks the door behind her.*)

CHRIS. (*To Claire.*) Mai Li and the butler are here.

CLAIRE. You're kidding. Where's Ernie and Cookie.

GLENN. I just met Ernie. Isn't he the butler?

CHRIS. Oh. No. Okay. We've got that one cleared up.

GLENN. Then they're just back from the Orient?

CHRIS. I imagine so. You're so well informed.

GLENN. Why is everyone up in Charley's room?

CHRIS. Oh. There was something on TV they all wanted to watch.

CLAIRE. Right. Very good, Chris.

(*Charley's bedroom door opens, and LENNY comes out.*)

LENNY. (*Jovial.*) Well, this is beginning to look like a party.

GLENN. What were you all watching up there?

LENNY. Up where?

GLENN. On TV.

CHRIS. (*To Lenny.*) The thing you went up to watch with Ken and Charley and Myra.

LENNY. Oh. OH! That thing. That show. The PBS Special on what's-his-name?

CLAIRE. . . . Hitler?

LENNY. Yes. The thing on Hitler. (*HE comes downstairs, glaring at Claire.*)

GLENN. On their tenth anniversary you wanted to watch a special on Hitler?

LENNY. Hitler as a boy. A whole new slant on him.

ERNIE. (*Comes out of the dining room door. HE carries two drinks.*) Dinner's coming along. (*To Glenn.*) Double Scotch, straight up.

GLENN. Oh, thanks.

ERNIE. Lenny, have you got the bandages?

LENNY. The bandages? Yes. I have them. I left them on Hitler . . . on the television. I'll be right back. (*HE runs back upstairs and into Charley's room, closing the door behind him.*)

GLENN. Listen, I'm sorry. I mistook you for the butler.

ERNIE. I kind of thought you did. No, I'm an analyst.

GLENN. Oh, for pete sakes. I'm Glenn . . . How's your wife doing?

ERNIE. The spaghetti's boiling, but the duck is still frozen.

GLENN. No, I meant her arm.

ERNIE. Oh, not too bad. She's a trouper. Her fingers are cramping up a little.

GLENN. Maybe she ought to see a doctor. Charley has one ten minutes from here, Dr. Dudley.

CHRIS. Oh. We called him. He's busy.

ERNIE. You called about Cookie's arm?

CLAIRE. No, about Lenny's neck.

GLENN. Lenny's neck?

CHRIS. And when the doctor called back, we told him about Ken's ears.

ERNIE. (*To Glenn.*) Isn't that incredible? From a can of shaving cream exploding?

GLENN. I thought it was a manhole cover.

CLAIRE. It was. But the pressure from the manhole cover made the shaving cream can explode.

ERNIE. (*To Glenn.*) I didn't hear that.

LENNY. (*Coming out of Charley's room with the bandages. HE runs downstairs.*) I got 'em. I got 'em.

GLENN. There certainly is some excitement around here.

CLAIRE. (*To Lenny.*) Guess who Glenn's doctor is?

LENNY. You're kidding. I wish I did his taxes.

ERNIE. Wait a minute! Glenn Cooper! From Poughkeepsie. You're running for the State Senate.

GLENN. That's right.

ERNIE. I have a good friend who knows you very well.

GLENN. Really? Who's that?

ERNIE. Harold Green.

LENNY. Harold Green! (*LENNY drops the bandages.*)

CLAIRE. Harold Green?

GLENN. Sure. I know Harold Green. We went to the University of Pennsylvania together. I haven't seen him in years. What's he doing now?

LENNY. He's a proxy new social member who just eats lunches and doesn't play tennis.

GLENN. Oh. At your club? (*GLENN hands the bandages to Ernie.*)

LENNY. Ernie, Cookie's waiting in the emergency room.

ERNIE. Right. (*To Glenn.*) There's your wife's Perrier. Nice to meet you, Glenn. (*As HE exits to the kitchen.*) . . . Thought I was the butler.

(*Charley's door opens and KEN comes out.*)

KEN. Somebody! Please! I need a drink real bad.

GLENN. How's your ears, Ken?

KEN. (*Coming downstairs.*) A beer would be fine, thanks.

GLENN. Maybe Charley has some ear drops. (*To Lenny.*) Did you see any in the medicine cabinet when you were getting the bandages?

LENNY. No, I didn't think of that.

GLENN. I'll go up and look.

(*HE starts to go up the stairs. LENNY and KEN block him.*)

LENNY. No. I remember. I looked. There weren't any. I forgot I looked.

(*The TELEPHONE rings.*)

KEN. Is there a cat in here?

CHRIS. A cat?

KEN. I just heard a cat meow. (*The TELEPHONE rings again.*) There it is again.

GLENN. That's the *phone*, Ken.

KEN. Why would he want a bone? It's a cat, not a dog.

(*The TELEPHONE rings again.*)

LENNY. I'll get it.

KEN. We're hungry, too, pussy. We haven't eaten either.

LENNY. (*Into phone.*) Hello? . . . Who? . . . I'm sorry, operator. We have a bad connection . . . Oh, yes. Yes. (*To Others.*) It's Harry and Joan from Venezuela. They're calling Charley and Myra.

CLAIRE. This is going to be good.

GLENN. Joan? That's Cassie's cousin. Wait, I'll get Cassie. I'm sure she'll want to speak to her. (*HE knocks on the powder room door.*) Cassie?

LENNY. (*Into phone.*) Hello, Joannie. It's Lenny. How are you? . . . Yes, everybody's here . . . Yes, we're having a great time . . .

GLENN. Cassie?

LENNY. (*Into phone.*) Charley and Myra? Of course they're here. What did you think? (*HE laughs and motions for CLAIRE and CHRIS to laugh, too.*) Sure. Just a minute. (*Covering the phone.*) Claire! Speak to her.

CLAIRE. Me? She's calling Charley and Myra.

LENNY. *Will you speak to her!!* (*HE shoves the phone at Claire.*)

GLENN. (*Knocking on the powder room door.*) Cassie? It's your cousin Joan from Venezuela.

CLAIRE. (*Into phone.*) Joan? What a nice surprise. No, it's Claire . . . Yes, a terrific party . . . Myra? Oh, she looks beautiful. She's wearing a red kimono. Mai Li's mother sent it to her . . . Wait, I'll let you speak to her. Hold on. (*Covering the phone, to Chris.*) Here. Talk to her.

CHRIS. Don't give me the phone. I'll drive your kids to school for a year.

CLAIRE. (*Dumping the phone in Chris's lap.*) I've done my part. I'm not the Red Cross.

GLENN. (*Knocking on the powder room door.*) Cassie? It's Joan and Harry. Don't you want to speak to them?

CHRIS. (*Into phone.*) Joan? Hi, sweetheart. How's Venezuela? . . . No, it's Chris. You sent a gift? A crystal vase from Steuben's? Gee, I think it's broken. Wait, Myra will tell you about it.

GLENN. (*Still knocking.*) Cassie, are you all right?

CHRIS. Who didn't speak to her yet?

CLAIRE. Ken. Ken didn't speak to her.

LENNY. (*Shouting at KEN, on the balcony.*) Ken? Do you want to speak to Joan?

KEN. What?

LENNY. *Joan! Do-you-want-to-speak-to-Joan?*

KEN. Sure. I'd love to go home.

CHRIS. (*Into phone.*) Joan? This connection is bad. I think I'm losing you.

GLENN. (*Banging on the bathroom door.*) Cassie, will you hurry up! We're losing the connection! *Come on, will you!!*

(*ERNIE and COOKIE come out of the kitchen. SHE holds a hot casserole, HE holds two bottles of wine.*)

COOKIE. It's din-din, everyone.

(*The bathroom door opens and CASSIE comes out in a state of shock.*)

CASSIE. *Who did that? Who banged on the door?*

GLENN. I did. Your cousin Joan is on the phone from Vene-zuela.

CASSIE. You scared the life out of me! I dropped my crystal down the toilet. A TWO-MILLION-YEAR-OLD CRYSTAL! !

CHRIS. I can't take this. (*SHE shoves the phone into Ken's hand.*) Here. You can't hear anyway, what's the difference?

(*KEN holds the phone, bewildered. As SHE walks away, SHE trips on the phone wire and falls flat on her face.*)

CASSIE. (*To Glenn.*) Don't just stand there, idiot, get my crystal.

GLENN. Hey, just cool it, Cassie, okay?

KEN. (*Into phone.*) Hello? . . . Hello?

ERNIE. (*Starting up the stairs.*) I'll go get Myra and Charley.

LENNY. (*Dashing up the stairs, cutting of Ernie.*) No, I'll get them, I'll get them. Myra and Charley! Myra and Chaaaaa . . . (*HE grabs his neck.*) Oh, shit! There it goes. This time it's perma-nent.

KEN. Hello? . . . Hello? . . .

CASSIE. (*Crying.*) It's a sin to lose a crystal. It's like killing your own dog.

LENNY. Oh, fuck a duck!

COOKIE. Everybody grab a plate, kids. (*As SHE hands out plates, her back goes out.*) Whoops. Oh, no. Oh, Christ. Oh, man. Oh, Momma.

KEN. Hello? . . . Hello? . . .

CURTAIN

ACT II

Scene: One hour later.
Plates of eaten food are about. Opened wine and champagne bot-tles are scattered about.
It's quiet. Very quiet.

At Rise: The only sound is of KEN eating. HE sits in an armchair finishing his dinner. The OTHERS have all eaten. GLENN and CLAIRE are seated on the sofa. LENNY is on the love seat, drinking wine. COOKIE sits on a chair near KEN, drinking coffee. CASSIE is standing on the balcony, holding the rail with her hands and drawing in deep breaths. ERNIE and CHRIS sit on the stairway. CHRIS is smoking a cigarette, like it was her last, and ERNIE smokes a pipe.

No one is talking. THEY are ALL deep in thought. NO ONE looks at each other.

The silence continues.

KEN's fork scratches on his plate as HE eats the last morsel of food. HE looks up.

KEN. *(Panicky.)* What was that?

GLENN. It was you, Ken. It was your fork scraping the plate.

KEN. My what?

CHRIS. Your fork scraping your plate.

KEN. *(To Glenn.)* You're fading out again, Glenn.

GLENN. That wasn't me, Ken. It was Chris.

KEN. I can make out voices now. Just a little here and there.

CHRIS. *(To Ernie.)* You think I can have another cigarette?

KEN. No. No cigarettes.

GLENN. *(Crossing to Lenny at the love seat.)* I still can't get over it. I find the entire story so hard to believe.

LENNY. He finds the story hard to believe. Because we acted our asses off to keep the truth from you.

GLENN. Myra is gone?

LENNY. Right.

GLENN. The servants are gone?

LENNY. Right.

GLENN. Charley shoots himself in the ear lobe?

LENNY. Right.

GLENN. It doesn't make any sense.

CLAIRE, CHRIS, & LENNY. Right!

ERNIE. Why didn't I see it? People running up and down stairs, no one answering the door, cans of shaving cream exploding. I'm on the staff of Bellevue Hospital, how could I believe such a story? *(To Chris.)* You never let on.

CHRIS. Listen, I was so desperate for a smoke, I went into Charley's bathroom and tried to light up a Q-tip.

COOKIE. Don't you have any self-control?

CHRIS. Of course. I only smoked half.

(KEN suddenly stands and looks around at everyone. HE is breathing hard and clenches his fists. HE looks as though HE's about to explode.)

CHRIS. Something's wrong with Ken.

COOKIE. Maybe he's still hungry. YOU WANT SECONDS, KENNY?

ERNIE. No, no. He wants to say something. Be quiet a minute, everyone . . . What is it, Ken?

KEN. I can't take it anymore . . . The pressure is killing me. I'm sorry, but I have to do this. *(To Ernie and Glenn.)* Myra isn't here! The servants aren't here! Charley's upstairs and he shot himself through the ear lobe! Maybe it was attempted suicide, maybe it wasn't, I don't know. I don't care. I'm just glad it's over with. *(HE sits back down in his chair, sobbing.)*

ERNIE. It's all right, Ken. We know. Lenny told us.

KEN. *(Looking at him.)* You know?

ERNIE. Yes.

KEN. Who told you?

ERNIE. Lenny told us.

KEN. Glenn told you?

ERNIE. No. Lenny. LENNY. LENNY TOLD US.

CLAIRE. I wish he were deaf again.

KEN. *(Looks at Lenny.)* Is it true, Lenny? Did you tell them?

LENNY. Oh, finish your goddamn dinner and leave us alone, will you?

ERNIE. All right, take it easy, Lenny. He's been under a big strain.

LENNY. And I haven't? I was acting my goddam head off that Myra was here. I had actual conversations with her up there. I even did her voice in case someone was listening.

COOKIE. Was that you? You could have fooled me.

LENNY. I *did.*

COOKIE. That's right. You did.

GLENN. So you really weren't watching Hitler on PBS?

LENNY. No, we stopped everything to watch "The Rise and Fall of Adolf Hitler" . . . I don't believe you people.

GLENN. It sounded so real, I believed it.

ERNIE. *(To Cassie.)* What about you, Mrs. Cooper? *(To Glenn.)* What's her name?

GLENN. Cassie.

ERNIE. *(To Cassie.)* What about you, Cassie? Did you think something strange was going on?

CASSIE. Yes. For about six months now.

ERNIE. What do you mean? *(To Glenn.)* What does she mean?

GLENN. You have to forgive her. She's still very upset about losing her crystal.

COOKIE. We could call a plumber. They get everything out. Wedding rings, car keys. I had an aunt who lost her dentures down the toilet and they got them out.

CLAIRE. And she wore them?

COOKIE. Well, obviously you clean them.

CLAIRE. They could be blessed by the Pope, I wouldn't put them in my mouth again.

GLENN. Unless you're into crystals, you wouldn't understand. Apparently, they have very special properties. You have to wash them in clear, spring water. They must be kept in direct sunlight. Cassie scrubs them every night with a soft, wet toothbrush. You never dry them in a towel. You pat them in a sort of leathery cloth. They really are very delicate.

CLAIRE. Have you got them enrolled in a good school yet?

ERNIE. Oh, come on, Claire. If crystals work for her, if they give her a sense of comfort and pleasure, what's wrong with it?

CASSIE. You don't have to defend me, Ernie. Crystals will be here millions of years after this planet is gone.

LENNY. If the planet is gone, don't the crystals go with it?

ERNIE. Lenny, don't.

CHRIS. *(To Glenn.)* I don't know if this would help her any, but there's a big crystal chandelier in the dining room. Should I mention it to her?

GLENN. Thanks, Chris, but I don't think so. Best leave her alone now.

CASSIE. (*Coming downstairs.*) I'm not dead, you know. I can hear. Maybe Ken can't, but I can. (*SHE exits into the powder room.*)

COOKIE. I can unscrew the toilet myself. I've done it before.

ERNIE. I don't think it's the time or the place to fix toilets, sugar.

CLAIRE. Yes. Perhaps another time, another place.

LENNY. (*To Cookie.*) Bleeding arm and all, Cookie, that was one hell of a meal. My hat's off to you.

GLENN. Hear hear.

ERNIE. Bravissima.

CHRIS. Arregeno! Arregeno!

EVERYBODY. I liked the duck. The duck was great. Really crispy. And the pasta was especially good. Didn't you think so? How long did you boil it?

KEN. (*Gets up with that mad look on his face again.*) Doesn't anybody . . . doesn't *anybody*—?

ERNIE. Quiet, everybody. Quiet . . . What is it, Ken? Doesn't anybody what?

KEN. Doesn't anybody—want to go upstairs and see if Charley is still alive? It's been awfully quiet up there, hasn't it?

CLAIRE. How would you know?

KEN. What?

ERNIE. You're right. My God, he's right. We've all been so busy eating and explaining to each other, we forgot all about Charley.

KEN. (*Pointing to Ernie.*) YES. YES. That's what I'm saying.

LENNY. All right, I'll go up and settle this now.

GLENN. Wait, wait. We're all in a precarious situation. Not only Charley, but a lot of people's futures depend on how we deal with this issue.

CLAIRE. Meaning you?

GLENN. Well, no. Cassie and I were the last ones to arrive. We just heard about it. We're hardly involved.

COOKIE. And Ernie and I were cooking the whole time. Nobody told us. Sorry.

LENNY. I *wanted* to call the police. Ken wouldn't let me call the police. Claire, didn't I want to call the police?

CLAIRE. Lenny wanted to call the police.

CHRIS. So what are you saying? That it's Ken's responsibility? He takes the rap for this?

ALL THE OTHERS. Oh, no. No, of course not . . . We didn't say that . . . Nobody's saying that. I didn't hear anyone say that. No one's accusing anyone of anything.

LENNY. . . . What we're saying is, if it comes down to it, he's the most logical, that's all.

CHRIS. I can't believe this. Ken almost went deaf trying to protect Charley and everyone else here. I expected a little bit more from his friends. My God, what a bunch of wimps . . . Have you heard any of this, Ken?

KEN. Well, answer her, Glenn, have you?

COOKIE. (*Screams, as SHE bends way over.*) Oh, God! Oh, no! Oh, Christ! Oh, Momma!

LENNY. What is it?

COOKIE. I lost my earrings. My good earrings! My grandmother's earrings!

CHRIS. (*Bending over, looking.*) Where did you lose them?

COOKIE. Right here. Right around here.

ERNIE. We'll find them, honey.

CLAIRE. What did they look like?

COOKIE. Old! Very old! With pearls. And a little ruby. (*Starting to cry.*) My grandmother gave them to me. I'm sick about this.

(*THEY are ALL on the floor, crawling around looking for the earrings.*)

COOKIE. (*Screams.*) AHHHH! Oh, God! Oh, my God!

CLAIRE. What?

COOKIE. They're in my hand. (*Shows them.*) I forgot I had them. I'm so stupid. Forgive me, everybody, I'm sorry . . . So, what were we saying?

(*THEY ALL glare at Cookie as THEY struggle to their feet.*)

ERNIE. Glenn, I'm a little worried about your wife. Do you think she's all right.

GLENN. Oh, she's fine. She's just in there trying to figure some way to get back at me. She'll come up with something.

(*The powder room door suddenly opens and CASSIE stands there with one arm extended up the door. Her hair is brushed over one eye. SHE looks sexy as hell, with a malevolent grin on her face. EVERYONE turns to look at her.*)

GLENN. Yeah, she's got one.

(*CASSIE crosses to the sofa, sits on the arm next to Lenny, practically leaning on him.*)

CASSIE. Please forgive me, everyone. I know I behaved badly tonight.

(*SHE smiles right at Lenny. HE smiles back, then looks away.*)

CASSIE. No, I really did . . . and I apologize. I've had—well, I've had a rough day today, and I'm just not here tonight.
LENNY. That's okay. Neither are Charley and Myra.
CASSIE. (*Smiles at Lenny.*) That's funny. That's truly funny, Lenny. I can never think of anything funny. How do you do that?
LENNY. (*A bit flustered.*) I don't know . . . I just . . . (*Sees CLAIRE glaring at him.*) Can I get up and get you a glass of wine?
CASSIE. Why? Do I look like I need one?
CLAIRE. Who is she getting back at, Glenn, you or me?
GLENN. (*Without looking at her.*) All right, Cassie, cut it out.
CASSIE. What do you mean, sweetheart.
GLENN. You know what I mean. Push your hair back up and sit on a chair.
CASSIE. (*Smiles at Glenn, then to Lenny.*) Do you know what he's talking about, Len?
CLAIRE. Excuse me. I'm going up to get Charley's gun.
ERNIE. Cassie, everyone here is your friend. Why don't you and I go out on the terrace and have a nice, quiet talk?
COOKIE. (*To Ernie.*) You do and you'll have a back worse than mine.
CASSIE. Oh, my goodness, I see what you're thinking. That is really incredible. Because the exact same thing happened to Glenn and me last week at a cocktail party for the Democratic Fund Raising Committee. There was the nicest woman there—very

attractive, very sweet, very refined—and because sometimes I can feel so silly and so insecure, I thought she was coming on to Glenn. They got up to dance and they were as close as freshly-laid wallpaper.

GLENN. Okay, Cassie, I think we're going.

(The INTERCOM on the phone buzzes.)

KEN. *(Holding his chest.)* Excuse me. I must have eaten too quickly.

CHRIS. That was the intercom, Ken. Not you.

LENNY. *(Crossing to the phone.)* I'll get it. *(Picking up the phone.)* Hello? . . . Charley? Are you all right? *(To others.)* It's Charley.

KEN. Molly? Who's Molly?

GLENN. *(Losing it.)* CHARLEY! CHARLEY! NOT MOLLY!

LENNY. *(Into phone.)* Yes, Charley, we're all here . . . Len, Glenn, Ken, Ernie, Claire, Chris, Cassie, and Cookie.

CLAIRE. Isn't that odd that all the women's names begin with a C?

CHRIS. That's right.

COOKIE. Except Myra.

CHRIS. Her middle name is Clara.

CLAIRE. And the men's names are all the same. Len, Glenn, Ken.

CHRIS. That's right.

CLAIRE. Except for Ernie and Charley.

COOKIE. Charley begins with a C.

ERNIE. What is this, anagrams, for pete sakes? Let him talk on the phone.

LENNY. Yes, Charley, I understand. No, it's perfectly reasonable. You do what you have to do . . . We'll be here. *(HE hangs up.)* He needs time to think.

KEN. More time to drink? He shouldn't drink with Valium.

GLENN. *(Shouting into Ken's ear.)* THINK! THINK! NOT DRINK.

KEN. Oh! Oh, my God! Oh, Jesus!

CHRIS. What? What is it?

KEN. My ears popped! They just opened up. My God, it sounds like a subway in here.

ERNIE. This is remarkable, but I'm having the first headache I've ever had in my life.

COOKIE. I just remembered.

CLAIRE. What?

COOKIE. Ernie's last name is Cusack. It begins with a C.

CLAIRE. You just remembered your husband's last name?

KEN. I can hear my own pulse. It's slightly up, but not too bad.

CASSIE. (*Smiles sexily at Ken.*) Can I take it, Ken? I'm very good at things like that.

GLENN. I'm warning you, Cassie. You're going to end up in the same place where your crystal is.

CASSIE. Don't threaten me, sweetheart, because I'll start naming names.

GLENN. That's it! That's it! I've got to stay, but I'm putting you in a taxi.

CASSIE. (*Screams.*) Never mind! I'LL WALK.

(*KEN grabs his ears in pain and drops to the floor. CASSIE storms out the front door.*)

GLENN. Walk? Twenty-two miles? Cassie, wait for me. Will you wait!! (*HE runs out after Cassie.*)

CLAIRE. I feel badly for her. Especially because one day she'll grow old and die.

COOKIE. I just thought of something else. Glenn went to Penn.

CHRIS. Oh, sit on it, will you, honey.

ERNIE. If I had you all in my group, I would never need another group again.

KEN. (*At the Stage Right wall, near the window.*) Shh. Quiet. I can hear them.

LENNY. Hear who?

KEN. Glenn and Cassie. They're in the driveway. I swear, I can hear them talking.

CLAIRE. The man is a German shepherd.

ERNIE. I don't think it's your business to listen, Ken.

LENNY. If he can hear through walls, it's his business.

KEN. She's talking about a woman. She's very upset.

COOKIE. (*Looking out the window.*) I'll say. She just kicked a car with her foot. Who owns the BMW?

LENNY. Ah, shit. The good side too, I bet.

CHRIS. (*Leaping to her feet.*) I just figured it out.

CLAIRE. I know what she's going to say. Glenn, Ken and Len are all men.

CHRIS. No, no, no. It's Glenn Cooper . . . Glenn is the one that Myra's having the affair with.

COOKIE. You think so.

CHRIS. Figure it out. Myra's been working very hard on Glenn's campaign. Two, three nights a week. *Late* nights.

CLAIRE. Of course. Charley's not dumb. He puts two and two together, confronts Myra with it, she confesses, Charley kicks her out of the house, tells the servants to go home and tries to blow his brains out.

ERNIE. You don't know that. That's an assumption on your part. That is a very, very dangerous statement to make. Don't you agree with me, Len?

LENNY. No.

ERNIE. Why not?

LENNY. I don't feel like it.

ERNIE. Listen, I think we have to bring this thing to a head. I'm going to go up and speak to Charley and find out what's what. (*HE starts for the stairs.*)

KEN. Wait a minute. Hold it! As far as Charley's concerned, only Chris and I know about Charley shooting himself in the ear, am I right?

LENNY. Right. He never said a word to me. He had the pillow covering up his ear the whole time.

CLAIRE. So what you're saying is, he doesn't know we know anything.

ERNIE. Well, he's got to know that we all haven't seen Myra. And that there's no servants here.

KEN. Exactly. But he doesn't know the *rest* of you know about the gunshot.

CHRIS. Slower. Go slower. Talk like we're children.

KEN. My point is, I told him we wouldn't tell anybody.

CLAIRE. And then you went ahead and told everybody.

KEN. No, no. I told only you and Lenny. Lenny told everybody.

LENNY. But you were deaf then. You didn't hear me telling everybody.

CLAIRE. (*To Ken.*) And then you told everybody *after* Lenny told everybody.

CHRIS. Go fast again. It doesn't make any difference.

(*COOKIE stands up and goes to the window.*)

KEN. What I'm trying to say is, as long as Charley doesn't think the rest of you know—

ERNIE. —Why tell him now? I see your point. We've got to keep up the subterfuge. If we confront him with everyone knowing about the gunshot, he could go to pieces. So until he tells us his own story himself, we have to pretend we don't know anything.

KEN. I should be the one who goes up. I tell Charley that everyone is here. And he asks me does everyone know what's happened.

ERNIE. You say, "No."

KEN. I say, "No." Then Charley asks me, well, if I'm not down there and Myra's not down there and the help's not down there, what did you tell them?

COOKIE. (*Looking out the window.*) Something's wrong with Cassie. Woops.

LENNY. Woops? What's woops? She threw up in the car?

COOKIE. She hit Glenn. His nose is bleeding.

CLAIRE. Tell me when he hits her back. I'd love to watch that.

KEN. Will you all please be quiet. I can't hear myself think. What was I saying?

CHRIS. (*Quickly.*) You said, "I should be the one who goes up. I tell Charley that everyone is here." And he asks "Does everyone here know what's happened?" Ernie said, "You say, 'No.'" You said, "I say 'no.' Then Charley asks me, 'Well, if I'm not down there and Myra's not down there—'"

KEN. Allrightallrightallright!!

ERNIE. I've got it. I've got it. Here's what we do. Charley's going to want to know what Ken told us. Ken tells Charley that he told us that Charley had a large benign wart removed from his ear this morning, but he's okay. Then suddenly Myra's mother broke her hip this afternoon and that Myra took her to the hospital and is going to stay there the night. The help, thinking the party was off, left the food and went home. It all happened so fast, they forgot to call us. We all got here, we understood and decided to cook the dinner ourselves . . . That's the story.

CLAIRE. I wouldn't believe the mother breaking her hip.

ERNIE. Why not?

CLAIRE. She died six years ago.

ERNIE. Then her father broke his hip.

CLAIRE. Her father lives in California.

ERNIE. Does she have a relative in the city?

CHRIS. She has a cousin Florence.

ERNIE. Then Florence broke her hip.

CHRIS. Florence is married. Why didn't her husband take her?

ERNIE. Then Myra broke her hip. The neighbors took her.

COOKIE. If he only had a wart removed, Charley could have taken her.

CLAIRE. Can't you think of something else?

ERNIE. (*Upset.*) I did! I thought of the mother, the father, the cousin, the wart and the hip. Nothing satisfies you people.

KEN. There's no logic to it. Nothing in that story is plausible.

ERNIE. (*Losing it.*) We don't need plausible. The man is in shock, mental anguish and emotional despair. Logic doesn't mean shit to him right now. (*He sits down, composes himself.*) Excuse my language.

(*The PHONE rings. THEY ALL look at it. The PHONE rings again. THEY ALL look at each other.*)

ERNIE. The telephone!

LENNY. Don't you think we know it's a telephone? We all have telephones, Ernie. We're all wealthy people here.

(*The PHONE is still ringing.*)

ERNIE. Just calm down, everybody. (*HE picks up the phone.*) Hello? . . . Yes? . . . Yes, he is . . . Who's calling, please? . . . I see. All right . . . Just a moment, please. (*Covering the phone.*) It's a woman. For Glenn.

CLAIRE. So?

ERNIE. It sounds like Myra.

COOKIE. Oh, fuck-a-doodle-doo.

KEN. Should I go get him?

ERNIE. Wait a minute. (*Into phone.*) Er, Glenn is outside just now. Can I tell him who's calling? . . . I see. All right. Hold on. (*Covering the phone.*) I can't tell. Maybe it is, maybe it isn't.

COOKIE. What did she say when you asked who's calling?

ERNIE. She said, "Just a friend."

LENNY. How did she say it?

ERNIE. She said, "Just a friend." How many ways are there to say it?

LENNY. I'll tell you how many ways. Nervous, phony, sincere, drunk—

CHRIS. Scared, guilty, lying—

COOKIE. Off-handed, perplexed, deceitful—

CLAIRE. Ominous, anonymous—

ERNIE. THIS ISN'T SCRABBLE, for God's sakes.

LENNY. Let me talk to her.

ERNIE. She didn't ask for you.

LENNY. She didn't ask for you, either. I know Myra's voice. Give me the phone. (*HE grabs the phone from Ernie.*) Hello? . . . No, it isn't. It's Glenn's friend, Len . . . No, Ken is getting Glenn . . . You sound awfully familiar. Do I know you? . . . I see . . . Well, hold on, please. (*Covering the phone.*) I don't think it's her.

COOKIE. Well, who does it sound like?

LENNY. Meryl Streep.

COOKIE. Meryl Streep? Why would Meryl Streep call here?

LENNY. I didn't say it *was* Meryl Streep. But you know how she sounds in the movies? Like she always does the character perfectly but it's not really her. That's how she sounds.

COOKIE. Like she's not Meryl Streep?

ERNIE. Now we're playing "Trivial Pursuit!" This is not a game show. Ken, will you please get Glenn? (*Grabbing the phone from Lenny.*) Hello? . . . Somebody went to get Glenn . . . Hello? . . . (*HE hangs up.*) She hung up. She must have gotten suspicious.

KEN. Quiet down everyone. I hear something!

CLAIRE. I'll bet it's the Concorde landing in London.

KEN. It's a car coming up the driveway.

(*HEADLIGHTS flash on the window.*)

CLAIRE. Maybe it's Myra.

LENNY. Maybe it's Harry and Joan from Venezuela.

(*The front door opens quickly and GLENN rushes in holding a bloody hanky to his nose.*)

GLENN. We got trouble. Oh, God, have we got trouble.

KEN. What is it?

GLENN. The police. It's a police car.

LENNY. (*Loudly, pointing at Ken.*) Okay! I warned you! I *told* you we should have called the police. Now look what's happened. The police came.

KEN. Who could have called the police?

CLAIRE. Maybe it was Myra.

CHRIS. Maybe it was Charley.

LENNY. Maybe it was Cassie. (*To Glenn.*) You were fighting with her, weren't you? Did she use the phone in my car?

GLENN. Not to call. She hit me with it.

LENNY. She broke my phone? My new phone in my new car?

ERNIE. Will everybody calm down. We've got to figure out what to say when they come in.

COOKIE. (*Looking out the window.*) They're trying to talk to Cassie. She won't roll down the windows.

LENNY. *My* windows? They're going to bust my windows? I'm going to take my car home in an envelope.

ERNIE. (*To Glenn.*) Why did you leave her out there in the car? She's in no condition to answer police questions.

GLENN. She's in good enough condition to smash my nose . . . Goddam, I got blood on my shirt.

LENNY. And you're running for the State Senate? I wouldn't let you run for Chinese food.

CHRIS. What's wrong with you people? I've got a six-year-old child at home who behaves better than we do.

LENNY. Fine! Then get him over here and tell *him* to talk to the police.

KEN. Take it easy, Len. She's been doing her share. She's the one who called Dr. Dudley.

LENNY. EVERYBODY CALLED DR. DUDLEY. HE'S IN THE YELLOW PAGES IN CHINA!!

CLAIRE. Maybe Dudley called the police.

(The TELEPHONE rings.)

ERNIE. It's the phone again.

LENNY. He's right. He guessed it was the phone twice in a row. This genius is going to save our lives.

ERNIE. *(Picking up the phone.)* Hello? . . . Yes? . . . Just a minute, please. *(To Glenn.)* Glenn, it's for you. *(Announcing to the Group.)* It's the same woman who called before.

GLENN. *(Crossing to the phone.)* What same woman?

CLAIRE. She wouldn't say. Maybe it was Myra, maybe it was Meryl Streep.

GLENN. Meryl Streep?

CLAIRE. You know how she sounds in the movies? Like she always does the character perfectly, but it's not really her? That's how this person sounded.

LENNY. *(At the front door, looking out.)* We've got two policemen coming in, she's giving us a resume of the party.

COOKIE. *(Looking out the window.)* Oh, oh. They're walking over here.

GLENN. *(Into phone.)* Hello?

COOKIE. *(Hobbling away from the window.)* They're on the way over.

GLENN. *(Into phone.)* Oh, hi. How are you? . . . No, it's not a cold, it's a telephone injury.

KEN. Now listen. The thing we can't do is let them see Charley. We can't let him downstairs or them upstairs.

GLENN. *(Into phone.)* I tried talking to Cassie, but she's very upset.

ERNIE. *(Gesturing importantly.)* Above all, no false statements. We must keep within the law. This above all, agreed?

LENNY. *(Mocking Ernie's gestures.)* Yea! To thine own self be true. Wherein the hearts of better men—are you fucking crazy? They're outside the door.

GLENN. *(Into phone.)* Of course I think you should talk to her, but I can't get her out of the car.

KEN. They're going to ask about the gunshots. What do we tell them about the gunshots?

GLENN. *(Into phone.)* All right, I'll call you back in fifteen minutes. Are you at the nine-one-four number?

LENNY. Kill him! Somebody kill him! Choke him with the telephone wire.

(The DOORBELL chimes.)

CHRIS. I'm very serious about this, but I'm not going to be able to hold my bladder.

ERNIE. All right, I've got it. We tell them we never heard the gunshots.

CLAIRE. You mean lie to them?

LENNY. What happened to "this above all?"

ERNIE. It won't work tonight. Maybe some other time.

CHRIS. If you let me go to the bathroom, I promise I'll come back.

GLENN. *(Still on the phone.)* Listen, I know you're a good friend. And I thank you for all your wonderful support.

LENNY. Leave him here. Let's run for our lives and leave that schmuck for the cops.

GLENN. *(Into phone.)* I can't talk anymore. I'll call you back later . . . I will . . . Goodbye. *(Hangs up and turns to the others.)* All right, what's going on?

LENNY. Well, about six weeks ago we got an invitation to this party—

ERNIE. Stop it, Lenny . . . All right, think everybody. Think. Why didn't we hear the gunshots?

COOKIE. *(Raising her hand.)* We're all deaf people. We meet once a week. That's why we didn't hear the doorbell.

LENNY. *(To Claire.)* Now you know why they call her Cookie.

CHRIS. I've got it! We were listening to the Hitler program. The cannons were bombing Berlin, we couldn't hear anything else.

(THEY all consider.)

LENNY. THERE WAS NO HITLER PROGRAM. WE MADE THE FUCKING THING UP TO FOOL THIS ASSHOLE. *(Points to Glenn.)*

GLENN. Hey, I've had just about enough from you, Lenny.

(The DOORBELL chimes. ALL drop to the floor.)

KEN. We've got to let them in.

LENNY. All right. Claire, open the door.

CLAIRE. I can't. I'm in charge of the music.

GLENN. The music! That's it!

CHRIS. What is?

GLENN. The music was on. We were all dancing. We couldn't hear the gunshots. Claire, put on the music.

(CLAIRE goes to the stereo cabinet.)

KEN. *(To Claire.)* WAIT!! Don't turn it on yet. There's one last thing to do.

CLAIRE. What?

KEN. Somebody has to be Charley. Just in case.

LENNY. Just in case what?

KEN. Just in case the police want to speak to Charley.

ERNIE. Ken is right. Charley is in no condition to tell them the real story.

LENNY. Of course not, because no one has *heard* the real story yet.

KEN. Exactly. But we have to be sure whatever story the police hear, has to be one that's not going to get us all in trouble.

CHRIS. I never saw a sinking ship empty so fast.

GLENN. I agree. Ken is absolutely right. *(To the Men.)* One of you three guys has to be Charley.

LENNY. When did *you* move to France?

GLENN. Well, let's be honest. I never even heard the gunshots.

LENNY. *(Shouting in Glenn's ear.)* BANG BANG, you bastard!

COOKIE. Isn't it against the law to impersonate another real person?

ERNIE. Yes, it is dear, but not if you do it well.

CHRIS. *(To the Women.)* Can you believe we actually married these men?

LENNY. This is a major felony we're talking about. You want to spend thirty years in a maximum security prison wearing a tuxedo?

KEN. *(Coming downstage and taking charge.)* We're all in this together, Glenn. Here's how we do it. You put out two fingers or one finger. If three guys are the same and one is different, that guy is Charley . . . Are we ready?

LENNY. Who made you Don Corleone?

KEN. You have a better idea?

LENNY. Yeah. Let the women wrestle for it.

GLENN. Come on. Let's get it over with, for crise sakes.

KEN. Okay. Here we go. One—two—three!

(The MEN put out fingers.)

KEN. Two and two. No good . . . Try again. Ready? One—two—three!

(The MEN put out fingers.)

KEN. All the same. No good . . . Again!

(The DOORBELL rings.)

KEN. Ready one—two—three!

(The MEN put out fingers.)

KEN. Aha! Lenny!

LENNY. *(Quickly putting his hand behind his back.)* What do you mean, Lenny?

GLENN. We all have two fingers out, you have one finger.

LENNY. Bullshit! I had two stuck together. *(HE shows them.)* I got duck grease on my fingers.

ERNIE. It was one finger, Lenny.

LENNY. It was two, I swear to God.

ERNIE. No, no. It was one. ONE FINGER. ONE! I SAW IT!!

COOKIE. And that man graduated from Johns Hopkins.

GLENN. Go on upstairs, Lenny. And don't come down unless we call you.

LENNY. No, I'm anxious to come as Charley. *(HE goes into Charley's room and closes the door.)*

(The DOORBELL rings again.)

KEN. Okay, Claire, put on the music.

ERNIE. Let's go, kids. Hurry up. Get your partners.

(THEY do.)

ERNIE. Okay.

(CLAIRE turns on the stereo. It is a loud rendition of "La Bamba" . . . the THREE COUPLES dance furiously.
We hear loud BANGING on the front door, and then it is opened.
TWO POLICEMEN stand there. One, OFFICER WELCH, a strong, vigorous man. The other, OFFICER PUDNEY, is a woman in her late twenties.
THEY stand watching the COUPLES dance. NO ONE seems to notice the POLICE.)

WELCH. *(Yells.)* Can you shut that thing off, please!

(NO ONE notices.)

WELCH. SOMEBODY PLEASE SHUT THAT DAMN THING OFF!

(KEN turns the MUSIC off. THEY ALL look surprised that the Police are in the room.)

ERNIE. *(Indignant.)* I beg your pardon. May I ask what you're doing here?
WELCH. I'm sorry. I didn't mean to bust the door open.
ERNIE. Then why didn't you ring first?
WELCH. I did. Five times.
ERNIE. *(Crossing near the Police.)* Five times? We didn't hear it.
WELCH. I guess the music was on so loud, you couldn't hear anything.
ERNIE. Of *course.* The *music.*
KEN. That's why we didn't hear you.
CLAIRE. No wonder we didn't get any phone calls. We wouldn't hear them.
CHRIS. That's what it was. The music.
COOKIE. It was on . . .
ALL. . . . *so loud.*
ERNIE. *(Congenial.)* Now, what seems to be the trouble, officer?

WELCH. Well, just sort of routine investigation, sir. My name is Officer Welch. This is Officer Pudney. Is this your house, sir?

ERNIE. *My* house? No, no. I live elsewhere. Other than here.

KEN. As I do. Live elsewhere. Could you tell us what this is about, officer?

EVERYONE. Yes, what's this about? Is anything wrong? Why are the police here? I can't imagine what's going on.

WELCH. All right, all right, take it easy. Calm down. I just want to ask a few questions . . . May I ask who the owner of this house is?

KEN. We'd be delighted to tell, Officer, but I believe it's customary first for you to inform us as to why these questions are being asked of us.

WELCH. You're a lawyer, aren't you.

KEN. Yes, I am.

WELCH. Well, as a lawyer you understand you're not obligated to answer these questions. I was hoping someone would be cooperative enough to tell me the owner's name.

(THEY ALL look at each other.)

CLAIRE. Brock. Charley Brock.

WELCH. Could you tell me if Mr. Brock is at home at present?

(THEY ALL look at each other.)

CLAIRE. I'm not sure. Chris, is Charley at home?

CHRIS. Charley? I think he went to walk the dog.

WELCH. Then he'll be back soon?

COOKIE. I don't think so. It's a Dachshund. They take very small steps.

KEN. *(Wanting no trouble.)* He's home. He came back, Officer.

WELCH. Well, then could I possibly see Mr. Brock for a moment?

KEN. *(Coming Downstage, taking charge.)* Well, it's an awkward time, Officer. As you can see, we're celebrating a party.

WELCH. Yes, I've noticed. What's the occasion?

KEN. The tenth wedding anniversary of Charley and Myra Brock.

WELCH. (*Crossing to Ken.*) I wouldn't take long. I just need a minute of his time.

KEN. Well, unfortunately, Mr. Brock is sleeping.

WELCH. Sleeping? In the middle of his anniversary party?

KEN. He was feeling depressed. He took a sleeping pill.

WELCH. Well, could I see *Mrs.* Brock?

KEN. Mrs. Brock is not here.

WELCH. She's not?

KEN. That's why Mr. Brock is depressed.

WELCH. Where is she?

(*THEY ALL look at each other.*)

ERNIE. . . . Her father broke his hip. She had to take him to the hospital.

(*THEY ALL glare at him.*)

WELCH. During her anniversary party? Couldn't someone *else* take him to the hospital?

CLAIRE. Her father lives in California.

CHRIS. It has to do with cousins and warts and hips. It's very complicated.

WELCH. (*Crossing to GLENN who is hiding his face with his hand.*) You, sir? Something wrong with your eye?

GLENN. Me? Yes. I put some drops in tonight and the cap fell off. Most of the bottle went in.

WELCH. May I have your name, sir?

GLENN. My name?

WELCH. Yes, sir.

GLENN. You mean, my name?

WELCH. Yes, sir . . . Is there a problem with giving me your name?

GLENN. I'm sorry. I just can't see you very well.

WELCH. You don't have to see to talk, sir. The drops didn't go in your mouth, did they?

KEN. Officer, I feel you're being unnecessarily abusive to these people. If you're going to ask any more questions, you'll have to tell us what this is all about.

WELCH. Yes, sir. I will . . . Can you please tell me who owns the BMW outside?

CLAIRE. It's my husband's car.

WELCH. And what is his name, please?

KEN. You don't have to answer that, Claire.

CLAIRE. His name is Len. Leonard Ganz.

WELCH. And where is Mr. Ganz now?

KEN. (*Like in court.*) I object.

WELCH. (*Annoyed.*) I ain't a judge! This ain't a court! I don't have a gavel! I just want to know where the man is.

KEN. You still haven't told us what this is about, so we're still not telling you where Mr. Ganz is.

WELCH. I don't know why I always have trouble in this neighborhood . . . Okay . . . (*Consulting his notebook.*) At approximately eight-fifteen tonight, an auto accident occurred on Twelfth and Danbury. A brand new red 1990 Porsche convertible with New York license plates smashed into the side of a brand new BMW four door sedan. Now, we know it wasn't the BMW's fault because the Porsche was a stolen car. Stolen at eight-fifteen tonight right off the dealer's lot. The man and the Porsche got away. Now do you know who that brand new Porsche belonged to?

CLAIRE. How would I know?

WELCH. It belonged to Deputy Mayor Charles M. Brock. Purchased today as a gift from his wife, Myra. A surprise wedding anniversary present.

CLAIRE. Surprise hardly says it.

KEN. Aha! So, you're here to investigate the car accident?

WELCH. That's right. Now if Mr. Ganz is here, I'd like to speak to him. And if he's not here, the police department would like to know where he is.

KEN. I see . . . Do you think you could wait outside for one moment, officer?

WELCH. Why?

KEN. Mrs. Ganz is my client. I would like to consult with her before any further questioning. It's within my rights.

WELCH. . . . One minute. That's all you get.

(WELCH *motions to* PUDNEY *and* THEY BOTH *go out the front door.*)

KEN. All right, we don't have much time. One of us has to be Lenny.

ERNIE. What are you talking about?

KEN. The man doesn't even know about the gunshots. He just wants to ask Lenny about the accident. But Lenny can't be Lenny because we need Lenny to be Charley in case he wants to ask Charley about the new car, and we can't let him see Charley because Charley has a bullet hole in his ear.

COOKIE. *(To Chris.)* Do you understand him in real life?

CHRIS. We don't actually talk that much.

KEN. All right. Glenn! Ernie! We have to choose again.

ERNIE. Oh, leave me alone with this stupid game. *(Walks away.)*

KEN. I know it's stupid, but we have to do it. We need a Lenny.

CHRIS. *(To Boys.)* Never mind. The girls will do it. Come on, girls. The odd woman's husband is Lenny.

CLAIRE. My husband *is* Lenny.

CHRIS. No, Lenny is Charley. You're playing for Glenn. Get in a circle.

(THEY bunch together, just like the Men.)

COOKIE. I don't know how to play this.

CHRIS. Just put out your fingers. We'll do the counting . . . Odd finger loses . . . All right? Ready? One—two—three.

(The GIRLS puts out fingers except COOKIE who puts out a fist.)

CHRIS. No! . . . No no no no! Your fingers, Cookie, open your fist.

COOKIE. I don't want to lose my earrings again.

CHRIS. Just one or two fingers! All right? Here we go. One—two—three!

(The GIRLS put out fingers.)

CHRIS. Aha! It's me! Fuck! . . . Sorry, Ken.

KEN. It's okay. All right, I'm Lenny. Open the door, Ernie.

(*ERNIE crosses to the front door. The front door opens. WELCH and PUDNEY come in. WELCH is unhappy.*)

WELCH. I'm glad to see you're not dancing again. Now where is Mr. Leonard Ganz?

KEN. He's right here in this room. I am Leonard Ganz.

WELCH. (*Looking at him sideways.*) You are?

KEN. Yes.

WELCH. How come it took you a whole minute to think of your name?

KEN. Never rush your answers. Harvard Law School.

WELCH. Never trust a man who doesn't know if he's here or not. Police Academy.

(*CHRIS involuntarily puts her arm through Ken's to protect him. WELCH sees this.*)

WELCH. Who are you, ma'am?

CHRIS. I'm his wife. His wife's best friend. (*Pointing to Claire.*) Her. Mrs. Ganz. (*Takes her arm away.*)

WELCH. Are you here alone, ma'am?

CHRIS. No. I'm here with my husband. Mr. Gorman.

WELCH. Where is he?

CHRIS. (*Looks around.*) Must have gone home early.

WELCH. Not much of a party, is it?

CHRIS. It's had its up and downs.

WELCH. (*To Ken.*) All right, Mr. Ganz. Tell us about the accident. In full and complete detail.

KEN. . . . Do you think you could step outside just one more time.

WELCH. I AIN'T GOING NO PLACE NO WHERE NO TIME!!! THIS IS IT!! This is where I live till I get what I came for, even if my whole family has to move in.

(*We hear the WALKIE-TALKIE squawk in Pudney's holster.*)

WELCH. What's that?

PUDNEY. 1047 Pudney. Over . . . (*The RADIO squawks at her.*) Check . . . Got it . . . Hold it. (*To Welch.*) Red 1990 Porsche con-

vertible located at Fifth and Market in Tarrytown. Suspect appre-
hended. They said call it a night.

WELCH. (*Nods.*) Well, I guess that ties that little bundle up.

EVERYBODY. Isn't that wonderful? Terrific! I'm so happy.

WELCH. Sorry to disturb you, folks.

EVERYBODY. Hey, it's okay. No problem. We understand.

WELCH. There'll be some further questioning for you tomorrow,
Mr. Ganz. No need to take any more of your time tonight. Thank
you and goodnight, folks.

EVERYONE. It's okay. Our pleasure. Anytime, officer.

(*GLENN goes to Welch and shakes his hand.*)

WELCH. I *know* I've seen you some place before. What's your
name again?

GLENN. (*Happily.*) Glenn. Glenn Cooper.

WELCH. Were you ever on TV?

GLENN. Well, as a matter of fact, yes. I'm running for the State
Senate.

WELCH. Right. I saw you do an interview on PBS. Why were you
so afraid to give me your name?

GLENN. Well, you know. When you're in politics, you don't want
to get mixed up with these things.

WELCH. Yes, but you weren't involved with this. Unless you witnessed the accident. Did you?

GLENN. No, no, no. My wife and I arrived late. We didn't even
hear the gunshots.

(*A moment of frozen silence. The OTHERS look to heaven for
help.*)

WELCH. . . . What gunshots?

GLENN. Hmmm?

WELCH. I said, what gunshots?

GLENN. I suppose the gunshots that were fired when they
chased the stolen car?

WELCH. That was twelve miles away over in Tarrytown. You got
twenty-twenty hearing, Mr. Cooper?

(PUDNEY's WALKIE-TALKIE squawks again.)

PUDNEY. 1047 Pudney. Over . . . *(SHE listens. It SQUAWKS.)* Right . . . Check . . . Will do. *(SHE turns it off. To Welch.)* Neighbors reported two gunshots were fired about nine P.M. from inside 1257 Peekskill Road, Sneden's Landing. Investigate.

WELCH. 1257 Peekskill Road . . . Well, we've got ourselves a double header, don't we? . . . Anybody want to tell us about the gunshots?

EVERYBODY. No. Not really. We didn't hear any gunshots. The music was so loud.

WELCH. Nobody heard them, I suppose. *(To Glenn.)* Who's the woman sitting outside in the BMW?

GLENN. She's my wife, Cassie.

WELCH. I'd like to have a little talk with Mrs. Cooper . . . Connie, get her in here.

COOKIE. *(Portentously.)* Connie? With a C?

(PUDNEY exits through the front door.)

WELCH. *(Coming downstage.)* Looks to me like you all had a fine dinner . . . I'd like to speak to the help, please.

KEN. There is no help.

WELCH. Then who did the cooking?

COOKIE. I did.

WELCH. What's your name?

COOKIE. Cookie.

WELCH. I mean your real name.

COOKIE. That *is* my real name. I have two sisters named Candy and Taffy. I swear to God.

WELCH. *(Looks at Ken.)* Is that blood on your shirt, Len?

KEN. Blood? Oh, yes. I cut myself with a fork during dinner.

WELCH. *(Nods doubtingly, looks at Glenn.)* Is that blood on *your* shirt, Glenn?

GLENN. Oh, yes. I must have rubbed against Len . . . when we were dancing.

WELCH. Ken, Len and Glenn. That's really weird.

KEN. It's just a coincidence.

WELCH. I guess it is. My name is Ben.

(The front door opens, and CASSIE comes in with PUDNEY. CASSIE is still angry. The shoulder pad on her suit jacket has been ripped open at the seam, and the white padding hangs out.)

WELCH. Are you all right, Mrs. Cooper?

CASSIE. I'm not pressing any charges. My lawyer will handle this.

GLENN. It was an accident. She dropped the electric cigarette lighter in the car on the leather seat, and I grabbed her jacket to pull her out of the car.

WELCH. *(To Glenn.)* And how'd you get that nasty blow on your nose?

GLENN. My wife was hanging up the car phone in the dark and my head was a little too low.

WELCH. My my my. We got a lot of cartoon humor in this case, don't we?

COOKIE. *(In pain, as SHE tries to sit.)* Ahhhh!

WELCH. You hurtin' too, ma'am?

COOKIE. Oh, I have a chronic back spasm. It's very hard for me to sit, stand or walk.

WELCH. And you didn't hear the gunshots either, I suppose?

COOKIE. No. I was dancing.

(WELCH looks at her in disbelief.)

COOKIE. Dancing is good for my back.

WELCH. And to think I was almost out the door with this one. *(To Chris.)* Mrs. Gorman?

CHRIS. Is that me? *(Looks around.)* Yes. Mrs. Gorman. Right.

WELCH. And what do you do?

CHRIS. Well, mostly, I've been helping with the drinks.

WELCH. Your occupation!

CHRIS. Oh, nothing . . . No, not nothing. Well, I'm a liar—a lawyer! . . . Sorry . . . And I'm a mother. I have two children . . . A boy . . . No, one child . . . Sorry. I'm very nervous.

WELCH. You and everybody else, ma'am. I'm going to say something now that is not really a part of my official capacity. But I don't believe one God damn thing I've heard in this room. I think there were gunshots here tonight. I think someone or *everyone* is trying to cover up something. A man gets hit in the nose, another man stabs himself with a fork, someone's BMW gets smashed up, the host takes a short-legged dog for a walk and then goes to sleep, the hostess takes her father to a hospital in California with a broken hip, and nobody hears two gunshots because everybody is dancing, including a woman named Cookie who's been cooking all night who can't stand or walk! You people have to deal with me. I'm a real cop, you understand? I'm not somebody named Elmer that your kids watch on the Disney Channel . . . Now, I want some *real* answers, intelligent answers, believable answers, and answers that don't make me laugh. But first, I want to see Mr. Charley Brock and find out what the hell's going on here—including the possibility of him having two bullet holes in him. Now, I'll give you five seconds to get him down here, or I'll take two seconds and go upstairs and find him.

(*KEN and GLENN argue silently behind Welch's back.*)

WELCH. Don't mess with me now. I'm so close to a promotion, I can smell it. And I'm not going to screw it up with *this* case . . . Do I start counting or do I start climbing up steps? It's up to you.

(*NOBODY moves. WELCH starts up the steps.*)

GLENN. Okay, just wait, will you? Wait a second. Wait. Okay? Can you wait? Just wait . . . Ernie! Ken! I mean Len. I think it's time to call Charley and ask him to come down, don't you?
ERNIE. Definitely.
KEN. Absolutely.

(*ERNIE goes to the phone and rings Charley's room.*)

ERNIE. . . . Charley? . . . It's Ernie. We're ready for you now . . . Are you ready for us now? . . . Relax, Charley, that's just an hysteric nerve reaction.
KEN. What's wrong with him?
ERNIE. (*To Ken.*) He thinks he went temporarily blind. (*Into phone.*) Just put some cold water on your eyes and come down.

There are two police officers who want to speak to you . . . Why? . . . BECAUSE YOU PUT OUT ONE FINGER, THAT'S WHY! ! (*Hanging up and smiling at Welch.*) He's fine. He's coming down.

GLENN. The truth is, Officer, we were trying to protect Mr. Brock because he's a dear friend of ours. But we know we're all in jeopardy if we hold back the truth. (*Crossing away from Welch.*) There *were* two gunshots here tonight. I, personally, did not hear them, but I share equal blame with those who *did* hear the shots and did not come forth with that information . . . despite the fact that I didn't hear them.

KEN. Stop helping so much, Glenn.

GLENN. Nevertheless, Mr. Brock is willing to tell us the full and complete story, the details of which none of us has heard yet. About the missing help, about the disappearance of his wife, Myra, and about the two gunshots, which I didn't hear.

COOKIE. Oh, God, I'm getting another spasm in my back.

CHRIS. Oh, who gives a shit?

(*Charley's bedroom door opens. LENNY stands there as Charley, wearing a robe, pajamas and slippers, and a large bandage over his ear. THEY ALL look at him. HE looks at them, furious for making him do this.*)

GLENN. Hello, Charley.

KEN. Hi, Charley.

ERNIE. Feeling all right, Charley?

(*LENNY comes slowly down the stairs.*)

WELCH. I'm Officer Welch, Mr. Brock. This is Officer Pudney. Please sit down.

(*LENNY sits.*)

WELCH. Take this down, Connie.

(*SHE takes out her notebook.*)

WELCH. Now, Mr. Brock, tell us from the beginning exactly what happened in this house tonight.

COOKIE. Does anyone want lemon tarts?

LENNY. Yes, a tart would be wonderful.

WELCH. Not now, ma'am . . . Go ahead, Mr. Brock.

LENNY. Okay . . . Let's see . . . the story . . . as it happened . . . as I remember it . . . as I'm telling it . . . oh, God . . . Well, here goes . . . At exactly six o'clock tonight I came home from work. My wife, Myra, was in her dressing room getting dressed for the party. I got a bottle of champagne from the refrigerator and headed upstairs. Rosita, the Spanish cook, was in the kitchen with Ramona, her Spanish sister and Romero, her Spanish son. They were preparing an Italian dinner. They were waiting for Myra to tell her when to start the dinner. As I climbed the stairs, I said to myself, "It's my tenth wedding anniversary and I can't believe I still love my wife so much." Myra was putting on the perfume I bought her for Christmas. I purposely buy it because it drives me crazy . . . I tapped on her door. Tap tap tap. She opens it. I hand her a glass of champagne. I make a toast. (*Looking at Claire.*) "To the most beautiful wife a man ever had for ten years." She says, "To the best man and the best ten years a beautiful wife ever had" . . . We drink. We kiss. We toast again. "To the loveliest skin on the loveliest body that has never aged a day in ten wonderful years" . . . She toasts, "To the gentlest hands that ever stroked the loveliest skin that never has aged in ten wonderful years" . . . We drink. We kiss. We toast . . . We drink. We kiss. We toast . . . By seven o'clock the bottle is finished, my wife is sloshed and I'm completely toasted . . . And then I smell the perfume. The perfume I could never resist . . . I loved her in that moment with as much passion and ardor as the night we were first newlyweds. (*Rising. To Welch.*) I tell you this, not with embarrassment, but with pride and joy for a love that grows stronger and more lasting as each new day passes. We lay there spent, naked in each other's arms, complete in our happiness. It's now eight o'clock and outside it's grown dark. Suddenly, a gentle knock on the door. Knock knock knock. The door opens and a strange young man looks down at us with a knife in his hands. Myra screams. (*HE begins to act out the story.*) I jump up and run for the gun in my drawer. Myra grabs a towel and shields herself. I rush back in with the pistol, ready to save my wife's life. The strange young man says in Spanish, "Yo quito se dablo enchilada por quesa in quinto min-uto." But I don't speak Spanish and I never saw Rosita's son, Romero, before, and I didn't know the knife was to cut up the salad and he was asking should they heat up the dinner now? So I aimed my gun at him, Myra screams and pulls my arm. The gun goes off and shoots me in the earlobe. Rosita's son, Romero, runs down-stairs and tells Rosita and Ramona, "Mamasetta! Meela que paso el hombre ay baco ay yah. El hombre que loco, que bang-bang"—the crazy man took a shot at him. So, Rosita, Ramona and Romero leave in a huff. My ear lobe is bleeding all over Myra's new dress. Suddenly we hear a car pull up. It's the first guests. Myra grabs a bathrobe and runs downstairs to stop Rosita, Ramona and Romero, otherwise we'll have no dinner. But they drive off in their Alfa Romeo. I look out the window, but it's dark and I think someone is stealing my beautiful old Mercedes, so I take another shot at them. Myra runs down to the basement where we keep the cedar chest. She's looking for the dress she wore last year for Bonds for Israel. She can't find the light, trips down the stairs, passes out in the dark. I run downstairs looking for Myra, notice the basement door is open and afraid the strange-looking kid is coming back, so I lock the door, not knowing that Myra is still down there. Then I run upstairs to take some aspirin because my earlobe is killing me from the hole in it. But the blood on my fingers gets in my eyes and by mistake I take four Valium instead. I hear the guests downstairs and I want to tell them to look for Myra. But suddenly, I can't talk from the Valium, and I'm bleed-ing on the white rug. So I start to write a note explaining what happened, but the note looks like gibberish. And I'm afraid they'll think it was a suicide note and they'll call the police and my friend Glenn Cooper was coming and it would be very bad for his cam-paign to get mixed up with a suicide, so I tore up the note and flushed it down the toilet, just as they walked into my room. They're yelling at me, "What happened? What happened?" And before I could tell them what happened, I passed out on the bed. And that's the whole goddamn story, as sure as my name is . . . (*HE opens his robe to expose the monogram "CB" on the pajamas.*) . . . Charley Brock.

WELCH. (*Crossing to Lenny.*) I buy it. I buy the whole thing. You know why I buy it? I buy it because I *liked* it! I didn't *believe* it, but

I liked it! I love my wife, too, and that's why I want to get home early . . . (*Crossing to the front door.*) . . . Sorry to bother you, folks. Take care of that ear, Mr. Brock, and happy anniversary.

(*WELCH and PUDNEY leave. The OTHERS turn and look at Lenny.*)

GLENN. Where—where in the whole wide world did you find the guts to tell a story like that?
LENNY. (*Beaming.*) I made it up.
KEN. Of *course* you made it up. But when?
LENNY. As I was telling it. Sentence by sentence. Word by word. I didn't know where the hell I was going, but I just kept going.

(*We hear the POLICE CAR drive away.*)

CLAIRE. You don't even speak Spanish.
LENNY. I made the Spanish up, too.
CHRIS. You shit, we all could have gone to jail for perjury.
LENNY. (*Smiling.*) I know. That was the challenge. The ultimate chutzpah. It was the best goddamn time I ever had in my life.
ERNIE. I am impressed. I am sincerely and deeply impressed. You have, without a doubt, Lenny, one of the weirdest minds I've ever come across.
CLAIRE. (*Holding up her glass.*) A toast to my husband, Lenny. Just when I was getting bored with our marriage, I fell in love with him all over again.
EVERYBODY. To Lenny!
CHRIS. I have an interesting question.
COOKIE. What?
CHRIS. What do you think really happened to Charley and Myra?

(*The INTERCOM buzzes.*)

ERNIE. (*Picks it up.*) Hello? . . . Yes, Charley . . . We're all here . . . Are you up to having some visitors? . . .Wonderful . . . We're dying to hear the story. We're on the way. (*HE hangs up.*) Charley is going to tell us the entire story.

(THEY ALL begin to troop upstairs.)

CHRIS. I hope it's shorter than Lenny's story.

CASSIE. *(To Glenn.)* Can we go back later and look for my crystal, honey?

GLENN. I'll buy you a thousand crystals, angel.

*(THEY are ALL on the stairs. Suddenly, we hear a KNOCK from
inside the basement door. ALL stop and turn.)*

MYRA. *(From behind the door.)* Open the door. Open the door.
Let me out!

KEN. Who is it?

MYRA. *(From behind the door.)* It's Myra!

(THEY ALL look at Lenny in disbelief.)

CURTAIN

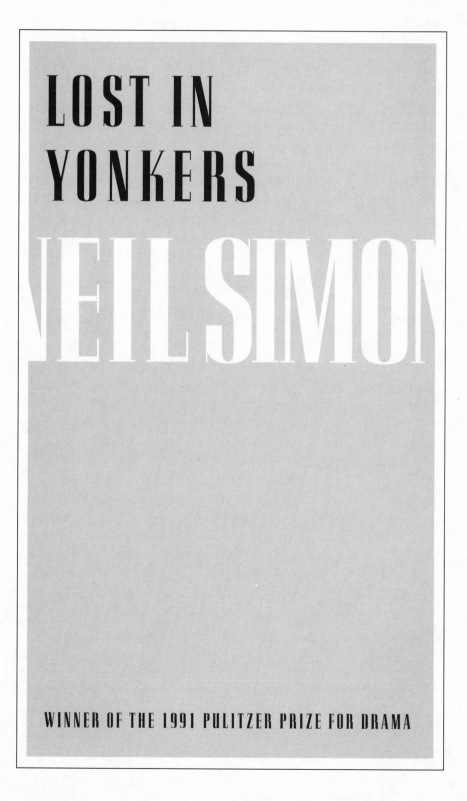

LOST IN
YONKERS

NEIL SIMON

WINNER OF THE 1991 PULITZER PRIZE FOR DRAMA

ACT I

Scene: Yonkers, New York . . . 1942.

An apartment that sits just above "KURNITZ'S KANDY STORE" . . . It consists of a living room, dining room, a small kitchen, one bathroom and two bedrooms. The entrance door leads from downstairs directly to the candy store.

At Rise: About six-thirty in the evening on a hot, sultry day in August. It's still quite light outside. A fan blows in the living room.

TWO YOUNG BOYS are in the living room. One, ARTHUR KURNITZ, about thirteen and a half, sits on an old armchair, looking apprehensive. HE is wearing an old woolen suit, his only one, with knickered pants, a shirt, tie, long socks and brown shoes.

The other boy is his brother, JAY KURNITZ, not quite sixteen. HE sits on the sofa, in a suit as well, but with long pants, shirt, tie, and shiny black shoes. HE looks more sullen and angry than apprehensive.

ARTY keeps wiping his sweaty brow with his handkerchief.

JAY. I hate coming here, don't you?

ARTY. *(in front of fan.)* It's hot. I'm so hot.

JAY. I'd hate coming here if I was cool. Pop doesn't even like to come and it's his own mother . . . I was so afraid of her when I was a kid. She'd come out of that door with a limp and a cane and looked like she was going to kill you. When I was five, I drew a picture of her and called it "Frankenstein's Grandma."

ARTY. Did she ever see it?

JAY. If she did, you'd be an only child today. Pop said she could swing her cane so fast, she could have been one of the greatest golfers in the world.

ARTY. All I remember was, I hated kissing her. It felt like putting your lips on a wrinkled ice cube.

JAY. Yeah, she's cold all right. She was the only one at Mom's funeral who didn't cry . . . I wonder what Pop's talking to her so long for.

ARTY. Because she's deaf in one ear, isn't she?

JAY. Yeah . . . Did you ever notice there's something wrong with *everyone* on Pop's side of the family? Mom used to tell me that.

ARTY. She didn't tell me. Like who?

JAY. Like all of them. Like Aunt Bella . . . She's a little (*Points to his head.*)—you know—closed for repairs.

ARTY. I don't care. I like her. Nicer than "hot house" Grandma.

JAY. I didn't say she wasn't nice. But she's got marbles rolling around up there . . . Mom said she got that way because when she was a kid, Grandma kept hitting her in the head every time she did something stupid . . . which only made her stupider.

ARTY. (*Lays on the floor, in front of the sofa.*) She wasn't stupid at making great ice cream sodas.

JAY. Hooray! Wonderful! She's thirty-five years old and she can make ice cream sodas. They don't give you a high school diploma for getting the cherry on top of the whipped cream.

ARTY. She went to high school?

JAY. A little. She missed the first year because she couldn't find it.

(*The bedroom door opens. Their father, EDDIE KURNITZ, about forty-one, steps out into the room. HE wears a suit and tie and seems hot and nervous. HE wipes his brow with a hanky.*)

EDDIE. You kids all right?

JAY. Yeah, Pop. Fine.

EDDIE. I'll be through talking to Grandma in a few minutes. (*To ARTY.*) Why are you lying on the floor? Don't do that, Arty. You'll crease your pants. You want Grandma to see you with creased pants? (*HE goes back in, closes the door.*)

ARTY. (*Stands.*) What's he want me to do, carry an iron with me?

JAY. He's afraid of her the same as Aunt Bella. Like Aunt Bella couldn't count so good, so instead of two scoops of ice cream in a soda, she'd put in three or four. For the same price. And if Grandma saw it, Whacko! Another couple of I.Q. points gone. (*Picks up a photo from behind the sofa.*) Here, look at this. Aunt Gert when she was a kid. See how her head is down. Probably ducking. The old cane was coming at her . . . You don't think Aunt Gert's a little coconuts too?

ARTY. No. She's just sick. She's got bad lungs or something.

JAY. Bad lungs, my eye. She can't talk right. She says the first half of a sentence breathing out and the second half sucking in. You've seen it.

ARTY. Do it for me.

JAY. I don't want to.

ARTY. Come on, do it.

JAY. No, I don't want to.

ARTY. Do it!

JAY. (*Imitates Aunt Gert. HE breathes out.*) "Oh, hello, Jay, how are you? And how is your father? And—(*Then talks as HE sucks in breath.*)—How is your little brother, Arty?"

ARTY. (*Laughs.*) I love it! I love when you do that.

JAY. I once saw her try to blow out a candle and halfway there she sucked it back on.

ARTY. You didn't.

JAY. With these two eyes. Mom says she talks that way because she was so afraid of Grandma. She never allowed her kids to cry.

ARTY. Never?

JAY. Never.

EDDIE. (*Comes back in.*) Grandma's worried about the doilies. Don't lean your head back on the doilies. It gets grease on them. She just had them laundered. (*HE goes back in.*)

ARTY. (*To JAY.*) You mean only people who just had a shampoo can sit here?

JAY. And what about Uncle Louie? You know what *he* is don't you?

ARTY. Yeah. A gangster. You believe that?

JAY. You bet. They say he's some big mobster's henchman.

ARTY. You mean he's got a bad back?

JAY. Not a hunchback. A *henchman*? . . . And real tough. He's a bag man.

ARTY. What do you mean, a bag man? He puts people in bags?

JAY. Not people. Money. *Hot* money. He collects bags of it from one guy and delivers it to the mob . . .

ARTY. *(Looks out the window.)* Hey! There's Aunt Bella . . .

JAY. Is she coming up?

ARTY. No. She's walking past the house.

JAY. I'll bet she's lost again. *(HE looks out window, calls down.)* Aunt Bella? . . . Hi! . . . It's Jay and Arty . . . Up here. *(HE waves to her.)* That's right. Up here . . . Here she comes.

(THEY walk away from the window.)

JAY. She ought to wear a compass or something!

(The bedroom door opens. EDDIE comes out again.)

EDDIE. Will you keep your voices down? Grandma said, "What are they yelling for?"

JAY. We were calling down to Aunt Bella. She's on her way up.

ARTY. Can I take my jacket off?

EDDIE. After Grandma sees you. And no ice cream sodas from Aunt Bella. Even if she asks you. I don't want to get Grandma upset now. Fix the doilies.

JAY. Is she all right?

EDDIE. Her back is bothering her. When Aunt Bella comes in, tell her Momma wants a back rub . . . Comb your hair, Arty, and don't make a mess. *(EDDIE goes back in. We hear a KNOCK on the front door.)*

BELLA. *(Offstage.)* Jay? Arty? It's me. Aunt Bella. Can I come in?

JAY. Guess who forgot how to open a door? . . .

(Jay opens the door. BELLA KURNITZ, in her mid-thirties, stands there. Although SHE's a mess at dressing, nothing matches at all, SHE is neat and sweet and pretty, although looking a little older than her age. SHE's as warm and congenial as SHE is emotionally arrested.)

BELLA. *(Smiles.)* I forgot my key.

JAY. How'd you get in downstairs?

BELLA. I used my spare key. I'm glad you called me. I walked right by the house, didn't I? Sometimes I daydream so much, I think I should carry an alarm clock . . . Oh, God, I'm so happy to see you. Arty! Jay! My two favorite cousins.

JAY. Aren't we your nephews?

BELLA. Of course you are. My cousins, my nephews, my boys. Come here, give your Aunt Bella a kiss. *(SHE puts down her purse, pulls JAY and ARTY into her arms and kisses them both.)* Let me look at you. You both got so much bigger. You're growing up so fast, it almost makes me cry . . . Where's your father? I haven't seen your father in so long . . . *(Calls out.)* Eddie! It's Bella . . . Is he here?

ARTY. He's in there, talking to Grandma.

BELLA. *(Suddenly nervous.)* Oh, I'd better not disturb them . . . Did she ask for me?

JAY. Pop said her back was hurting. She wanted you to give her a back rub when you came in.

BELLA. Oh. Did you tell her I was here?

JAY. No. You just came in.

BELLA. Did you tell her where I went?

JAY. We didn't know where you went.

BELLA. Well, let's not tell her I'm here yet. Then we won't be able to visit. *(SHE takes off her sweater.)* Oh, you're both getting so handsome.

JAY. Thank you.

ARTY. Thank you, Aunt Bella.

BELLA. I bet I look much older to you two. Do I? The truth. Tell me.

JAY. I don't think so.

ARTY. No.

BELLA. I was hoping you'd say that. I'm thirty-five. And I don't even look it, do I?

JAY. No.

ARTY. Not to me.

BELLA. And how old are you boys now? About twenty?

ARTY. I'm thirteen and a half.

JAY. I'm fifteen and a half.

BELLA. Well, that adds up to about thirty-five. So we could be brother and sisters. Isn't that wonderful?

JAY. Yeah.

BELLA. Yeah . . . I just got back from the movies. I had the most wonderful time. I wish I knew you were here, we all could have gone.

JAY. What did you see?

BELLA. I don't know. I couldn't find the theater I was looking for, so I went to the one I found. But it was better than the picture I wanted to see. It was with Bette Davis and George Brent . . . Maybe we could all go again next week, if I can find the wrong theater again.

ARTY. Sure. I'd love to.

BELLA. Why don't you take your jackets off, you two? Look at you both perspiring.

ARTY. We're fine, we're cool in here with the fan.

BELLA. They had air conditioning at the movie house. I was actually cold. I felt so happy for the actors to be in an air-conditioned theater.

JAY. (*Looks at ARTY, then at BELLA.*) I don't think the actors feel it. They're just pictures on the screen.

BELLA. Well, I know that, silly. I meant they'd be happy to know that people who were watching their movies were nice and cool so we enjoyed the movie better.

JAY. Oh. Right. I bet they would.

BELLA. I bet I know what would make you two cool in a second. How about a big ice cream soda deluxe? With everything in it? Look at your faces lighting up. Come on. I'll make it for you downstairs.

JAY. I think we have to wait here. Pop'll be out in a second and he wants us to see Grandma.

BELLA. Well, I'll bring them up here. That's no trouble. What kind? Chocolate? Vanilla? Butter Pecan? What's your favorite, Arty?

ARTY. All of them.

BELLA. I can make that. With three different kinds of ice cream. I used to make one with *four* different kinds. They were selling like crazy, but we lost a fortune . . . How long ago did she ask for me?

JAY. Grandma? A couple of minutes ago.

BELLA. Did you tell her I was here?

JAY. No, we told Pop we saw you from the window. But maybe he didn't say anything to her.

BELLA. It doesn't make any difference. She heard my footsteps coming up the stairs.

ARTY. How? Isn't she partly deaf?

BELLA. Oh, sure. But the other part hears perfectly . . . What about a small sundae? Chocolate ice cream with hot-fudge sauce and some whipped cream and chopped walnuts? Are you going to say no to that, Arthur? I bet you can't. Say no. Let me hear you.

ARTY. (*Looks at JAY.*) It sounds like just a small one.

JAY. (*To BELLA.*) He can't. We're having dinner soon. It's just that Pop told us to wait.

BELLA. Oh, your father. He never takes anything from anybody. I couldn't even give your mother a cup of coffee . . . Did you know that? . . . Where is she, anyway?

JAY. (*Looks confused.*) She's dead. Mom is dead.

BELLA. (*Looks confused a moment.*) Yes. I know . . . I mean where is she buried?

JAY. At Mount Israel Cemetery in the Bronx. You were at the funeral. Remember?

BELLA. You mean the first time?

JAY. What do you mean, the first time?

BELLA. When I came in the car. Not the bus.

ARTY. The bus?

BELLA. (*Thinks . . .*) No. No. I'm thinking of someone else. Sometimes my mind wanders. The kids in school used to say, "Hey, Bella. Lost and found called and said, 'Come get your brains'" . . . (*SHE laughs.*) . . . but I didn't think that was funny.

(*The BOYS nod.*)

BELLA. I bet you miss Mom a lot, don't you? Don't you, Arty?

ARTY. Yeah. A lot.

BELLA. She was a lot like your father. Very independent. Stuck to her own family mostly. (*SHE lowers her voice.*) She didn't get along too well with your grandmother. Nobody does. My sister, Gert, was once engaged to a man. She brought him over to meet Grandma. The next day he moved to Boston.

JAY. That's too bad.

BELLA. Don't tell Grandma I said that.

ARTY. I won't.

BELLA. You're both so shy. I used to be shy. Grandma didn't like me to talk too much . . . I had a lot of friends, but I didn't talk to them . . . It's a shame your mother couldn't have had more children . . . She didn't, did she?

JAY. No.

BELLA. No . . . Because it would be easier for you now that she's gone. Big families are important when you have trouble in your life. We were a big family . . . Me and your father and Louie and Gert . . . That was before Rose and Aaron died . . . Rose was just a baby but Aaron was almost twelve so I didn't know Rose as well as Aaron . . . You never knew them, did you?

JAY. I don't think we were born yet.

BELLA. No. I don't think so . . . My father died before I was born. But I wasn't sad about that.

JAY. That's good.

BELLA. Because I loved him so much. Did you know you could love somebody who died before you were born?

JAY. I guess so.

BELLA. Because I know he would have taken care of me . . . Like your father takes care of you. You know what I mean?

JAY. I think so.

BELLA. Yeah . . . So what about that sundae? It's going to sit down there melting on the counter if I make it and you don't eat it . . . Last time I'm asking, Arthur. Yes or no?

ARTY. I'd . . . I'd like to . . . (HE looks at JAY, who shakes his head "No.") Maybe later.

BELLA. (Snaps coldly, angrily.) NO! NOT LATER!! IT'S TOO LATE NOW!!! . . . I'm not asking you again. You hurt my feelings, the both of you. You tell your father to teach you better manners before I'm ever nice to you again . . . I know you miss your mother but that doesn't mean you can be disrespectful to me . . . I *always* liked your mother whether she took coffee from me or not. And you can tell that to your father, the both of you. You hear me? . . . I'm sick of it.

(SHE goes into the bathroom and SLAMS the door hard. JAY and ARTY just look at each other.)

JAY. You see why I don't like to come here too much?

(The bedroom door opens and a bedraggled EDDIE comes out, looks around.)

EDDIE. Where's Aunt Bella? I thought I just heard her.

JAY. She's in the bathroom.

EDDIE. I heard the door slam. Did you say anything to upset her?

JAY. Yeah. Everything.

ARTY. Is it time to go yet, Pop?

EDDIE. We'll go when I tell you. You haven't even seen your grandmother. Stop rushing me. You just got here, didn't you?

EDDIE. *(HE KNOCKS on the bathroom door.)* Bella! It's Eddie. Momma wants to see you. It's her back again . . . Bella? *(No answer. To the BOYS.)* Is she all right?

JAY. How do you know when she's all right?

EDDIE. Hey! No remarks about Aunt Bella, you hear me? She loves you boys. Always has. So just sit there and be quiet. God, my head is splitting. *(HE goes back into bedroom, closes door.)*

(The bathroom door opens and BELLA steps out, holding a towel and oil.)

BELLA. Was that your father banging on the door just now?

JAY. Yes.

BELLA. Is he angry with me?

JAY. With you? No.

BELLA. I hope not. Do I look better?

ARTY. Better than when?

BELLA. Than before. When you said I wasn't looking well.

ARTY. I didn't say that.

BELLA. Then who said it? . . . Jay?

ARTY. Maybe. Did you say it, Jay?

JAY. Nobody said anything.

BELLA. Oh. I know. It was Grandma. She didn't like the way I looked today. She hates this dress . . . I made it myself.

ARTY. Really?

BELLA. *(Nods.)* It took me almost a year.

JAY. . . . Grandma wants you, Aunt Bella.

BELLA. Oh yeah . . . As soon as I finish Momma's rub, I'll start dinner . . . Are you boys hungry?

ARTY. I don't know. Jay knows. Tell her, Jay.

JAY. I'm not so sure we're staying for dinner.

BELLA. Of course you are. You think I'd let you go all the way home without dinner? . . . Are you going to say no to me again, Arty?

ARTY. (Quickly.) I'm not. I'm eating. I'm hungry. No matter what Jay does. I'm eating.

BELLA. Well, we're *all* eating. It's Sunday. And you think about what you want for dessert, Arty, because whatever you want is what you're going to get . . . Start thinking now.

ARTY. I started! I started! I want a big ice cream soda with a sundae with whipped cream and hot fudge sauce. Is that okay?

BELLA. Sounds perfect to me. And don't give any to Jay. He missed the deadline. (SHE *puts her nose up to JAY and goes into Grandma's room.*)

ARTY. (*To JAY.*) Don't be mad. I had to say it. I was afraid she was going to strangle me with the towel.

JAY. It's up to Pop. We'll see what Pop says.

(ARTY *lies on the sofa. The bedroom door opens. EDDIE comes out. HE looks strained . . . HE crosses to the open window and takes a deep breath of air.*)

EDDIE. Jay! Get me a glass of water, please.

JAY. Right, Pop. (HE *rushes into the kitchen.*)

EDDIE. It must be over a hundred in here. (HE *looks at ARTY.*) Get your shoes off the sofa, what's wrong with you?

ARTY. (*Moves shoes.*) I'm feeling kind of faint.

EDDIE. What do you mean, faint? Kids your age don't faint.

ARTY. Maybe I'm getting older.

JAY. (*Comes in with the glass.*) Here you go, Pop. Nice and cool.

EDDIE. Don't spill it on the rug. (HE *takes the glass and drinks. Puts the glass down.*) All right . . . Time to talk. Sit down, Jay. Next to Arty.

(*Jay sits on the sofa next to ARTY. EDDIE sits on the stool. HE is thinking about how to start.*)

EDDIE. I er . . . I wanted to tell you boys—(*And suddenly HE breaks and tears come to his eyes. HE quickly tries to stifle it. HE wipes his eyes. HE goes to the window for some air.*)

ARTY. Is anything the matter, Po—

EDDIE. It's so damn hot in here, isn't it? . . . So, I just had a talk inside with your grandmother . . . Because I've had a problem . . . When your mother and I had a problem, we always tried to keep it from you boys because we didn't want to worry you . . . Well, you can't keep cancer a secret forever . . . You knew without me telling you, didn't you, Jay?

JAY. Yes, Pop.

EDDIE. I did everything I could. The best doctors, the best hospitals I could get into . . . She had a nice room, didn't she? Semi-private, no wards or anything . . .

JAY. I know, Pop.

EDDIE. We're not rich people, boys. I know that doesn't come as a surprise to you . . . but I'm going to tell you something now I hoped I'd never have to tell you in my life . . . The doctors, the hospital, cost me everything I had . . . I was broke and I went into debt . . . So I went to a man . . . A loan shark . . . A moneylender . . . I couldn't go to a bank because they don't let you put up heartbreak and pain as collateral . . . A loan shark doesn't need collateral . . . His collateral is your desperation . . . So he gives you his money . . . And he's got a clock . . . And what it keeps time of is your promise . . . If you keep your promise, he turns off the clock . . . and if not, it keeps ticking . . . and after a while, your heart starts ticking louder than his clock . . . Understand something. This man kept your mother alive . . . It was his painkillers that made her last days bearable . . . And for that I'm grateful . . . Jay! Remember what I taught you about taking things from people?

JAY. (*Nods.*) Never take because you'll always be obligated.

EDDIE. So you never take for yourself . . . But for someone you love, there comes a time when you have no choice . . . There's a man in New York I owe . . . Nine thousand dollars . . . I could work and save four more years and I won't have nine thousand dollars . . . He wants his money this year. To his credit, I'll say one thing. He sent flowers to the funeral. No extra charge on my bill . . .

JAY. Pop—

EDDIE. Let me finish . . . There is no way I can pay this man back . . . So what'll he do? Kill me? . . . Maybe . . . If he kills me, he not only loses his money, it'll probably cost him again for the flowers for *my* funeral . . . I needed a miracle . . . And the miracle happened . . . This country went to war . . . A war between us and the Japanese and the Germans . . . And if my mother didn't come to this country thirty-five years ago, I could have been fighting for the other side . . . Except I don't think they're putting guns in the hands of Jews over there . . . Let me tell you something. I love this country. Because they took in the Jews. They took in the Irish, the Italians and everyone else . . . Remember this. There's a lot of Germans in this country fighting for America, but there are no Americans over there fighting for Germany . . . I hate this war, and God forgive me for saying this, but it's going to save my life . . . There are jobs I can get now that I could never get before . . . And I got a job . . . I'm working for a company that sells scrap iron . . . I thought you threw scrap iron away. Now they're building ships with it . . . Without even the slightest idea of what I'm doing, I can make that nine thousand dollars in less than a year . . .

JAY. That's great, Pop.

EDDIE. Don't say it till I finish . . . The factories that I would sell to are in the South . . . Georgia, Kentucky, Louisiana, Texas, even New Mexico . . . I'd be gone about ten months . . . Living in trains, buses, hotels, any place I can find a room . . . We'd be free and clear and back together again in less than a year . . . Okay? . . . So now comes the question, where do you two live while I'm gone?

(There is a deafening silence as JAY and ARTY turn and look at each other.)

ARTY. *(Wipes his brow.)* . . . God, it's so hot in here.

JAY. Please, Pop, don't make us live here . . . That's what you're thinking, isn't it?

EDDIE. I have no choice, Jay. I don't know where else to turn.

JAY. *(To EDDIE.)* Why can't we stay where we are?

EDDIE. I gave the apartment up. I told the landlady yesterday.

ARTY. *(Astonished.)* You gave it up?

EDDIE. She raised the rent. *Every*body's looking to make money out of this war. And the truth is, by the end of the year, I'll owe eleven thousand. While I'm away, the clock doesn't stop ticking.

JAY. Grandma wouldn't be happy with us. We're slobs. We leave everything on the floor. Arty's always breaking things.

ARTY. *(To EDDIE.)* Remember when I broke the good water pitcher? And the ink stains on the sofa. All mine! . . . I'm danger-ous, Pop.

EDDIE. Listen to me, both of you. It took me an hour and a half to convince her. It's not that she doesn't like you. But she's old. She's set in her ways. And she's worried about people being around Bella.

ARTY. Me too.

EDDIE. She hasn't even said positively yet. She's thinking about it. She'll come out. She'll talk to you. She'll see how it goes. It's up to us to convince her that you two won't be any trouble . . . That's why I want you both looking so neat. Don't you see how important this is?

JAY. And what if she *did* take us in? Then you'd be obligated, Pop. Don't you think you have enough obligations now?

EDDIE. I'm not asking for myself. I'm asking for my boys. For my boys, I'll be obligated . . . There's nothing to discuss anymore . . . It's up to Grandma now . . . And it's up to you. *(HE crosses to Grandma's bedroom door.)* I'll see if she's ready. *(HE turns back to them.)* If she says no, I can't take this job. I can't pay back the man I gave my promise to . . . Just show Grandma what a terrific present she's getting to have you boys live with her . . . Fix your tie, Jay. Straighten your collar, Arty . . . Stand straight, both of you . . .

(They stand straight. HE nods.)

EDDIE. That's my boys. *(HE goes into Grandma's room.)*

(The BOYS look at each other.)

JAY. Oh, my God. What if Grandma says "Yes"?

ARTY. She won't. Because I'm going to break something. What's her favorite thing in this room?

JAY. You're not breaking anything. Because we have to stay here and save Pop's life.

ARTY. And what about *our* lives? We could grow up like Aunt Bella. I could be in the seventh grade for the next twenty years.

JAY. Listen, if you act like this when Grandma comes out, that's like putting a gun to Pop's head and pulling the trigger.

ARTY. Oh. So we stay here and get whacked in the head every time we cry . . . or suck candles back on like Aunt Gert. *(HE sucks his breath in and says)* "Hello, Arty. How are you?"

JAY. *(Grabs ARTY by his shirt collar.)* One more word from you and I'll whack you, I swear to God.

(ARTY pulls away but JAY holds on . . . and Arty's collar gets torn halfway off and dangles there.)

JAY. Oh, my God. It tore!

ARTY. Well, that's it. The war is over for us . . . I hope Pop bought the grave next to Mom.

JAY. *(Looking in a drawer.)* Jesus! It's all your goddamn fault . . . *(Starts to cry.)* Dammit! I hate you so much. I hate Mom for dying. I hate Pop for putting us in this spot. I hate Grandma for being such a rotten old lady. I hate everybody in the whole Goddamn world.

(And the bedroom door opens and EDDIE comes out with a smile.)

EDDIE. You ready, boys? *(And then HE looks at them.)* . . . What the hell's going on here? . . . What are you crying about? What happened to your collar? *(HE quickly closes the bedroom door.)*

ARTY. Nothing.

EDDIE. Don't tell me nothing. Were you fighting? Of course you were fighting, just look at you. I don't believe it. If I can't trust you for two minutes, how can I trust you for a year? . . . And do you think I would do this to my mother? To my sister, Bella? . . . I'm ashamed of you. I'm ashamed of you both . . . Wait outside for me. Out in the street. I don't want to look at you . . . Go on, get out.

ARTY. We weren't fighting. It was an accident. I was trying to straighten my tie and I straightened it too tight.

JAY. I was crying about Mom. She'd be so sad to see you in such trouble . . . We really want to stay here. We like Yonkers.

EDDIE. Are you serious? Or you just trying to lie your way out of this?

JAY. Serious. Very serious.

ARTY. It's the most serious we've been in our lives.

EDDIE. I hope so. For all our sakes . . . All right. Fix yourself up. Tuck in your collar. Wipe your eyes . . . I'll get Grandma.

(*The door opens and BELLA comes out. SHE rushes to the sofa and throws herself on it, sobbing.*)

EDDIE. Oh, Jesus! Bella? . . . What's wrong? . . . What is it, Bella?

(*SHE buries her face in a pillow, like a five-year-old child. ARTY and JAY look at each other . . .*
EDDIE sits next to BELLA and puts his arm around her shoulder.)

EDDIE. (*To BELLA, softly.*) . . . Did Momma say something? . . . Was she angry with you?

(*BELLA whispers in Eddie's ear.*)

EDDIE. No, no, Bella. She does too love your back rubs, she told me that . . . She's just got a lot on her mind today. (*HE looks at the BOYS disapprovingly, then back to BELLA.*) You all right now, sweetheart?

(*BELLA whispers again to him.*)

EDDIE. Yes, I know you're lonely . . . I know it's hard to be alone with her all the time . . . But, Bella, I have good news for you . . . Maybe you won't be alone anymore . . . You know who's going to stay here, Bella? If Momma says yes . . . Arthur and Jay . . . Wouldn't that be nice? . . . To have Arthur and Jay here? . . . They'd live here and spend time with you and you'd have someone to talk to at nights.

(ARTY and JAY look at each other.)

EDDIE. Would you like that, honey?

BELLA. *(Beams.)* Yes.

EDDIE. All right. Then give me a smile and a hug.

BELLA. *(Throws her arms around Eddie's neck.)* Don't go away, Eddie . . . Stay and live with us . . . I miss you so much . . . She's so mean sometimes.

EDDIE. No, she's not. She's just getting old . . . I can't stay, honey. I have to go away for a while. But the boys will be with you. They're looking forward to it . . . Would you like to lie down in your room for a while, Bella? Momma has to talk to the boys now.

BELLA. *(Grabs his hand.)* No. I want to stay here with you.

EDDIE. It would be easier, I think, if Momma and the boys talked alone.

BELLA. *(Sternly.)* I want to stay here with you.

EDDIE. Ohh, God . . . All right. You sit right there. But you be very quiet now, all right? . . . Just don't interrupt because we don't want to get Momma upset . . . Okay. Here we go. *(HE crosses to the bedroom door, knocks and goes in.)*

(JAY and ARTY look at BELLA. SHE looks up at the ceiling.)

JAY. Er . . . Arty and I are really hoping it works out, Aunt Bella.

BELLA. *(Puts finger to her lips.)* Shhh. Mustn't interrupt.

JAY. Oh, yeah. Right.

(EDDIE comes out of the bedroom and arranges the BOYS to greet GRANDMA.)

EDDIE. Her back is killing her but she doesn't want me to help her. *(Calls in.)* Okay, Momma.

(There is a beat as MOMMA is going to make her entrance when SHE wants.

GRANDMA KURNITZ enters slowly from the bedroom. SHE is a big woman, or, hopefully, gives that appearance. Not fat, but buxom, with a strong, erect body, despite her seventy-odd years. SHE has white hair pulled back in European style with buns

*in the back. SHE carries a cane and walks with a slight drag-
ging of one foot. SHE wears rimless glasses and has a pasty
white complexion. SHE wears a large-print dress of the period
with a cameo brooch pinned on. Authority and discipline seem
to be her overriding characteristics and SHE would demand
attention in a crowd. SHE speaks with few, but carefully cho-
sen words, with a clear German accent.
SHE walks to the armchair, not looking at anybody, least of all the
BOYS. Then SHE sits and looks at EDDIE.)*

GRANDMA. So?

(EDDIE motions with his head to the BOYS.)

JAY. *(On cue.)* Hello, Grandma.
ARTY. Hello, Grandma.

*(EDDIE looks at them again and gives them another head signal.
JAY steps up and kisses her quickly on her cheek and steps
back. ARTY does the same and steps back. GRANDMA KUR-
NITZ hardly reacts.)*

EDDIE. I know you haven't seen the boys in a long time, Mom.
They wanted to come but with their mother sick so long, they felt
they should spend as much time as they could with her . . . I bet
they've grown since you've seen them, haven't they?
GRANDMA. *(Looks at them, then points her cane at ARTY.)* Dis iss
da little one?
EDDIE. Yes. Arthur. He's two years younger, right, Arty?
ARTY. Yes. I'm two years younger . . . than him.
GRANDMA. *(Looks at JAY, points cane at him.)* Dis one I remem-
ber more . . . Dis one looks like his mother.
JAY. Yes. A lot of people tell me that.
GRANDMA. Vot's wrong with your eyes?
JAY. My eyes? Oh. They're a little red. I got something in them
and I scratched them too hard.
GRANDMA. You vere crying maybe?
JAY. Me? No. I never cry.
GRANDMA. Big boys shouldn't cry.

JAY. I know. I haven't cried in years. A couple of times when I was a baby.

EDDIE. Oh, they're strong kids, Ma. Both of them.

GRANDMA. *(Looks at JAY.)* Yakob, heh?

JAY. Yes, but they call me Jay.

GRANDMA. No. I don't like Jay . . . Yakob iss a name.

JAY. Sure. Yakob is fine.

GRANDMA. And Artur.

ARTY. Arthur. But they call me Arty.

GRANDMA. I don't call you Arty.

ARTY. Sure. I *love* Arthur. Like King Arthur.

GRANDMA. You go to school?

ARTY. Yeah.

GRANDMA. Vat?

ARTY. Yes. I go to the same school as Yakob.

GRANDMA. Vitch one iss da smart one?

(JAY and ARTY look at each other.)

EDDIE. They both do very well in school.

GRANDMA. *(Points cane at EDDIE.)* They'll tell me. *(SHE looks at them.)* Vitch one iss da smart one?

ARTY. *(Points to JAY.)* Yakob is. He gets As in everything. I'm better at sports.

GRANDMA. Shports?

ARTY. Baseball. Basketball. Football.

GRANDMA. You play in the mud? In the dirt? You come home with filthy shoes and make marks all over the floor?

ARTY. No. Never. I clean them off at the field. I bring a brush and polish them up on a bench. *(HE looks at EDDIE to see if HE got away with that.)*

GRANDMA. If the smart one iss smart, he'll make sure you do.

EDDIE. No, the boys are very neat. Even their mother said so.

GRANDMA. *(Taps her cane a few times on the floor, like an announcement.)* So tell me . . . vy do you vant to live with Grandma?

(The BOYS look at each other.)

ARTY. . . . Why don't *you* tell Grandma, Yakob?

JAY. (*Glares at him.*) . . . Well . . . because . . . Pop has to go away. And we had to give up our apartment . . . and when Pop said we had the opportunity to live here with you—our only living grandmother . . . and our only living Aunt Bella . . . I thought that families should sort of stick together now that our country is at war with Germ—Japan . . . so we can all be together during times like this . . . and I also think that—no. That's all.

GRANDMA. (*Nods.*) . . . And this is the smart one?

EDDIE. I thought he said that very well, Momma.

GRANDMA. (*Points cane at ARTY.*) And what about this King Artur? . . . Vy do you vant to live with Grandma?

ARTY. (*After looking at GRANDMA.*) . . . because we have no place else to go.

EDDIE. I . . . I think what Arty is trying to say, Momma—

GRANDMA. (*Points cane at EDDIE.*) No! . . . he knows vot he vants to say . . . (*SHE looks at ARTY.*) I tink maybe *diss* is da smart one.

EDDIE. He's always been very honest. But he's just a boy, Momma—

GRANDMA. So! You haff no place else to go. Dot's vy you vant to live with Grandma . . . All right . . . So now Grandma vill tell you vy she doesn't tink you should live vit her . . . Dis house is no place for boys. I'm an old woman. I don't like to talk. I don't like noise. I don't like people in my house. I had six children once, I don't need more again . . . Bella and I take care of the store six days a veek and on Sunday ve rest. Today is Sunday and I'm not resting . . . Bella is not—she's not goot vit people too long. A little bit yes, then she gets too excited . . . You understand vot I'm saying? . . . Vot vould you do here? There's no games in dis house. There's no toys in dis house. I don't like the radio after six o'clock. The news yes, dot's all . . . Ve go to sleep nine o'clock, ve get up five o'clock. I don't have friends. Bella don't have friends. You vould not be happy here. And unhappy boys I don't need.

EDDIE. Momma, can I just say something—?

GRANDMA. (*Holds up cane.*) No! I'll just say someting . . . I think about dis inside. Because anger hass been in me for a long time . . . Vy should I do dis? . . . Vot do I owe your father? . . . Ven did he ever come around here after he married your mother? I never saw him . . . Because she turned him against me. His own mother . . . She didn't like me, I didn't like her. I'm not afraid to tell da truth either . . . I don't vish anybody's death. Maybe she vas a goot mother to you, may she rest in peace, to me she vas nothing . . . And your father vas afraid of her. Dot's vy he stopped coming here. You're big boys now, how many times haff I seen you since you were born? Four, five times? . . . Dose are not grandchildren. Dose are strangers . . . And now he comes to me for help? . . . He cried in my bedroom. Not like a man, like a child he cried. He vas always dot vay . . . I buried a husband and two children und I didn't cry. I didn't haff time. Bella vas born vit scarlet fever and she didn't talk until she vas five years old, und I didn't cry . . . Your father's sister, Gertrude, can't talk vitout choking und I didn't cry . . . Und maybe one day, they'll find Louie dead in da street und I von't cry . . . Dot's how I vas raised. To be strong. Ven dey beat us vit sticks in Germany ven ve vere children, I didn't cry . . . You don't survive in dis vorld vitout being like steel. Your father vants you to grow up, first let *him* grow up . . . Ven he learns to be a father, like I learned to be a mother, den he'll be a man. Den he von't need my help . . . You think I'm cruel? You tink I'm a terrible person? Dot a grandmother should say tings like dis? I can see it in your faces vot you tink . . . Goot, it'll make you hard. It'll make you strong. Den you'll be able to take care of yourselves vitout *any*body's help . . . So dot's my decision. Maybe one day you'll tank me for it. *(SHE gets up.)* Give da boys an ice cream cone, Bella. Den come inside and finish my legs.

(SHE starts for the bedroom. THEY ALL stand, stunned. BELLA, who has remained seated, seems impervious to this.)

EDDIE. *(Without anger.)* . . . You're right, Momma. I am the weak one. I am the crybaby . . . Always was. When you wouldn't pick me up and hug me as a child, I cried . . . When my brother and sister died, I cried . . . And I still haven't stopped crying since Evelyn died . . . But you're wrong about one thing. She never turned me against you. She turned me towards *her* . . . To loving, to caring, to holding someone when they needed holding . . . I'm sorry about not bringing the boys out here more. Maybe the reason I didn't was because I was afraid they'd learn something here that I tried to forget . . . Maybe they just learned it today . . . I'm sorry I bothered you on your Sunday. I'm sorry I imposed on your rest. I'm sorry about what they did to you as a child in Berlin. I'm sure it was terrible. But this is Yonkers, Momma. I'm not angry at you for turning me and the boys down. I'm angry at myself for not knowing better . . . Take care of yourself, Momma . . . Never mind the ice cream cones, Bella. I used up all my obligations for this year. (*HE crosses to the door.*) Come on, boys. We're going.

(*JAY and ARTY are too dumbstruck to move, to have been in the middle of all this.*)

EDDIE. . . . I said let's go.

(*THEY start for the door.*)

BELLA. Arty? (*SHE gets up with a warm, sweet smile on her face.*) We'll have dinner another night . . . Why don't you and Jay go home and pack your things and I'll get your bed ready and make room in the closet for you when you move in.

(*The BOYS stop, look at EDDIE.*)

EDDIE. Thank you, Bella . . . but Momma and I just decided it's not a good idea.

BELLA. (*Still smiling, SHE begins to make up the sofa bed.*) And, Jay, you make a list of all the things you boys like for breakfast, and I'll make sure we have it . . . And don't forget your toothbrushes because we don't carry them in the store . . . And each of you bring something from your house that you really love, even if it's big, and we'll find someplace to put it.

GRANDMA. Dot's enough, Bella. Diss is not your business.

BELLA. (*To the BOYS.*) How about a picture of your mother? We can put it right here on the table. It'll be the last thing you see at night and the first thing you see in the morning . . . It's going to be such fun with you both here . . . Momma's right. I do get so excited around people but it makes me so happy.

GRANDMA. Bella! Nicht sprecken! Enough!! . . . They're going. Dot's the end of it.

BELLA. (*Quite calmly.*) No, Momma. They're not going. They're staying. Because if you make them go, I'll go too . . . I know I've said that a thousand times but this time I mean it . . . I could go to the Home. The Home would take me . . . You're always telling me that . . . And if I go, you'll be all alone . . . And you're afraid to be alone, Momma . . . Nobody else knows that but me . . . But you don't have to be, Momma. Because we'll all be together now . . . You and me and Jay and Arty . . . Won't that be fun, Momma?

(THEY *stand there,* ALL *frozen, except* BELLA, *who is beaming . . .*
The stage goes to BLACK.)

SCENE TWO

Over the sound of the TRAIN, *in the* BLACK, *we hear* EDDIE's *voice.*

EDDIE. (VO.) "Dear Jay and Arty . . . I tried phoning you the other night, but I forgot the phone is in the candy store and you probably couldn't hear it . . . Well, I've been through Kentucky, Georgia, Tennessee and West Virginia . . . Don't complain about Aunt Bella's cooking to me because I haven't eaten anything down here that wasn't fried, smoked, hashed, gritted or poned . . . or wasn't caught in a swamp, a tree, or coming out of a hole in the ground . . . Right now I'd go into debt again just to eat an onion roll . . . "

(The LIGHTS *come up and the letter continues to be read by* JAY. *THEY are both in bed, one lamp on. It is late at night.*)

JAY. (HE *reads.*) "Although business is good, I've had one minor setback. I've developed what the doctor calls an irregular heartbeat. He says it's not serious, but doesn't think I should be traveling so much. But I can't afford to stop now." (HE *looks at* ARTY.) An irregular heartbeat doesn't sound too good . . . God, I wish there was some way we could make some money. Not "kid" money. I mean *real* money.

ARTY. What if one night we cut off Grandma's braids and sold it to the army for barbed wire?

JAY. I can't believe we're fighting a war to make this a better world for someone like you.

(*The front door opens and BELLA comes in, closing the door quietly. SHE looks at the BOYS, puts her finger to her lips to be quiet.*)

BELLA. Is Grandma sleeping? Don't tell me, you'll wake her up . . . Arty! Jay! The most wonderful and exciting thing happened to me tonight. But don't ask me. I can't tell you. You're my good luck charms, both of you.

GRANDMA. (*Appearing suddenly out of her room. To BELLA.*) You tink I don't hear you coming up the stairs? You tink I don't know it's eleven o'clock? You tink I don't know where you've been?

BELLA. Just to the movies, Ma.

GRANDMA. Movies, movies, movies. You waste your money and your life in da movies. Und den you walk home by yourself. Do you know what kind of men are on the street at eleven o'clock?

BELLA. I didn't see a soul, Ma.

GRANDMA. Ya, ya, ya! Look for trouble, you'll find trouble.

BELLA. No one bothers me, Ma.

GRANDMA. Then you waste money on movie magazines? Fill your head with Hollywood and dreams that don't happen to people like us?

BELLA. Sometimes they do.

GRANDMA. Never. NEVER!! . . . (*Holds out her hand.*) Give it to me. I don't want trash in this house.

BELLA. It's my magazine, Ma. I bought it with my own money.

GRANDMA. No! *My* money. I pay for everything here. You don't have anything unless I give you. Give-me-the-magazine!

BELLA. Please don't do this to me in front of the boys, Momma.

GRANDMA. You bring it home in front of the boys, you'll give me the magazine in front of the boys. (*Holds her hand out.*) Give it to me now, Bella.

(*BELLA looks at the BOYS embarrassed, then gives her the magazine. GRANDMA looks at magazine, nods disgust.*)

GRANDMA. When I'm dead, you can buy your own magazine.
BELLA. No, I won't, Momma. Because you'll find a way to get them anyway.

(*She rushes into her room. GRANDMA looks at the BOYS.*)

GRANDMA. . . . You like to pay my electric bill?

(*JAY quickly turns out the light. It is DARK, except for the LIGHT from GRANDMA's room.*)

GRANDMA. . . . And you try cutting my braids off, you'll get your fingers chopped off. (*SHE goes in and slams her door.*)

(*The lights go to BLACK and we hear the TRAIN again.*)

SCENE THREE

In the DARK, we hear the voice of EDDIE again.

EDDIE. (*VO.*) "Dear Boys . . . This'll just have to be a short one. I'm in Houston, Texas, and I just got plumb tuckered out. That's how they talk down here. I had to take a week off and rest. Nothing to worry about. I'll be on the road again real soon and I promise I'll make up the time . . . Love, Pop."

(*The LIGHTS come up. It is Sunday afternoon, weeks later. ARTY stands on Grandma's chair, his hand upraised, and HE is jubilant.*)

ARTY. (*Yelling.*) Alone at last! Grandma's out! Aunt Bella's out! We have the house to ourselves. We're *free*! Ya ya ya ya ya!!!
JAY. Will you shut up! She could walk back in any minute. You know what she'd do if she found you jumping on her chair?

ARTY. (*With German accent.*) Ya! She vould chop off my legs . . . And Aunt Bella vould cook dem for dinner. (*HE jumps on the bed.*)

JAY. (*Looks out the window.*) Hey! Arty! There's that car again.

ARTY. What car?

JAY. The black Studebaker. It's the two guys who came looking for Uncle Louie. They look like killers to me . . . What do you think they want?

ARTY. (*Looks out window.*) I don't know. Let's give 'em Grandma. Ya ya ya ya ya!

JAY. (*Pulls him away.*) Get out of there. (*HE peeks again.*) They just keep circling and circling. Aren't you afraid of guys like that?

ARTY. No. I lived up here for a month. I can take anything.

(*The front door opens and BELLA comes in.*)

BELLA. Is Momma home?

JAY. No. She's still at Aunt Gert's.

BELLA. I don't want to cry. I don't want to cry. I don't want to cry.

JAY. Is there anything we can do? . . . You can talk to us, Aunt Bella.

BELLA. Do you think so? Do you think I can trust you? You're still so young.

JAY. You don't have to be old to be trusting.

BELLA. And you'd never tell Grandma what I tell you? Because if she ever found out, she'd put me in the Home . . . She would. For the rest of my life.

JAY. I don't think she would do that. She just says that to scare you sometimes.

BELLA. No. She would do it. Sometimes she'd take me on the trolley, and we'd go by the Home and she'd say, "That's where you'll live if you're not a good girl."

ARTY. You said she wouldn't do that because she's afraid to be alone.

BELLA. But she's not alone anymore. She's got you two here.

ARTY. Oh, no. If you left, we'd go with you to the Home.

JAY. Arty, knock it off . . . if you don't want to tell us, Aunt Bella, you don't have to. We're your friends.

BELLA. . . . I wish Eddie was here. Eddie would know what to do.

JAY. We're Eddie's sons. That's almost the same thing.

BELLA. Yes. That's true . . . All right . . . Come here. Sit down, both of you.

(SHE crosses to sofabed and sits.
THEY sit on either side of her.)

BELLA. This is our secret now, all right? . . . A sacred secret. Say it, the both of you.

ARTY and JAY and BELLA. This is a sacred secret.

BELLA. All right then . . . *(SHE smiles.)* I'm going to get married . . . I'm going to be a wife and I'm going to have lots and lots of children and live in a place of my own . . . isn't that wonder-ful news?

(The BOYS look at each other.)

BELLA. You're the only ones that know this . . . Jay! Arty! I'm going to get married.

(THEY're, of course, dumbstruck.)

JAY. Gee, that's swell, Aunt Bella.

ARTY. Have you met anybody yet?

BELLA. What do you mean, have I met anyone? . . . Of course I have . . . I met him ten days ago at the movies. At the Orpheum Theatre . . . I saw him there four times this week.

JAY. You both went to the same movie four times?

BELLA. I didn't mind. And he has to, because he works there. He's an usher . . . And he looks so wonderful in his uniform.

ARTY. He's an usher?

BELLA. And his name is Johnny. I always thought I would marry someone named Johnny.

ARTY. What a great guess.

BELLA. Anyway, we went out later for some coffee . . . And we went for walks in the park . . . and down near the river. And then today, just like in the movies, at exactly two o'clock . . . or two-fifteen . . . or two-thirty . . . he asked me to marry him . . . And I said I would have to think it over, but the answer was yes.

ARTY. That was pretty quick thinking it over.

BELLA. I know. I didn't want him to change his mind . . . Are you as happy about this as I am?

JAY. Oh, sure . . . sure . . . How old is he?

BELLA. He's thirty . . . Maybe not. Maybe about forty . . . But he's so handsome. And so polite. And quiet. I had to do all of the talking. All he said was, "Would you marry me?"

JAY. Was he ever married before?

BELLA. Oh, no. I would never marry someone who was married before. I want it to be the first time for both of us.

JAY. If he has no children, how come he's not in the army?

BELLA. Oh, he wanted to go but they wouldn't take him because of his handicap.

JAY. What handicap?

BELLA. He has a reading handicap.

JAY. You mean he has bad eyes?

BELLA. No. He just has trouble learning things. The way I did. He went to a special school when he was a boy. The one near the Home. He was there once, in the Home, for about six months, and he said it was terrible . . . So his parents took him out . . . And now he's much happier.

JAY. I can tell why you're not anxious to tell Grandma . . . I mean, because it's so sudden like.

BELLA. And he doesn't want to be an usher forever . . . He wants to open up a restaurant . . . I would be the cook and he would be the manager. I would love that more than anything in the whole world.

JAY. Could he do that? Manage a restaurant? If he couldn't read the menus?

BELLA. Well, I would do all that. I would help him . . . The only thing is, his parents are poor and he doesn't make much money and we'd need about five thousand dollars to open a restaurant . . . And I don't know if Momma would give it to me.

JAY. Your mother has five thousand dollars?

BELLA. Oh, more. Ten or fifteen thousand. I'm not supposed to tell anyone.

JAY. Where does she keep it? In the bank?

BELLA. No. It's here in the house somewhere. She changes the hiding place every year. No one knows she has it . . . Not Eddie or

Gert or Louie. No one . . . So my problem is, I have to get her to say yes to marrying Johnny, and yes to opening the restaurant and moving away, and yes to giving me the five thousand dollars. But I don't think she's going to say yes, do you?

JAY. I don't think she's going to let you go to the movies much anymore.

BELLA. She won't know if I don't tell her. You won't tell her, will you, Jay?

JAY. I swear.

BELLA. Arty?

ARTY. She and I have very short conversations.

BELLA. I have to go inside now and think this one out. I'm not good at thinking things out. I'm much better with my hands . . . But you're smart. Both of you. Maybe you'll think it out for me . . . Please do. I'd be grateful to you for the rest of my life. (*She starts to go, then stops.*) Oh. I thought of a name for the restaurant, too . . . "La Bella Johnnie."

JAY. That's nice.

BELLA. Yeah. I just hope he can read it. (*SHE goes into her bedroom.*)

ARTY. Wait'll he meets Grandma. He'll be back in the Home in a week.

JAY. Fifteen thousand!! Wow! You think she would have loaned some of it to Pop. (*Looking around.*) Where would be the safest place to hide it? Where no one would think of looking?

ARTY. You're not really thinking of stealing it, are you?

JAY. No, but what if we just borrowed it? I would just love to send Pop an envelope with nine thousand dollars in it.

ARTY. And who would he think sent it to him? *God???*

JAY. He had an uncle in Poland who died. He left the money in his will for Pop.

ARTY. You think the Germans would let some Jew in Poland send nine thousand dollars to some Jew in Alabama?

BLACKOUT

SCENE FOUR

We hear the TRAIN . . . then EDDIE's voice . . .

EDDIE. *(VO.)* ". . . Dear Boys . . . Traveling through the South has been a whole new education for me. Some people are very warm and polite and educated and very well spoken. And then there are some on the train who spit tobacco juice on the windows . . . A lot of people have trouble with my New York accent. I didn't even know I had one till I got here . . . I met a nice Jewish family in Atlanta, but I couldn't understand them either. This woman, Mrs. Schneider, said to me, 'You all come over to the Synagogue this Shabuss and you'll meet some mighty fine folks.' I didn't want to hurt her feelings so I said, 'Sho nuff.' And she just looked at me and said, 'Who's Shonuf?' . . . I guess it takes a while to learn the dialect. Love, Pop."

(The LIGHTS come up. It is one week later, about 12 o'clock at night. The room is dark except for the FULL MOON that shines brightly in through the window.
The Boys' bed is open. NEITHER of them is in the bed. ARTY, in pajamas, is standing near the door that leads downstairs.)

ARTY. Jay! Hurry up! What if Grandma wakes up? . . . This is crazy. Why would she hide money in the store?

(Suddenly, we see the FLASHLIGHT coming from downstairs. ARTY rushes back into bed. JAY comes in with the flashlight.)

JAY. I looked everywhere. There's no money down there. *(HE shivers.)* God, I'm freezing. I was looking under the ice cream cartons. *(He gets into bed.)* I think I got frostbite.
ARTY. Why would she keep money under ice cream? We use those cartons up every week.
JAY. Not the boysenberry. Boysenberry sits there for months. Nobody's ever going to look under boysenberry.
ARTY. I can't believe we're stealing money from out own grandmother.

(THEY put out the FLASHLIGHT and turn to go to sleep . . . A moment passes . . . then the front door opens. We see a MAN in a hat enter, closing the door, then slowly, quietly cross toward the window. HE carries a small black bag.)

JAY. Who's that? *(Turning flashlight on MAN.)*
MAN. Get that light outa my face and go back to sleep, kid.
JAY. There's nothing here to steal, mister. I swear.
MAN. Is that you, Jay?
JAY. Yeah. Who are you?
MAN. It's Uncle Louie.
JAY. Uncle Louie? No kidding? . . . Arty! It's Uncle Louie.
ARTY. Uncle Louie? . . . Really? Hi, Uncle Louie.
LOUIE. Is that Arty?
ARTY. Yeah. It's Arty . . . Hi, Uncle Louie.
LOUIE. Wait a second. *(LOUIE turns on the lamp. LOUIE KUR-NITZ is about thirty-six years old. HE wears a double-breasted suit, with a hanky in the breast pocket, black pointy shoes, a dark blue shirt and a loud tie. HE also wears a fedora hat and carries a small, black satchel, not unlike a doctors' bag.)* Whaddya know? Look at you! Couple a big guys now, ain't you? . . . You don't come around for a while and you grow up on me . . . Come here. Come on. I want a hug. You heard me. Move it.

(The BOYS look at each other, not thinking LOUIE was the hugging type. THEY quickly climb out of bed and go to him. HE puts his arms around both their shoulders and pulls them in to him. HE looks at JAY.)

LOUIE. Picture of your mother. Pretty woman, your mother . . . *(To ARTY.)* And you. You look like a little bull terrier. Is that what you are, a bull terrier? *(HE musses Arty's hair.)*
ARTY. Yeah, I guess so.
LOUIE. *(Fakes a punch at Jay's mid-section.)* Hey, watch it! What are you now, a middleweight or what? Who's been beefin' you up?
JAY. Aunt Bella. She's a good cook.
LOUIE. *(Taking off his hat.)* And a couple a midnight trips down to the ice cream freezer, heh? Diggin' into the boysenberry with your flashlight? . . . That's breakin' and enterin', kid. Two to five years.

JAY. You saw me?

LOUIE. (*Crosses to Grandma's door and listens.*) I been down there since Ma closed the store.

JAY. Sitting in the dark?

LOUIE. Yeah. Waitin' for her to go to sleep. I wasn't in no mood for long conversations.

JAY. (*Looks at ARTY, then at LOUIE.*) I just took a finger-full, that's all. I love boysenberry.

LOUIE. Big mistake, kid. Mom reads fingerprints. She'll nail you in the morning.

JAY. Are you serious?

LOUIE. Get outa here. What are you? A couple a pushovers? Like your old man . . . You think your pop and I didn't do that when we were kids? That was the beauty part. Never took nothin' durin' the day. A ton a ice cream, a store full a candy, anything we wanted. Never took nothin' . . . But as soon as Ma let her braids down and turned out the lights, we were down there lappin' up the cream and meowin' like cats . . . Ain't that the way? It's only fun when there's a chance a gettin' caught. Nothin' sweeter than danger, boys, am I right?

JAY. I guess so.

LOUIE. Damn right.

ARTY. I didn't know Pop was like that.

LOUIE. Yeah, well, he was no good at it anyway. Ma knew what was goin' on. She could tell if there was salt missin' from a pretzel . . . But she wouldn't say nothin'. She'd come up from the store with the milk, siddown for breakfast, knowin' that two scoops of everything was missin', and she'd just stare at you . . . right into your eyeballs, pupil to pupil . . . never blinkin' . . . Her eyes looked like two district attorneys . . . and Eddie couldn't take the pressure. He'd always crack. Tears would start rollin' down his cheeks like a wet confession . . . and whack, he'd get that big German hand right across the head . . . But not me. I'd stare her right back until her eyelids started to weigh ten pounds each . . . And she'd turn away from me, down for the count . . . And you know what? She loved it . . . because I knew how to take care of myself . . . Yeah, me and Ma loved to put on the gloves and go the distance.

JAY. Nobody told us you were coming over tonight.

LOUIE. Nobody knew. It was even a surprise for me. I gotta stay here a couple days, maybe a week. They're paintin' my apartment.

ARTY. You didn't know they were going to paint your apartment?

LOUIE. They just found the right color paint tonight. Hard to find with the war on. (*HE takes off his jacket, revealing a holster with a pistol in it.*) So, you kids been keepin' your nose outa trouble?

(*The BOYS look at the gun, mesmerized.*)

JAY. Huh?

LOUIE. How's Pop? Ma tells me he's in the junk business. Is that right, Arty?

ARTY. (*Looking at the gun.*) Huh?

LOUIE. Sellin' scrap iron or somethin', ain't that it?

BOTH BOYS. Huh?

LOUIE. Whatsamatter? (*Looks at the gun.*) This? (*HE smiles.*) Hey, don't worry about it. (*Takes it out of holster.*) I'm holdin' it for a friend. This policeman I know went on vacation, he didn't want to lose it. They have to pay for it when they lose it . . . (*He puts it in his pants, under the belt, just over the fly.*) Also, the ladies like it. You dance with 'em close, gives 'em a thrill. (*HE winks at them.*)

JAY. Is it . . . is it loaded?

LOUIE. Gee, I hope not. If it went off, I'd have to become a ballerina. (*HE winks at BOYS. HE hangs the gun and holster on a chair, comes back and resumes getting undressed.*) Does your pop ever send you some loose change once in a while?

JAY. Oh, yeah. Whenever he can.

LOUIE. Like never, right? You think I don't know what's goin' on? The sharks are puttin' the bite on him, right? He shoulda come to me. There's lotsa ways of borrowin' money. Your pop don't unnerstand that. Sometimes bein' on the up and up just gets you down and down, know what I mean, Jay?

JAY. Yeah . . . I never knew a policeman could lend his gun to someone.

LOUIE. (*Looks at him, then at ARTY.*) You got a smart brother there, Arty, you know that? You're right, Jay. It's my gun. I'm a bodyguard for a very prominent and distinguished political figure. It's sort of like an FBI man, only they call it something else.

ARTY. You mean a henchman?

LOUIE. (*Glares at him.*) Who's been telling you stories like that? Jay?

ARTY. No. I swear.

LOUIE. Don't ever repeat that word around to anyone again, you understand?

ARTY. I didn't mean to say it. I was thinking of hunchback.

LOUIE. A couple of jokers here, heh? Don't pull my leg, Arty, it might come off in your hands . . . So, we got a little business to discuss. You boys got any problem with makin' a little after-school money?

JAY. You mean a job? I've been looking, but Grandma wants us in the store after school. To help pay our expenses.

LOUIE. Tell you what. How'd you like to work for me? Five bucks a week, split between you, cash on the barrel. Only first you gotta guess what number I'm thinkin' of. Make a mistake and the deal's off . . . Take a guess, boys.

ARTY. Three.

JAY. Seven.

LOUIE. Thirty-seven. That's right. Good guess. You're on Louie's payroll now. (HE *takes a five dollar bill out of his garter and hands it to JAY.*) . . . Now, Arty, can you drive a car?

ARTY. Me? I'm only thirteen and a half.

LOUIE. Too bad. I need someone who can drive a car.

ARTY. I'm a pretty good roller skater.

LOUIE. (*Smiles.*) That's good 'cause I'm spinnin' your wheels, kid. Now your leg's bein' pulled. Wake up and live. It's a fast world out there.

JAY. Uncle Louie . . . This five dollar bill . . . It has your picture on it.

LOUIE. (*To ARTY.*) He ain't no faster than you. Look in your pocket, Arty.

ARTY. (*Feels in his pajama pocket. Takes out a five dollar bill, unfolded.*) It's five dollars. A real one. How'd you do that?

LOUIE. These fingers were touched by genius. I could have been a concert violinist, but the handkerchief kept fallin' off my neck.

JAY. What do we have to do for the money?

LOUIE. Nothin'. Like if anyone comes around here lookin' for me, you don't know nothin', you ain't seen nothin', you ain't heard nothin'. You think you can handle that?

ARTY. There were two men here the other day looking for you.

LOUIE. Yeah? What'd they look like?

ARTY. One had a broken nose and the other one had—

LOUIE. —a Betty Grable tie.

ARTY. Right.

LOUIE. Hollywood Harry. Got all the stars hand-painted on silk . . . So if they show up here again askin' questions, what do you say to 'em?

BOTH. Nothing.

LOUIE. Smart boys. Look in Jay's pocket, Arty.

ARTY. (*Looks in Jay's pocket, takes out a bill.*) Another five dollars.

LOUIE. I could have played Carnegie Hall.

JAY. We wouldn't be doing anything wrong, would we?

LOUIE. You're my brother's kids, you think I'm gonna get you involved with somethin' stupid? Don't be stupid. There's a couple of guys who don't like me 'cause I've been seein' a lady I shouldn't a been seeing. A minor neighborhood problem . . . Okay. It's late. I'm gonna wash up. We'll bunk up together tonight, okay?

ARTY. Sure. There's plenty of room.

LOUIE. Oh. One last thing. (*Points to black satchel.*) Don't touch this. I got my valuables in there. My draft card. My driver's license. My good cuff links. I'll put it somewhere you won't have to worry about it. (*He starts for the bathroom with bag, then stops.*) Oh, Arty. See if there's anything else in your pajama bottoms.

ARTY. (*Looks.*) No. There's nothing there.

LOUIE. Well, don't worry. You're young yet. (*HE chuckles and goes into bathroom.*)

ARTY. He's incredible. It's like having a James Cagney movie in your own house.

JAY. We're not taking that money. They're not painting his apartment at midnight. He's a bag man and he's got a bag and a gun and Pop wouldn't want us to get paid for saying "Nothin'" to Hollywood Harry in the Betty Grable tie. Forget it.

(*Bella's door opens and SHE comes out quietly.*)

BELLA. Jay? Arty? Have you thought of anything yet? About how I should tell Grandma about you-know-who?

JAY. Gee. No. We've been very busy ourselves.

BELLA. Sure. I understand. But if you *do* think of something, I'm going to give you each a dollar. I know you could use it. I'll let you go back to sleep. I was having such a good dream. I'm gonna go back and finish it. (*SHE goes back in her room and closes the door.*)

JAY. You know, we could make a great living just from this family.

(*The bathroom door opens and LOUIE comes out carrying his black bag. HE puts it where HE can see it from bed, then sits, takes off his garters and socks and gets into bed.*)

LOUIE. You guys have to go to the bathroom?

JAY. No. Why?

LOUIE. I don't like anybody getting up while I'm sleeping.

ARTY. Sure . . . How late do you sleep?

LOUIE. Until I see something I don't like. (*HE looks around contentedly.*) Yeah, it's good to be home. In my own bed.

ARTY. Is this where *you* slept?

LOUIE. Yeah. Me and Eddie. And Gert slept with Bella. And Ma slept with her cane . . . There's nothing like family, boys. The one place in the world you're safe, is with your family . . . Right?

JAY. Right.

ARTY. Right.

LOUIE. Right. So unless something unforeseen goes wrong, I'll see you in the morning, pals . . . (*Turns out the lamp.*) Sleep tight. (*HE turns on his side, away from them. There is a silence . . . then:*)

ARTY. Jay?

JAY. What?

ARTY. I have to go to the bathroom.

LOUIE. (*Without moving.*) Save it.

(*In the dark we hear:*)

EDDIE. (*VO.*) "Dear Boys . . . The one thing that keeps me going is knowing you're with my family. Thank God you're in good hands. Love, Pop."

CURTAIN

ACT II

In the dark, we hear the "TRAIN" sounds and a letter from
  EDDIE.
As the LIGHTS come up, we see ARTY in bed, wrapped up in a
  bathrobe, a comic book on his lap. HE is reading a letter as
  EDDIE's voice continues:

EDDIE. *(VO.)* "Dear Boys . . . Sorry I haven't kept up my letter writing. The truth is, I was in the hospital a few days. Nothing serious. The doctor said it was just exhaustion. I remember when I was a boy, if I got sick, my mother used to give me the worst tasting German mustard soup. God, how I hated it. Luckily, they don't serve it in Mississippi. I'll write soon. Love, Pop."

(The front door opens and JAY comes in carrying a bowl of soup.)

JAY. You got it real tough. Reading comic books and missing school. I wish *I* had a fever. Here. Drink this.
ARTY. *(Looks at it suspiciously.)* What is it?
JAY. Grandma made you soup.
ARTY. Forget it. I'm not drinking it.
JAY. Don't start in with her, Arty. She's in a rotten mood today.
ARTY. You mean all those other days she was in a *good* mood?
JAY. Just drink it . . . Where's Uncle Louie?
ARTY. Taking a nap in Aunt Bella's room.
JAY. Well, tell him he got a phone call this morning. One of the guys from the Studebaker.
ARTY. But you said you don't know nothin', right?
JAY. Right. And he said, "You tell Louie that Friday night the dance is over."
ARTY. What dance?
JAY. The "Goodbye Louie" dance.
ARTY. You mean he's double-crossing the mob?

JAY. You got it.

ARTY. Wow! . . . You think they're going to kill him?

JAY. Maybe all three of us. We work for him, don't we?

(The front door opens. GRANDMA walks in wearing her candy store apron, looking angry.)

GRANDMA. *(To JAY.)* It takes twenty minutes to bring up soup? . . . I got one sweeper not sweeping downstairs, I don't need two.

JAY. I was just going.

GRANDMA. And don't let the kids sit on the stool all day. One buys a malted and the other two steal pretzels. If they steal, you pay for it.

JAY. Sure. That's only fair. *(HE crosses to the front door.)*

GRANDMA. Vot was dot?

JAY. I said, "Yes, I hear."

GRANDMA. He's fresh to me, dat one. *(SHE pulls the covers off of him.)* Come on. Out of da bed. It's enough lying around already.

ARTY. *(Pulls sheet back up.)* I'm freezing. And I'm burning up with fever. You can feel my head.

GRANDMA. You lay in bed, you get fever. You get up and walk, da fever looks for somebody else. *(SHE hits the bed with her cane twice.)* Out! Out!

ARTY. *(Gets out of bed, stands and shivers.)* My mother always kept me in bed when I had a fever.

GRANDMA. *(Straightens the sheets and starts to fold the bed back into a sofa.)* You're not in your mother's house no more. *(Pointing to the chair at the living room table.)* You sit in dat chair and you do your homevork. And no funny books. And you finish dat soup. All of it.

ARTY. I tried. I can't get it down.

GRANDMA. If you eat it quick, you von't taste it.

ARTY. I would taste this if I didn't have a tongue.

GRANDMA. You listen to me. You're not fresh yet like da other one, but I see it coming. No, sir. Not in dis house . . . You live vith me, you don't stay in bed two days . . . You get better qvick und you get dressed und you come downstairs und you vash up the soda fountain und you sveep up the store. I didn't ask to take care of you, but if I take care of you, you'll do vot I tell you. *Don't turn away from me!* You'll look at me!! . . . You're not going to vin dis argument, I tell you dot right now. You understand me?

ARTY. . . . Yes.

GRANDMA. Den put da soup in your mouth right now or I do it for you.

(*HE looks at her. SHE obviously means business. HE quickly puts the soup in his mouth. HE keeps it there.*)

ARTY. . . . I can't swallow it.

(*GRANDMA crosses to him, pulls his head back and the soup goes down.*)

ARTY. You could drown me like that . . . Why are you so mean to me? I'm your own grandson.

GRANDMA. Dot's right. And vot am I?

ARTY. What do you mean?

GRANDMA. *Vot am I??* . . . Am I a nobody?

ARTY. No. You're my grandmother.

GRANDMA. Den vere's da respect? Da respect I never got from you or your family since da day you vere born?

ARTY. You're just mad at my mother and you're taking it out on me. You don't care about your rotten soup or making me get better. You just want me to be miserable because somebody made you miserable in Germany. Even Pop said it . . . Well, that's not my fault. Take it out on Hitler, not on me.

GRANDMA. Und if you vere a boy growing up in Germany, you vould be dead by now.

ARTY. That's right. Maybe I would. And if I ate this soup, I would be just as dead. Would that make you happy then? You want to be happy, Grandma? Watch! (*And HE quickly eats six or seven spoonfuls of the soup.*) Okay? Now you can stand there and watch me die.

GRANDMA. No. You von't die. You'll be better dis afternoon. It's not so important dat you hate me, Artur . . . It's only important dat you live. (*SHE crosses to the door and opens it.*) Dot's something dot I could never teach your father. (*SHE exits.*)

(*Bella's bedroom door opens and LOUIE comes out with sleepy eyes and mussed hair. HE wears an undershirt, pants and socks, no shoes.*)

LOUIE. Ever hear of General Rommel?

ARTY. Who?

LOUIE. General Irwin Rommel. German tank commander. Right now he's rollin' right across Egypt, cuttin' through the whole British Army. Tough as they come . . . But if Momma wanted him to eat the soup, he would eat the soup.

ARTY. Did you eat it when you were a kid?

LOUIE. Oh, yeah.

ARTY. I thought you weren't afraid of her.

LOUIE. I wasn't. That's how I proved it to her. I hated that soup worse than you. But I would drink three bowls of it and ask for more. She knew she couldn't win with me.

ARTY. I wish I was as tough as you.

LOUIE. Hey, you're gettin' there. You took her on, kid. That took guts. That took moxie.

ARTY. What's moxie?

LOUIE. (*Stands in a defiant position, in his body and in his face.*) *That's* moxie! . . . Where's Jay-Jay?

ARTY. Downstairs guarding the pretzels . . . Uncle Louie . . . There was a phone call for you.

LOUIE. For me?

ARTY. Jay took it. He told them he never heard of you.

LOUIE. But they left a message, right?

ARTY. Yeah. They said, "Tell Louie that Friday night the dance is over."

LOUIE. (*Smiles.*) Yeah. Well, that don't mean nothin'. A couple a Bronx boys like to talk tough . . . Whatsa matter? Grandma got you down?

ARTY. I think she loves doing it.

LOUIE. Hey, let me tell you somethin'. Guess who hates livin' here more than you? (*HE points to Grandma's door.*) The old lady with the cane. That's right. Grandma hates runnin' this store. She hates livin' in Yonkers. You know how many friends she's made here in thirty years? . . . Zippo.

ARTY. She doesn't exactly put herself out with people.

LOUIE. I never said she was a lot a laughs. I'll tell you the truth. I don't like her much myself. She knows it. Why should I? She used to lock me in a closet for breakin' a dish. A ten-cent dish, I'd get two, three hours in the closet. And if I cried, I'd get another hour . . . No light, no water, just enough air to breathe. That's when I learned not to cry. And after a few times in the closet, I toughened up. But I also never broke another dish . . . No, I didn't like her, but I respected her. Hell of a teacher, Ma was.

ARTY. Wouldn't it have been easier if she bought paper plates?

LOUIE. Then where's the lesson? There's no respect for paper plates. Hear me out . . . She was no harder on us than she was on herself. When she was twelve years old, her old man takes her to a political rally in Berlin. The cops broke it up. With sticks on horse-back. Someone throws a rock, a cop bashes in her old man's head, a horse goes down and crushes Ma's foot. Nobody ever fixed it. It hurts every day of her life but I never once seen her take even an aspirin . . . She coulda had an operation but she used the money she saved to get to this country with her husband and six kids. That's moxie, kid.

ARTY. Did she ever put my father in the closet?

LOUIE. Not a chance. She'd open the closet door and he'd tie himself to the radiator. Even if it was hot. No, he was too afraid to go up against her. He was careful. He never broke nothin' except maybe himself . . .

ARTY. Didn't you ever want to run away?

LOUIE. I did. Twelve times. Still a record in Yonkers. The last time she wouldn't take me back. Tole the policeman she didn't know me. I had no place to go so I lived under the house with a couple of cats for two weeks. Dead of winter. Bella would come out and bring me sandwiches, a blanket, couple of candles. Mom caught her and put her in the closet overnight. But Bella don't understand anything so she thought it was kinda fun. Or maybe she thought it was the safest place to be . . . Now, Gert— Gert was more scared than your old man. Gert used to talk in her sleep and Mom heard her one night sayin' things she didn't like. So Gert didn't get supper that week. Until she learned to sleep holdin' her breath.

ARTY. I don't blame you for hating her.

LOUIE. I didn't say "hate." I didn't *like* her. That's different. How you feelin'?

ARTY. I think my fever's gone.

LOUIE. Lousy soup but it works . . . When Jay comes up, tell him to bring me some coffee and a doughnut. I'll be in the shower. I wanna clean up before I go.

ARTY. You leaving? When?

LOUIE. Tonight. No point waitin' till the dance is over. (*HE winks, starts for bathroom.*)

ARTY. Uncle Louie . . . ?

(*LOUIE stops.*)

ARTY. Are you in trouble?

LOUIE. (*Smiles.*) Arty! I was never *not* in trouble. (*HE goes into the bathroom and closes the door.*)

(*The front door opens and JAY storms in, looking furious. HE slams the door closed.*)

JAY. I hate her! . . . I hate her guts. No wonder Mom never wanted us to come here.

ARTY. What did she do?

JAY. She charged me for three pretzels. Three pretzels that some kids while she was downstairs and I was upstairs with your soup . . . She says, "No, there were twelve pretzels in the glass when I went upstairs and nine pretzels when I came down." . . . Not even Sherlock Holmes would notice that . . .

ARTY. Two cents a pretzel, it's only six cents.

JAY. Oh, is that all it is? Then *you* pay it . . . Is Uncle Louie still sleeping?

ARTY. He's taking a shower. He's leaving tonight.

JAY. Leaving? I have to talk to him.

ARTY. About what?

JAY. It's private business.

ARTY. Jay, you don't *have* any business. All you got is a job that costs you six cents a day . . . Come on, tell me, Jay. I'll find out sooner or later.

JAY. . . . I'm going to ask Uncle Louie to take me with him.

ARTY. *WHAT???*

JAY. Will you be quiet!

ARTY. Are you crazy? Go with Uncle Louie?

JAY. I have to make money. Get a good job somewhere. But I can't leave here with minus six cents in my pocket. Uncle Louie is my ticket out.

ARTY. Running away. That's all Pop has to hear.

JAY. Well, we just can't count on Pop anymore. Maybe I can take care of him better than he's taking care of us.

ARTY. Doing what?

JAY. Maybe Uncle Louie can teach me a few things.

ARTY. Oh, great. To become what? A junior bag man? "The Pocketbook Kid"?

JAY. If Uncle Louie says yes, you can't stop me.

ARTY. . . . Then take me with you.

JAY. Take *you*? You're only a kid. Besides, she doesn't treat you the way she treats me.

ARTY. I'm afraid of her, Jay. A horse fell on her when she was a kid and she hasn't taken an aspirin yet.

JAY. Look, if I can get set up somewhere with a good-paying job, I'll send for you.

ARTY. You promise?

JAY. I swear on Momma's grave.

ARTY. Artur and Yakob, the gangster. I can't believe it.

(The front door opens and BELLA comes in.)

BELLA. *(To JAY.)* Oh, here you are. Momma sent me up to look for you. She didn't know where you were for twenty minutes.

JAY. I'm coming right down. I just have to ask Uncle Louie something. He's in the shower.

BELLA. *(To ARTY.)* Are you feeling better, Arty?

ARTY. Yeah.

BELLA. I'm glad. Because we're having company tonight. My sister Gertrude. Do you remember her?

JAY. Sort of.

BELLA. She hasn't been well. She doesn't breathe right. I think it's because she used to sleep with her head inside the pillow.

ARTY. *Inside?*

(*BELLA nods, quickly closes the front door, then crosses closer to the BOYS.*)

BELLA. (*Whispers.*) Tonight's the night.
JAY. Tonight's what night?
BELLA. The night that I talk to Momma. About you-know-what.
JAY. Just the two of you?
BELLA. No. With Aunt Gertrude and Uncle Louie here. And you and Arty. I wouldn't dare talk to Momma without the family here. To back me up . . . You *are* going to back me up, aren't you? You promised.
JAY. It's not going to go very late, is it?
BELLA. Not if everybody backs me up . . . You're not going any-place, are you?
JAY. Me? No. Where would *I* be going?
BELLA. My heart hasn't stopped pounding all day. I'm so ner-vous, I can't stop eating. I ate three pretzels before and I *never* eat pretzels.
JAY. *You* ate the pretzels? . . . If you eat anything else, would you tell Grandma first?
BELLA. Oh, she knows I ate the pretzels. She even said to me, "Why are you eating so much? You nervous about something?" . . . I'd better get downstairs. (*SHE crosses to the door.*) You too, Jay. I don't want to do anything to upset Momma before tonight. (*SHE opens the door.*) Arty, if you want more soup, just let me know. (*SHE goes and closes the door.*)
JAY. (*Furious.*) She *knew* Aunt Bella ate the pretzels!! . . . Grandma's crazy, Arty. Where did that horse fall, on her *head?*

(*LOUIE comes out of the bathroom, his hair wet and combed straight back. HE has a towel around his neck and HE carries the little black satchel.*)

LOUIE. Perfect timing, Jay-Jay. (*HE looks around.*) You got my coffee and doughnut?
ARTY. Oh. I forgot to tell him.
LOUIE. So tell him.

ARTY. *(To JAY.)* Uncle Louie wanted some coffee and a dough-nut.

JAY. Coming right up . . . Would you tell Grandma it's for you? Because doughnuts are expensive.

LOUIE. *(Smiles.)* What is she doing, charging you for missing doughnuts?

JAY. No. Missing pretzels. How did you know?

LOUIE. It's her favorite trick. I once owed her two dollars for a missing bag of pistachio nuts. One minute they were on the counter, the next minute they were gone. She blamed me. Until I found them in her drawer. She said, "You're responsible if some-body steals from this store. Even me." . . . Hey, Arty. Get my shirt, will ya? It's on the bed.

(ARTY crosses into Bella's room.)

JAY. Did you pay her the two dollars?

LOUIE. No. I stole the nuts back that night. But I got the lesson.

JAY. You've learned a lot in your life, haven't you, Uncle Louie?

LOUIE. No one takes me for pistachios no more.

(ARTY comes out with Louie's shirt.)

JAY. I can see . . . A guy could learn a lot from you, I bet.

LOUIE. *(Takes the shirt, puts it on.)* I could write a book.

JAY. You wouldn't have to write. I mean, if someone just hung around you watching, they would pick up a lot, don't you think?

LOUIE. *(Sits on the sofa, begins to shine his shoes.)* A lotta what?

JAY. A lot of anything.

LOUIE. I don't think so. 'Cause I don't like nobody hangin' around watchin' me.

JAY. *(Looks at ARTY, then at LOUIE.)* Uncle Louie . . . I have an important question to ask you.

LOUIE. Don't ask questions, kid. That's probably the best thing I could teach you. Never ask questions.

JAY. I'm sorry . . . I'll just tell you then . . . I want to leave here . . . Tonight . . . I made up my mind. I'm definitely going . . .

LOUIE. Where you goin'?

JAY. As far away as I can get.

LOUIE. How far is that? Five-dollars far? Ten-dollars far? A dozen pretzels far?

JAY. No. Just a-pair-of-shoes far. Until they wear out.

LOUIE. And then what? You better have better transportation than a pair of shoes.

JAY. I never did this before. That's why I'm asking your advice.

LOUIE. You're gonna make your grandma very unhappy, Jay-Jay.

JAY. No, I won't. Besides, that never stopped you.

(LOUIE stops brushing and looks at JAY.)

ARTY. Would you like me to brush your shoes, Uncle Louie?

LOUIE. *(To ARTY.)* Hey! One guy work on me at a time, okay? *(HE brushes again; to JAY.)* So why you wanna go? It's cold out there. It's lonely out there . . . and it's dangerous out there.

JAY. I know that . . . but there's money out there.

LOUIE. Oh, I see . . . You lookin' to get rich fast?

JAY. Not for me. For Pop.

LOUIE. Ain't that nice? Like Robin Hood, heh?

JAY. I don't want to rob people.

LOUIE. No? . . . Who *do* you want to rob?

JAY. No one.

LOUIE. That sorta rules out gettin' rich fast.

JAY. *Some* people do it.

LOUIE. Yeah? How?

JAY. You'll think this is a question.

LOUIE. *(Angrily.)* Then don't ask it. I can't help you, kid. I got nothin' to teach you and nothin' I *wanna* teach you . . . Is that what you think I do? Rob banks? Rob liquor stores? Grocery stores? Little old ladies in the park? Is that what you think I am?

JAY. No . . . I don't think so.

LOUIE. You don't think so? What is that, a compliment? . . . You wanna know what I do? I'm a businessman. I'm a freelance money manager. A twenty-four-hour-a-day investment adviser. You been dyin' to ask me that all day so now I told you. School's out. You graduated. Now find a girl and go to your prom, okay?

JAY. Thank you . . . I just have one minor question to ask.

LOUIE. *(Smiles.)* You got balls, kid . . . Did you know you got balls?

JAY. I'm aware of them, yes.

LOUIE. (*To ARTY.*) I love your brother . . . Reminds me of me. (*To JAY.*) What's your minor question?

JAY. Are there any openings in your business?

LOUIE. (*Stares at him.*) . . . You got balls but I think they're in your head.

JAY. I'll do anything and I won't ask any questions.

LOUIE. There are no openings. The reason there are no openings is because there's no business no more. I'm relocating. It's a one-man operation outa town . . . That's the end of this conversation. As far as I'm concerned, this conversation is deceased. Okay?

JAY. . . . Take me with you . . . I'll get off wherever you want me to, but please, take me with you tonight.

LOUIE. Are you deaf or somethin'? (*To ARTY.*) Is he deaf? Doesn't he hear what I just said? Did *you* hear what I just said?

ARTY. I caught most of it, yeah.

LOUIE. (*To JAY.*) Take you with me for what? For company? Your company's starting to pester me already. What do I need you for? What can you do for me? Heh? (*HE exits into the bathroom.*)

JAY. . . . I could carry your little black satchel.

LOUIE. (*LOUIE comes out, wearing his shoulder holster. HE has fire in his eyes. LOUIE moves toward JAY.*) . . . You interested in my little black satchel?

JAY. No . . . I just thought—

LOUIE. No? But you want to carry it . . . Why? Does it look heavy to you? . . . You think I got a broken arm, I can't carry a little bag like that?

JAY. No.

LOUIE. So maybe you have some other interest in it . . . You been foolin' around with this bag?

JAY. I swear. No.

LOUIE. So what are you curious about? How much it weighs or something? . . . You want to pick it up, go ahead, pick it up.

JAY. I don't want to pick it up.

LOUIE. Pick it up, Jay. It ain't gonna bite you . . . You won't be happy till you pick it up. Go ahead, kid. Pick it up.

JAY. I really don't want to.

ARTY. Come on, Jay. Please pick it up.

JAY. Stay out of this.

LOUIE. No, no . . . Arty, come here.

ARTY. Me?

LOUIE. That's right. You're Arty.

(ARTY comes to him. LOUIE puts his arm around Arty's shoulder.)

LOUIE. I want you to go over to that stool and pick up the black bag.

ARTY. Jay is closer.

LOUIE. Jay is not interested. I want you to do it.

(ARTY goes over and stands next to the stool where the black bag sits.)

LOUIE. Okay, Arty. Pick it up.

ARTY. *(His face screws up.)* I don't know why but I think I'm going to cry.

LOUIE. Just pick it up, Arty.

(ARTY picks it up.)

LOUIE. Is it heavy?

ARTY. No.

LOUIE. Is it light?

ARTY. No.

LOUIE. So what is it?

ARTY. . . . Medium.

LOUIE. Okay, so it's medium . . . So what do you think is in the bag? . . . Money? . . . fives and tens and twenties and hundreds all stuck together with rubber bands? . . . WHAT?? . . . I said WHAT!!!

ARTY. I don't know.

LOUIE. You don't know . . . Well, then, maybe you'd better look in the bag and see . . . Why don't you do that, Arty? . . . Open the bag . . . Okay?

ARTY. Please, Uncle Louie—

LOUIE. *(Takes a step closer.)* I'm only gonna ask you one more time, Arty . . . because I'm runnin' out of patience . . . Open—the bag!

(ARTY looks at him, helpless, terrified . . . and then suddenly.)

JAY. Don't do it, Arty . . . Leave him alone, Uncle Louie. You want the bag open, do it yourself. *(HE takes the bag from ARTY and tosses it at Louie's feet.)* Maybe you don't rob banks or grocery stores or little old women. You're worse than that. You're a bully. You pick on a couple of kids. Your own nephews. You make fun of my father because he cried and was afraid of Grandma. Well, everyone in *Yonkers* is afraid of Grandma . . . And let me tell you something about my father. At least he's doing something in this war. He's sick and he's tired but he's out there selling iron to make ships and tanks and cannons. And I'm proud of him. What are *you* doing? Hiding in your mother's apartment and scaring little kids and acting like Humphrey Bogart. Well, you're no Humphrey Bogart . . . And I'll tell you something else—No. That's all.

LOUIE. *(LOUIE has hardly blinked an eye. HE shifts his body and takes one small step toward JAY. Smiles.)* That was thrilling. That was beautiful. I had tears in my eyes, I swear to God . . . You got bigger balls than I thought, Jay. You got a couple of steel basketballs there . . . You know what you got, Jay? You got moxie.

JAY. What's moxie?

LOUIE. Tell him, Arty.

ARTY. *(ARTY makes Louie's gesture of what moxie is. To JAY.)* That's moxie.

LOUIE. Yeah . . . Your father's a lucky guy, let me tell you . . . that's why I don't think you should go with me, Jay. You take care of Arty here. And Momma and Bella. And maybe one day you'll be proud of your old Uncle Louie, too. *(HE picks up the bag, puts it on table.)* And don't worry what was in the bag. It's just laundry. Dirty laundry, boys. That's all.

(HE crosses to mirror to finish getting dressed as GRANDMA walks in.)

GRANDMA. *(Sternly, to JAY.)* Are you a banker? Is this your lunch hour? Well, dis is not a bank. Go down and help Bella close up da store . . . Artur, get your clothes on. Ve haff company tonight.

(ARTY runs into the bathroom.)

LOUIE. I don't think I can stay, Ma.

GRANDMA. I didn't ask you to. Bella asked you. You'll stay. *(To JAY.)* You haff someting to say to me? No? Den get downstairs . . . Und you und I haff someting else to talk about later.

JAY. About what?

GRANDMA. About a jar of pistachio nuts dat are missing, dot's about what.

(JAY looks at LOUIE, then goes. LOUIE puts on his suit coat and hat. GRANDMA looks at him. It is more of a scowl. SHE takes a few bills out of her pocket.)

GRANDMA. You're getting careless, Louie. You dropped this money on my dresser this morning.

LOUIE. Louie's never careless, Ma. It's for you. I had a good week.

GRANDMA. A good week for you is a bad week for someone else . . . I don't want your profits, Louie.

LOUIE. It's just a hundred bucks. Happy Birthday, Ma. It's tomorrow, right?

GRANDMA. *(Puts the money on the table.)* Don't pay me for being born. I've paid enough.

LOUIE. *(Picks up the money.)* Then take it for putting me up. You know how I hate hotels. *(HE offers it to her.)*

GRANDMA. *(Angrily.)* I don't take from You!!! . . . Not what you haff to give . . . You were always the strongest one. The survivor . . . *Live*—at any cost I taught you, yes. But not when someone else has to pay the price . . . Keep your filthy money, Louie. *(SHE starts to go.)*

LOUIE. *(Smiles.)* You're terrific, Ma. One hundred percent steel. Finest grade made. Eddie's out there lookin' for scrap iron and the chump doesn't know he's got a whole battleship right here . . . Nah. You can't get me down, Ma. I'm too tough. You taught me good. And whatever I've accomplished in this life, just remember—you're my partner. *(HE blows her a ferocious kiss.)*

BLACKOUT

SCENE TWO

In the dark, we hear the voice of EDDIE again.

EDDIE. *(VO.)* "Dear Momma . . . The boys tell me you're getting along fine with them. I told you they wouldn't be any trouble. Enclosed, I'm sending you twenty-five dollars to cover their food and Arty's medicine . . . Yakob tells me some kids have been stealing pretzels and pistachio nuts. It's amazing that hasn't stopped in almost thirty years . . . Love, Eddie."

(Later that night.
BELLA and JAY are cleaning off the dining table of its remaining
    dishes and straightening out the chairs.)
GRANDMA sits in her usual chair, wearing a sweater and cro-
    cheting or doing needlepoint. LOUIE, wearing his suit jacket,
    paces, looking like HE's anxious to go. AUNT GERT, in her
    mid- to late-thirties, sits on the sofa. SHE holds a purse and
    her handkerchief, which SHE uses now and then to wipe her
    mouth. ARTY is in the kitchen, unseen, helping clean off the
    dishes.)

BELLA. Would anyone like more coffee? Momma? Gert?

(GRANDMA doesn't answer.)

GERT. *(Nods.)* Mmm.
BELLA. Strudel with it?
GERT. *(Hoarsely.)* No.
BELLA. Jay, go in and get Aunt Gert some more coffee, but no strudel.

(JAY goes in.)

BELLA. Louie? Wouldn't you like another piece?
LOUIE. *(Distracted.)* I had enough, Bella.
BELLA. You always have two pieces.

LOUIE. One strudel is enough tonight, okay, Bella?

(HE looks at his watch . . . BELLA starts to put chairs from the dining table into the circle of seats in the living room.)

BELLA. Don't help me with the chairs, anyone. I know just how I want it to be.

(LOUIE looks at his watch as BELLA puts the chair in the right spot.)

LOUIE. Listen, Momma. I'm gonna run along, now. I'll call you next week. Gert, it was good seein' you, sweetheart. You're lookin' terrific.

BELLA. Louie, you're going to sit right here.

LOUIE. Bella, I'm sorry. I really gotta go. It was a top notch dinner, no kiddin'. *(HE kisses her cheek. HE calls off into kitchen.)* Jay! It'll work out. Trust me. Where's Arty? I'm leavin'.

BELLA. Noo! You can't go yet, Louie . . . You promised.

LOUIE. I promised I'd stay for dinner. I stayed for dinner. How many dinners you want me to stay for?

BELLA. But the family hasn't had a talk yet.

LOUIE. We did. We talked all through dinner. I never had a chance to swallow nothin'. I'm all talked out, Bella.

BELLA. There's still something that hasn't been talked about. It wasn't something that could be talked about at dinner . . . You sit here. This is your place.

LOUIE. *(Exasperated.)* I told you I had to go right after the coffee. I had my coffee. I had my strudel. I had my dinner. I have to go, Bella.

BELLA. *(Nervously.)* Momma! Gert! Tell him to stay . . . Louie, you can't go, you have to be here. The whole family has to be here. Momma, tell him.

GRANDMA. *(Sternly.)* You're getting excited, Bella.

BELLA. I won't get excited. I promise. I'm fine, Momma . . . Just ask Louie to stay. Let me get the boys in.

GERT. He'll stay, Bella.

BELLA. *(Calls out.)* Jay? Arty! Forget the dishes. We'll do them later . . . Everybody inside.

(JAY comes in with Gert's coffee. ARTY follows, eating the last bite of a piece of strudel. HE is dressed now.)

JAY. Here's your coffee, Aunt Gert.

GERT. Thank you.

BELLA. Jay! Arty! Sit on the sofa with Aunt Gert. Momma, you stay there. I'll sit here and, Louie, sit on the chair.

LOUIE. I've been sittin' all night, Bella. I can stand up, okay?

BELLA. But it would be so much better if you were sitting, Louie. I pictured everybody sitting.

LOUIE. *I don't wanna sit!!* Change the picture. Picture everybody sittin' and me standin', all right?

(This is about to be the first time we hear AUNT GERT talk her full first sentence, where her affliction becomes apparent. SHE speaks normally for the first half of the sentence and then somewhere past the middle, SHE talks by sucking in her breath, so the words go to a higher pitch and it sounds very difficult for her.)

GERT. Louie, can't you just sit for a few minutes until Bella tells us what it is—*(SHE sucks in now.)*—she wants to talk to us all about?

(ARTY and JAY look at each other.)

LOUIE. Okay. Okay. *(HE sits on the window seat.)* Here? All right? Is this the way you pictured it, Bella?

BELLA. No. I pictured you sitting on the chair I picked out.

LOUIE. *(Crosses to the "his" chair, but doesn't sit.)* Bella! It's *very* important that I leave here soon. Very important. I don't want to upset you, sweetheart, but I can't spend the rest of the night getting the seating arrangements right . . . I'm gonna stand up, I'm gonna listen and then I'm gonna go.

BELLA. *(Puts her head down, sulks, childlike.)* I pictured everybody sitting.

LOUIE. Jesus!

GERT. Louie, stop arguing with her and sit down, for God sakes, before—*(SHE sucks in.)*—she gets into one of her moods again.

GRANDMA. Louie, sit! Gertrude, stop it.

LOUIE. Louie sit! Louie stand! Louie eat! . . . You don't scare me anymore, Ma. Maybe everyone else here, but not me. You understand?

GRANDMA. (*Still crocheting.*) Sit down, Louie!

(*LOUIE sits.*)

BELLA. All right. (*SHE sits.*) Are we all seated now?

LOUIE. Yes, Bella. We're all seated. You wanna take a picture of what you pictured?

GERT. Stop it, Louie.

BELLA. (*Looks around, smiles, content with the seating.*) Now . . . who wants to start?

LOUIE. (*Rises.*) Who wants to *start*? . . . Start *what*? . . . Momma, I haven't got time for this. Maybe when I was twelve years old, but not tonight. It's one of her games. Her crazy games, for crise sakes.

GERT. Is this a game, Bella? Are you just playing—(*Sucks in.*)— a game with us, darling?

BELLA. It's not a game. It's very important . . . But I don't know how to start to say it. So somebody else has to help me and start first.

LOUIE. (*To BELLA.*) You have something important to tell us and you want *us* to start? (*HE starts toward the front door.*) Listen, Gert. You understand her better than I do. When you figure out what it is, let me know.

JAY. (*To BELLA.*) Aunt Bella, have you . . .

(*LOUIE and EVERYONE ELSE stop and look at JAY.*)

JAY. . . . Have you been going to the movies lately, Aunt Bella?

BELLA. (*Smiles.*) Thank you, Jay . . . Yes. I have been going to the movies a lot lately . . .

(*LOUIE looks at her in disbelief.*)

BELLA. . . . Three times last week.

JAY. Really? . . . Did you see anything good?

BELLA. Oh, yes. I saw a picture with William Holden and Jean Arthur . . . I really liked it . . . That's why I saw it three times.

LOUIE. This is what I stayed to dinner for? This is what I had to sit in the right seat to listen to? Jean Arthur and William Holden? Are they in the picture you pictured here?

GERT. Is that what this is about, Bella? Is this all about what movies—(*Sucks in.*)—you went to last week?

BELLA. No, but I'm getting to it. Ask me more questions, Jay. You're good at this.

JAY. Uh, let's see . . . Did you—go alone?

BELLA. Oh, yes. I always go alone. But it's interesting you asked me that . . . Because I met a friend there . . . You can ask me questions too, Gert.

GERT. I don't know what kind of questions—(*Sucks in.*)—to ask you.

ARTY. Ask her who the friend was.

GERT. Who was the friend?

BELLA. Well, his name is Johnny, I always see him there because he's the head usher. He's very nice.

JAY. So you just saw him in the theater?

BELLA. Well, once or twice we went out for coffee and once we took a walk in the park.

LOUIE. . . . You went to the park with this guy?

BELLA. Just to talk . . . You have to sit down if you're going to ask me questions, Louie.

(*LOUIE comes back and sits down.*)

BELLA. Now whose turn is it?

GRANDMA. Dis is ven you came home at eleven o'clock?

BELLA. Maybe. I think so. Was that it?

GERT. What did you do until eleven—(*Sucks in.*)—o'clock?

BELLA. We walked and we talked . . . And we got to know each other . . . He doesn't want to be an usher forever. One day he wants to open up his own restaurant.

LOUIE. His own restaurant? And he's an usher? What is he, fifteen, sixteen?

BELLA. No. He's forty . . . And he wants to open up the restaurant with me.

(There is silence. SHE has finally gotten their attention.)

LOUIE. Why with you?

BELLA. *(Starting to get nervous.)* Because I can do all the cooking . . . and write out the menus . . . and keep the books.

GERT. And what would he do?

BELLA. He would be the manager. *(SHE sees this isn't going too well.)*

LOUIE. If he's the manager, why doesn't *he* write out the menus and keep the books?

BELLA. Well, he has a—*(She looks at ARTY and JAY.)*—a reading handicap.

LOUIE. A what?

BELLA. A reading handicap.

LOUIE. Okay, hold it. Wait a minute. *(Rises.)* What do you mean? He can't read?

BELLA. You're not supposed to get out of your chair. That's not how I pictured it.

LOUIE. Yeah, well, now I'm getting my *own* picture . . . This guy is what? Illiterate?

BELLA. He can read . . . a little.

LOUIE. What's a little? His *name*? . . . This guy is either pulling your leg or he's after something, Bella . . . Is he after something?

BELLA. Maybe this isn't a good time to talk about it.

LOUIE. No, it's the *perfect* time to talk about it . . . What is this guy after, Bella? Has he touched you? . . . Has he fooled around with you?

BELLA. NO!!! He's not that kind of person.

LOUIE. Well, what kinda person *is* he? . . . He's forty years old, he takes you to the park at night. He wants to open up a restaurant with you and he can't read or write . . . How are you going to open up a restaurant? Who's going to put up the money?

BELLA. It'll only cost five thousand dollars.

LOUIE. *(Laughs.)* Five thousand dollars? Why not five million? And who's got the five grand? Him?

BELLA. I don't think so . . . He doesn't have any money.

LOUIE. Oh. Too bad . . . Well, then who does that leave?

BELLA. Don't yell at me, Louie.

LOUIE. I'm not yelling at you, Bella. I'm just asking you a question. Who does that leave to put up the five thousand dollars?

GERT. This is too terrible. Momma, please tell them—(*Sucks in.*)—to stop this awful thing.

LOUIE. Who does that leave, Bella?

BELLA. I'll get the money somewhere.

LOUIE. Where is somewhere, Bella? . . . There is no somewhere. You want Momma to sell the store? Is that what this guy asked you to do?

BELLA. He didn't ask me anything.

LOUIE. Then he's either very smart or very dangerous. Well, he doesn't sound too smart to me. So that just leaves dangerous.

BELLA. He's *not* dangerous.

LOUIE. How do you know that?

BELLA. Because they don't take you at the Home if you're dangerous.

LOUIE. . . . *The Home???*

GRANDMA. Oh, my Gott!!

GERT. I don't understand this. Can somebody please—(*Sucks in.*)—explain all this to me?

LOUIE. (*To BELLA.*) Bella, honey. This man sounds very troubled . . . Is he living at the Home now?

BELLA. No. With his parents. He didn't like the Home. They weren't very nice to him there. (*Looks at GRANDMA, pointedly.*) . . . It's not a *nice place*, Momma!

LOUIE. Bella, sweetheart. Don't go to that movie anymore. Don't see that fella again. He may be very nice but he sounds like he's got a lot of whacky ideas, you know what I mean, sweetheart?

BELLA. You promised you would support me . . . Jay! Arty! You said you would back me up. You promised.

LOUIE. Back you up with what, Bella? . . . The restaurant? The money? Is that what this guy is after?

BELLA. He wants *more* than that.

LOUIE. What could possibly be more than that, Bella?

BELLA. Me! He wants *me*! He wants to marry me! (*SHE starts to cry.*) I want to marry *him* . . . I want to have his children . . . I want my own babies.

LOUIE. (*Sits back.*) Jesus Christ!

GRANDMA. (*Shocked at this.*) Dot's enough! . . . I don't vant to hear dis anymore!

BELLA. You think I can't have healthy babies, Momma? Well, I can . . . I'm as strong as an ox. I've worked in that store and taken care of you by myself since I'm twelve years old, that's how strong I am . . . Like *steel*, Momma. Isn't that how we're supposed to be? . . . But my babies won't die because I'll love them and take care of them . . . And they won't get sick like me or Gert or be weak like Eddie and Louie . . . My babies will be happier than we were because I'll teach them to be happy . . . Not to grow up and run away or never visit when they're older and not be able to breathe because they're so frightened . . . and never, *ever* to make them spend their lives rubbing my back and my legs because you never had anyone around who loved you enough to want to touch you because you made it so clear you never wanted to be touched with love . . . Do you know what it's like to touch steel, Momma? It's hard and it's cold and I want to be warm and soft with my children . . . Let me have my babies, Momma. Because I have to love somebody. I have to love someone who'll love me back before I die . . . Give me that, Momma, and I promise you, you'll never worry about being alone . . . Because you'll have us . . . Me and my husband and my babies . . . Louie, tell her how wonderful that would be . . . Gert, wouldn't that make her happy? . . . Momma? . . . Please say yes . . . I need you to say yes . . . Please?

(*It is deathly silent. No one has moved. Finally, GRANDMA gets up slowly, walks to her room, goes in and quietly closes the door.*)

BELLA. (*Looks at the OTHERS.*) Hold me . . . Somebody please hold me.

(*GERT gets up and puts her arms around BELLA and rocks her gently.*
We go to BLACK.)

SCENE THREE

ARTY. (VO.) Dear Pop . . . Things are really bad here. Really, *really* bad. I wish you were home. Even just for a weekend. Last night I cried for you . . . and for Mom . . . but Jay was afraid Grandma would hear, so he stuck a sock in my mouth. I miss you and love you. Your son, Arty . . . Not Artur.

(*Sunday, the following week. About midday.*
ARTY is seated at the table, writing in his notebook. JAY stands looking out the window.)

JAY. Where do you think Aunt Bella could be? Missing for two nights, somewhere out there in the city. I'm worried.
ARTY. Maybe Uncle Louie took her with him.
JAY. If he didn't take me, you think he's going to take Aunt Bella and her forty-year-old usher from the Home? . . .

(*The door to Grandma's room opens and AUNT GERT comes out.*)

GERT. I'm going now. I think Momma feels better since—(*A breath.*)—Aunt Bella called me.
JAY. No idea where she is?
GERT. Yes. (*Moves away from Grandma's door.*) . . . She's at my house.
JAY. *Your* house?
GERT. Shhh. She doesn't want Momma to know.
ARTY. You mean she's been there all the time?

(*Gert nods "yes."*)

JAY. Is she ever coming back?
GERT. She's meeting with that man today . . . We'll know soon.
ARTY. Do you think they'll get married?
GERT. Who knows? . . . She's been crying for—(*Sucks in.*)—two days now. I'm sorry. It's hard for me to talk.

JAY. Isn't there anything the doctors can do about that, Aunt Gert?

GERT. I don't have it that much. It's mostly—(*Sucks in.*)—when I come here.

JAY. Oh.

GERT. You boys take care of Grandma now. If Bella doesn't come back you're all she has.

JAY. I know.

GERT. If you run into trouble, do you have my number?

JAY. I don't think so.

GERT. It's Westchester seven—(*Sucks in.*)—four-six-six-nine.

ARTY. What?

GERT. Westchester seven—(*Sucks in.*)—four-six—

JAY. I have it! I have it!

GERT. Goodbye, darlings. Take care. I love you. (*SHE goes, closing the front door.*)

ARTY. It could be worse. Suppose we were left with *her* instead?

JAY. That's not funny.

ARTY. Yes, it is.

JAY. All right. It's funny. But I feel sorry for her. I feel sorry for this whole family . . . Even Grandma . . . Don't you?

(*ARTY looks at JAY, says nothing.*)

JAY. Well, I do. And you should, too.

(*Grandma's door opens. SHE comes out, looking tired.*)

JAY. Hi, Grandma. How you feeling?

ARTY. Is there anything we can get you?

GRANDMA. (*SHE sits.*) Vot are you doing in the house on Sunday? Vy don't you go for a walk or something?

JAY. We thought we'd keep you company.

GRANDMA. I don't need to be kept company.

ARTY. You want the radio on, Grandma? They have Sunday news on today.

GRANDMA. I had enough news already this week.

JAY. Things are getting better in North Africa. They captured twenty thousand Germans this month.

GRANDMA. Twenty thousand Germans . . . Goot. Dot's goot news . . . How is your father?

JAY. He's feeling better. He thinks he could be home for good in about eight months.

GRANDMA. Eight months . . . You'll be glad to go home, ya?

ARTY. Ya . . . Yes . . . Sort of.

JAY. But we'll still come out and visit you, Grandma.

GRANDMA. Maybe I von't be here . . . Maybe I'll sell da store.

JAY. Sell the store? What would you do without the store?

GRANDMA. Don't worry so much about your grandma. Your grandma knows how to take care of herself, believe me . . . Go on outside, both of you. You talk too much.

JAY. You sure you don't mind being alone?

GRANDMA. (*SHE sits back and closes her eyes.*) . . . Maybe dis is da first Sunday I'll get some rest.

(*The front door opens and BELLA comes in. SHE is wearing a hat and coat and carries her purse and a small suitcase. SHE also has a cake box.*)

JAY. Aunt Bella!

ARTY. Are you okay?

GRANDMA. (*SHE doesn't react to this. SHE remains sitting back with her eyes still closed.*) Go already. How many times do I haff to tell you?

(*The BOYS look at her, then turn and leave, closing the door. BELLA stands there looking at her MOTHER, who has still refused to open her eyes.*)

BELLA. Hello, Momma . . .

(*GRANDMA doesn't respond.*)

BELLA. . . . Would you like some tea? It's chilly in here . . . I bought a coffee cake at Grossman's. It's still warm . . . It's all right if you don't want to talk to me, Momma. I know you must be very angry with me.

GRANDMA. *(Looks away from BELLA.)* You're home for goot or dis is a visit?

BELLA. I don't know . . . I thought I'd come back and talk to you about it.

GRANDMA. Like you talked to me da night you left? . . . Vidout a vord?

BELLA. You're the one who didn't talk, Momma. You never gave me a chance to say anything.

GRANDMA. I heard vot you had to say. I didn't haff to hear no more.

BELLA. *(Nods.)* Look, Momma, I'm not crying . . . I know you're very angry with me but I'm not crying. And it's not because I'm afraid to cry. It's because I have no tears left in me. I feel sort of empty inside. Like *you* feel all the time.

GRANDMA. How vould you know how I feel?

BELLA. You don't think I know anything, do you? You think I'm stupid, don't you, Momma?

GRANDMA. No. You're not stupid.

BELLA. Then what? Am I crazy? Do you think I'm crazy, Momma?

GRANDMA. Don't use dot word to me.

BELLA. Why not? Are you afraid of it? If that's what I am, Momma, then don't be afraid to say it. Because if I'm crazy, I should be in the Home, shouldn't I? But then you'd be alone and you wouldn't like that. Is that why you don't use that word, Momma?

GRANDMA. . . . You vant to know vot you are, Bella? . . . You're a child. Dot's vot da doctors told me. Not crazy. Not stupid . . . A child! . . . And dot's how I treat you. Because dot's all you understand . . . You don't need doctors. You're not sick. You don't need to live in da Home. *Dis* is vere you live. Vere you can be vatched and taken care of . . . You'll always be a child, Bella. And in dis vorld, vere dere is so much hate and sickness and death, vere nobody can live in peace, den maybe you're better off . . . Stay a child, Bella, and be glad dot's vot Gott made you.

BELLA. Then why did he make me look like a woman? . . . And feel like a woman inside of me? And want all the things a woman should have? Is that what I should thank him for? Why did he do that, Momma, when I can do everything but *think* like a woman? . . . I know I get confused sometimes . . . and frightened. But if I'm a child, why can't I be happy like a child? Why can't I be satisfied with dolls instead of babies?

GRANDMA. I'm not so smart I can answer such things.

BELLA. But I *am* smart, Momma. Maybe only as smart as a child, but some children are smarter than grown-ups. Some grown-ups I've seen are very stupid. And very mean.

GRANDMA. You don't haff responsibilities, Bella. And responsibilities is vot makes meanness.

BELLA. I don't want to be your responsibility. Then maybe you won't be so mean to me.

GRANDMA. Den who will be responsible for you? Yourself? Dot man you ran away with? Who vants money from you? Who wants other things from you? God only knows vot else. Things you vould never know about. Stay the way you are, Bella, because you don't know vot such feelings would do to you.

BELLA. Yes, I do, Momma. I know what other things you're talking about . . . Because they've happened to me, Momma . . . They've happened because I *wanted* them to happen . . . You angry at me?

GRANDMA. *(Turns away, dismissing this.)* You don't know vot you're saying, Bella.

BELLA. You mean am I telling you the truth? Yes. I know what the truth is . . . Only I've been afraid to tell it to you for all these years. Gertrude knows. She's the only one . . . Do you hate me, Momma? Tell me, because I don't know if I did wrong or not.

GRANDMA. You're angry so you tell me lies. I don't vant to hear your childish lies. *(SHE waves BELLA away.)*

BELLA. No! You *have* to listen, Momma . . . When I was in school, I let boys touch me . . . And boys that I met in the park . . . And in the movies . . . Even boys that I met here in the store . . . Nights when you were asleep, I went down and let them in . . . And not just boys, Momma . . . men too.

GRANDMA. Stop dis, Bella. You don't know vot you're saying . . . You dream these things in your head.

BELLA. I needed somebody to touch me, Momma. Somebody to hold me. To tell me I was pretty . . . *You* never told me that. Some even told me they loved me but I never believed them because I knew what they wanted from me . . . Except John. He *did* love me. Because he understood me. Because he was like me. He was the only one I ever felt safe with. And I thought maybe for the first time I *could* be happy . . . That's why I ran away. I even brought the five thousand dollars to give him for the restaurant. Then maybe he'd find the courage to leave home too.

GRANDMA. (*Looks at her disdainfully.*) Is dis someting else you dreamed up? Vere vould you get five thousand dollars?

(*BELLA opens her purse and takes out a stack of bills tied in rubber bands. SHE puts it on the table.*)

BELLA. Does this look like a dream, Momma?

GRANDMA. (*Picks up the bills and looks at them.*) Vere did you get dis? (*SHE turns quickly, looks toward her room.*) Did you steal from me? You know vere I keep my money. Nobody else but you. (*SHE throws her cup of tea in Bella's face.*) You thief!! You steal from your own mother? *Thief!!*

BELLA. (*Screams at her.*) Go on, hit me, Momma! Crack my head open, make me stupid and crazy, because that's what you really think anyway, isn't it?

GRANDMA. Get out of my house. Go live with your thief friend. You vant da rest of the money, go, take it . . . It von't last you long . . . You'll both haff to steal again to keep alive, believe me.

BELLA. I don't want the rest of your money . . . You can have this too . . . Louie gave it to me. I stayed in Gertrude's house the last two nights . . . Louie came to say goodbye and he gave me this out of his little black satchel and God knows how much more he had . . . I didn't ask him. Maybe he's a thief too, Momma, but he's my brother and he loved me enough to want to help me . . . Thieves and sick little girls, that's what you have, Momma . . . Only God didn't make them that way. *You* did. We're alive, Momma, but that's all we are . . . Aaron and Rose are the lucky ones.

GRANDMA. (*Crushed.*) NOOO!! . . . Don't say dat! . . . Please Gott, don't say dat to me, Bella.

BELLA. I'm sorry, Momma . . . I didn't mean to hurt you.

GRANDMA. Yes. You do . . . It's my punishment for being alive . . . for surviving my own children . . . Not dying before them is my sin . . . Go, Bella. Take Louie's money . . . You tink I don't know vot he is . . . He stole since he vas five years old . . . The year Aaron died . . . And I closed off from him and everybody . . . From you and Louie . . . From Gert and Eddie . . . I lost Rose, then Aaron, and I stopped feeling because I couldn't stand losing anymore . . .

BELLA. Momma!

GRANDMA. Go open your restaurant, live your own life, haff your own babies. If it's a mistake, let it be your mistake . . . If I've done wrong by you, then it's for me to deal with . . . That's how I've lived my life and no one, not even you, can change that for me now.

BELLA. . . . There is no restaurant, Momma . . . He's afraid to be a businessman or a manager . . . He likes being an usher . . . He likes to be in the dark all day, watching movies whenever he wants . . . Then he can live in a world he can feel safe in . . . He doesn't want babies . . . He doesn't want to get married . . . He wants to live with his parents because he knows that they love him . . . And that's enough for him.

GRANDMA. Then maybe he's more lucky than you.

BELLA. Maybe he is . . . But I'll never stop wanting what I don't have . . . It's too late to go back for me . . . Maybe I'm still a child but now there's just enough woman in me to make me miserable. We have to learn how to deal with that somehow, you and me . . . And it can never be the same anymore . . . (*SHE gets up.*) I'll put my things away . . . I think we've both said enough for today . . . don't you? (*BELLA picks up her things, crosses into her room and closes the door.*)

(*GRANDMA sits, stoically . . . and then her hand goes to her mouth, stifling whatever feelings are beginning to overcome her.*
We go to BLACK.)

SCENE FOUR

BELLA. *(VO.)* Dear Eddie . . . This postcard is from Bella. I just want to tell you that Arty and Jay are all right and I have good news for you except I don't have no more room. Love, Bella.

(Nine months later. We hear the CHURCH BELLS chime.
ARTY and JAY are dressed in the same outfits they wore on that first
day. THEY each have a suitcase sitting in the middle of the
room.)

ARTY. . . . How long you think Pop's going to be in there?

JAY. I don't know, but we made it, Arty. Ten months here and we're still alive. We got through Grandma and we're all right.

ARTY. You know who I miss? Uncle Louie . . . I'm glad those two guys never caught him.

JAY. No, but maybe the Japs will. You think he's safer fighting in the South Pacific?

ARTY. No. But he's probably the richest guy on Guadalcanal.

(The front door opens and AUNT BELLA comes in carrying two
shopping bags.)

BELLA. Oh, thank God. I thought you'd be gone before I got back. I ran all over Yonkers looking for these . . . *(SHE puts the bags down.)* Okay. Close your eyes.

(THEY do. SHE takes out a basketball and a football. SHE gives
the basketball to JAY.)

BELLA. The football is for you, Jay. *(SHE gives the football to ARTY.)* And the basketball is for you, Arty. Do you like 'em?

ARTY. Ho-lee mackerel!

JAY. This is incredible.

BELLA. I hope it's the right size. I just took a guess.

JAY. This is one of the best gifts I ever got, Aunt Bella.

BELLA. Well, you two were the best gifts I ever got too. I hate to give you up.

JAY. You don't have to. We're coming out all the time.

ARTY. I really love this, Aunt Bella. Thank you.

BELLA. Well, it's not just from me. It's from Grandma too. I just have to tell her later.

(The bedroom door opens and Eddie comes out.)

EDDIE. Well, Grandma and I are through talking, boys. You ready to go?

JAY. Hey, Pop. Look! It's from Aunt Bella. And Grandma.

ARTY. Aunt Bella, go out for a pass.

(GRANDMA comes out of the bedroom, just as ARTY throws the football to JAY.)

GRANDMA. Vot's dis? Vot did I tell you about games in da house?

EDDIE. They're not playing games, Momma. They know better than that.

GRANDMA. If dey break someting, dey'll pay plenty, believe me.

JAY. Thank you for the ball, Grandma. I love it.

ARTY. I never owned a football in my life, Grandma.

EDDIE. All right. Grandma's tired, boys. Let's say goodbye and go.

GRANDMA. Ve said goodbye dis morning. Two goodbyes is too much.

EDDIE. *(With some sincerity.)* Well, Momma . . . I just wanted to say thank you. You did a lot for me and the boys. I don't know how to repay you for that.

GRANDMA. I'll tell you how. Don't do it again.

EDDIE. I pray to God I won't have to.

GRANDMA. And if you have to, I'll say no again. And this time I'll mean it . . . When Louie left for the Army, I thought about sending you the money. Even Bella asked me to. But then I said no . . . Eddie has to do things for himself. And you did it. That's good.

EDDIE. Yes, Momma. I'm glad you finally approve of me.

GRANDMA. I didn't say that. All I said was "Good."

EDDIE. I'll accept that, Momma.

GRANDMA. So, I suppose you'll get married again, and I won't see your boys for another ten years.

EDDIE. I'm not ready for marriage yet, Momma, but from now on the boys won't be strangers anymore. They'll be grandchildren . . . And I'm going to kiss you goodbye whether you like it or not. (*HE leans over her and kisses her.*) Thank you for not putting up a fight. (*Nods, turns to BELLA.*) Goodbye, Bella . . . What can I say?

BELLA. I know, Eddie. I know.

EDDIE. (*Hugs her.*) I love you so much. (*HE turns.*) . . . I'll meet you downstairs, boys. Thank Grandma, go on. (*And HE goes before the tears come.*)

JAY. I er . . . I just want to say thank you for taking us in, Grandma. I know it wasn't easy for you.

GRANDMA. Dot's right. It vasn't.

JAY. It wasn't easy for us either. But I think I learned a lot since I'm here. Some good and some bad. Do you know what I mean, Grandma?

GRANDMA. (*SHE looks up at him.*) You're not afraid to say the truth. Dot's good . . . You want to hear what my truth is? . . . Everything hurts. Whatever it is you get good in life, you also lose something.

JAY. I guess I'm too young to understand that.

GRANDMA. And I'm too old to forget it . . . Go on. Go home. Take care of your father. He's a good boy but he always needs a little help.

(*JAY nods and crosses to the door, waiting for ARTY.*)

ARTY. Well, you sure gave me and Yakob a lot of help, Grandma. Danker Schein . . . That means, "Thank you."

GRANDMA. He's sneaky, dis one. Tries to get around me . . . Don't try to change me. Sometimes old people aren't altogether wrong.

ARTY. You're absolutely right . . . Can King Artur give you a kiss goodbye? (*HE kisses her and crosses to the door.*)

GRANDMA. . . . What were you two looking for that night under the boysenberry? My money maybe?

ARTY. No! I swear!

GRANDMA. You should have looked behind the malted machine.

(*The BOYS hit themselves for their stupidity and leave. BELLA looks at her MOTHER.*)

BELLA. Well, I'll get dinner started . . . Do you mind eating early because I'm going out tonight. With a friend.

(GRANDMA looks at her.)

BELLA. It's a girl, Momma. I have a new girlfriend. She likes me and I like her . . . And she also has a brother I like . . . He works in the library . . . He can read everything . . . I'd like to have them both over for dinner one night . . . Can we do that, Momma?

(GRANDMA looks away, not knowing how to deal with this.)

BELLA. It's all right . . . It's no rush. You don't have to make up your mind right now. *(SHE turns on the radio.)* . . . I thought Thursday would be a good night. *(The music, "Be Careful It's My Heart" sung by Bing Crosby, comes up. BELLA hums along happily.)* It's called music, Momma. *(And SHE disappears into the kitchen.)*

(GRANDMA watches BELLA, then nods her head as if to say, "So it's come to this . . .")

CURTAIN

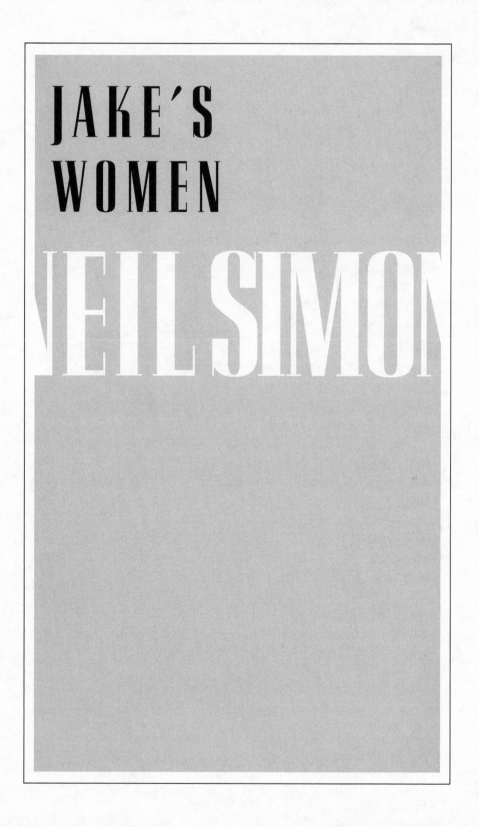

JAKE'S
WOMEN

NEIL SIMON

ACT I

The action of the play takes place both in Jake's apartment and in his mind. The apartment is minimal, his mind is overflowing. There are no walls, no windows, no sense of place and even time is indefinite.

There is, however, a staircase that goes up at an angle, stops at a second level. This is Jake's office. A desk, a chair and a word processor. Nothing else. Next to it, a single door.

Downstairs is a sofa and a few chairs.

The people in Jake's imagination hopefully or seemingly appear from nowhere and leave the same way. Lights should help achieve this. It's important that they can appear and leave almost instantly.

At Rise: JAKE, a man in his early fifties, is upstairs at work at his processor. HE types, leans back to think, types again. The PHONE RINGS. HE stays lost in thought. It RINGS twice more before HE picks it up, irritated by the interruption.

JAKE. (*Into phone.*) Hello? . . . Yes, Karen, I'm working . . . No, I'm not *always* working, I'm just working now . . . Okay, so I'm working every time you call, what is it, Karen? . . . No, Maggie isn't home yet. (*Losing patience.*) We're all having dinner Saturday night, yes, I know.

(*MAGGIE, an attractive woman in her late thirties, appears downstairs, unnoticed by JAKE. SHE stands, thumbs through a magazine.*)

JAKE. (*Into phone.*) Primolo's restaurant on 63rd, I know . . . Karen, why do you always have to confirm what we've already confirmed? . . . I don't talk to you like a stranger, I talk to you like my sister . . . You don't feel I do? . . . Do you want me to confirm that you're my sister? . . . Karen, I have to get back to work . . . I don't know what I'm writing, I haven't read it yet . . . I'm hanging up now, Karen. Please don't call back to confirm I've hung up on you. Goodbye . . . (*HE hangs up.*)

MAGGIE. (*Looking through magazine.*) You are, you know.

JAKE. I am what?

MAGGIE. Always working.

JAKE. I stop when you come home, don't I?

MAGGIE. You stop typing but your mind keeps working.

JAKE. Not out of choice. My mind has a mind of its own . . . Why did I send for you?

MAGGIE. Beats me. I'm still out there on 48th Street looking for a cab. You see what I mean? I'm just a thought in your head right now and you're so busy working, you can't even think of why you just thought of me.

JAKE. No, no. I remember. I was just thinking about the first day we met.

MAGGIE. You love to play back that tape, don't you?

JAKE. Do it with me, Maggie. The way we met.

MAGGIE. You do it too much, Jake.

JAKE. I must need it. Come on, Maggie, do it.

MAGGIE. (*Looks at her watch.*) Well, I've got ten minutes before I get home. Why not? Okay . . .

(*SHE pretends to pick up a glass. THEY stand on opposite sides of stage.*)

MAGGIE. East Hampton. Eight years ago. The July 4th party at the Tabacks . . . A sunset.

JAKE. A beautiful sunset.

MAGGIE. A beautiful sunset. I'm wearing a light blue Laura Ashley dress that I borrowed from my friend, Laura Ashley, who unfortunately is *not* the designer, so it hangs a little . . . I'm on my second Margarita, feeling a little nervous because this is the In Crowd and I'm an Out Girl and don't know a soul here including the guy who brought me . . . Then I notice you noticing me so I pretend not to notice because you look kind of sexy and intelligent and I don't think I can handle sexy and intelligent on two Margaritas on an empty stomach.

JAKE. Will you just skip to the part when we meet?

MAGGIE. Hey, Jake. These words are coming out of your mind. You're the one who just made yourself sexy and intelligent.

JAKE. Okay okay okay . . . So I notice you and you notice me. Then you turn to talk to this Yuppie couple.

MAGGIE. So I turn to talk to this Yuppie couple, both dressed in white slacks, white blazers and white buckskins, looking like two bandaged index fingers. *(To the imaginary couple, SHE laughs heartily.)* Oh, God, I haven't made up my mind *who* to vote for . . . No, I understand the issues, I just don't know who's running.

JAKE. *(To imaginary friend.)* Frank! Hey, Frank. Who's the girl in the light blue dress? . . . *That's* Laura Ashley? . . . No, not the dress. The girl. Well, ask because I'd like to know.

MAGGIE. *(To couple.)* It's Maggie . . . No, I don't think we have . . . Oh, my God. You're *that* Ralph Lauren . . . How nice. I thought you two were always on safari. *(SHE drinks.)*

JAKE. *(Pushing through crowd.)* Pardon me. Coming through . . . Oh, hi, Barbara . . . You *did* like the book? Oh, I'm so glad . . . The *L.A. Times?* No, I didn't read it . . . You *mailed* me a bad review? How thoughtful . . . Excuse me.

MAGGIE. *(To a man.)* Oh, hello. Nice to meet you, Ed. *(SHE shakes his hand.)* You look so familiar. Are you an actor? . . . What do you mean, sort of? . . . Oh, God. You're Mayor Koch, aren't you?

JAKE. Excuse me. Coming through . . . Oh, hi, Martha . . . Of course I'll give. What's the charity? . . . The Homeless of East Hampton? . . . You mean the ones who couldn't rent a house this summer?

MAGGIE. Would you excuse me, Mr. Ed? Mr. Koch . . . I see someone who knows where the bathroom is.

(MAGGIE and JAKE turn and bump into each other. SHE spills her drink.)

MAGGIE. Oh, God, I am *so* sorry.

JAKE. *(Looks at his crotch.)* That's okay . . .

MAGGIE. Would you like my napkin?

JAKE. *(Looks at crotch again.)* Well, it's an awkward place to be rubbing.

MAGGIE. Well, *I* wasn't going to rub it. I thought *you* would.

JAKE. It'll dry. No one will notice if you stand in front of me for a while.

MAGGIE. Well, I'm not feeling all that well. There's Mayor Koch. He might want to stand in front of you.

(SHE starts to go, HE blocks her.)

JAKE. Are you—here with anyone?

MAGGIE. Yes, I'm with a date . . . Charley something.

JAKE. That's odd. My date is Sybill something.

MAGGIE. Oh? Maybe they're married.

JAKE. Gee, I hope so . . . Are you here for the summer?

MAGGIE. Nooo . . . Are you?

JAKE. Nooo . . . Amazing how many things we have in common . . . Is your name Jake?

MAGGIE. No. It's Maggie. Do I look like a Jake?

JAKE. No. I do. I'm just looking for a hook in this conversation . . . Could I er . . . buy you dinner?

MAGGIE. Oh, that's very nice of you but I think the food here is free . . . Well, it was nice meeting you, Jake.

JAKE. This can't be goodbye.

MAGGIE. It won't be. We'll meet again.

JAKE. When?

MAGGIE. *(Looks at her watch.)* Well, I'll be home for dinner in ten minutes. Go back to work, Jake. Living out the past is not going to get us through the future. *(SHE puts down the glass and starts out.)*

JAKE. Dammit, Maggie! Can't we just have ten good minutes together? Because I'm afraid tonight may not be so wonderful.

MAGGIE. Really? Well, I don't know what's going to happen tonight, Jake, do I? And that scares you. Because you can never control what I say when reality begins.

(SHE leaves. JAKE faces audience.)

JAKE. *(To audience.)* She's right, you know. Reality is a bummer. God, how much better writing is. *(HE points to his office.)* That little room up there is eight by ten feet but to me it's the world. The universe! You don't get to play God, you get to *be* God! . . . Push time backward or forward or put it on hold. Bend it, twist it, tie it in knots or tie it in ribbons, the choice is yours. And oh, what choices . . . The downside? You get to be a slave to the things you love. Eight hours go by up there in ten minutes and that ten minutes is captured forever on paper . . . but the eight hours of your life is gone and you'll never see those again, brother . . . How much living have I missed these last thirty years? . . . And is creative pleasure better than real pleasure? . . . We're all writers in a sense, aren't we? . . . You're driving in your car to work, having an imaginary conversation with your wife. She says this, you say that, she says that, you say this. She's so damn stubborn and intractable— only she's not saying it. You wrote it! You're bright, witty and clever and she's a pain in the ass. You win the argument and she's not even there, what the hell kind of victory is that? *(HE looks at his watch.)* Maggie'll be home soon, knowing something is up with us and she'll be armed to the teeth with honesty. Honesty can bring a writer to his knees and Maggie's got enough to bring me to my hips. *(HE calls out.)* Karen! I need help. *(To the audience.)* My sister Karen is no wizard but she *is* family. Married, divorced, went to NYU Film School. Made a three-hour student film of *her,* just sitting on a kitchen chair, called *Loneliness* . . . But she'll be on my side. Loving, encouraging, sympathetic, because that's how I need her and that's how I'll make her. And no matter what she's doing, she'll come the minute I think of her. *(HE calls out.)* Karen! It's Jake.

(*KAREN comes out. SHE's about forty, dressed in a rather unflattering dress.*)

KAREN. What? I'm here. Stop yelling. You have to think of me now? I was watching *The Godfather I, II* and *III* . . . If he makes four, five, and six, forget it, I need a life . . . What's wrong, Jake?

JAKE. It's Maggie and me. We're having trouble and I need advice, Karen.

KAREN. Is she here? Do you want me to speak to her? Where is she; I'll talk to her?

JAKE. If she were here, how could you talk to her, Karen? *(Points to his head.)* You're here, here in my head.

KAREN. I never know how that works. When I'm here, I can talk to you. But when someone *else* is here, I can't talk to *them*. It's very confusing, Jake. I feel like I'm in a Woody Allen movie.

JAKE. *(Turns to audience.)* The interesting dilemma here is not "Why is Karen irritating me now?" but why am I making her irritate me?

KAREN. I'm irritating you now, aren't I?

JAKE. A little. It's nothing. It's a mind exercise. I keep writing in my head like magicians twirl a coin over their fingers.

KAREN. Don't write me, Jake. Let me be me. You have such a distorted picture of me these days.

JAKE. *I* do?

KAREN. Where did you find this dress I'm wearing? This dress is not me. Bette Midler does a concert in a dress like this.

JAKE. I'm sorry. I was working. I didn't have time to go shopping for clothes. Karen . . . I wanted to talk to you now. I need advice and you're the only one in the world who can help me now . . . Would you?

KAREN. Of course. I *want* to hear. I care about you. I worry about you. You're my brother, I love you . . . See, that's a good speech. That's how I should talk. Giving, caring, nurturing. Make a note of that.

JAKE. *(To audience.)* They make you pay for these conversations. I used to think of my mother and she'd make me eat a whole imaginary dinner while I talked.

KAREN. So what is it, Jake? Tell me what's wrong.

JAKE. I think Maggie's getting ready to leave me.

KAREN. Don't tell me. Oh, my God, no. Why? What happened?

JAKE. A lot of things that never should have happened.

KAREN. Alright, don't jump to conclusions . . . Don't try to guess what's going on in someone else's mind. I used to worry that Harry was going to leave me too.

JAKE. But he *did* leave you.

KAREN. Because I kept saying, "You're going to leave me one day, I know it." It drove him crazy . . . Besides, we had big problems. You and Maggie had eight good years together. She loves you, that I would bet my life on.

JAKE. She's been seeing another man.

KAREN. I'm such a bad judge of character. Are you positive, Jake?

JAKE. It's someone new in her office. I don't know if he means something to her or if it's just a symptom of what's wrong with us.

KAREN. What *is* wrong with you?

JAKE. Something stopped.

KAREN. I am so depressed. Is there something wrong with our family, Jake? Mom got divorced. Pop got divorced. I got divorced. Now you're getting divorced.

JAKE. Mom and Pop is one divorce. And I'm not divorced yet. Don't make it an epidemic, Karen.

KAREN. Have you been seeing anyone?

JAKE. Me? No.

KAREN. You haven't been seeing another woman?

JAKE. Didn't I just say no?

KAREN. Who's the other woman?

JAKE. An actress, about a year ago. It only lasted about three weeks.

KAREN. You mean if it's under a month, it's not an affair? Every man in America is looking for a calendar like that.

JAKE. I expected you to be supportive.

KAREN. No, you expected me to say what you want to hear. Alright, how's this? . . . "You're entitled to an affair, Jake. You work hard. It would kill Momma to hear but she's dead anyway so what do *you* care?"

JAKE. Karen, I don't need you to make me feel guilty.

KAREN. Yes, you do. I don't mind. I'm not working anyway . . . So tell me, are you still seeing this tramp?

JAKE. She's not a tramp . . . No. It's over. The truth is, I love Maggie more now than I ever have in my life. I don't want to lose her, Karen. If I lose her, I lose everything.

KAREN. Oh, Jake, Jake. You're so dependent on women. I've always known that. I wish I could hold you right now. I want to grab you in my arms the way Momma did and make you feel wonderful and safe and loved. I'm sorry Julie died. I'm sorry Maggie is so unhappy. But you have me, Jake. You can count on me . . . This is another good speech. Give me more lines like this. This is a woman you could like.

JAKE. Everyone likes you, Karen.

KAREN. So why can't I make a marriage work? Don't end up alone like me, Jake. I live in the movies, night after night, and you can't be happy living in a popcorn world . . . No! See, that's crappy dialogue. You're getting even with me now for that crack about Momma.

JAKE. I'm sorry. I'll fax you the rewrites tomorrow, okay?

KAREN. Does that mean I'm going?

JAKE. *(Turns his head.)* No. I hear Maggie coming up the stairs. Stay a few minutes.

KAREN. I'm in your head. How am I going to get out, when you sneeze?

JAKE. *(To audience.)* Maggie'll come in with a big smile on her face, always hiding her true feeling . . . "Hi, hon. Sorry I'm late."

MAGGIE. *(Comes in carrying her leather case.)* Hi, hon. I actually found a taxi.

JAKE. *(To audience.)* Close enough.

MAGGIE. Do you mind if we call in for Chinese? I'm too tired to eat low-fat food tonight.

KAREN. She gets to dress so pretty and I have to wear this ugly shmata.

MAGGIE. *(Crosses, gives Jake a cheek kiss.)* Ohh, you smell good. You took a shower. That's what I need. You get so grimy from ambition. *(SHE starts upstairs.)*

JAKE. You going to be long?

MAGGIE. Not if I use soap. Why?

JAKE. I just thought we'd talk.

MAGGIE. Before dinner?

JAKE. *(Shrugs.)* Before. During. After.

MAGGIE. Really? It's been years since we had a marathon conversation . . . Sure. Just let me wash my face, I'll be right down . . . Anything I should feel nervous about?

JAKE. Depends on what makes you nervous.

MAGGIE. . . . Answers like that. *(SHE is gone.)*

KAREN. Oh, Jake, Jake! You're asking for trouble.

JAKE. What do you want me to do, forget about this other guy?

KAREN. No. Just wait. Bring it up on your fiftieth anniversary.

JAKE. I really love you, Karen. I make you sound silly and foolish and irritating. The clown with a heart of gold. You'll meet the right man. Trust me. I'll look myself.

KAREN. Find him, don't think of him. I don't want a man who dresses worse than me. (*SHE is gone.*)

(*MAGGIE appears upstairs, a towel around her neck.*)

JAKE. (*Quietly.*) Round one!

MAGGIE. (*Makes a drink.*) So what kind of day did you have . . . she asks cautiously.

JAKE. I worked. I spoke to Karen.

MAGGIE. Oh. How is she?

JAKE. Lonely, miserable, frustrated. Not bad, actually . . . She's having a dinner party this Saturday. We're invited. We have to find her a date, which is why she's having the party.

MAGGIE. *This* Saturday?

JAKE. Yes.

MAGGIE. I have to go to Philadelphia on Saturday. I told you that.

JAKE. No. You said you *thought* you had to go.

MAGGIE. Yes. I said, "I think I have to go to Philadelphia on Saturday."

JAKE. I think I'm going is indefinite. I'm going is "I'll be back on Sunday." Or do you *think* you'll be back on Sunday?

MAGGIE. I will be back on Sunday. Are you in a lousy mood or do I just *think* you are.

JAKE. Sort of a lousy mood.

MAGGIE. Yes, I sort of noticed . . . This isn't what you wanted to talk about, is it, Jake?

JAKE. No.

MAGGIE. Something else then.

JAKE. Yes.

MAGGIE. (*Smiles.*) Okay. What?

JAKE. I'm thinking.

MAGGIE. (*Lightly.*) You looking for a topic?

JAKE. No. I have a topic.

MAGGIE. What is it, Jake? You look so pained. (*HE doesn't answer.*) Tell me. I'm not going anywhere.

JAKE. I want to get the first sentence right. It's important.

MAGGIE. The first sentence is?

JAKE. It's the writer in me. Always afraid I'll lose my audience. Did you ever read *The Naked and the Dead*? . . . Great first sentence.

MAGGIE. What was it?

JAKE. "Nobody could sleep."

MAGGIE. Yeah. Great first sentence alright . . . What's yours, Jake?

JAKE. (*HE pauses.*) . . . Do you want out of this marriage?

MAGGIE. (*Looks at him, stunned, then lets out a breath of her own.*) Well, you've just topped Norman Mailer . . . Is this what this conversation is going to be about?

JAKE. Well, let's see if it turns into a conversation first.

MAGGIE. Where did this come from, Jake? And why now? Isn't this the kind of talk one prepares for? Take the phone off the hook, get out a bottle of scotch?

JAKE. You get the phone, I'll get the scotch.

MAGGIE. I thought the reason you were in a lousy mood was because I couldn't have dinner with Karen on Saturday. Shows you where my mind must be.

JAKE. I don't *know* where, Maggie. Tell me.

MAGGIE. Whoa, Jake. I gave you time to think of your first sentence. Give me a chance to get my second wind . . . Why not yesterday, Jake? Or last week or last month? Did something happen today that never happened before?

JAKE. Yes.

MAGGIE. What?

JAKE. I decided to ask you.

MAGGIE. I see. Well, I guess sleeping back to back for the last few weeks doesn't make this *too* much of a surprise . . . Okay. You want to know if I want out of this marriage? The answer is "No," I do not want out of this marriage.

JAKE. I'm glad to hear it. So everything is fine.

MAGGIE. I didn't say it was.

JAKE. I didn't think it was.

MAGGIE. No, everything is *not* fine, Jake. Does that come as a shock to you?

JAKE. No. It's been obvious for months. So why haven't either of us talked about it before?

MAGGIE. We talk about it every day. In the lack of warmth we show each other. The way you sometimes don't even acknowledge me when I walk in the door.

JAKE. On the nights I'm lucky enough to still be up when you walk in.

MAGGIE. Yes, I've been working a lot more than I used to. Moving up the corporate ladder has its drawbacks, I'm sorry. Are we just going to stand here matching complaints? Where are we going with this?

JAKE. I don't know. It's our first trip . . . Are we in trouble, Maggie, or are we in *big* trouble?

MAGGIE. I love how *I* get to be the one on the witness stand. I don't know, Jake. We're in trouble. That's more than we've ever been before so the size of it seems irrelevant.

JAKE. Really? I'd hate to get a report like that from my radiologist. "Well, there's something there, Jake, but the size of it is irrelevant."

MAGGIE. Jesus, I love what you consider a "talk before dinner". . . What have you got in mind for "during and after"?

JAKE. It's amazing but I don't even know what you're feeling right now. Are you hurt? Are you frightened? Angry? Defensive? What?

MAGGIE. (*Snaps it out.*) Claustrophobic! Isolated! Airless! Atrophying! . . . Christ, I can't believe I'm saying these things. This is dangerous, Jake. Let's put it off for a while. Please! Maybe it'll even go away in the morning.

JAKE. Go away?? After "Claustrophobic? Airless? Atrophying?". . . Those words have a certain permanency. They tend to stick to your ribs.

MAGGIE. Christ, you wanted this conversation, Jake. Not me. Isolated and airless are painful things to say and I'm sure to hear, but probably a lot less terrifying than the death of a marriage . . . but I guess we'd better get on with it . . . Okay. I have a first sentence for you, Jake . . . How about separating for six months just to give us some breathing space?

JAKE. (*Stunned.*) Separate for six months? . . . That's a lot of breathing space. That's about as big as Arizona . . . How long have you been thinking about this?

MAGGIE. It just came up. More or less impromptu.

JAKE. Do you actually think after six months apart, we'd be able to get together again?

MAGGIE. Why not?

JAKE. Why not? Half our problems are based on the fact that we're apart three or four months of the year to begin with. I don't understand how separating is the answer to being separated too much.

MAGGIE. I need the time, Jake.

JAKE. For what?

MAGGIE. For myself. I feel lost, out of control. I feel like I'm skiing down a mountain without a pole and there's nothing but trees and rocks at the bottom.

JAKE. Maybe I could be there to catch you.

MAGGIE. Catch me? I thought you were the one who pushed me . . . I didn't mean that. Oh, God, I'm so lousy at being unhappy.

JAKE. Don't you want this marriage?

MAGGIE. I have always wanted this marriage. I would give anything to go back and start it over from the beginning. But you only get one beginning to a marriage.

JAKE. Who says? Why can't we go back? Why don't we get married again. (*SHE dismisses it.*) I'm serious. New wedding ring. New party. Different hors d'oeuvres. They're probably cold by now . . . It's possible if you want it badly enough.

MAGGIE. Thank you, Jake. That's a very sweet offer.

JAKE. Then take it.

MAGGIE. We're having enough trouble making this marriage work, let alone starting a new one.

JAKE. I don't think we should separate. I think it would be the end of us.

MAGGIE. Jake, don't you see me? Don't you see how much I've changed? I can't stop running. I run for taxis, for planes, for elevators. I run for analyst sessions and lunch appointments. I run ten miles every weekend and it's still not far enough or fast enough. I'm no good for anybody until I learn to stop running and find out what it is I'm running from. And if I'm still running six months from now, there won't be anything left of me worth being married to.

JAKE. I love you, Maggie.

MAGGIE. I love you too, Jake. At least we have that to hang on to. That's worth waiting six months for, isn't it?

JAKE. It's also worth staying here and fighting for.

MAGGIE. NO!!! I don't *want* to fight for it. I've tried so hard this year to *talk* to you but I always ended up just listening. We started off with a marriage and ended up with a monologue. You never listen, Jake. Not even to what I'm trying to say now. You just want it to be better without even wanting to know what's wrong. We shouldn't be fighting for our marriage, we should have been living it.

JAKE. Then let's start tonight because six months apart will kill us.

MAGGIE. So will forcing me to stay. I'm sorry, Jake. Maybe there is a chance for us but not with a quick resolution. I have to get in a hot tub and just be alone for an hour. I don't know what else to say. We're not going to settle this right now anyway . . . Okay? . . . Jake? . . . Did that go by you too?

JAKE. No. I caught it.

(SHE looks at him, then starts up the stairs.)

JAKE. . . . How much does Michael Jaffe have to do with this?

MAGGIE. *(Stops, turns.)* What?

JAKE. Michael Jaffe . . . Wrong name or just the wrong time to say it?

MAGGIE. *(Nervously.)* What are you talking about?

JAKE. I'm talking about Michael Jaffe.

MAGGIE. What about him?

JAKE. Right. What about him? I know very little except he's extremely bright, that he's brought a new "energy" to your office, that everyone likes him and that things have really "perked up" since he's come to work there . . . And a jogger too, didn't you tell me that? You went jogging with him when you were all in Chicago, I believe you said. It's nice for someone like you who's always running to have someone to run with, am I right, Mag?

MAGGIE. I'm not going to get into one of these discussions. *(SHE turns.)*

JAKE. *(HE snaps.)* Oh, come on, Maggie, get into it. I want to know just how "perked up" things are with you two . . . Is that an unfair question to ask, seeing as it comes on the heels of you asking me for a separation? . . . Are you having an affair with him or not?

(*SHE looks at him, speechless.*) . . . No answer? Does that mean you're not having an affair with him?

MAGGIE. . . . No.

JAKE. No . . . So you're *not* having an affair with him.

MAGGIE. No.

JAKE. Alright, let me rephrase the question . . . Have you slept with him?

MAGGIE. (*As if it's the last words she'll ever speak.*) . . . Yes.

JAKE. Yes?

MAGGIE. Yes.

JAKE. Jesus Christ, what did I ask that for?

MAGGIE. I'm sorry, Jake.

JAKE. Oh, shit, Maggie.

MAGGIE. Jake—

JAKE. I was smart enough to figure it out and dumb enough to make you say it.

MAGGIE. I shouldn't have said it, Jake. The truth doesn't fix anything.

JAKE. No. It just makes it clearer.

MAGGIE. It's not an affair because it stopped as soon as it started. But it happened and I'm sorry . . . Jake? I don't think we should say anything more. We're just going to hurt each other.

JAKE. I thought we passed that a minute ago.

MAGGIE. (*About to go, stops, turns.*) Did—did you—I'm sorry. The guilt is so great. I'm trying to make it easy on myself . . . Did you ever do anything? In all the years we were married? . . . You don't have to answer it, but maybe I'd feel better if I knew . . . Did you?

JAKE. (*Sits there, thinking.*) . . . If I said yes, would it make any difference? About the separation?

MAGGIE. No.

JAKE. Then my answer would be meaningless, wouldn't it?

MAGGIE. Nothing we do is meaningless.

JAKE. Alright. Then I'll tell you.

MAGGIE. No . . . It doesn't really matter. Exchanging guilts isn't exactly going to save the day.

(*SHE turns, goes upstairs and is gone. JAKE turns to the audience.*)

JAKE. I didn't even get the opportunity to lie . . . which I don't think I would have . . . Of all the imaginary conversations I have, ten, twenty, fifty a day, why did this have to be a real one? *(HE points upstairs.)* Up there I could have fixed all this. Turn on the machine and rewrite it . . . "No, Jake. There was no affair and I never slept with anyone. Michael Jaffe is a twerp . . . Don't you know you've spoiled me so, I could never let another man ever touch me". . . . Click! Turn off the processor, get a beer and turn on the Knicks-Laker game.

(MOLLY, a twelve-year-old girl, appears and stands there. HE doesn't see her but senses her.)

JAKE. Molly? Is that you?
MOLLY. Yes, Daddy.
JAKE. *(Turns, looks at her.)* You're so young. Eleven, twelve? Why am I thinking of you now?
MOLLY. You need someone to tell you they love you.
JAKE. That doesn't count. All little girls love their daddies.
MOLLY. Sandra Gerstein *hates* hers.
JAKE. Why?
MOLLY. I don't know. I made it up. I thought it would make you feel better.
JAKE. No, honey. *I* made it up. Not you.
MOLLY. I know. Did it make you feel better?
JAKE. Yes.
MOLLY. You fool yourself a lot, don't you?
JAKE. You got it.
MOLLY. Why are you and Maggie breaking up?
JAKE. I don't know, Molly.
MOLLY. Is it because you both had an affair?
JAKE. Jesus, I'm not going to discuss this with a twelve-year-old.
MOLLY. Then when?
JAKE. When you come back like you are today. All grown up.
MOLLY. Alright. I will.

(YOUNG MOLLY moves out as OLDER MOLLY, at twenty-one, appears from the opposite side.)

OLDER MOLLY. So tell me, Dad.

JAKE. *(To audience.)* Gee, time flies when you're neurotic.

OLDER MOLLY. I know what's wrong with you and Maggie. It's not about Michael Jaffe *or* your actress friend.

JAKE. It's not? Then what *is* it about?

OLDER MOLLY. It's about Mom.

JAKE. Your mother's been dead for ten years.

OLDER MOLLY. I know. Ghosts are a bummer; aren't they?

JAKE. *(Nods.)* Life's a bummer, kiddo.

OLDER MOLLY. I thought self-pity was a no-no.

JAKE. Only on the stage. In life it's very comforting.

OLDER MOLLY. Boy, do you need help, Dad.

JAKE. I didn't have to think *you* up to tell me that.

OLDER MOLLY. Why don't you talk to Edith? Come on, talk to her.

JAKE. Analysts don't work nights. That's when they have their *own* breakdowns.

OLDER MOLLY. I don't mean *really* talk to her. Make *up* that you talk to her.

JAKE. Some session. I make up Edith, the questions *and* the answers. What's the point?

OLDER MOLLY. Complete control. Your favorite thing in life.

JAKE. It isn't really. It's being at the mercy of someone else that scares me. Been that way since I was a baby. My mother was always afraid I'd fall out of my high chair so she tied me in with a rope. Couldn't move my hands, couldn't push away the baby food I hated. I had to fight her off with my nose.

OLDER MOLLY. That's awful.

JAKE. I grew up thinking that's the way life was. First time she took me to a restaurant I couldn't eat because the waiter forgot to tie me up.

OLDER MOLLY. No wonder you're in analysis.

JAKE. That was a problem too. By now I had claustrophobia. For the first year in Edith's office, I wouldn't let her close the door. Everyone in the waiting room heard my life story. I'd walk out and someone sitting there would say, "You're sounding better today". . . Then it got worse. On airplanes I was always afraid of being locked in the john. So I kept testing the door, opening it and closing it. The sign above would light up, "Occupied, Vacant, Occupied, Vacant"... I think maybe that's why I became a writer. I could write when I wanted, where I wanted and what I wanted.

OLDER MOLLY. Maybe Maggie doesn't want to be tied up either.

JAKE. Smart observation.

OLDER MOLLY. So maybe you better talk to Edith.

JAKE. For you, anything. See you later, babe.

OLDER MOLLY. Anytime . . . You're on, Edith.

(OLDER MOLLY goes off just as EDITH, a woman in her late forties, comes on.)

EDITH. Just what I need. A session *he* makes up that I don't even get paid for . . . So what is it this time, Mr. Creative?

(SHE sits on chair. HE sits on sofa.)

JAKE. Please, Edith, I'm shopping for a little compassion.

EDITH. *(Like a mother to an infant.)* Ahh, wassa mawa, baby?

JAKE. *(To audience.)* She actually does that in sessions. It's the New Age analysis. Make the patient look like a schmuck.

EDITH. Is that what I'm here for, Jake? To set up straight lines for you?

JAKE. I'm lost, Edith. Confused. I had an affair with someone but I don't want to leave Maggie. She *slept* with someone and she *does* want to leave.

EDITH. So what's your point? Your affair wasn't as good as the guy she slept with?

JAKE. Forget it, Edith. You're not an analyst. You're a mother with a diploma.

EDITH. And what are you? A martyr! A self-made sufferer! Don't you know you're better than that, Jake? You're a warm, loving, giving human being with incredible sensitivity. And Maggie doesn't even appreciate that.

JAKE. You really think so?

EDITH. I don't know. They're your words, I'm just moving my lips.

JAKE. *(To audience.)* See? I'm a schmuck again. *(To Edith.)* Edith, I need help. Real help. I'm giving you temporary freedom. Make up your own words.

EDITH. Alright. Why do you like to deprive yourself so much, Jake?

JAKE. Oh, Christ, Edith. We do that question every week. I hate that question. Don't you have another question?

EDITH. Yes. Here's one. Why don't you like me to ask you why you like to deprive yourself?

JAKE. This is my last session, Edith. Real or not. And then I'm going to find another analyst to help me understand why I went to you so long.

EDITH. Can I suggest someone? My son, Arthur, just started his own practice. It's in California, but he's worth the trip.

JAKE. God, you make me so furious. Do you know what I'd like to do to you right now, Edith?

EDITH. *(Infant talk again.)* Wha, baby? Tell mawa what Jakey wanna do?

JAKE. *(To audience.)* She could lose her license for this, you know. *(To Edith.)* I'd like to either punch your face out with my fist or rip your clothes off and hump the life out of you.

EDITH. I know what *my* choice is . . . Which do you prefer?

JAKE. Forget it. It's just wishful thinking.

EDITH. When you wish, you wish upon the child in you. Do you know who said that?

JAKE. Jiminy Cricket?

EDITH. No, Me! . . . Didn't you read my book?

JAKE. *Love Yourself, Fuck Them?* Was that the title?

EDITH. You are so naughty . . . How's your sex life, Jake?

JAKE. My sex life? You think Maggie and I are screwing eight hours a day while we discuss our breakup?

EDITH. Maybe if you did, you wouldn't be breaking up.

JAKE. Edith, I am so tired of your fortune cookie wisdom. I picture some patient coming to you with no arms, no legs, no eyes, no ears, no mouth and you asking him how his sex life is.

EDITH. Well, if he found a way to get to my office, why not?

JAKE. Edith, did you ever *actually* cure anyone?

EDITH. Analysis doesn't cure you, Jake. It just makes you feel better between sessions.

JAKE. You know, I should have married you instead of Maggie. Then I wouldn't be so unhappy about the marriage breaking up.

EDITH. You know what I think, Jake? And listen to this because I think I'm going to say something very profound.

JAKE. Oh, good. *60 Minutes* will be one hour late tonight in order to bring you this CBS Special, *Edith Reports*. And now, Dr. Edith Hassenberg.

EDITH. *(Out front.)* Thank you, Don, and good evening. *(To Jake.)* I'll tell you what I think. I think you won't hit me so you can deprive yourself of anger and you won't hump me so you can deprive yourself of losing. And then you make fun of it so you can deprive yourself of feelings.

JAKE. How did you work that out?

EDITH. Easy. You're a Sagittarius.

JAKE. You'd better let me have your son's number . . . You-are-ludicrous.

EDITH. You make Karen foolish and you make me ludicrous! Is this your way of getting back at women because Julie died and Maggie stands up to you?

JAKE. I'm handling this the best way I can . . . I have one dead wife and one on the way out the door. What do you want, a tap dance?

EDITH. Why not? You're unhappy if you want to be. You're lonely if you want to be. It's your choice.

JAKE. My choice that Julie died? That Maggie's leaving?

EDITH. I didn't say your fault. I said your choice.

JAKE. I don't get it.

EDITH. If you want to suffer, you suffer. If you want to be fat, you're fat. We make our own destiny, Jake.

JAKE. Is that why you're still unmarried?

EDITH. No. Most men are shits.

(HE walks away, throwing his hands up.)

EDITH. Oh, this is pointless, Jake. Do you want the Comedy Store or do you want help? Don't mock me, use me.

JAKE. Okay. Alright. What do you want?

EDITH. Answers. *Real* answers. If you could have anything you wanted in the world, right now, this minute, this second, what would you ask for?

JAKE. Don't do this to me, Edith.

EDITH. Answer me, Jake. What would you ask for?

JAKE. You *know* what I would ask for.

EDITH. Then say it.

JAKE. Stop it. STOP IT!!!

EDITH. Ask for it, then I'll stop it . . . Ask for it, Jake. Please!

JAKE. JULIE! I . . . I WANT JULIE!!!

(*Suddenly, JULIE, a lovely young girl about twenty-one, in jeans and a shirt, lies on a bench with the* New York Times Magazine *section and a pen.*)

JAKE. (*Sees her, crosses to her.*) I want her alive, the way I remember her. I want to be twenty-four when she was twenty-one. I want to be lying on the grass in Central Park on a Sunday morning, watching her do the *Times* crossword puzzle, knowing the first true happiness I ever felt in my life.

JULIE. (*Without looking up.*) Jake? Who's the Iron Man of Baseball? Nine letters.

JAKE. Lou Gehrig.

JULIE. Right. Very good. *Ninotchka* director, thirteen letters.

JAKE. Ernst Lubitsch.

JULIE. My God, you're a genius. (*We hear BELLS. SHE turns, looks.*) Hey! There's the ice cream man. I'm buying. What do you want?

JAKE. Chocolate. Seven letters.

JULIE. Seven letters is Vanilla. You pay. I'll be right back. (*SHE runs off.*)

JAKE. . . . And I lay there, looking up at the sky, dreaming about what the rest of our lives would be like . . . And I want the rest of our lives . . . Can you get me Julie, Edith?

EDITH. No.

JAKE. Then don't play games with me.

EDITH. I don't play games, Jake. You do.

JAKE. Yes . . . I do.

EDITH. Why?

JAKE. Because in games, I never lose. And what I lose, I can rewrite.

(MAGGIE comes out of the upstairs bathroom in a terry cloth robe. SHE crosses to the stairs.)

MAGGIE. Can we talk for a minute?
JAKE. *(Looks up.)* Sure . . . Would you like a drink?
EDITH. No, thanks, I have to leave now.
MAGGIE. Yes, please. A vodka.

(EDITH turns and sees MAGGIE who has come down the stairs.)

EDITH. Oh. I didn't see her. *(SHE crosses closer to Maggie.)* She looks beautiful. I've always loved her face. And that wonderful skin. So English and clean. I have skin like lost luggage.
JAKE. *(JAKE has crossed to the bar to make Maggie's vodka.)* Feeling any better?
MAGGIE. No. Just cleaner.
EDITH. Listen to her, Jake. Hear her out. Don't say no to everything. You always have options. *(SHE starts to black out.)* That's what life's about . . . Options . . . Options . . . I love how my voice trails off . . . Options . . . Options . . . *(And SHE's gone.)*

(JAKE hands MAGGIE her drink.)

MAGGIE. How are *you* feeling?
JAKE. Tired. Trauma always exhausts me.
MAGGIE. . . . . I'm scared, Jake. I've never been this scared in my life. Not since I left Michigan to go on my own. So here I am, seventeen years later, doing the same thing I did then and feeling the same emptiness in the pit of my stomach. I haven't made much progress, have I?
JAKE. Maybe we shouldn't have married until you stopped running.
MAGGIE. My fault, Jake. I thought you were the finish line . . . This isn't going to turn ugly, is it?
JAKE. Maybe. I don't know. But at least I'm fighting with every goddamn thing I have to save this. What are *you* doing?

MAGGIE. Trying to save this marriage the only way I know how. By giving it up for a little while.

JAKE. You can't keep what you give up.

MAGGIE. Why not? You did it with me for eight years.

JAKE. *I* did? What did I keep?

MAGGIE. Well, Julie, for one thing. She may have died but you never let go. Wherever we moved to, whenever we traveled, we always took Julie with us. Some nights I was tempted to put down an extra dinner plate for her, but I didn't think you'd be amused . . . I had to live *your* memories for so long. It was always *your* friends, *your* family, your work, as if I were a replacement, a substitute, always trying to make the first team.

JAKE. The first team? Jesus, you devoted so much of this marriage trying to become chairman of the board, I never saw you for half those eight years. I don't know whose dream you were trying to fulfill, but it sure as hell wasn't mine.

MAGGIE. Well, unfortunately, it wasn't mine either. For as long as I can remember, I was molded and shaped in the form of somebody *else's* concept of a woman, never mine. The church taught it to me, parochial schools taught it to me, my mother, my father—God, you couldn't get out of the Midwest without its stamp of approval. I was taught to be a good girl, a wife and a mother but never a person. You could be a carbon copy but don't mess with being an original. That's what you married eight years ago, Jake. A good girl. As good and as obedient as my mother, never suspecting, of course, that it was three martinis a day that kept her obedient . . . And then one day I woke up and said to myself, "I don't want to be anyone's concept of me except me . . . not even Jake's". . . You are so important to me, but you're also so consumed with creating your own images and characters, planning every detail of their life, molding them and shaping them into *your* creations, *your* concepts. And I said, "Jesus, I just left all this in Michigan, what do I want it in New York for?". . . And the minute I tried to step out on my own, to try to be someone *I* created, that *I* controlled, you made me pay so dearly for it. You made me feel like a plagiarist . . . And so one day in Chicago, I let myself become a very bad little girl. The next morning I looked in the mirror and I sure didn't like what I saw. But I saw the possibility of becoming someone who would have to be accepted on *her* terms and certainly not someone who was considered a rewrite of someone else. And until you begin to see *me,* Jake, *my* Maggie, I am getting out of this house, out of this life and out of your word processor . . . I may be making the biggest mistake of my life but at least it'll be mine . . . Dear Lord, Creator of the Universe, forgive me. And if not, not.

JAKE. . . . You're not assuming I'm the Creator of the Universe, are you?

MAGGIE. No, Jake, but thanks for telling me . . . I'm leaving. Give us both a break and don't fight it.

JAKE. Fight what? You've made up your mind.

MAGGIE. There were two of us in the ring, Jake. I'll try to move some of my things out tomorrow.

JAKE. Tomorrow? Then we still have an interesting night ahead of us.

MAGGIE. I'm not staying tonight. I thought I'd drive out to the beach house. Is that alright with you?

JAKE. It's your house too.

MAGGIE. Thank you.

JAKE. I'll keep the half facing the ocean.

MAGGIE. This is going to be hard on Molly.

JAKE. She's a strong kid. She'll be alright.

MAGGIE. Still, it's the second time she's losing a mother . . . and the third time I'm losing a child. Maybe that's why she means so much to me.

JAKE. I wanted those babies as much as you, Maggie. Maybe things might have been different for us.

MAGGIE. Maybe. But as bad as those two nights in the hospital were I thought that was the closest we've ever been to each other.

JAKE. We didn't get any breaks, did we?

MAGGIE. Will you be here tomorrow?

JAKE. To watch you pack? No, thanks. I'll spare myself that. I've always hated the sight of a wife leaving.

MAGGIE. Then there isn't much left to say, is there?

JAKE. I guess not.

MAGGIE. (*SHE starts up stairs, stops at the top.*) Jake! I know nothing in life ever hurt you as much as Julie dying . . . Well, tonight is the worst thing that's ever happened to me. (*SHE leaves.*)

JAKE. (*To audience.*) I haven't hung on to Julie . . . I swear to you, I have tried over and over and over to get Julie out of my mind. I *never* summon her up. She just bursts in on me.

(*JULIE, still at twenty-one, but dressed differently, bursts in on him.*)

JULIE. (*Angrily.*) Where were you?

JAKE. When?

JULIE. Last night. This morning. Right now. This minute. How could you not call me? How could you not want to know how I feel?

JAKE. About what?

JULIE. About *what?* About what happened to us?

JAKE. I don't know. What happened to us?

JULIE. Oh, my God. I don't believe this.

JAKE. Julie, I had a *very* busy day. People in and out of here. I'm sorry . . . What happened to us?

JAKE. *WE MADE LOVE!!!*

JAKE. We did?

JULIE. "We did," he says. We slept together. For the first time, Jake. Not just *our* first time. It was *my* first time . . . Ever!! And you don't remember it?

JAKE. Oh, *that* first time. Yes, I do. I just didn't realize you were going back twenty-nine years.

JULIE. I'm not going back twenty-nine years. I'm going back to last night.

JAKE. I know. I know.

JULIE. Well, aren't you going to ask me how I feel?

JAKE. Sure. How do you feel, Julie?

JULIE. (*Exasperated.*) Forget it. Never mind. It doesn't matter.

JAKE. No, it does, Julie. I swear. It's just that it comes at a bad time. Maggie's upstairs getting ready to leave me.

JULIE. Who's Maggie?

JAKE. My second wife.

JULIE. Well, she can be your first wife for all I care because I'm not sure you and I are ready for marriage.

JAKE. Julie, please don't mix up my time periods. It confuses me. I'm a writer, not a computer.

JULIE. You're a writer? You go to law school.

JAKE. Yes, *then*. But later I gave up law school and became a writer.

JULIE. Really? What did you write?

JAKE. Well, you wouldn't have heard of them because I didn't write them yet. I mean, I did write them but I just thought of you *now* and you're here before they would have been written. In other words, if you were here *later*—

JULIE. Alright. I get it. I got it. Okay. God!

JAKE. You *do* get it?

JULIE. I *said* I did. I get it.

JAKE. How old are you?

JULIE. Twenty-one.

JAKE. And how old am I?

JULIE. Twenty-four.

JAKE. No, you don't get it . . . Look at me, Julie. Closely.

JULIE. *(SHE looks at him closer.)* Oh!

JAKE. See what I mean?

JULIE. You're in your mid-thirties.

JAKE. I wish . . . Look closer, Julie. At the gray in my hair, at my skin, in my eyes.

JULIE. *(Looks him over.)* Oh, God, Jake. You're *old!* . . . You're my father's age.

JAKE. *(Annoyed.)* No, I'm not. He was fifty-eight then. I'm only fifty-three.

JULIE. You're fifty-three? . . . And I slept with you last night?

JAKE. It wasn't last night. It was twenty-nine years ago . . . You see when I bring you back—

JULIE. Okay okay okay, I get it.

JAKE. Why? Do you think I look awful?

JULIE. No, not *awful* . . . Mature! . . . Look, it's okay. It happens.

JAKE. Am I that different?

JULIE. Well, you're a little—bulkier . . . Is that the wrong word?

JAKE. You can't imagine.

JULIE. I do like the little wrinkles around your eyes . . . and under them. It gives you—character. It's nice.

JAKE. Stick around, you'll love senility and arthritis.

JULIE. I don't care how old you are, Jake. Last night was still wonderful. God, I was scared. That I wouldn't like it. That *you* wouldn't like it. Did you know that out of all my girl friends, I'm the last one to do it? It's just that there was never a boy I wanted to get that close to. Never . . . But when we walked home last night, I said to myself, if he tries, if he even puts a hand on my shoulder, he's going to know just how much love I have to give him . . . And it was easier than I thought it would be, Jake . . . It was *wonderful*. I am *so* glad we picked each other because I could never be with anyone else and neither could you. You know that, don't you?

JAKE. Julie, don't.

JULIE. Is that the wrong thing to say?

JAKE. Wrong? You make me want to hear more. To say more. To crawl in that place you're in now and stay there forever. But I can't do it. We're not *in* the same place, Julie.

JULIE. We're not? *Now* I'm confused . . . Is this some sort of dream?

JAKE. Yes. For me . . . It's a memory, Julie. You're the memory and I'm the present. And there's no future. Not a *real* future. Because we can never be together the way we once were. In life, I mean . . . That life is gone . . . Can you understand what I'm saying?

JULIE. Oh, God . . . Oh, my God, Jake . . . Are you dead?

JAKE. *(Exasperated.)* Jesus!

JULIE. Oh, Jake, I'm so sorry. When did it happen? Was it terrible? Well, of course, it would *have* to be terrible. No wonder you look older. They say your whole life flashes in front of you just before you die. That would age somebody, wouldn't it?

JAKE. *(To audience.)* I haven't got the heart to tell her. *(To Karen.)* Karen, help me.

(KAREN rushes out.)

KAREN. *(Upstairs.)* What is it, Jake?

JAKE. She thinks *I'm* the one who died. What'll I tell her?

KAREN. That's not for us to do, Jake. Maybe a policeman or a rabbi.

JAKE. *(To Julie.)* It wasn't me, Julie. It was you.

JULIE. That died? Oh, I'm so relieved. I hate it when someone I love dies.

KAREN. Such a sweet girl, but a little naive, no?

JAKE. *(To Karen.)* No. She's just young.

JULIE. *(To Jake.)* Now I see why you bring me back. It's mostly when you're in trouble, isn't it?

KAREN. Join the club, honey.

JAKE. No, not exactly—

JULIE. Yes, it's true, Jake. Every time I come here, your life's in turmoil.

KAREN. Remember the heart attack?

JULIE. I remember when you had a heart attack. I was here, wasn't I?

JAKE. Well, after you left I found out it was just a bad shrimp.

JULIE. Then why didn't you get me back here and tell me?

JAKE. Well, you were so comforting, I really enjoyed it.

EDITH. *(Appears upstairs, opposite side of Karen.)* What about that tragedy in the paper?

JULIE. And I was here the night that terrible tragedy was in the paper.

JAKE. That was just a bad review in *Time* magazine . . . Look. I panic sometimes. I admit it.

JULIE. And now I'm here because Maggie is leaving you.

EDITH. He uses people like Kleenex.

JAKE. *(To Julie.)* There's hardly a day in my life that I don't think of you, Julie.

JULIE. But you don't send for me unless you're in trouble. That's not fair, Jake. That's not honest. Because I come here with such expectations. You use the beginning of the best part of my life to get you through the worst part of yours. Make up your mind, Jake. Is this time for me or for her?

EDITH. *(To Karen.)* This is interesting. *This* is fascinating. I can't follow it but it's riveting.

JAKE. *(To Julie.)* Julie, would it be alright if this time was just for *me*? Because right this minute I don't think I could give either one of you what you need.

JULIE. If you need me now, that's alright. I'll do whatever I can. The thing is, I don't know if I can do it like this.

JAKE. Like what?

JULIE. Being twenty-one. I'm too young, too inexperienced. How can I help you when I don't even know what life is about yet . . . Make me older, Jake. Make me—thirty-six.

JAKE. I can't do that, Julie.

JULIE. Sure, you can. I want to see what I'd look like anyway. If I'm going to be fat, I'll start dieting now.

KAREN. *(To Edith.)* He wants her younger. She wants to be older. Can you imagine? Only a dead woman would think like that.

JULIE. I'm doing it, Jake. I'm going out. I'll see you in fifteen years. Don't go away, otherwise I can't come back. *(SHE starts out.)*

JAKE. Stop it, Julie. I can't do it.

JULIE. Why not?

JAKE. Because . . . you never *were* thirty-six.

JULIE. I wasn't? . . . Oh . . . How old did I get to be?

JAKE. Thirty-five.

JULIE. That's very young, isn't it?

KAREN. *(To Edith.)* This is the sad part. I'm going to see what else is on. *(SHE leaves.)*

EDITH. Don't make it too depressing, Jake. You just slept with the girl last night. *(SHE goes.)*

JULIE. How did it happen?

JAKE. Don't you remember?

JULIE. No.

JAKE. How can you not remember that?

JULIE. Because I'm twenty-one. It hasn't happened yet . . . Tell me, Jake.

JAKE. It was an auto accident. Coming back from Vermont. The end of June.

JULIE. Were you in the car?

JAKE. No. The night before, in Vermont, I got a call my mother was sick in Florida. I got a flight out in the morning. You drove back yourself.

JULIE. What were we doing in Vermont?

JAKE. We were taking Molly up to camp.

JULIE. Molly?

JAKE. You don't know who Molly is?

JULIE. *(Shakes her head "no," then realizes.)* . . . Oh, God . . . We had a girl. *(JAKE nods.)* When?

JAKE. You were twenty-four. No, twenty-five.

JULIE. *(Smiles.)* We had a baby . . . We had a little girl . . . What is she like, Jake?

JAKE. Like you. Pretty. Smart. Impetuous . . . She's at college now. At Amherst.

JULIE. Amherst?

JAKE. Is that alright?

JULIE. Yes. It's wonderful. Why did you pick Amherst?

JAKE. I didn't. You did. You said if we had a child, you wanted her to go to Amherst.

JULIE. No, I said Dartmouth.

JAKE. Oh. I thought you said Amherst . . . She only has six months left. She could transfer.

JULIE. No, no. Too much packing to do . . . So tell me about us. Were we a happy family? What did we do in the summers? Did we have a dog?

JAKE. Yes. A yellow Labrador.

JULIE. Perfect. What was his name?

JAKE. Bark.

JULIE. Bark?

JAKE. Yes. I asked him his name and he said—

JULIE. (*Laughs.*) Bark! Alright . . . What about the summers? Where did we go?

JAKE. We rented a farmhouse in New Hampshire.

JULIE. All my dreams are coming true. Was Molly a happy baby?

JAKE. Oh, laughed all the time. Even in her sleep. She loved everything . . . Only kid I knew who couldn't wait to get her shots at the doctor's.

JULIE. Are you exaggerating?

JAKE. Well, maybe embellishing.

JULIE. Oh, God. I wish we could have lived there for the rest of our lives.

JAKE. We did.

JULIE. (*Gets it.*) Oh. Right . . . I got everything I wanted, Jake. Didn't I?

JAKE. Almost.

JULIE. Do you think I could see her?

JAKE. Molly? Sure. There's pictures all over here. (*HE opens a drawer.*) I took some great ones out at the beach this summer.

(*SHE looks at one.*)

JAKE. Here.

JULIE. Is that her? Oh, Jake . . . She looks so grown up.

JAKE. (*Looks.*) Well, actually, she's six months older than you are now.

JULIE. Not pictures, Jake. I want to see Molly.

JAKE. You mean *Molly* Molly? She's not here. She's up at school.

JULIE. Send for her.

JAKE. Send for her? You mean call her and tell her to drive down here and see what I'm thinking?

JULIE. No. Think of her too. Snap your fingers. I don't know how you do it. Just do it. I just want to see her. To talk to her.

JAKE. About what?

JULIE. None of your business. Mother and daughter things. Private stuff. Without you here.

JAKE. Julie, if I go, my thoughts go with you. They're attached to my brain.

(*The PHONE RINGS.*)

JULIE. You owe this to me, Jake.

JAKE. I do?

JULIE. For making me come only when you need me. Well, now I need you.

(*The PHONE RINGS again.*)

JAKE. (*HE picks up phone.*) Hello? . . . Oh. Molly. (*To Julie.*) It's Molly. The real Molly. (*Back into phone.*) We were just thinking about you. *I* was.

JULIE. Can I listen? Can I hear her voice?

JAKE. Please. AT&T is having enough trouble. (*Into phone.*) Sorry, hon. I was on long distance. How are you? How's school? . . . Oh, stop worrying. You always think you're going to fail your exams.

JULIE. I was the same way. Can I tell her that?

JAKE. (*Into phone.*) Molly, could you hold it one second. I want to turn down the TV. (*To Julie.*) I'll try. Another time. I promise.

JULIE. On my birthday? Can I see our daughter on my birthday?

JAKE. Your birthday?

JULIE. Instead of a present. I don't even want a cake. Just Molly. Say yes, Jake.

JAKE. Okay. Yes. I promise.

JULIE. Write it on your calendar. October 12th. Lunch with Molly and Julie.

JAKE. *Lunch??* I'm not taking you two to lunch. Julie, please. Don't turn this into Science Fiction. Just say goodbye.

JULIE. *(Backing off.)* Goodbye, Jake. I love you . . . Last night was great . . . Even if it was twenty-nine years ago. See you October 12th. *(SHE is gone.)*

JAKE. *(Back into phone.)* Molly? Sorry . . . A little hectic today . . . Listen, hon. There's a little trouble here . . . No, no . . . Domestic . . . Can we talk about it later? . . . Thanks . . . Maggie's upstairs . . . Listen, don't tell her I said anything . . . I love you too . . . Hold on. *(HE presses another button, then into phone.)* Hi. It's Molly. Do you want to talk to her? . . . No, I just said there were problems but I didn't go into any details . . . I think so too . . . Alright. Hold on. *(HE switches buttons again, then hangs up. HE looks up at the audience. To audience.)* Molly knew what was wrong without me even telling her. She knew me better than I knew myself . . . I have a theory that wisdom doesn't come with age. It comes at childhood, peaks around eighteen, then slides slowly down the scale into adulthood . . . Parents express anger at a child by saying, "You ungrateful little brat. You'll never amount to anything" . . . But kids are creative. They express anger by going to school and drawing a picture of you with the head of a gargoyle . . . God has protected children with a purity of spirit and the ability to see things as they really are. They have an uncanny knack for speaking simple truths . . . Molly, as young as she is, had the one quality I was never able to find, or worse still, never able to accept in another human being . . . Trust! *(HE crosses.)* For example, on the first day that she and Maggie met eight years ago, as certain as I was about Maggie, it was Molly alone whose stamp of approval I needed. I remember it as if it were yesterday.

(HE snaps his fingers . . .
MAGGIE comes on. This is MAGGIE eight years ago. Her clothes are less fashionable but her eagerness is infectious. SHE carries a gift-wrapped book and a wet floppy hat that is crushed and dirty.)

MAGGIE. I'm late, I know. I'm sorry.

JAKE. What is it?

MAGGIE. A bus went by and blew my hat off. I chased it five blocks all the way downtown . . . And then a cab ran over it and dragged it back *up*town . . . And by the time I got it, a dog was chewing on it. I bought it just for tonight. I wanted to look nice for your daughter. I wanted to make a good impression on her.

JAKE. Then wear it. That's the way *she* dresses.

MAGGIE. Don't make fun of me, Jake. Tonight is important . . . I bought her a book. Does she like books?

JAKE. Loves books. What did you get her?

MAGGIE. I don't know.

JAKE. You don't know?

MAGGIE. No. I was rushing in the store. I didn't want to be late, so I just grabbed a book in the children's section and had them wrap it up.

JAKE. She'll love the book and she'll love you.

MAGGIE. Maybe I'm trying too hard to please her. Listen, maybe there's a chance I won't like *her*.

JAKE. That's right. Maybe you won't.

MAGGIE. What would you do?

JAKE. Well, as soon as your hat dried, I'd ask you to leave.

MAGGIE. You wouldn't.

JAKE. Of course I wouldn't. It's a joke.

MAGGIE. Don't ever kid me, Jake. I have absolutely no sense of humor.

JAKE. Don't worry. We'll get you a tutor.

MAGGIE. You will?

JAKE. No. That's a joke too.

MAGGIE. So where's Polly?

JAKE. Molly. She's inside, trying on every outfit in her closet.

MAGGIE. Where are we going to eat?

JAKE. Sung Foo's. It's Szechuan Chinese. Her absolute favorite.

MAGGIE. Oh, God. Sung Foo's. I got sick there once.

JAKE. Okay, we'll go somewhere else.

MAGGIE. No, I don't want to disappoint her. We'll go. I'd rather get sick.

JAKE. Good. Get sick. She'd love that.

MAGGIE. Why?

JAKE. She wants to be a doctor.

MAGGIE. Okay, now *that* was a joke.

JAKE. No, it wasn't.

MAGGIE. Damn, they're so hard to spot.

JAKE. She's going to love you, Maggie. I promise.

MAGGIE. God, I hope so, Jake.

JAKE. You don't have the slightest idea of how special you are, do you?

MAGGIE. Oh, please don't say that, Jake. I have trouble taking compliments.

JAKE. Didn't your parents ever give them to you?

MAGGIE. Please. I graduated from high school second in my class and for a year my father called me "his little runner up."

JAKE. I'm sorry.

MAGGIE. Our backgrounds are so different, Jake. I wish I were born in New York, like you. Everyone's so talkative, so open here. You and Julie had so much in common, I know. Maybe that's why I'm nervous about Molly. I can picture being your wife but will she want me as a mother?

JAKE. Why don't you just start out as friends and the rest will take care of itself.

MAGGIE. You're smart, you know that? Well, of course, you know it. I have to be told. But I know we're good for each other, Jake. You and I must have come together for some important reason. And you're what I want, what I need. Someone to center my life on. Sometimes I run on supercharged batteries and if you don't watch me, I could spin right out into another galaxy.

JAKE. Perfect. Because my head is in the clouds most of the—

(*Before HE can finish, SHE kisses him. HE puts his arms around her.*
MOLLY, at twelve, comes out. SHE stops when SHE sees them, embarrassed.)

MOLLY. Oh. Hi. I'm sorry.

MAGGIE. (*Nervously.*) Hi . . . I must be Maggie.

JAKE. (*To Molly.*) She's got a very quick sense of humor.

MAGGIE. (*Extends hand to Molly.*) I'm real glad to meet you, Sally.

MOLLY. Molly.

(THEY shake.)

MAGGIE. Molly. Sorry . . .

(SHE sits, followed by MOLLY.)

MAGGIE. So, your dad tells me you go to school at Walton.
MOLLY. Dalton.
MAGGIE. Dalton. Right . . . I went to high school in East Lansing, Michigan. And then I went to Michigan State.
MOLLY. Right. What did you major in?
MAGGIE. Political science . . . I wanted to become a political scientist . . . or something like that . . . And then I switched to premed . . . which led to advertising.
MOLLY. Right.
JAKE. Sort of like throwing darts, wasn't it?
MAGGIE. *(Looks at Jake.)* Yes, wasn't it? *(To Molly.)* Have you thought about where you want to go to college?
MOLLY. Mm hmm. Amherst. Dad says my mother always wanted me to go to Amherst.
MAGGIE. Oh. Good school. Good sports program. Do you play sports?
MOLLY. Not well.
MAGGIE. Me neither. Although I was a cheerleader in high school. But I depressed everyone so they let me go.
MOLLY. *(Laughs.)* That's funny.
MAGGIE. It *is?* Oh, thank you, Molly. That means so much to me.
JAKE. Why don't you give Molly her present?
MAGGIE. I'll give it to her when I'm good and ready. *(To Molly.)* I have a present for you, Molly. *(SHE gets book and gives it to her.)* I hope you like it.
MOLLY. *(Feels it.)* It's a book, isn't it?
MAGGIE. I'm hoping it is, yes.
MOLLY. Should I open it now?
MAGGIE. Please. The suspense is killing me.
MOLLY. *(Tears off the wrapping paper and looks at the book. Reading title.)* The 1981 World Atlas.

(MAGGIE looks at Jake. JAKE looks at the ceiling.)

MAGGIE. *(To Molly.)* Did you read it?

MOLLY. No.

MAGGIE. Oh. Well, I hear it's very good.

JAKE. Universal bought the movie rights.

MAGGIE. *(To Molly.)* It's a dumb choice, isn't it? I'll be honest. I grabbed it without even looking.

MOLLY. No, I really need this for school because the names of the countries are changing all the time. *(Opens book, looks at pages.)* This is terrific.

MAGGIE. *(To Jake.)* See! She loves it.

JAKE. You certainly know how to grab a book . . . Is anyone besides me hungry?

MAGGIE. So starved you wouldn't believe it. Can we go to my favorite favorite place? Sung Foo's?

MOLLY. That's my favorite favorite too.

JAKE. What a small world small world this is.

MOLLY. Oh! Sung Foo's was in the paper last week. Three men were killed there.

MAGGIE. Really? What were they eating?

MOLLY. *(Puzzled.)* . . . No. They were shot.

MAGGIE. Shot?

JAKE. It's not on the menu. You have to ask for it . . . Are we ready to go, guys?

MOLLY. I just have to turn off my TV. *(To Maggie.)* Is it alright if I call you Maggie?

MAGGIE. Maggie? Sure, that's the only name I got right.

MOLLY. *(Laughs.)* I love your humor. *(SHE runs off.)*

MAGGIE. Oh, Jake. We like each other. And I'm crazy about her. I want more, just like her . . . What a terrific day. What a terrific opportunity for all of us . . . Oh! Where's the bathroom? I forgot to go today. I am so happy.

(JAKE points, and MAGGIE rushes off.
MOLLY comes back on.)

MOLLY. I'm ready.

JAKE. Come here. I want to talk to you . . . The truth now. Do you like her?

MOLLY. She is the absolute best most perfect one you ever brought home. I mean *some* of them were really doozies.

JAKE. I didn't ask for an in-depth review of my social life . . . What do you like about her?

MOLLY. Everything. She's fun and she's pretty and she dresses nice and she's very smart. I can tell.

JAKE. How can you tell?

MOLLY. I spoke to her.

JAKE. That's right. You did . . . So do you think I should be—you know . . .

MOLLY. Serious?

JAKE. Serious about her?

MOLLY. No.

JAKE. No?

MOLLY. I think you should just marry her. This week. I can't wait for her to move in.

JAKE. What's the rush?

MOLLY. She might change her mind.

JAKE. Hey! I'm the catch of the year.

MOLLY. I know. But the years go by fast.

JAKE. Oh, thanks.

(The TELEPHONE RINGS inside.)

MOLLY. That's my phone. I'll be right back. *(SHE starts to go.)*

JAKE. Molly? What's the absolute best thing about her?

MOLLY. That she'll make us all a good family again.

JAKE. Thank you, Molly. That's a nice thing to say.

(Her PHONE RINGS again.)

MOLLY. If you two elope, can I go too?

JAKE. Sure. Bring your friends. I'll get a bus.

MOLLY. Oh, great. I will.

(SHE turns and runs off into her room. JAKE sits there a moment, happy.)

*(There is another LIGHT CHANGE and MAGGIE comes out of
the upstairs bathroom wearing a raincoat, a scarf on her head
and carrying a small suitcase. SHE looks bleak, sees Jake.)*

MAGGIE. I didn't tell Molly too much, but she senses what's
going on . . . She's driving into town on Saturday. We'll have lunch.
(SHE's downstairs by now.) I told the service to hold my calls. I don't
think I'll go into work this week . . . I'm not even sure that job is the
right thing for me now anyway. *(SHE starts for the door.)* . . . Can I
call you from the beach?

JAKE. If you like.

MAGGIE. God, I just don't know how to get through that door.

JAKE. Would you like me to open it?

MAGGIE. No. If I can get through that, I can get through anything . . . Goodbye, Jake.

JAKE. I hope not, Maggie.

*(SHE looks over at Jake, then goes. JAKE sits, looking morose . . .
YOUNG MOLLY and OLDER MOLLY come on together.)*

OLDER MOLLY. Hi, Dad.

YOUNGER MOLLY. Hello, Daddy.

JAKE. *(Looks at them.)* Well!! I never saw the both of you together
before? . . . Any more Mollys coming? Like Molly at twelve months?

YOUNGER MOLLY. No. Molly couldn't talk at twelve months.

JAKE. And you figure I feel like talking now, right?

OLDER MOLLY. Or not talking. Whatever you want, Dad. We
just want to stay and keep you company.

(THEY sit with him, one on either side.)

JAKE. I may be sitting here all night. Maybe all week.

OLDER MOLLY. We don't mind.

YOUNGER MOLLY. We could play games. How about Actors and
Actresses?

OLDER MOLLY. He doesn't want to play games now.

JAKE. No, no. That's alright. Maybe it'll take my mind off
things . . . I'll go first . . . M.L. English actress.

OLDER MOLLY. Maggie Leighton.

JAKE. Right . . . M.S. Another English actress.

OLDER MOLLY. Maggie Smith.

JAKE. Right . . . The lead in *Cat on a Hot Tin Roof?*

YOUNGER MOLLY. Maggie the Cat.

JAKE. Right . . . This wasn't such a good idea, was it?

ALL THREE. No.

JAKE. No . . . Maybe just sitting quietly is the best idea.

YOUNGER MOLLY. Yes, Daddy.

JAKE. *(He holds their hands.)* Thank you, Molly . . . You too, Molly . . . We got through this once . . . We'll get through it again . . .

(THEY sit quietly, looking at him.)

Curtain

ACT II

About six months later.
JAKE is sitting at his word processor. HE types, then leans back
in thought.
MAGGIE enters, wearing the same clothes she left in at the end
of Act I, carrying the same overnight bag.
SHE stands there looking up at him. HE sees her.

JAKE. . . . Forget something?

MAGGIE. Yes . . . Our marriage.

JAKE. I thought you packed it when you left.

MAGGIE. I thought so too. Apparently I was wrong . . . about a lot of things.

JAKE. I thought you were pretty clear about what you wanted.

MAGGIE. I found out what I wanted wasn't out there . . . I missed you, Jake. I missed the little things. The way you stare at the ceiling when you're lost in thought. The way you always find the right words to say even in the most painful situation. And I fumble through, tripping over my own tongue, trying to say to you that I was wrong. Wrong about everything. And praying to God that you haven't rented out my half of the bed or that somebody else's soap isn't sitting up there in my soap dish.

JAKE. Do you mean it, Maggie? Is that what you really want?

MAGGIE. Oh, yes, Jake, yes. Oh, God, yes. (*And suddenly SHE starts to laugh.*) I'm sorry, Jake. (*SHE laughs again.*) I don't mean to laugh. But honestly, this is the *dumbest* scene you've ever written in your life.

JAKE. (*Angrily.*) I didn't write it. I'm just *thinking* of it.

MAGGIE. Oh, good. Then you didn't waste any paper. (*This really breaks her up.*)

JAKE. What I wasted was even *thinking* about you . . . Go on. Get out of here. I have important work to do.

MAGGIE. (*Still laughing.*) Don't lose the line about somebody else's soap in my soap dish. (*SHE picks up her bag, holding her sides laughing as SHE heads out.*) Oh, God. I needed a good laugh. (*SHE is gone.*)

JAKE. *(To audience.)* What you just witnessed is a man at the end of his rope . . . with nothing to hold on to because his wife took the rope with her . . . I don't know, I used to fantasize lust, romance, power. Now I'm into humiliation. It was six months since Maggie left and I haven't written a single word worth processing. To tell you the truth, I miss Maggie . . . Not that I haven't been dating now and then. Man does not live by abstinence alone . . . But recently, here in the privacy of my home, my mind and my thoughts, I was visited by a new and fresher hell than my warped imagination could ever dream of . . . No longer did I summon up the Karens and Ediths and Mollys of my life to help brighten up the endless sleepless nights . . . Now they came on their own. Uninvited. Unsummoned. Unstoppable.

KAREN. *(Appears.)* Jake, could I speak to you for a minute?

JAKE. Karen, I didn't send for you. Please go away. Isn't there an Ingmar Bergman Festival somewhere?

KAREN. I just came from one. But in the middle of *Cries and Whispers,* I began to worry about you.

JAKE. Everyone who sees *Cries and Whispers* gets worried. Well, stop it because I'm fine.

KAREN. You're not fine. You need rest. You're overwrought, overworked, underweight. How can you sleep, running around like a lunatic with every woman you bump into?

JAKE. I am not running around with every woman I bump into. I'm very selective.

KAREN. Sure. If they're a woman, you select them. Like that new one. That—Sheila woman.

JAKE. Don't say "That Sheila Woman." I hate that expression. It sounds like a bad television series.

KAREN. I only use that expression because I can't keep up with all your women.

JAKE. Four! Four women in six months . . . Peggy, Kathy, Dana, Myra and Sheila—Five! Five women in six months.

KAREN. Susan wasn't a woman?

JAKE. Two nights. That lasted two nights.

KAREN. So what does that make her? Half a woman?

JAKE. It makes her someone I wasn't interested in.

KAREN. You go out with women you're not interested in?

JAKE. You have to go out with them before you find out you're not interested, don't you?

KAREN. You can't tell right away? *I* can.

JAKE. Good. Then *you* go out with her. If you have a good time, let me know and *I'll* go out with her.

KAREN. Why is it whenever I try to help you, you push me away? You're that way with *all* women. You're so—so—standoffish.

JAKE. *I'm* standoffish with women? I'm a thousand times more comfortable with women than I ever am with a man. I love being around them. I never even *think* of a man. Watch! . . . I'm thinking of Pop. Of Uncle Josh. Of my best friend, Marty . . . Do you see a man in here? No! . . . I happen to love women. That's my trouble. I can't seem to exist without them.

KAREN. What you love is to *love* women. You love to have women in love with you. You even love to love women who love you because you're standoffish. But intimacy, aha, *that* you're afraid of.

JAKE. *(Incredulous.)* What??

KAREN. I said, "Aha, *that* you're afraid of." I think you're afraid to lose control in a relationship with a woman. To let a woman in so close, so deep inside of you, that she'll gobble you up and you'll lose whatever you think you are. You always have to be the master, Jake. The master, the conductor, the director and the attorney general. You don't think it's strange that you sit around here thinking about women and making up what they say to you? And then you think up that *we* make up that we come over here on our own? Come on! How much more control do you want? . . . They love you, they leave you, they come back to you, they worry about you, they die, they live, they grow up, they fall down, they fight for you, they cry for you—it's a three-ring circus in here and all the horses and lions and elephants are women . . . You're the star of the show, Jake. You're the one they shoot out of a cannon and you fly around the tent with an American flag in your mouth and all the women go crazy and faint and they take them away to hospitals . . . The trouble is—it's very hard to get close to a man who's flying around in a tent with a flag in his mouth. That's what I call trouble with intimacy.

JAKE. I couldn't be more intimate with women. I'm an open book. I tell them everything. My feelings, my hurts, my pains, my vulnerabilities. My intimacy scares them, if you want to know the truth. And if I'm the ringmaster of the circus, how come all the acts are leaving? Mom is gone, Julie is gone, Maggie's left, Molly's on her own, Peggy, Kathy, Dana, Myra, none of those worked out. That's why you're here seven days a week. There's no one left for me. This house used to be filled with people laughing, living, loving . . . and now it's just me talking to you telling me what I'm telling you to say . . . You think I'm crazy, don't you?

KAREN. Well, you're in a peculiar line of work, Jake.

EDITH. *(Appears.)* He picked it because he likes to deprive himself.

JAKE. *(To Edith.)* Who asked you? If this is a session, Edith, I'm not paying for it. Charge it to Karen.

EDITH. *(To Jake.)* Have you seen Maggie since she's back from Europe? I hear she looks beautiful.

JAKE. How would I know where Maggie is? You think that's all I have on my mind? I happen to be seeing someone now, Edith.

EDITH. Who?

KAREN. That Sheila woman.

EDITH. Well, I know for a fact that you dialed Maggie's number last night, got scared and hung up on the first ring.

JAKE. *I* hung up? Jesus, even discussing a confidential thing like that in front of my sister is the most unethical goddamn thing I ever heard.

KAREN. *(To Edith.)* I think he should get away. He could make believe he was in Paris for two weeks.

JAKE. *(Looks at himself in the imaginary mirror.)* My God, I can see them in the mirror. They're really here.

EDITH. *(To Karen.)* I'm just trying to point out to him that he's going to keep turning down every woman he meets until he lets go of the past.

JAKE. Excuse me, girls. I'm going to the bathroom. *(HE starts to cross.)*

KAREN. And I'm saying if he took the time to meet the right woman, he wouldn't turn her down.

EDITH. The trouble is, he wouldn't know who the right woman is if he—

(*On that word, JAKE goes into the bathroom and closes the door.
    EDITH and KAREN stop talking. THEY don't freeze, but
    THEY have nothing to say without JAKE there.*
*Finally, we hear the TOILET FLUSH and JAKE comes out of the
    bathroom.*)

EDITH. —met her, for God's sake.

(*JAKE crosses to the phone and starts to dial.*)

EDITH. (*To Jake.*) Who are you calling?
JAKE. I'm calling you!
EDITH. (*Looks at her watch.*) At four twenty? I'm with a patient.
JAKE. I pity whoever it is. (*Into phone.*) Hello? Edith?
EDITH. That's not me. It's my answering machine. Wait for the
beep.
JAKE. (*Waits, listens.*) Christ! Do I have to listen to the entire
album of *Man of La Mancha*?
EDITH. (*Looks at her watch.*) . . . Okay! *Now!*
JAKE. (*Into phone.*) Edith. It's Jake. I'm at home. I'm having one
of those things we talked about. This time it's you and my sister.
Could you call me on your break? Please, just call me back as soon
as you can. (*HE hangs up.*)
EDITH. (*To Karen.*) By the way, Karen, I think I met a man. Very
attractive, very wealthy, recently widowed. As a matter of fact, he's
the patient I'm having the session with right now.
KAREN. Isn't it unethical to date your own patient?
EDITH. Yes. But if this thing gets serious, I'll tell him he's cured.
JAKE. (*Exasperated.*) Christ Almighty!

(*The PHONE RINGS. HE quickly picks it up.*)

JAKE. Hello? . . . Yes, Edith. Thanks for calling back. Yes, they're
sitting in here now. You and Karen. Dissecting me like a frog in biol-
ogy . . . And Karen just made a twelve-minute speech about me
being a ringmaster and flying around a circus tent with a flag in my
mouth.
KAREN. (*To Jake.*) Tell her the whole speech. It was wonderful.

EDITH. *(To Karen.)* Shh. He's talking to me.

JAKE. *(Into phone.)* No, no. This is real. I can even see them in the mirror. In the beginning it just used to be my thoughts. Like when I'm writing. But now I can see them. I hear them. I can smell their perfume.

KAREN. *(To Edith.)* Some crap he must have me wearing.

JAKE. *(Into phone.)* It scares me, Edith. Does it scare you?

EDITH. No, Jake. It doesn't scare me.

JAKE. *(To Edith.)* *Will you let me talk to you,* for God's sake? *(Back into phone.)* Excuse me, Edith . . . It's driving me nuts. I have to get rid of them. My sanity is at stake here. What should I do? . . . Please tell me . . . Yes? . . . Uh uh . . . Uh huh . . .

KAREN. *(To Edith.)* I hope this isn't going to be like *Ghostbusters.*

JAKE. *(Into phone.)* Alright. If I have to, I have to. Thank you, Edith. Goodbye. *(HE hangs up and starts up the stairs.)*

EDITH. *(To Jake.)* Where are you going?

JAKE. Upstairs. To take a bunch of Seconals. If you won't leave, at least I can *sleep* you away. *(HE starts up again.)*

EDITH. Jake, no. You'll kill yourself.

JAKE. *(Points to the phone.)* It was your suggestion.

EDITH. It *was?*

KAREN. *(As SHE goes.)* Pills! Pills! That's all you doctors know . . . Then what does he need a psychiatrist for?

EDITH. Who else is going to get him the pills?

(THEY are both gone.)

JAKE. *(Turns to the audience.)* You want to know how low I've sunk? *(HE points to the phone.)* I never spoke to Edith. I called my service. I actually made a phone call pretending I was speaking to the *real* Edith to scare the Edith and Karen in my head out of here . . . I tricked myself and I fell for it . . . The thing about going crazy is that it makes you incredibly smart, in a stupid sort of way. *(HE starts down.)* But I do feel like I'm losing a grip on myself. As if I'm spiraling down in diminishing circles like water being drained from a bathtub, and suddenly my big toe is being sucked down into the hole and I'm screaming for my life . . . No. Not my life. My mother . . . Why, tell me why, it's always your mother. It's never your father or an uncle or a second cousin from Detroit . . . I was five years old in a third-floor apartment in the Bronx, waking up from a nap and there's no one there. My mother is on the *fourth* floor visiting a neighbor. I'm terrified. Why doesn't she hear me? Why doesn't she come? And by the time she comes, it's too late. Your basic Freudian mother abandonment trauma has set in like cement . . . I never trusted her again.

(*The INTERCOM BUZZES.*)

JAKE. What was that? . . . Oh, the buzzer . . . God, I'm a bundle of nerves . . . (*HE picks it up.*) Yes? . . . Oh, Sheila . . . What a surprise, Sheila . . . Where are you, Sheila? . . . Oh, of course. Downstairs . . . Sure. Come on up, Sheila. (*To audience.*) But is Jake doomed? Not by a long shot. There's Sheila. Another woman to the rescue . . . Another woman . . . It's always another woman . . . Stop it, Jake . . . You can handle it, Jake. Get a hold of yourself, Jake . . . Get a grip on yourself . . .

(*SHEILA appears, an attractive woman in her early thirties.*)

SHEILA. Hi.
JAKE. Sheila! Oh, Sheila, it's so good to see you. God, I'm glad you're here. Where were you so long? I've been waiting all day for you.
SHEILA. You were?
JAKE. Of course I was. You look so good. So pretty. So sweet. So how are you?
SHEILA. Are you alright? . . . You look—discombobulated.
JAKE. No, no. I'm bobulated. I was just working.
SHEILA. You look exhausted. Have you been sleeping?
JAKE. While I work? No. You have to be awake to work . . . No, I'm just tired . . . Hungry. I forgot to eat . . . Oh, my God. I forgot our lunch date. Dammit, I'm sorry.
SHEILA. We didn't have a lunch date.
JAKE. We didn't.
SHEILA. Not today. You forgot *yesterday's* lunch date. I called you four times. You had your service on. Don't you check your messages?
JAKE. No. I didn't want to interrupt my train of thought.

SHEILA. Since yesterday?

JAKE. Well, it was a long train . . . I'm sorry, Sheila. I know I'm not making sense. Did I say bobulated? . . . I can't get my thoughts together. My mind keeps stuttering. *Sputtering* . . . skittering. What's the word I want?

SHEILA. For what?

JAKE. For when your mind makes jumps. Splintering. Scattering. Jesus, I can't think straight . . . staggering. Stammering . . . *faltering!!*

SHEILA. Stop it, Jake. Give your mind a rest.

JAKE. I can't. I've been going through this thing. A writer thing.

SHEILA. A block.

JAKE. No, not a block. *Yes,* a block. Digressions. Distractions. Dissections . . . No, not dissections. *Delusions!*

SHEILA. Delusions?

JAKE. Like delusions. I veer off. I wander. I stray. I roam. I fade off into other places.

SHEILA. I can see that.

JAKE. You can? Oh, no, not about you. I'm so grateful for you, Sheila. I depend on you. You comfort me, you support me, you hold me together.

SHEILA. I hardly see you.

JAKE. Well, I've been busy. But when you *are* here, you're so real, Sheila. I *love* that you're real. Nobody is real anymore.

SHEILA. I *try* to be real.

JAKE. Well, you look real. You smell real. You *feel* real. (*HE holds her.*) Oh, God! Flesh and blood. I *love* flesh and blood . . . Some people don't have it, you know.

SHEILA. Flesh and blood?

JAKE. They're superficial. You can see right through them. Oh, maybe you can see their reflection in a mirror, but they're not really there.

SHEILA. I've met people like that.

JAKE. Oh, I could introduce you to a roomful. But *you,* Sheila. You're so vivid. So colorful. So dimensional.

SHEILA. What do you mean, dimensional?

JAKE. Dimensional. You have sides. You have a left side, a right side, a front side, a back side. You have form as a person. You have matter. Good, firm, solid matter.

SHEILA. Well, I work out in a gym a lot.

JAKE. No! That kind of matter doesn't matter . . . Listen to me. You know how people come in and out of your life? In a door, out the door. This one's here, that one's here. You know that feeling?

SHEILA. I don't entertain as much as you.

JAKE. Exactly! Exactly! That's my point. You know what my trouble is, Sheila? I work too much. I don't want work to be my life. I want my life to be my life. I let so many things go by. So many things I don't do.

SHEILA. Like what?

JAKE. Like travel. I should travel a lot more.

SHEILA. I loved our trip to Quebec.

JAKE. Okay. There you are. But there's more than Quebec. There's Europe. There's Africa. There's the Middle East. Well, no, not the Middle East, but there's Japan. Have you ever been to Japan?

SHEILA. No.

JAKE. Oh, Japan is the greatest, I was there with Maggie once. And with Julie once. And once with another girl. I'd love to go with you.

SHEILA. They must know you very well there.

JAKE. Hey! There's Australia. Have you ever been to Australia?

SHEILA. No. Just here and Quebec. I don't fly too well.

JAKE. Okay. A ship. A slow boat to China. How does that sound? China? Hong Kong? The Orient?

SHEILA. When are you talking about?

JAKE. Next month. Next week. How about next week?

SHEILA. Go to China next week? My vacation isn't for eight months.

JAKE. You could ask them. Tell them it's an emergency.

SHEILA. An emergency vacation to China?

JAKE. Okay, forget China. Forget Hong Kong. What about India? Bombay? Calcutta?

SHEILA. I can only get a three-day weekend, Jake. I could *go* there, but I'd have to quit my job when I *got* there.

JAKE. Alright. Forget Bombay. Forget Calcutta. Forget traveling . . . I'll tell you what I'd really like to do. What would really shake my life up.

SHEILA. What's that, Jake?

JAKE. I want to move. It's time I moved, Sheila.

SHEILA. I thought you loved this place.

JAKE. I *did* love it. I don't love it now. I want a new place, Sheila. A new start. A new beginning for you and me. Do you understand what I'm saying, Sheila?

SHEILA. You want me to move in with you?

JAKE. Yes!!! . . . Not *now*. Some day. Later on. In the future.

SHEILA. So what are you saying?

JAKE. I just said it. Move in with me. But not now. Some day. Later on.

SHEILA. Why does that sound negative to me?

JAKE. It's *not* a negative. It's a *positive* negative. It's a cautious enthusiasm.

SHEILA. Like an uncommitted commitment?

JAKE. No. That's an oxymoron. What I'm saying is, I love you and I want you to be with me . . . someday, somewhere, somehow.

SHEILA. This is all new to me, Jake. You never talked like this before. I know you care for me but I never thought it was about loving.

JAKE. Didn't I just say I love you?

SHEILA. Yes, but it didn't have any immediacy to it. I feel like I have to wait for a delivery date.

JAKE. Are you saying you don't know how I feel?

SHEILA. Well, I always felt like I was needed but I never felt loved. I like being needed but being loved is better.

JAKE. So what are you saying? Have I been—what? Cold to you?

SHEILA. No. Never cold. You're warm and funny and affectionate. But you always keep your distance. An arm's length away. Sort of—standoffish.

JAKE. Oh, shit.

SHEILA. Did I say something wrong? Am I the first one who ever said that?

JAKE. Standoffish? I don't know. I can't recall anyone ever saying it.

SHEILA. Maybe standoffish is too strong. Maybe a lack of intimacy.

JAKE. Can we get off this, Sheila? We're in a holding pattern here. We're not moving this along.

SHEILA. Where do you want to move it to?

JAKE. All I'm trying to do is move from here to there. I'm here now but I want to get to there. Do you understand that, Sheila?

SHEILA. Yes. You're here but you want to get to there.

JAKE. Right!! Right!! That's right!! From here to there, that's all.

SHEILA. Jake, I mean this as a constructive positive, but you seem very confused.

JAKE. I'm not confused. Well, a *little* confused. I can't keep my visions focused.

SHEILA. Is it an eyeglass thing?

JAKE. No, I see fine. I see great. Why am I having trouble with this? What is it I'm trying to say?

(*MAGGIE appears. SHEILA never sees her.*)

MAGGIE. That you're really not interested. That you're just kidding yourself. (*SHE goes.*)

JAKE. I am *not* kidding myself.

SHEILA. About what?

JAKE. (*To Sheila.*) About us. About you and me. I think we should start seeing each other on a regular basis, Sheila.

SHEILA. You mean every night?

JAKE. Yes. Every night. Well, no, not every night. A *lot* of nights. The nights that you don't have something else to do. Or *I* don't. But most nights. Can we do that?

SHEILA. I was hoping we could spend more time together.

JAKE. Oh, there are so many things we can do.

SHEILA. Like what?

JAKE. I don't know. We'll make a list. A "things we can do together" list. Or *you* can make the list and I'll check off what I like.

SHEILA. Sure.

JAKE. And then I'm going to move. I really never liked this neighborhood anyway. A bunch of old remodeled factories, that's all it is.

(*MAGGIE appears on opposite side of stage.*)

MAGGIE. Ah, but Jake, it has such charm.

JAKE. And it has no charm. Some people *think* it has charm but it doesn't, believe me.

MAGGIE. Why don't we ask Sheila?

JAKE. STAY OUT OF THIS!!

SHEILA. I *am*. You say it doesn't have charm, I believe you.

JAKE. *(To Sheila.)* Now uptown is the place. The Upper East Side. Do you like the Upper East Side?

SHEILA. Everybody likes the Upper East Side.

MAGGIE. *(To Jake.)* I thought you liked Brooklyn Heights.

JAKE. I *do* like Brooklyn Heights.

SHEILA. I didn't say you didn't.

JAKE. *(To Sheila.)* I know. I meant Brooklyn Heights is a good idea too. Great views of the river. And nobody from New York ever comes over to visit you.

MAGGIE. Of course Bedford Village is beautiful.

JAKE. I *know* Bedford Village is beautiful.

SHEILA. Yes, I hear it is too.

JAKE. *(Smiles to Sheila.)* Yes, isn't it? The leaves turning brown in the fall. There was a house on a lake up there I always dreamed of living in.

MAGGIE. Why don't you go and see it, Jake?

JAKE. *(To Sheila.)* You want to go and see it, Jake? . . . Sheila? Come on, Sheila. Let's go up and see it, Sheila.

SHEILA. Now? It'll be dark by the time we get there.

MAGGIE. You could stay at the Bedford Inn.

JAKE. *(To Sheila.)* We could stay at the Bedford Inn. Then we could see the house first thing in the morning.

SHEILA. Jake, I wish you could listen to yourself. You want to go to China, Japan, Australia, Calcutta. Then you want to move to the Upper East Side and Brooklyn Heights and Bedford Village. *Nobody* can change their mind that fast.

MAGGIE. *He* can.

JAKE. I can.

SHEILA. Well, I can't. I'm not a writer, Jake. I'm a business-woman. I make up my mind slowly and carefully. If I wanted to live on the Upper East Side, I would investigate the Upper East Side.

JAKE. I know.

SHEILA. And if I wanted to live in Brooklyn Heights—

JAKE. I know.

SHEILA. I would investigate—

ALL THREE. —Brooklyn Heights.

JAKE. I know.

SHEILA. Or if I wanted to live in Bedford Village—

JAKE. I know I know I know I know.

SHEILA. (*Defensive.*) I'm sorry. Live where you want, Jake. I just think you should investigate one place at a time.

JAKE. I will I will I will I will! . . . I will! . . . I'm sorry. Forgive me . . . I will.

SHEILA. Can't we just go a little slower? You move in so many directions. I never know where it is you want to get to.

MAGGIE. (*Points from Sheila to herself.*) Form there to here, honey.

JAKE. (*To Maggie.*) No, it's not.

SHEILA. What's not?

JAKE. (*To Sheila.*) It's not the way I am. I don't want to go in a lot of directions. I want to live in the country. In Bedford Village.

SHEILA. You sure you wouldn't get bored in the country, Jake?

MAGGIE. (*To Sheila.*) He'd kill himself.

JAKE. (*To Maggie.*) Will you butt out of this?

SHEILA. Listen, I don't have to talk at all.

MAGGIE. (*Gets up.*) Let's take her up on that, Jake. (*MAGGIE stands behind Sheila and mimics every word and gesture she utters, in complete unison.*)

SHEILA. I don't know when I'm being negative or constructive or logically positive or conventionally destructive . . . You tell me I have a front side and a back side and an inside and an outside. I have form and dimension and matter that doesn't matter. You love me, you want me to move in with you but not today, later, in the future, someday, somehow, somewhere over the rainbow . . . Then you want to get from here to there, from there to here, MAKE UP YOUR MIND, JAKE!! I CAN'T TAKE ANY MORE. MY HAIR IS STARTING TO FALL OUT.

(*THEY finish with their arms and bodies in the same position, like the finish of a musical number.*)

JAKE. Alright. I'm sorry. I didn't mean it. Forgive me.

MAGGIE. Don't *beg* her, Jake.

JAKE. I'M NOT BEGGING!

SHEILA. Who *asked* you to? (*SHE starts to walk away.*)

JAKE. Don't leave, Sheila.

SHEILA. Where am I going? To Calcutta? Don't corner me. I get very nervous when I get cornered.

JAKE. I won't corner you. We should get out of here. We should go up to Bedford. Right now.

SHEILA. Alright. Fine. I'll go to Bedford. If you want to go to Bedford, I'll go.

MAGGIE. There's a lot of traffic now. You waited too long.

JAKE. Well, there's a lot of traffic now. We waited too long.

SHEILA. YOU ASKED ME TWO MINUTES AGO!!! . . . What is wrong with you, Jake?

MAGGIE. Yes, what *is* wrong with you, Jake?

JAKE. (*To Maggie.*) You know goddamn well what's wrong. It's *you!!*

SHEILA. Oh, it's *me*! It's *my* fault. I'm the one who wants to take a slow boat to Brooklyn Heights. I'm the oxymoron who can't get her visions focused.

MAGGIE. (*To Jake.*) How'd you like to hear that voice the rest of your life?

JAKE. (*To Maggie.*) Will you shut up, goddammit!!

SHEILA. (*Nervous, backs away.*) Jake, you're making me nervous. I've never seen you like this.

JAKE. I know. I know. It's a phase. It'll go. It'll pass. It'll stop.

SHEILA. Jake, I'm calling your doctor. What's your doctor's name?

MAGGIE. Edith! Let's get Edith here. Let's have a party.

JAKE. (*To Maggie.*) I'm telling you for the last time. SHUT UP!!!

SHEILA. What's happening, Jake?

JAKE. (*To Maggie.*) Get out! I want you out of this house *now!!* Do you hear me?

SHEILA. (*Frightened.*) Yes, I hear you. (*Backing away.*)

JAKE. (*To Sheila.*) Don't go, Sheila. You promised to stay. I'll get rid of her. I'll call Edith. Edith will help.

MAGGIE. (*To Sheila.*) Edith won't help, Sheila. I'm a prisoner in his head. Go for help.

JAKE. (*To Maggie.*) If you don't stop, I swear, I'll kill you.

SHEILA. (*Backs up, screams.*) Ohhhhhh!

MAGGIE. (*To Sheila.*) Run, Sheila, run. That's what I did, honey.

JAKE. (*To Maggie.*) Go on. Keep talking. You'll never leave this room alive!

SHEILA. *(Screams.)* Oh, God!!! . . . Oh, my God!!! *(And SHE goes running from the apartment.)*

JAKE. Sheila . . . Sheila!

MAGGIE. That was fun, Jake. Bitchy but fun.

JAKE. Why did you do that, Maggie? What was the point of it?

MAGGIE. I suppose because you didn't have the guts to tell her yourself. So you made me the hit man. To dump her would be cruel and you're not cruel, Jake. So you act like a lunatic, Sheila thinks she's well out of it and you're off the hook. You never get your hands dirty, do you?

JAKE. You don't think much of me, do you, Maggie?

MAGGIE. See what I mean? You're so afraid to face who you really are, you leave me to pass judgment on you and then blame *me* for what you don't like about yourself.

JAKE. Well, since I'm making up what you say, I might as well take advantage of it.

MAGGIE. You're cute, Jake. Nuts but cute . . . Come on, leave your work upstairs where it belongs. *(Points upstairs.)* That's writing—*(Points downstairs.)*—this is living . . . If surgeons lived like you, they'd be cutting people up in elevators. *(SHE starts to go.)*

JAKE. Where are you going?

MAGGIE. Hopefully, out of your mind. Which is where I think *you're* going.

JAKE. Then help me.

MAGGIE. How?

JAKE. *(Points up to his office.)* I want to get from there to here . . . Up there I trust what I do . . . but down here, it's people I have to trust and that's hard.

MAGGIE. For everybody, Jake. That's why women carry mace in their pocketbooks. *(SHE starts away again.)*

JAKE. Will I see you again?

MAGGIE. I don't know. That's between you and Maggie. *(SHE leaves.)*

JAKE. *(Turns to the audience.)* I have the feeling I'm trying to put together a jigsaw puzzle that has no picture on it . . . I'm a blank, waiting to fill in who I am . . . How did I get to be this way? . . . That's not a rhetorical question. I mean, if you know, please tell me . . . Okay, Jake. Go back to the beginning. That's what Edith always says . . . Here's another Mother story . . . I'm six years old,

sitting in the kitchen with my mother, watching her shell peas . . .
And on the floor I see a roach . . . My mother, faster than a speeding train, takes a newspaper and splats it against the baseboard . . .
"Where do roaches come from?" I ask my mother . . . "From the
dirt," she answers . . . "You mean," I say, "the roaches like to live in
the dirt and eat it?" . . . "No," says Mom. "The dirt turns *into*
roaches" . . . And I go back into my room, lay on the bed and say
to myself, "The dirt turns into roaches" . . . And the realization
hits me . . . My mother is dumb . . . And I know instinctively that
six years old is too soon to find out that your mother is dumb . . .
Because I'm banking my whole childhood on this woman taking
care of me . . . And so I decided on that day, I would never depend
on anyone except myself . . . I loved my mother, but I never asked
her any more questions . . . The trouble is, here I am today
at the age of fifty-three, without any answers . . . Oh my God,
Julie!

(JULIE *suddenly appears. This is* JULIE *at thirty-five.* SHE *wears
a skirt and a brown suede bolero jacket.*)

JULIE. You remembered! I didn't sleep a wink last night wondering if you were going to send for me or not.

JAKE. Of course I was.

JULIE. Maybe you heard me praying, "Please don't forget, Jake.
You've *got* to think of me today". . . And you did, didn't you, Jake?

JAKE. Yes. I guess so. Sure. I mean otherwise what would you be
doing here? . . . The thing is, it's not a good time for me right now,
Julie.

JULIE. Oh. Are you writing?

JAKE. I don't know. I can't tell *what* this is anymore.

JULIE. I read some of your books. Just the first few. I didn't get to
the rest yet.

JAKE. Really? What did you think?

JULIE. I liked them.

JAKE. But you didn't love them.

JULIE. No. But I see each one getting a little better than the last.

JAKE. What was wrong with them?

JULIE. They weren't you. Just be you, Jake. And don't rush the endings. You always rush the endings as if you're anxious to get on with the next one.

JAKE. I know what you mean. I sort of do that with people too . . . Julie, this has been a long day for me. Do you think we could do this tomorrow?

JULIE. Tomorrow is too late, Jake. *Today* is October 12th.

JAKE. October 12th?

JULIE. My birthday . . . I'm thirty-five.

JAKE. Oh, God, Julie. Yes! . . .

JULIE. So what am I wearing? Where's the mirror? I want to see how you dressed me. (*SHE sees the imaginary wall mirror, crosses and looks at herself.*) Of course. My brown suede jacket. Your favorite . . . And that little chocolate stain is gone.

JAKE. I had it cleaned. Then I gave it to Molly. She asked for it.

JULIE. I'm glad. (*SHE turns around, looks at herself again.*) So this is thirty-five.

JAKE. Feel any different?

JULIE. No. I don't *look* much different either. I've hardly aged.

JAKE. I know. It's your birthday. I didn't have the heart.

JULIE. Damn you, Jake, will you stop controlling everything? If I'm thirty-five, make me *feel* thirty-five.

JAKE. Okay. Okay. You're thirty-five.

JULIE. (*Like a bolt hit her, grabs her head and stomach.*) Wow! That was a kick in the head . . . What does fifty-three feel like?

JAKE. The kick gets a little lower.

JULIE. (*Stands next to him, looks in mirror.*)But this looks righter. You and me. We seem more like a couple now . . . Promise me you'll live a very long time, Jake.

JAKE. Why?

JULIE. I need you to. Otherwise who'll bring me back?

JAKE. I'm not the only one who thinks of you.

JULIE. No, but you think of me the way I want to be thought of.

JAKE. Maybe I shouldn't.

JULIE. What does *that* mean?

JAKE. You're too perfect, Julie. Too beautiful, too smart, too sweet, too understanding. No other woman can hold a candle to you. They're all standing in the dark, waiting to get a compliment from me.

JULIE. Why do you do it? Was I so terrible that you don't want to see me the way I was?

JAKE. Don't you understand, Julie? When you come back, I even make *myself* better than I am. I'm charming, I'm witty, I'm romantic, I'm "cute," I'm goddamn irresistible.

JULIE. Well, don't do it to me. I don't want to be a shrine. I don't want to be a touched-up photo in a family album. I want to be me because even a memory deserves some self-respect. Otherwise I'll never know if you would have loved me if we were still together.

JAKE. Of course I would.

JULIE. No! That's the idealization. That's the fantasy. Every man's dream—His wife never grows old . . . Well, we do, Jake. And if you keep bringing me back here looking like a young Natalie Wood and acting like Sally Field in *The Flying Nun*, I'll lose respect for you. I want to be woman enough for you because if I'm not, you won't be man enough for me. If you had died before me, I would have kept you funny and loving and sexy, but I wouldn't leave out the petulant son of a bitch you can sometimes be, because I want the whole package, dammit! . . . God, it feels so good to have a little fire in me again.

JAKE. (*To audience.*) I've created Mrs. Jakenstein.

(*The PHONE RINGS. HE picks it up.*)

JULIE. Husbands and wives fight, Jake, what's wrong with that? It's normal.

JAKE. (*Into phone.*) Hello?

JULIE. It's human.

JAKE. (*Into phone.*) Maggie?

JULIE. God, we really used to go at it sometimes.

JAKE. (*Into phone.*) How are you?

JULIE. Remember the day I threw the frozen veal chop at you. Hit you right in the head and you suddenly started to—

JAKE. (*To Julie.*) Julie, could you hold it a second. It's Maggie.

JULIE. Oh. Sorry. Go ahead.

JAKE. (*Into phone.*) . . . Where have you been? . . . Ballooning in France? . . . You don't mean getting fat, do you? . . . Oh, good . . . No, I'm fine . . . Where are you? . . . Really? That's just around the corner.

(JULIE nods to him, "Yes, let her come.")

JAKE. Well, I was just finishing some work.

(JULIE waves at him, shakes her head, "No. Tell her to come.")

JAKE. Could you hold it a second, Mag? *(HE covers phone. To Julie.)* What?

JULIE. See her, Jake. Let her come. It'll be good for you.

JAKE. With *you* here? Please! I just went through that. There's a poor girl named Sheila who's probably in Montana by now.

JULIE. I'll leave when she gets here. She's the one who called, Jake. It must be important to her.

JAKE. *(Looks at her, then into phone.)* Maggie? Yes, it's fine. Great . . . I'll see you in about ten minutes . . . I am too. Bye. *(HE hangs up.)* You really don't mind my seeing Maggie?

JULIE. *(Smiles.)* No. My time will come with you again.

JAKE. *(Worried.)* Why? Have you heard something? Did they mention dates or anything?

JULIE. Don't worry about it. I'm in no rush.

JAKE. Well, it was really good seeing you today. So I'll er . . . call you soon, okay?

JULIE. Aren't you forgetting something?

JAKE. What?

JULIE. I'm waiting for my birthday present.

JAKE. Your present? Gee, I didn't get you anything.

JULIE. Yes, you did. You just haven't delivered it yet.

JAKE. What?

JULIE. Molly! . . . You promised I could meet Molly on my birth-day.

JAKE. Oh, Julie. I can't do that now.

JULIE. You promised, Jake. Suppose you die? This could be my only chance. This could be Molly's only chance to meet me. You have to do it, Jake.

JAKE. But Maggie's coming up.

JULIE. In ten minutes. We can cover a lot in ten minutes.

JAKE. I can't believe I'm having a conversation with myself and losing the argument . . . Okay. Sit here . . . No. Stand back. Over there. In the shadow.

JULIE. Why?

JAKE. I don't know why. Because I'm nervous. I think we're playing with fire here.

JULIE. I'll take care of it, Jake. I'll treat it with respect.

JAKE. This is going to end up a famous case history. Right up there with the Elephant Man . . . Alright, here we go. (*HE turns to think, then stops.*) How old?

JULIE. Who?

JAKE. Molly. How old do you want her to be?

JULIE. Now. Today. All grown up. The way I've never seen her. The way she's never seen me . . . I'm ready, Jake. (*SHE goes back in the shadows.*)

JAKE. . . . Alright. Show time.

(*HE turns away and then MOLLY comes out. SHE is twenty-one and wearing the exact same brown suede jacket that Julie is wearing. MOLLY doesn't see Julie yet. SHE just looks at Jake.*)

MOLLY. Hi, Dad. You okay?

JAKE. Yes, honey. I'm fine.

MOLLY. So why am I here? You sure you're not sick or anything?

JAKE. No, no. I just er . . . well, this may seem very weird to you, Molly.

MOLLY. What is it?

JAKE. There's somebody here.

(*HE looks at Julie. MOLLY turns and sees Julie as well. SHE seems shocked at first. SHE takes a step back, frightened.*)

JULIE. Hello, Molly.

(*MOLLY is confused.*)

JULIE. It's alright, Molly. Don't be afraid . . . Jake, she's having trouble with it. It's not right this way. Help her to accept it. Oh, Molly, I didn't want to scare you.

JAKE. Okay. I didn't think it out. Let me start over . . .

MOLLY. NO!! It's alright . . . Now I understand. Now it's fine.

JULIE. Are you sure?

MOLLY. Yes. Positive . . . Hello, Mom.

JULIE. Hello, Molly . . . Would you like to sit down here with me? Would that be alright?

MOLLY. Yes. Of course. (SHE crosses and sits on sofa next to Julie.) I have a million things to ask you. It's like meeting someone you've always heard about. Like a movie star. Only it's my mom. I feel like asking you for your autograph.

JULIE. I love the way you look, Molly. We have a classy-looking daughter, don't we, Jake?

JAKE. Yes, Julie.

JULIE. Do I seem very different from the way you remembered me?

MOLLY. You're prettier than your pictures. And you look younger than I thought you'd be.

JULIE. Your father touched me up a little.

MOLLY. I didn't even realize it. We're wearing the same jacket.

JULIE. Isn't it great? Your dad prints them out like Xerox copies. (SHE looks at Molly's hand. SHE wears four different rings.) These rings are beautiful. Where did you get them?

MOLLY. Well, this one was yours.

JULIE. Yes. It was my favorite.

MOLLY. This one Dad gave me for my sixteenth birthday. And this one Maggie gave me for Christmas. And this one a friend of mine gave me.

JULIE. Okay. Let's hear about the friend. This is the kind of news I came back for. Who is he?

MOLLY. Well, he's at Yale. The Drama Department. I met him at the theatre. He did a play there.

JULIE. An actor?

MOLLY. No. Set designer. Graduated with an architectural degree . . .

(MOLLY and JULIE continue talking but THEY mime what they're saying, but keep up the same joy and exuberance. JAKE turns to the audience.)

JAKE. (To audience.) I'm standing there listening to a conversation that never existed and never could. And yet it's so real to me, and from the looks of it, so real to them . . . Their joy, their laughter, the reborn intimacy and love they're sharing were created by me. And I'm thinking, if I can create *this* intimacy, why can't I experience it in my own life?

MOLLY. What was the best thing we ever did together? Just you and me.

JULIE. Oh, gosh. So many things. The first movie I ever took you to see.

MOLLY. *101 Dalmatians.*

JULIE. Right. The first horse I ever put you on.

MOLLY. Chiquita. A palomino with a yellow mane.

JULIE. The first sleep-over date you ever had.

MOLLY. Cynthia Gribble. She got sick in the night and threw up all over me.

JULIE. And you came into my room and said, "Mommy. Cynthia just hurt my feelings."

(THEY BOTH laugh at this.)

JULIE. What were *your* favorite times?

MOLLY. That's easy. When we were in a hotel in Atlantic City. And you let me call room service and order my own dinner.

JULIE. And I came out of the shower and found two chocolate sundaes and a pineapple cheesecake.

MOLLY. And I thought you were the greatest mom in the whole world because you didn't send it back.

(THEY continue their conversation in mime. JAKE turns to audience.)

JAKE. *(To audience.)* Am I the only one who's ever done this? I don't think so. There's not one of you who hasn't thought, at three o'clock in the morning staring up at a ceiling, of what it would be like to talk to your father who died five or twenty years ago. Would he look the same? Would you still be his little girl? . . . Or the boy you loved in college who married someone else. What would your life be if he proposed to you instead? . . . You've played that scene out. We *all* do it . . . My problem is I never *stop* doing it.

MOLLY. *(To Julie.)* . . . I never wanted it to end. I never wanted to grow up . . . I never wanted you to grow old . . . Oh . . . I'm sorry.

JULIE. That's alright, sweetheart.

MOLLY. No, it was terrible of me to say.

JULIE. It was terrible of me to leave. You must have been so angry.

MOLLY. No, not angry. I just never knew where you went to. It happened so fast. I kept thinking you'd come back but all I had was your picture next to my bed. And I would talk to it every night. Sometimes it would smile at me and sometimes I could hear your voice so clear, so comforting. Telling me what to do. Telling me not to worry. Telling me that you loved me . . . Until one day I stopped hearing it. I would call out for you but there was no answer. I would shake the picture, "Talk to me. Talk to me" . . . but it would just stare back at me . . . and I felt so—cheated.

JULIE. I'm sorry about that, Molly. I'm sorry about all the years we didn't have together.

JAKE. (To audience.) And suddenly I felt this was going too far . . . (To Molly.) It's getting late, Molly. Maggie'll be here soon.

MOLLY. No, not yet. (To Julie.) Tell me other things, Mom. Anything. Just keep talking.

JULIE. I can't, hon. Maggie's coming over. We should go. We've taken enough of Dad's time.

MOLLY. It's not Dad's time. It's our time. I don't want you to go.

JAKE. We'll do it again, Molly. Another time.

MOLLY. What other time? I've been waiting for this day since I'm ten years old. I don't want her to go.

JULIE. It's alright, baby. Your father kept his promise to me, he'll keep it to you. I'll come back, I swear.

MOLLY. NO!!! You said that to me in Vermont and you never came back. I don't trust you anymore. I don't trust him. I don't trust anyone.

JAKE. (To audience.) That sounds familiar. That word doesn't keep coming up by accident.

MOLLY. (To Julie.) I need those years. I need you to fill in the eleven years I never had with you. Don't leave me now when we have a chance to make them up.

JAKE. Molly, nobody can make up eleven years. Not like this. This is just a game. We can't keep playing this game forever.

MOLLY. I didn't ask to play it. You brought me here. You brought Mom. You bring us together after eleven years and you give us ten lousy minutes together. What is that? Why did you do it? It's so damn cruel.

JULIE. Because I asked for it, Molly.

MOLLY. No, you didn't. *He* did. *He* brought us here. We can't get here until he thinks of it. *(To Jake.)* So what are you going to do? It's *your* Goddamn game, *you* get us out of it.

JULIE. Molly, don't.

MOLLY. *(To Jake.)* Why didn't you leave well enough alone? What is it you wanted to see?

JAKE. I wanted to see you both happy.

MOLLY. By doing the impossible?

JAKE. Not so impossible. I saw you both laughing, both together again. It made me happy to see that.

MOLLY. I think you're the one who doesn't know it's a game. So what happens to us now? Do we go back in some corner of your mind and wait till Mom's next birthday to hear the second installment of the Years That Never Happened?

JULIE. Jake, stop this. I don't want to hear anymore.

MOLLY. He can't stop it. He loves it too much. He'll never let go of it. He'll sit in this house alone, afraid to get on with his life because this *is* his life. Isn't that right, Dad?

JAKE. So everyone tells me.

MOLLY. Then please let go of this.

JAKE. I will. Eventually.

MOLLY. No, not eventually. Eventually has come. Eventually is today. I don't know what it is you're trying to work out. If it's Mom's death, that wasn't your fault. My loss wasn't your fault.

JAKE. You don't have to be at fault to feel guilty.

MOLLY. You don't have to feel guilty to make it better . . . So I think Mom and I ought to go now, don't you?

JAKE. It feels like someone's taking my toys away from me.

MOLLY. Everybody gives up their toys sometime . . . Come on, Mom. Let's go.

JAKE. Don't leave together.

MOLLY. Why not? The neighbors?

JAKE. It's too dramatic. Too final. Too wrapped up. I feel like Ethel Merman's going to come out and sing, "Everything's Coming Up Roses". . . Just leave, say goodnight, go back to school, say "See you next week."

MOLLY. That's still playing the game, isn't it?

JAKE. Sure. But indulge me.

MOLLY. Why not? *(Looks at her watch, grabs her books.)* My God, what am I doing here so late? I've got exams tomorrow. Goodnight, Dad. Get some sleep. You look tired. *(SHE kisses his cheek.)* Love you . . . Goodnight, Mom. It was real good seeing you. You look just great.

JULIE. *(To Jake.)* Can I kiss her goodbye? I won't make an opera out of it.

JAKE. Whatever you like. I'm not playing anymore.

(JULIE turns, looks at MOLLY, who rushes into JULIE's arms. THEY embrace.)

JULIE. I love you, baby.

MOLLY. I love you, Mom. *(SHE turns and rushes off.)*

JULIE. Thank you for my present, Jake.

JAKE. Next time you're getting a gift certificate from Bendel's.

(The DOORBELL RINGS.)

JAKE. That's Maggie. You'd better go.

JULIE. Not yet. You still have one more thing to do for me.

JAKE. Don't ask to see Bark. He died when he was twelve.

JULIE. I want a proper kiss goodbye.

JAKE. Oh, I don't think we should get physical, Julie. They have a nasty word for that.

JULIE. *(Moves closer, puts her arms around his neck.)* You don't have to do a thing. This one is my fantasy.

(THEY kiss, warmly and deeply. The DOORBELL RINGS again.)

JULIE. Goodbye, Jake.

MAGGIE. *(Enters.)* Hi.

JAKE. Hi.

MAGGIE. It's good to see you.

JAKE. You look wonderful.

JULIE. Don't screw this up, Jake. *(SHE leaves.)*

JAKE. *(To Maggie.)* How are you feeling?

MAGGIE. Tense but relaxed . . . How about you?

JAKE. I'm studiously nonchalant.

MAGGIE. The apartment looks nice. Anything new here?

JAKE. Just today's paper . . . How's your apartment?

MAGGIE. Ugly. But it has a very nice view of better apartments.

JAKE. You look very fit. Still jogging?

MAGGIE. No. Treadmill. I like running in place. I don't have that same urge to get somewhere.

JAKE. You can sit down, if you like. I think that's your half of the sofa there.

MAGGIE. Oh, er, if you get a letter from my lawyer about a legal separation, you can forget about it.

JAKE. Really? Change your mind?

MAGGIE. No. He died . . . I have to get a new lawyer.

JAKE. Doesn't everyone? . . . Can I get you anything? A drink? Coffee?

MAGGIE. No, thanks. I'm meeting dinner for someone . . . Someone for dinner . . . Okay, so I *am* a little nervous.

JAKE. Yeah, well, this smile is painted on too. So, what's this new job of yours I hear about?

MAGGIE. Yes. I'm working for Wang.

JAKE. *(Nods.)* What's he like?

MAGGIE. Well, there really isn't a Wang. It's that computer company with the oblique commercials. Five men and a woman sitting around a table with overlapping conversations and quick cuts to their shoes or scratching their earlobes. It's a very effective ad campaign except that most people still don't know what a Wang is.

JAKE. I *thought* I knew but it couldn't be the same thing.

MAGGIE. No, I don't think so . . . Oh, Christ, Jake. I'm so glad we got the first part of this conversation over with.

JAKE. I know. I felt like we wandered into a Noel Coward tribute or something.

MAGGIE. You *are* funny, Jake.

JAKE. And what about you? Are you happy?

MAGGIE. Happy? . . . No, not really. But at least I'm not running like mad trying to find it everywhere from here to Calcutta.

JAKE. *(Smiles.)* Calcutta! . . . That reminds me of that three-way conversation we had with Sheila. That was something, wasn't it?

MAGGIE. Who's Sheila?

JAKE. *(Pauses, looks at her.)* Shit! Sorry. Just having a minor lapse with my spatial concepts.

MAGGIE. Still can't keep them out, heh, Jake . . . God, the irony of it.

JAKE. Of what?

MAGGIE. That I'm still attracted to the very thing about you that drove me out of here.

JAKE. That sounds promising.

MAGGIE. I didn't make any. I still don't think a marriage can run on an attraction.

JAKE. No, I don't think so either . . . So what brings you here?

MAGGIE. I just wanted to see you. To talk to you.

JAKE. I sense something important is about to be said.

MAGGIE. I think the man I'm going to have dinner with tonight is going to propose to me.

JAKE. I see. Well, that qualifies as important. Probably in the same category as "My house is on fire". . . How do you feel about it?

MAGGIE. I'm scared I might say yes.

JAKE. Who isn't? . . . And what's the frightening part?

MAGGIE. That it would be over with us.

JAKE. Well, it would certainly slow us down . . . I don't suppose I could come along and coach you? . . . No . . . What does he do?

MAGGIE. He listens to me. He pays attention.

JAKE. You mean for a living?

MAGGIE. Jesus!

JAKE. What?

MAGGIE. I'm sitting here telling you that in twenty minutes I may be making the biggest decision of my life and I don't feel any concern from you or any interest in my life unless it's connected to you.

JAKE. I'm concerned. If you got sick, I would worry. If you got married, I'd be pissed . . . Since I still care for you, that seems pretty reasonable to me.

MAGGIE. I still care for you too, Jake. But it doesn't depend on our getting together or not.

JAKE. Am I dense because I'm not rooting for the other guy to get the girl?

MAGGIE. No matter what we talk about, it always seems to come out like a story conference.

JAKE. Well, if it is, I never seem to get past the editor. Christ, Maggie, if we're just going to pick up where we left off six months ago, you should have gone straight to dinner.

MAGGIE. I was hoping that things might have changed since six months ago.

JAKE. (*Shrugs.*) They have. You found a guy who listens better than I do.

MAGGIE. Don't listen to the words, Jake. Listen to the feelings. There's pain going on here. Your pain and mine. And we can't get anywhere until we get in touch with those feelings. We're like two people reaching out for each other with both hands tied behind our backs.

JAKE. (*Confused.*) Why can't I understand your concept of getting in touch with pain? I don't think I just speak words. I speak feelings and emotions. I care. I love. I'm miserable. I'm angry. I'm desperate. I'm hopeful and mostly I'm confused. Am I getting close?

MAGGIE. Yes, Jake. You're getting close.

JAKE. Thank God. Tell me what I did so I can hold on to it.

MAGGIE. I think part of you is standing right there in front of me, listening and talking to me . . . But there's that other part of you. The writer. The observer who's standing up there in his office, right now, watching and observing the two of us, detached as hell, and *he's* the one who's getting in our way, Jake. He's the one who's not involved in our problem. He's a voyeur. A manipulator. And unless you can let go of him and trust yourself, Jake, trust how you feel and not what he judges to be the truth, then you'll never feel safe with me or with anyone . . . And that would be such a loss . . .

JAKE. Jesus, Maggie, you make me feel so isolated. So inhuman.

MAGGIE. No. I think you're alone. I think you put yourself there a long time ago because it feels safe to you. All that I'm asking is that you come out of your hiding place and join the rest of us. There's a lot of people out here who love you, Jake. Trust it.

JAKE. (*Hoping to explain.*) I don't observe because I choose to. I'm not alone because I prefer it. I'm not a writer because I'm good at it . . . I write to survive. It's the only thing that doesn't reject me. My characters are the only ones I know who love me unconditionally, because I give them life. Do you love me unconditionally, Maggie?

MAGGIE. I'm not that selfless. And you didn't give me life, Jake. My mother did. And I like you much better than I like her.

JAKE. Do you? Funny, you look about ten miles away from where I sit.

MAGGIE. No, Jake. I think we're so close. I swear. I think we're only an inch or two apart.

JAKE. What's wrong with that? Most couples I know have the Grand Canyon between them and they don't even notice.

MAGGIE. I notice. But I want more than that for us.

JAKE. I mean this in all sincerity. I wish I were as smart as you.

MAGGIE. I wasn't this smart before I married you. You made me think. You made me observe.

JAKE. So why doesn't your observer run off with *my* observer and you and I can stay here?

MAGGIE. Okay. If you want me to stay, I'll stay. If you want me to come back, I'll come back.

JAKE. (*Smiles.*) You're tricky, you really are. You know I'd grab that in a minute. But you're also smart enough to know that I'm smart enough to know that wouldn't work. That I know you're right. That until I cross those two inches, until I can understand the *concept* of those two inches, we'd always be in trouble.

MAGGIE. You know something, Jake. Even though we've just been pretty tough on each other, this is one of the best talks we've ever had.

JAKE. Really? I hated it. I grew up seeing movies where saying "I love you" was a happy ending.

MAGGIE. Maybe it will be. Once we both realize this isn't a movie . . . I'm late for dinner.

JAKE. You're not really going to say "Yes" to him tonight, are you? I mean, is this guy only a quarter of an inch away from you or what?

MAGGIE. No, I'm not going to say yes . . . I'm going to wait till I hear from you.

JAKE. Oh, you're just going to leave me walking around here all day with a tape measure? What are you hoping is going to happen?

MAGGIE. A catharsis! A bolt of lightning! A miracle!

JAKE. Jesus, now I have to be the Messiah.

MAGGIE. No, I'll just settle for Jake . . . So long, Jake. (*SHE goes.*)

JAKE. (*To audience.*) Men have climbed mountains for women and crossed burning deserts for them, and I can't get to this one because I'm two lousy inches away . . . Maybe if I put a little weight on around the midsection, I could squeeze across the finish line . . . Okay, so I need a catharsis, a bolt of lightning and a miracle . . . Where the hell do you shop for that . . . Wait! Hold it! . . . One last Mother story . . . Make that a Mother and Father story . . . I feel a connection here . . . I am ten years old, walking down the street with my friend, Sal . . . And coming in the opposite direction is my father with a woman half his age . . . A chippie, they called them then . . . He doesn't see me but Sal says to me, "Hey, Jake. There's your father". . . And I say to protect my father or my shame, "No, it's not. He just *looks* like my father". . . What prompts me later that day to tell my mother about it is still unclear to me. I want to make things right but right for who? . . . When my father comes home later that night, my mother pulls him into my bedroom, turns on the lights and screams at me, "Tell him, Jake. Tell him what you told me you saw today". . . I want to run as fast as I can or die on the spot, but my mother won't be denied. I tell my father what I saw . . . And he looks me in the eye and says, "You're a liar. You saw someone else, not me". . . He makes me pay for his indiscretion . . . I hate my father for betraying my mother, hate my mother for betraying me and hate myself for betraying them both . . . It did, in time, pass and maybe was even forgotten in the forty years that eventually buried them both . . . But I can't help feeling that three betrayals in one day could eventually make two inches to cross—a very long trip for someone who never learned to trust again . . . So what would that be? A small catharsis? . . . (*Looks off.*) What do you think, Karen? . . . Karen? . . . Where are you? . . . Karen, I'm calling you. (*To audience.*) She's never done this before . . . Karen, it's Jake. I need you . . . Come on, wear anything you want, I'll pay for it. Where are you? (*To audience.*) This is scary. Don't go away. I don't feel like being alone right now . . . Edith!! . . . Please come out. I can't wait till our appointment on Tuesday . . . I need a quick fix. A couple of laughs . . . I need the jokes, the kidding around. *Love Yourself, Fuck Them*, that was funny, wasn't it? . . . Molly? Julie? Not even you? . . . You want to see each other again, I'll set it up. I'll order in pizzas, you can spend the whole day gabbing and gorging yourselves, whaddya say? *(To audience.)* Jesus! I've been praying to get rid of them, *begging* for them to be gone and now that they're not here I feel empty. I feel scared, I feel stark naked . . . Jesus, this is hard. My goddamn heart is palpitating . . . I can hardly breathe . . . what is this? . . . Is this going crazy? Is this going mad? . . . Or is this the miracle? . . . I mean she already got her catharsis, maybe this is the freaking miracle . . . *(Looks around.)* So what have we got left? A bolt of lightning . . . *(HE moves away.)* Better get away from anything metal . . . Rubber? Where's rubber? . . .

(HE looks around. We suddenly hear a VOICE, a VOICE not clear as to gender or age.)

VOICE. "Jake, are you alright?"
JAKE. *(Looks up.)* No! . . . I'm not alright . . . Who is that? Karen?
VOICE. *(From another speaker.)* Are you alright, Jake?
JAKE. I just said no, didn't I? . . . Why, do I look alright? I'm falling to pieces here . . .
VOICE. *(From another speaker.)* Jake, are you alright?
JAKE. *(To audience.)* What is this, *Field of Dreams*? "Build it and they will come"? *(To Voice.)* . . . Who are you? What do you want?
VOICE. *(From another speaker.)* Don't get scared, Jake. Don't get nervous. It's me.
JAKE. *(To audience.)* Oh, my God. I think it's my mother. *(To Voice, cautiously.)* Mom? Is that you? *(To audience.)* Gee, I hope she didn't hear me tell about the dirt turning into roaches.
VOICE. *(From another speaker.)* I love you . . . and I forgive you.
JAKE. You forgive *me*? *(Somewhat sarcastic.)* Well, that's very generous of you, Mom . . . Why can't I see you? Where are you?
VOICE. *(From another speaker.)* I love you . . . and I forgive you.
JAKE. What have you got, your own sound system? . . . What are you doing this for, Mom? . . . If you forgive me, what is it you forgive me for? *(To audience.)* Am I really hearing her or is this my imagination? . . . No, this is coming from someplace else . . . Some deep place I've never tapped into before. Only what's the point of it? *(To Voice.)* What are you doing this for, Ma?

VOICE. (*From another speaker.*) Think about it, Jake. You'll figure it out.

JAKE. (*To audience.*) Thank God Sheila isn't here, her hair would turn white by now . . . "Think about it, Jake. You'll figure it out". . . My mother was never articulate before and suddenly she gives me the hieroglyphics to work out . . . "Think about it, you'll figure it out". . . No, as I said, I loved my mother, but I didn't trust her before and I don't trust her now. (*HE starts up the steps, stops, comes back down.*) . . . Wait a minute, wait a minute, hold it . . . That's not my mother's voice. It didn't sound like her . . . It sounded like— like me . . . Jesus! It was *my* voice. I had it all turned around . . . It was *me* saying to my mother, "I love you, Mom . . . and I forgive you". . . (*HE stops, catches himself, moves Downstage.*) I love you, Mom . . . and I forgive you. (*HE takes a second, then looks at audience.*) I think you have to forgive those you love before you can forgive yourself . . . And so Maggie got her bolt of lightning. (*HE starts up to his office.*) So what do I do now? Call the restaurant and say to the maître d', "Please tell the pretty lady in the beige suit her husband called and said, 'Just had the big three. Hurry home'"? . . . (*HE sits at his desk.*) No. Nothing in life gets resolved that fast. (*HE turns, looks at the typewriter, when suddenly we hear MUSIC from downstairs. To audience.*) Did I leave the stereo on? . . . Or are my imaginary conversations turning into musicals now?

(*OLDER MOLLY, EDITH, KAREN, JULIE, SHEILA and YOUNGER MOLLY all appear suddenly from doors, from the balconies on both sides, ALL in party dresses.*)

ALL SIX WOMEN. Surprise!

JAKE. (*To audience.*) They're back! . . . Just when I thought it was safe to go back to the typewriter . . . Karen, don't! Edith, Molly, Julie, please! If you love me, you'll go and never come back.

EDITH. (*Baby talk again.*) But you need us, Jakey. You called for us.

KAREN. We were getting dressed. I paid a fortune for this.

YOUNGER MOLLY. Let us stay, Daddy. I love being twelve years old.

JULIE. (*Hugs Older Molly.*) And Molly and I can be together forever, Jake.

OLDER MOLLY. Can we, Dad?

SHEILA. If you want, I'll go to Calcutta, Jake. I'll quit my job.

JAKE. No! No! NO! I don't want that.

EDITH. Then what do you want? Ask for it, Jake. Please! ASK FOR IT!

JAKE. (Shouts.) MAGGIE! I WANT MAGGIE!

EDITH. Oh! (Smiles.) Well, it's about time, Jake.

(The DOORBELL RINGS. THEY ALL turn and look. MAGGIE comes in, in the outfit SHE was just wearing.)

JULIE. Let's go, ladies . . . I don't think we live here any more.

(One by one, THEY quickly disappear.)

MAGGIE. I let myself in, Jake. Is that alright?

JAKE. No, you didn't, Maggie. I think I just let you in.

MAGGIE. I didn't go to that restaurant. I called him and explained . . . I'd like to stay and work out those last two inches together, Jake. Is that alright?

JAKE. Yeah. That would be great.

(SHE starts up toward him.)

JAKE. NO! You stay there! I'll come down to you. (HE starts to take that first step cautiously.)

MAGGIE. Are you alright?

JAKE. Well, a little nervous. It's a ten-mile drop from here to there.

(HE starts again. HE steps down very cautiously, as HE and MAGGIE reach for each other, like God and Adam reaching out in the Sistine Chapel.)

Fade to Black

LAUGHTER
ON THE
23RD FLOOR

NEIL SIMON

ACT 1

We are in the offices of The Max Prince Show, *a television variety show. It is on the 23rd floor of a building on 57th Street between Fifth and Sixth Avenues.*

This is the Writers' Room. It is actually two rooms made into one large room, by breaking down the wall that separated them. We can still see where the molding has stopped between the two rooms.

The room is divided into two spaces. On Stage Left is where the actual writing takes place. There is a metal-top desk, a typewriter on it and a swivel chair behind it. A large leather sofa is to the left of the desk. On the opposite side of the desk and facing it, a large, comfortable sitting chair. This belongs to MAX PRINCE. Around this grouping are chairs of assorted kinds, room enough for eight people to sit down.

The other side of the room at Stage Right is more of a lounging area. There is a table against the wall with a coffee maker on it and coffee is now perking in it. There are paper cups and a few regular coffee mugs for the veteran writers. Also on the table is an assortment of fresh bagels, rolls, sliced pound cake and Danish.

There is a small desk in this area as well as two chairs on either side and a telephone on the desk.

There is also a cork board on the wall to which index cards are tacked on to denote the sketches that are being written. There are also piles of magazines, dictionaries and thesauruses about. There are two doors, one on each side of the room.

Also Emmies and awards on the shelves.

It is a few minutes before ten A.M. *on a crisp Monday morning in March 1953.*

At Rise: LUCAS BRICKMAN, about mid-twenties, sits at center desk, writing. HE looks up.

LUCAS. *(To audience.)* I guess this is what I've dreamed of my whole life. There was no comedy show in all of television that equaled *The Max Prince Show*. Not in 1953, there wasn't . . . *(HE gets coffee.)* An hour and a half revue every Saturday night, completely live. And now I was actually a writer on it. My name is Lucas Brickman. *(HE sips coffee.)* Max was unlike any comedian I had ever seen before. He didn't tell jokes. He didn't say funny lines. He was just funny. But on camera, when he had to be himself, like introducing a guest, he couldn't say four intelligent consecutive words without mumbling or coughing. I like Max a lot. Mostly because he treated his writers with respect. And he paid them more than anyone else. All young guys and they made more money than the governor of New York. Well, they were *funnier* than the governor of New York. *(HE looks at his watch.)* If I seem nervous to you, it's because it's only my second week here. One of the other writers left and I'm here on a four-week trial contract. So if I'm going to prove myself, I'm going to have to do it fast. My problem is, I'm shy . . . but I did manage to get one really funny line on last week's show. Unfortunately Max coughed on that line and no one in America heard it . . . My entire future depends on my finding a voice for my humor . . . or a cure for Max's cough.

(The door opens. MILT FIELDS, another writer, enters. HE wears a black cape over a sports jacket, a bow tie and a black beret on his head.)

MILT. *(In the doorway.)* I did it. Broke every record on the Henry Hudson Parkway. Door to door, Scarsdale to 57th Street, twenty-eight minutes, twelve seconds, made every light . . . Can you imagine if I had a car? *(Crossing to Lucas.)* Ba-dum-bum. How you doing, Arnie?
LUCAS. Fine. It's Lucas.
MILT. It's not Arnie?
LUCAS. No.
MILT. I called you Arnie all last week, you never said a word.
LUCAS. I didn't know you were talking to me.

MILT. You're going to have to learn to speak up, kid. Otherwise these killers'll eat you alive. (*HE throws his cape.*) Hang this up, willya? Be careful with it. It's an antique.

LUCAS. (*Touches it.*) Feels nice. Where'd you get it?

MILT. I took it off a dead bullfighter in Spain. What do I know? A junk shop. But it's got style, class. I got a flair for dressing, no?

LUCAS. A flair? You got a rocket. Where'd you get the beret?

MILT. The beret is legitimate. Got it in Paris. The last one sold.

LUCAS. The last beret in Paris?

MILT. MGM bought 'em all up for Gene Kelly movies.

(*LUCAS nods.*)

MILT. Look, he believes me. What do I know about berets? And I look like a putz in this. So why would I wear it?

LUCAS. Why?

MILT. Because people notice it. Look at me without a beret. (*HE takes it off.*) Invisible, right? A nothing. Who is he? But watch. (*HE puts beret back on.*) Now I'm someone. A diplomat. A traveler. Maybe I know Ernest Hemingway. I go to French movies, laugh at the jokes (*HE laughs.*), don't understand a fucking word they're saying, but people come over on the way out. "You like the picture?" "Eh, comme ci, comme ça." I don't even understand *that* but I get attention. I'm unique, right?

LUCAS. Well . . .

MILT. What am I, good looking? No. Am I smart? Eh. Am I funny? Yes. But compared to the comic minds in this room, I'm Herbert Hoover's kitchen help . . . So I wear yellow suede shoes on Christmas and a cowboy hat on Yom Kippur. And when I walk in here, Max Prince laughs. And if Max Prince laughs, my kids eat this week.

LUCAS. Max didn't talk to me once last week.

MILT. Alright. I'll rent you the beret. Fifty bucks a week. If he picks up your option, seventy-five.

LUCAS. No, that's okay.

MILT. (*Hands him the beret.*) Here. It's a gift. (*HE pulls a red one from one pocket and a green one from the other pocket.*) I'm up to my ass in berets.

LUCAS. (*Smiles.*) And you don't think you're funny?

MILT. (*Putting away the red and green berets.*) Cheap! Cheap laughs! These guys are Tiffany's. I'm a wholesaler. (*Crossing to the bagel table.*) What they have in quality, I make up in quantity. Bulk, volume, that's my humor. Where's the onion rolls? It's in my contract. My agent negotiated for onion rolls.

LUCAS. (*Points.*) Isn't that one?

MILT. (*Picks up a small dark roll.*) This? This is a Jewish hockey puck. Smell it. Does that smell like an onion roll?

LUCAS. I can't smell. I have a cold. I could listen to it if you want.

MILT. (*HE grabs the beret from Lucas.*) You're funny, Arnie. You're too quiet, but you're funny. Don't be *too* funny. I have a wife and two kids to support. It's murder on my mistress.

Both.(*Together.*) Ba-dum-bum.

MILT. Yeah. You'll be alright.

(*The door opens and VAL SKOLSKY enters in an old, worn top-coat over a somber suit and tie. HE is the senior member of the staff. An emigrant from Russia when HE was twelve, HE still carries his accent. HE is the most politically aware of all the writers.*)

VAL. (*Russian accent.*) Did Max get in yet? Excuse me. Am I interrupting? Forgive me. Pay no attention.

MILT. The man apologizes three times in one sentence and hasn't said good morning yet.

VAL. I'm sorry. Obsolutely unforgivable. I have a lot on my mind. It's an affliction common to geniuses. Just kidding. (*HE hangs up his topcoat.*)

MILT. You like his coat, Luke? Val buys all his clothes at Ellis Island.

VAL. Dot's right. Be funny before work starts. (*HE rubs his hands, looks at food table.*) So what have we got here? Nothing bot onion rolls. Ernie, do me a favor. Look for a pompernickel bagel.

MILT. His name is Arnie.

LUCAS. It's Lucas.

VAL. It's not Ernie?

MILT. It's not even Arnie . . . It's not even *pom*pernickel.

VAL. Don't start with me. I didn't sleep last night. I didn't have breakfast. I didn't get laid in a week. And Max calls my house at twelve A.M. midnight. He never calls at twelve A.M. midnight unless there's trouble.

MILT. Twelve A.M. *is* midnight, putz.

VAL. Milt! Don't bother me. It's too early in the day to say go fock yourself.

MILT. There's no such word as "fock." A person can't "fock" himself. You can't be a U.S. citizen until you say "Go *fuck* yourself."

VAL. Kiss my naturalization papers, okay? (*Looks at buffet table.*) I can't believe there's not one pompernickel bagel.

LUCAS. (*Points.*) There's one.

VAL. (*Picks it up.*) Thank you, Lukela. You'll go far on this show. (*HE opens the already split bagel.*) Look at this. Already sliced. *This* is why my father brought us to America.

LUCAS. For sliced bagels?

MILT. Mine came for chocolate pudding. In Poland they could make it but they couldn't get it in the cups.

VAL. (*Putting cream cheese on his bagel.*) I wonder if Max called anybody else last night? Did he call you, Lewis?

LUCAS. Lucas. No. Why would he call me? Is anything wrong?

VAL. I don't know yet. I was out last night. Oh, listen. I saw without doubt, the most focking brilliant play I have ever seen in my life. I'll remember it as long as I live.

LUCAS. What was it?

VAL. What the hell was it? Downtown. In the Village. The Grapes Theater. Not the Grapes. The Peach. The Pear. The Plum. Whot sounds like that?

LUCAS. The Cherry Lane?

VAL. Dot's it. God bless you. You obsolutely get a raise this Christmas, we'll see, maybe, who knows?

MILT. This is our head writer, Arnie. A man who learned to speak English from a dog who barked at night.

VAL. Is dot right? I got news for you. My dog *dreams* funnier than you.

MILT. My dog can say fucking pumpernickel.

VAL. Good. Then he can take your place on the show.

LUCAS. So what was the play?

VAL. What play?

LUCAS. At the Cherry Lane.

VAL. Ibsen. *Hedda Gobbler.*

MILT. *Hedda Gobbler?* Is this about a turkey?

VAL. You focking illiterate. I'll bet you five hundred dollars right now you don't know Henrik Ibsen's first name.

LUCAS. You just said Henrik.

VAL. I did? *(To Milt.)* Alright. I'll bet you two-fifty. *(VAL laughs. To Lucas.)* Dot's funny. My mistakes are funnier than what he makes op. *(Looks at his watch.)* It's after ten. Max is *never* this late. Now I'm worried.

LUCAS. *(To Val.)* You don't have *any* idea why he called?

VAL. *(Taking a sip of coffee.)* None. He spoke to my maid. In Swedish. Double talk Swedish. To a woman who's here three weeks from Peru. She was still crying when we came home . . . Something's op. I swear to God.

MILT. *(Into phone.)* Honey, can I have an outside line, please?

VAL. Goddammit, you know the rules, Milt. Is this a business call or a personal call?

MILT. I don't know. Let's see who answers.

LUCAS. It seems incredible, growing up in Russia, that you became a comedy writer. I mean, did they have television there?

VAL. Television? They don't have doorbells yet. *(To Lucas.)* And yet the greatest comedy in the world came from Russia. Gogol, Chekhov, Dostoyevsky. The best. Read *Dead Souls* sometime. Absolute genius. But in Russia today, comedy is dead. Lenin killed it. Stalin buried it. And what have they got now? The most corrupt and insidiously evil political regime since Ivan the son of a bitch . . . No, sir. Until there are humane reforms in that country, I wash my tongue of their language. Ptui! *(HE spits out.)* I'm sorry. I got cream cheese on you. Totally unforgivable.

MILT. *(Into phone.)* Hello? Who's this? . . . No, I'm calling Collette.

VAL. Collect? We've got a show to write and you're calling some girl collect?

MILT. *(To Val.)* Collette! Her name is Collette, not *collect.* Why don't you go to Berlitz and drive them crazy?

VAL. Hey! This is not a day to get me angry, Milt, I swear to God.

MILT. Alright, put me down for Wednesday. *(Into phone.)* Yes, I'm holding.

VAL. (*Looks at his watch.*) Where is everyone? Five after ten and we haven't put two lousy words down on paper.

MILT. He's right. Hey, Luke. Put two lousy words down on paper. (*Into phone.*) Collette? Milt. Listen, babe. We'll have to cancel tonight. It's my wife's birthday. Unless I can convince her she's wrong.

> (*The door opens and BRIAN DOYLE enters, a lit cigarette in his mouth. HE wears a rumpled dark tweed jacket with baggy pants. HE is starting to get bald but HE has newly made dots on his scalp from a recent hair transplant. HE is Irish, about twenty-nine, a heavy smoker, a heavy cougher and a heavy drinker, but with a biting sense of humor as caustic as his outlook on life.*)

VAL. Brian! Jesus! You picked a bad time to come late.

BRIAN. I'm sorry. I just stopped to—(*HE coughs.*) I stopped to—(*HE coughs again, almost uncontrollably, then stops.*) I stopped to get some cigarettes. (*Hangs up his coat.*)

LUCAS. (*To audience.*) Brian Doyle. Good guy, good writer, lousy smoker.

MILT. Hey, guys. Please. I'm cheating on the phone here and I can't hear a Goddamn thing.

VAL. That's it, dammit! Dot's a fifty-dollar fine.

MILT. I gotta go, honey. They just raised the rates. I'll call you. (*HE hangs up.*) Oh, Brian's smiling. Something happened. He met someone at the convent.

BRIAN. Five days! Count 'em, guys, that's all you get. Because on Friday this good-lookin' Irishman is leaving the show. The Gentile makes good.

LUCAS. Where you going?

BRIAN. I think they call it—Hollywood? Sold my screenplay to Metro. MGM? You must have heard of it.

LUCAS. MGM? That's great!!!

VAL. Every week he's leaving the show on Friday. Every week he's flying to Hollywood. Every week he sold a screenplay to MGM or Twentieth Century Fox.

MILT. Not Fox. *Fucks!* I keep telling you.

(*BRIAN enters humming.*)

VAL. That's it! I want a sketch started immediately right now before Max gets here. Who knows what shape he'll be in? Lucas, get *Newsweek, Time, Life,* every magazine. See what's in the news. Milt, see what ideas we got on the board. See what's a hit picture. Maybe there's a Marlo Brandon movie Max can do.

(*MILT takes idea board off the wall.*)

LUCAS. Marlon Brando.
VAL. What did I say?
LUCAS. Marlo Brandon.
VAL. My way was funnier.

(*BRIAN has pulled a piece of cake off with his fingers.*)

VAL. Hey, Brian. When you're through destroying the pound cake, maybe you'll find time to come up with an idea.
BRIAN. (*To Lucas.*) Come here, Luke. These guys still don't believe me.

(*BRIAN takes out a small piece of paper. HE hands it to LUCAS.
LUCAS looks at it.*)

BRIAN. That's history, kid. Right up there with David Selznick buying *Gone With the Wind.* Go on. Read it.
LUCAS. (*Reads small note paper.*) "Your agent called and said MGM will get back to you."

(*LUCAS, MILT and VAL look at each other.*)

VAL. . . . Go on. We're listening.
LUCAS. That's it.
MILT. That's it? "MGM will get back to you" is a deal? . . .
BRIAN. I got a call from the coast last night. They sign the contract soon as they okay the script.
LUCAS. They didn't okay it yet?

BRIAN. They'll okay it as soon as they read it.

LUCAS. They didn't read it yet?

BRIAN. They'll read it when I write it.

MILT. *You didn't write it yet?*

BRIAN. *(Points to his head with index finger.)* Here! It's all up here! Every page, every word, every comma.

VAL. They made a deal for your finger pointing to your head?

BRIAN. You jealous bastards. I told the idea to my agent, my agent told it to MGM. The whole studio is crazy about it. You see these guys, Luke? Thirty years from now they'll be writing game shows and I'll be VP of MGM, screwing Lana Turner.

MILT. When she's sixty-two? Why?

VAL. I categorically resent your remarks. Dis is without a doubt, the finest writing staff in the history of television. And I would rather stay here till my prostate falls out before I ever sold out to the dreck and garbage of Hollywood. God's truth, even if they asked me.

BRIAN. What if they asked you?

VAL. I'm open to everything. You can tell them.

(KENNY FRANKS walks in. Neatly dressed, sports jacket, tie, raincoat, tortoise-shell-framed glasses. HE is surely the most sophisticated of the lot.)

KENNY. *(Holding up* Time *magazine.)* Did you see this? This week's *Time* magazine? Pope Pius approves of psychoanalysis . . . This means from now on Confession will be eighty bucks an hour . . .

LUCAS. *(To audience.)* Kenny Franks, boy genius. They say he was writing jokes for Jack Benny when he was fourteen. I wasn't allowed to stay *up* for Jack Benny when I was fourteen.

VAL. *(Looks at the* Time *magazine that Kenny put on desk.)* You think maybe this Pope thing would make a sketch for us?

KENNY. Well, I think we'd all have to take Communion first.

BRIAN. Take it. It beats circumcision.

(KENNY pours hot water into a mug, puts tea bag in it, then lets it cool.)

MILT. *(To Brian.)* What the hell would a Gentile like you know about circumcision? *(To others.)* Did you ever see him in the men's room? He pisses straight up the wall.

(KENNY takes a pill with a cup of water.)

MILT. So, Mr. Vitamin, what kind of pill are we taking today?
KENNY. Nicotine tablets. *(HE drinks it down.)* Now I can get cancer without having to smoke.

(Brian laughs. Kenny stirs his tea.)

KENNY. How you doing, Luke?
LUCAS. I don't know. Nobody tells me.
KENNY. Don't worry. Max thinks you're going to be great.
LUCAS. Did he say so?
KENNY. No, but I'll tell him he did. He doesn't remember. *(HE sips his tea.)*
VAL. *(To Kenny.)* Did you hear about Max calling me at twelve A.M. midnight?
KENNY. Did you know he called *me* at eleven-thirty?
VAL. *Max* did?
KENNY. He was sitting in his den, piss drunk with a loaded shot-gun on his lap.
VAL. Son of a bitch. He told you this?
KENNY. Well, it sort of dribbled out of his mouth, but I got most of it.
VAL. Son of a bitch.
LUCAS. He had a loaded gun?
KENNY. He said he got another threatening letter in his mailbox last night.
MILT. It wasn't me. I sent my letter last week.
VAL. Son of a bitch. Did he call the police?
KENNY. Well, he said he was taking the matter in his own hands. It's him against them now.
BRIAN. Son of a bitch. Sorry, Val. There was one open.
VAL. *(To Kenny.)* What do you mean, him against them? Who's them? Did he say?

KENNY. The man was on tranquilizers and scotch. Every time he talked he blew bubbles.

LUCAS. Tranquilizers?

MILT. (*To Lucas.*) Max gets in his limo every night, after work, takes two tranquilizers the size of hand grenades and washes them down with a ladle full of scotch. His driver helps him into his house and he falls asleep on the floor of his den next to his dogs.

BRIAN. Exactly. That's why there are no letters. The man is paranoid.

VAL. Maybe Brian's right. Remember when Max accused his next door neighbor of shooting up the tires on his Cadillac?

BRIAN. Hey, guys. Max shoots up the tires himself. We all know that.

LUCAS. Why would he do that?

BRIAN. He has a gun. He has a Cadillac. He's free on Sundays. Why not?

LUCAS. Does Max have any enemies?

KENNY. Besides himself, I don't think so.

LUCAS. What do you mean?

KENNY. Nobody hates Max the way Max hates Max.

BRIAN. I love it when you talk like Gertrude Stein.

KENNY. (*To Lucas.*) They don't get it. We *write* comedy. Max *does* comedy. It's his ass out there in front of the cameras every week.

MILT. Is that his ass? No wonder he gets such big laughs.

VAL. No. Kenny's right. Max likes it in here, with us, not out there. The funniest man since Chaplin and he still throws up before every show.

BRIAN. For twenty-five grand a week, I'd put my fingers down my throat.

MILT. Hey, Brian. Don't ever knock Max in this room. He puts bread on my kids' plates and he's transplanted every hair on your head. (*HE takes Brian's cap off, revealing transplants.*)

BRIAN. (*Touches his hair.*) If I didn't tell you, you'd never know.

KENNY. So what are the dots on your head for? Tic-tac-toe?

MILT. I hear transplants grow in like pubic hair. That means you'll have to get a zipper for your face.

BRIAN. Gee, I'm really going to miss you guys in Hollywood.

(The OTHERS react.)

KENNY. Oh, Jeez. He sold another script? What putz studio bought it this time?

LUCAS. MGM.

KENNY. For how much?

BRIAN. Seventy-five grand.

KENNY. No, I mean how much you want to bet you're full of shit?

BRIAN. Name your price.

KENNY. Five hundred bucks if you win. If you lose, we all get to pull out your transplants . . .

(CAROL WYMAN enters, carrying a shoulder bag. SHE's about twenty-eight, with a strong and quick defense system that comes with being the only female writer on the staff.)

CAROL. *(Excited.)* Have you guys heard the news?

(THEY just stare at her.)

CAROL. . . . Of course not. No one else here cares about what's going on in this country. Am I the only one here who takes an interest in something besides jokes and cars and money and baseball?

ALL except VAL. *(THEY look at each other and nod.)* Yeah, you're the only one . . . Right . . . You got it . . . You do it, we're busy.

VAL. What's the news?

CAROL. I just heard it in the taxi. Joe McCarthy called General George Marshall a Communist.

VAL. Un-focking-believable.

CAROL. He calls a five-star General of the Army a card-carrying Communist.

BRIAN. Even if he *was* a Communist, why would he have cards printed up?

CAROL. Hey, children. Wake up. Time for school . . . You think this is a joke? America's on the brink of becoming a fascist state and this doesn't worry you?

BRIAN. McCarthy's a nut case. A drunken fanatic. How long you think he's going to last?

VAL. Some of them lasted long enough to kill six million Jews.

BRIAN. Hey, I met hotheads like McCarthy. He'll start a fight in an Irish bar one night and get a dart right between the eyes.

CAROL. I feel so badly for General Marshall. Such a nice man. Such a sweet face. Of all names to pick, why him?

MILT. I don't know. Val, did you ever see Marshall at any of the meetings?

VAL. ARE YOU OUT OF YOUR FOCKING MIND??? You don't make jokes like dot. Some secretary outside hears dot and the next thing I'm being subpoenaed in Washington.

CAROL. Val is right. No Communist jokes. None of us are safe today. *(SHE whispers.)* They got that blacklist thing, you know.

MILT. They got what?

CAROL. *(Whispers.)* Blacklist. Blacklist.

KENNY. Three bags full.

CAROL. Don't you guys realize they can put anyone—*(Whispers.)*—on the blacklist they want.

LUCAS. Without proof?

KENNY. In a second. They've got a wait list to get on the blacklist.

MILT. Not if you tip the maître d'.

CAROL. I can't believe they think this is funny. Did any of you see Edward R. Murrow last night?

MILT. I don't live in his neighborhood.

CAROL. What do I have to do to impress you this is serious?

MILT. Well, the whispering was good.

CAROL. Two top U.S. Senators told Murrow the FBI were tapping their phones.

VAL. You see? Same as Russia. First the politicians, then they go after the arts. The writers first because they're the intellectuals.

BRIAN. Well, this room looks pretty safe.

CAROL. You think so? Whoever has access to the public is McCarthy's enemy. That's us. *(Whispers.)* I bet they have a bug in this room right now.

MILT. Well, you leave crumbs, you're gonna have bugs.

(VAL glares at him.)

MILT. It was a political joke. I thought you'd like it.

KENNY. . . . Don't you see, you're playing right into McCarthy's hands. Fear through intimidation.

MILT. He doesn't intimidate you? A United States senator who giggles like Porky the Pig?

VAL. My God, this is a terrible time for all of us.

BRIAN. *(Looks at his watch.)* Twenty after ten, he's right.

CAROL. Oh, my God. Oh, Jesus, no.

VAL. *What?*

CAROL. I have a cousin. My mother's nephew. A nice, sweet, stupid boy. He was a Communist in college for three months, then he quit. What would I do if they asked me about him?

VAL. You take the Fifth Amendment.

MILT. Or the Sixth Avenue subway. You get off in China.

KENNY. Okay, guys. Enough. We're heading into the Cancer Zone of humor.

CAROL. You know how Max hates McCarthy. Wait'll he hears about this.

BRIAN. Wait'll you hear about Max.

CAROL. What?

LUCAS. He got a threatening letter.

CAROL. From McCarthy?

BRIAN. No. He writes them himself.

VAL. You don't know that.

KENNY. *(To Carol.)* He called me last night. Had one of his scotch-tranquilizer combos. Sitting there with a loaded shotgun on his lap.

VAL. Said he was going to shoot the bastards.

CAROL. Hasn't he got those two hunting dogs? Maybe that's all it is. He was just going to go hunting.

KENNY. Those dogs don't hunt. They point to food in supermarkets.

VAL. Okay, God forgive me for mentioning this word . . . Nervous breakdown.

MILT. That's two words. God'll never forgive you.

KENNY. Wait a minute. Let's not go off half-cocked . . . First one who makes a joke on that is in trouble.

MILT. Listen, if you're half-cocked, you're in *enough* trouble. *(Milt looks at Val, then Kenny, then takes a sip of coffee.)*

KENNY. Has Max ever missed a show? Has Max ever missed a rehearsal? Has Max ever missed a writing session? Never. He's in this room with us every day. Never an ego-inflated shit like most of the comics we've all worked with. Max is a professional. He's dependable. He's reliable. He's eccentric but he's not crazy.

VAL. Then why, for the first time, is he a half hour late?

KENNY. He probably stopped to shoot his dogs, his toes and his tires. But he'll be here.

(The PHONE rings.)

CAROL. *(Picks up phone.)* Hello? . . . Oh. Hi. Where are you? *(Covering mouthpiece.)* It's Ira. He's running late at his analyst's.

MILT. I thought his analyst died.

CAROL. He met another one at the funeral. *(Into phone.)* Ira, just get here, we have problems. *(SHE hangs up.)*

LUCAS. *(To audience.)* Ira Stone was a hypochondriac who came in late every day with a new ailment. His greatest wish in life was to have a virus named after him.

(The PHONE rings again.)

LUCAS. *(He picks up phone.)* Hello? . . . Oh. Okay. Thanks, Helen. *(HE hangs up quickly.)* Max just walked in. He stopped off in the john.

VAL. *(Nervously.)* Alright. Everybody calm down. Relax. What do we say to him?

CAROL. Do we mention anything about the letters or the loaded shotgun?

LUCAS. He must know because he told Kenny last night.

VAL. We should make a quick decision what we say. How long you think he's going to pee in there?

BRIAN. My friend had a German shepherd who flew from Paris to New York. When he landed, he peed for two hours and ten minutes.

LUCAS. Can you imagine what Lindbergh must have done?

VAL. You know what? I don't want the responsibility of being head writer anymore. I swear to God. I quit. Carol, you're head writer.

CAROL. I'm trying to get pregnant. I have enough to worry about.

BRIAN. Ask your husband. Why should *we* do everything?

(The door opens. MAX PRINCE enters. HE is in his early thirties. HE wears a trench coat over a gray double-breasted suit, black shoes, a white shirt and tie. HE appears to be taller than HE is because HE exudes great strength. His strength comes more from his anger than from his physique. HE dominates a room with his personality. You must watch him because HE's like a truck you can't get out of the way of. HE is quixotic, changing quickly from warm, infectious laughter to sullen anger. HE is often monosyllabic, offering a word or two to convey his thoughts. Today is not a good day for Max. HE storms across the room almost oblivious to them.)

VAL. Oh, just talking about you, Max. We were saying the response to Saturday's show was unbelievably good. Maybe the best ever.

CAROL. I got at least twenty phone calls.

MILT. I made ten myself, that's how good it was.

MAX. *(Paces angrily.)* Any reports on the show?

VAL. *(A little bewildered.)* Yes, Max. Unbelievably good. Maybe the best ever.

MAX. *(Still pacing.)* What did they say?

VAL. . . . They said unbelievably good. Maybe the best ever.

MAX. Mug. *(HE hangs up his trench coat.)*

LUCAS. What?

MAX. Mug.

VAL. *(To Lucas.)* Mug. He wants coffee in his mug. No cream, four sugars.

LUCAS. Oh right, Max. *(HE quickly goes to get the coffee.)*

MAX. Did we get any more memos from NBC?

VAL. What?

MAX. Memos! Memos! They love to send memos.

VAL. No, Max. No memos.

MAX. *(Mocks acting hurt.)* No memos? They skipped a day without memos? They're saving them so they can memo me to death. They'll bury me in a folded memo in the Mount Memo Cemetery in Memo Park, New Jersey.

LUCAS. *(Comes back with coffee.)* Here's your coffee, Max. Be careful. It's very hot.

MAX. *(HE takes cup and then drinks it all down without stopping.)* WHOOOOOOOH . . . that was hot.

VAL. You shouldn't drink hot things so fast, Max.

MILT. No. It's good. Boils the blood.

CAROL. You want an aspirin, Max?

MAX. Took a bottle at home.

BRIAN. Well, a bottle of aspirin should clear it up.

CAROL. Did you get any sleep last night, Max?

MAX. Oh, yeah. Slept like a bear.

KENNY. Those bear sleeps are great, heh, Max? You wake up in April, May, you feel like a million.

(MAX laughs and unzips his pants, taking them off over his shoes. Holding his pants and jacket HE crosses to the door and yells out:)

MAX. *HELEN! I'M READY!!*

HELEN'S VOICE. Coming, Max.

MAX. *(To others.)* We work today. Lotsa work. I want to do a great show this week. NO!! Not a great show. The best. Best show we ever did, you hear?

MILT. Sure, Max. It's always good to change it once in a while.

(MAX is standing in his shirt, shorts, socks, shoes and garters. HELEN enters. SHE is an attractive secretary, late twenties. MAX hands her his jacket and pants.)

MAX. Dry cleaned and pressed.

HELEN. Like always, Max.

MAX. And check my pockets. I don't want my keys pressed.

HELEN. Yes, Max. Oh, Mr. Revere of NBC sent you a big pile of memos.

(MAX looks furiously at the others. HELEN leaves with his suit and closes door. MAX crosses to his rack, gets his trench coat, puts it on.)

MAX. Ohhhhkay! . . . They started, we'll finish. You all heard it. NBC fired the first shot. Remember this day, everyone. A day that will live in infamy . . . March 6th, 1953.

BRIAN. . . . It's March 8th, Max.

MAX. *(Glares at him.)* What are you, a historian? . . . March 6th, March 8th, March 12th, who gives a damn? . . . *(HE sits, lights his cigar.)* The battle has started. The lines have been drawn. Now we have to plan our counterattack.

CAROL. *(To Kenny.)* What's it about?

KENNY. *(Shrugs, then to Max.)* What's up, Max?

MAX. What's up? What's not down is up . . . What's up could be down, what's down could be up. You understand?

KENNY. Certainly. It's Newton's Theory of Obscurity, isn't it?

MAX. *(Lights his cigar.)* They want to cut the show down to an hour.

CAROL. An *hour*?

VAL. Us?? We're the number one show in the country. Maybe two, three the worst.

MAX. Cutting us down. Right at the kneecaps. Chop chop chop chop chop.

KENNY. Can't you reason with these people, Max?

MAX. What people? NBC is not a people. They're not like us. They wear black socks up to their necks. Crew neck socks . . . They come home from work and before dinner, they dance with their wives . . . They put up wallpaper in their garages . . . You can't talk to them.

KENNY. Then what is it they want?

MAX. Alright. *(HE holds up his cigar.)* . . . What is this I'm smoking?

(THEY ALL look at each other.)

BRIAN. I'll take a chance, guys . . . *(To Max.)* A cigar?

MAX. Wrong.

BRIAN. Damn. I thought I had it.

MAX. *(To Brian.)* To *us* it's a cigar. To them it's power. To them it's control. To them it's grabbing our testicles and *squeezing* them. *(HE grabs them and squeezes, grimacing in pain. MAX then turns to Carol and squeezes his testicles.)* You understand?

(LUCAS and MILT look toward Carol.)

MILT. *(Aside to Carol.)* I'll explain what that feels like later.

VAL. Forgive me, Max. I don't mean to interrupt. Let me see if I can understand . . . The cigar is a phallic symbol, i.e., the penis . . . i.e., the penis is power, i.e., the penis is control. Right?

MAX. *(Nods.)* I ee I ee oh!

KENNY. So NBC is using their power to control us, right, Max? To do what?

MAX. To cut out my HEART! They want to cut the budget, save money. He says the show is too sophisticated. Too smart, he says. My own sister, my own brother, two people who never graduated from *spelling,* understand every word. The big money sponsors want out, he says. What do they sell? Raisins? Macaroni? Cream cheese? People who eat and chew can't understand this program? . . . Who does he think we're playing for, dogs and cats?

CAROL. Can they just say that, Max? "From now on you've got an hour and that's it"?

MAX. They can say what they want . . . let 'em. But I've got a plan.

CAROL. What's the plan, Max?

MAX. Okay. Close the doors.

LUCAS. *(Looks.)* The doors are closed, Max.

(MAX leans forward in his chair. Motions to them to lean in. THEY ALL do.)

MAX. When the Thracians fought the battle of the Modena Heights in 354 B.C., outnumbered by a hundred thousand men, what did Cyclantis, the greatest military mind in all of history, decide to do?

(THEY ALL look at each other again.)

MILT. *(To Carol.)* Was Cyclantis the giant with the big eyes?

VAL. Will you let the man finish? . . . What did Cyclantis do, Max?

MAX. He sent out one hundred women, old, young, whatever . . . placed them ten miles apart in a—in a—*(Makes circle with his finger.)*

KENNY. A circle?

MAX. (*Nods.*) A circle . . . covering two hundred miles. Then in the dead of night, each of the hundred women lit a—lit a—(*Makes upward hand gesture.*)

VAL. An umbrella?

MAX. A *torch*. Big torches . . . An umbrella? The enemy saw the torches all around them, thought they were surrounded, threw down their arms and sounded surrender. Y'hear? The surrounded sounded surrender . . . and that's what we're going to do.

MILT. Get a hundred women with torches and surround Rockefeller Center?

(*VAL glares at him.*)

MILT. I'm just asking. I was never *in* the army.

BRIAN. I say we just kill the fuckers.

MAX. You got it.

KENNY. Can you tell us *exactly* what NBC did, Max?

MAX. They sent me their Declaration of War. In the mail. Delivered to the house where my wife and children sleep. There's going to be blood spilled. Oh, yes. But not in my house. Their palaces will crumble and their kings will fall and their wheat fields will be scorched.

MILT. (*Aside to Carol.*) NBC has wheat fields?

KENNY. Let me ask you, Max. Is it NBC who's been sending you the threatening letters?

MAX. Who told you about that?

KENNY. You did. Last night. You called me, remember?

MAX. I called *you*?

KENNY. Yes.

MAX. Last night?

KENNY. Right.

MAX. That was you?

KENNY. I swear.

MAX. It didn't sound like you.

KENNY. I tried my best, Max.

MAX. You sounded foreign to me. Spanish maybe.

VAL. That was my maid from Peru.

MAX. She was at Kenny's house?

VAL. No. In *my* house. You called me after you called Kenny.

MAX. I never spoke to you.

VAL. No. I was at the theater.

MAX. I called you at the theater?

VAL. No. You called me at my house. I went to the theater. In the Village. The Peach. The Pear. The Plum.

LUCAS. The Cherry Lane.

VAL. The Cherry Lane. Thank you.

MAX. *(To Lucas.)* You were with Val?

LUCAS. No. I was at home. With my wife.

MAX. I called you at home?

LUCAS. No. Not me. Val wanted to know what theater he went to and I told him.

MAX. Val called you to ask what theater he was in?

LUCAS. No. He already came home. He asked me this morning.

MAX. I didn't even know you were married.

LUCAS. Well, this is the first time we ever talked.

MAX. *(Holds his head.)* I can't remember anything. I think somebody's drugging me, I swear to God.

VAL. Well, Max, that brings up another delicate subject.

MAX. I fell asleep the other night with my eyes open. I thought I was dreaming about a ceiling.

VAL. In the first place, Max, you know we all love you.

MAX. Sometimes I go in the kitchen in the middle of the night, get a hammer and smash walnuts. Why would I do that?

KENNY. I think Freud says that's a symptom of fear.

MAX. Why? I'm not afraid of walnuts . . . You want to hear the worst part?

CAROL. I thought we did, Max.

MAX. When I eat, I can't tell the difference between steak and fish anymore. Why is that? *(He is near tears.)*

BRIAN. Where did they catch your steak, Max?

(MAX glares at Brian. BRIAN looks away.)

MAX. *(To Val.)* What was the delicate subject?

VAL. Well, it's just that we feel for your own good, Max, for your own health, for your family's well-being . . .

MAX. I don't want to hear my fortune. I just want to hear the delicate subject.

KENNY. We don't think those pills you take before you leave here at night are good for you, Max.

MAX. *(Confused.)* What pills?

VAL. The pills, Max. That you take before you go home.

MAX. I take pills? What are you talking about? Those tranquilizers? They're prescription. Two little pills.

KENNY. *Little* pills? We could play nine innings of soft ball with one pill.

MAX. I hardly take them. Once a week.

BRIAN. You take them once a week every night, Max.

MAX. They're harmless. Carol, remember you weren't feeling well one night? I gave you half a pill. Did anything happen?

CAROL. I don't remember. I slept for nine days.

KENNY. It's not just the pills. It's the four jiggers of scotch you take to wash them down. Pills and liquor don't mix, Max. Or max, Mix, however you want.

MAX. I gotta sleep. If I don't sleep, who's gonna protect my family from them?

CAROL. NBC is threatening your family?

MAX. They're threatening my show. My show is my life. If they threaten my life, they threaten my family. You want to hear the letter they sent me? You want to know what they said, word for word for word?

MILT. Go ahead, Max. The doors are still closed.

MAX. *(Leans back in his chair, looks at his cigar.)* . . . They said . . . "Give the people shit."

(THEY ALL look at each other.)

CAROL. The president of NBC said that?

MAX. You heard me. "Give the people shit."

BRIAN. You mean as a gift?

CAROL. Why would he say that, Max?

MAX. Because—they can make money on shit. A pot full. Drive up to Connecticut, they got big Tudor shit houses wherever you look, that's why they invented television. They put shit on for people to watch, they advertise shit, the people run out and buy the shit, their kids break the shit, so they buy them more shit and the shit moguls go to France in the summer and the poor people stay here and watch more shit . . . That's why I got a letter saying, "Give the people shit."

MILT. (*Aside to Carol.*) Isn't that what Marie Antoinette said?

CAROL. (*Swatting Milt.*) Why do you always talk to *me*? Annoy somebody else once in a while.

KENNY. Let me take a whack at this. For four years in a row we sweep the Emmy Awards. Every critic in the country loves us. But suddenly television is expanding. They're going into the Midwest, the south. Different kinds of audience. They want to watch quiz shows, bowling, wrestling, am I right?

MAX. (*Nods.*) If you got shit, shovel it over.

KENNY. So they want to cut us to an hour. Don't make the shows too esoteric. Too smart. Don't do take-offs on Japanese movies, Italian movies.

MAX. Feed a horse hay, what are you going to get?

CAROL. You don't even have to say it, Max.

KENNY. So it's not only cutting the half hour, it's the kind of show they want us to do.

VAL. Can't we talk to them, Max?

MAX. Talk? No! No talk! Fight! We fight them on the sea, we fight them on the beaches. Or we'll get the bastards in an alley in Brooklyn somewhere. Remember what Churchill said? "Never have so many given so much for so long for so little for so few for so seldom" . . . (*HE nods to others . . . then MAX crosses to the coffee table and pours water into a paper cup. HE carries it back then sips it.*)

CAROL. My God! This ties up with everything that's going on in this country today. The censorship. The blacklisting. It's Senator McCarthy publicly disgracing a man like General George Marshall.

MAX. (*Spitting out water.*) What?? What did he say about Marshall?

CAROL. You didn't hear? It was on the radio all morning.

MAX. (*Crushes the paper cup. Water erupts.*) What'd he say? I want to hear it exactly. Say it slowly, I don't want to miss a word. (*MAX crosses to his chair, takes a final sip from his crushed cup and puts it on the coffee table.*)

CAROL. Joe McCarthy accused General George Marshall, a five-star general of the army, of being a member of the Communist Party.

(*MAX squeezes the arm of his chair so tightly, a piece breaks off. HE gets up, so angry, we can see the veins in his neck.*)

MILT. (*Aside.*) Somebody trade places with me.

(*MAX moves around, seething.*)

VAL. We know how you feel, Max. We feel the same way.

MAX. You feel the same way I do? . . . I don't think so. Would you like to know how I feel? Ask me. Ask me how I feel about McCarthy.

CAROL. Don't ask him, Val. I'm afraid to see.

MAX. You don't want to see, don't look. (*To Val.*) Ask me how I feel.

VAL. We can already *see* how you feel, Max.

MAX. (*To Val.*) Not yet. When you ask me, then you'll see . . . *Ask me!!*

(*MAX's hand beckons strongly to be asked. KENNY, who sits between Max and Val, turns slowly to Val.*)

VAL. How do you feel about McCarthy, Max?

MAX. Thank you. (*HE turns and smashes his fist through the wall. His hand remains in the hole. It's the wall that had the sketch ideas before MILT took it down.*) There! That's how I feel.

CAROL. Oh, my God!

VAL. Are you alright, Max?

BRIAN. Someone go in the other room and see how McCarthy is.

MAX. They want me to give them shit? There! I gave them shit.

VAL. Can you get your hand out, Max?

MAX. *LEAVE IT THERE!!* Get a knife. Cut if off. Send it in a box to that no good bastard. Let him know what I think of him.

CAROL. Someone get his hand out. It could be broken.

(*MAX pulls it out. It is still in a fist.*)

MAX. *(Calls out.)* HELEN!! GET IN HERE!! *(To Carol.)* Called him a Communist, heh? *(HE looks around.)* I want to hit something. Something big. Something expensive.

MILT. There's a bank across the street, Max.

HELEN. *(Rushes in.)* Yes, Max?

MAX. *(Points.)* You see this hole? Don't touch it. Leave it there. Call up a framer. No. Call Tiffany's. I want that hole framed in their *best* silver. And underneath I want a plaque. Gold! And on the plaque I want engraved, "In honor of General George Marshall, Soldier, Statesman, Slandered by that son of a bitch McCarthy."

HELEN. *(Writes this down.)* I'm not sure that Tiffany's would print that, Max.

MAX. You pay 'em enough, they'll print it.

HELEN. Yes, Max. *(SHE rushes out.)*

(BRIAN, who has exited Stage Left, sticks his head through the hole in the wall.)

BRIAN. I think this could be a national monument. Like Monticello.

MAX. *(An idea hits him.)* OKAY!! OKAY, I GOT THE SKETCH FOR THIS WEEK'S SHOW.

KENNY. What is it, Max?

MAX. I want to be the Statue of Liberty. I want to wear a long gown down to my toes.

VAL. I like that.

MAX. With big sandals. And a tiara. With a torch and a book. I want to be painted green. With bird shit on my shoulders from the pigeons. And I'm standing on this box that says, "Give me your poor, your hungry, your sunburned, your toothless" . . . whatever they got there.

MILT. We'll look it up.

VAL. Goddammit, dot's funny, Max.

KENNY. And what happens?

MAX. She gets subpoenaed. To Washington. She comes in the courtroom, the bottom of her dress is dripping wet from the harbor. With codfish in her hair. *(HE "squeezes" water out of imaginary bottom of dress.)*

LUCAS. This is terrific.

MAX. And he's sitting up there looking at her. Senator Joseph McNutcake.

KENNY. *McNutcake?* . . . We can't say that, Max. Not on the air.

MAX. You don't think it's funny?

KENNY. Yes, it's funny. I don't think eight years in jail would be funny. You can't say McNutcake.

MAX. (*Thinks.*) How about McBirdbrain? . . . McFruithead? . . . McFahrblungett. It means crazy in Yiddish, he'll never understand it.

VAL. Someone'll tell him.

MAX. So we do nothing? Is that what you all want to do? Nothing?

MILT. I don't think having a long life is nothing, Max.

MAX. Where I grew up, we took care of bullies. There was a big fat shlub in my class. We called him Tank Ass. He used to steal my sister's lunch. One day I put a rock in her sandwich. That taught him.

CAROL. He bit into it?

MAX. He ate it. The whole rock. He had to start wearing iron underwear. We gotta do *something*, guys.

VAL. We feel the same as you, Max.

MAX. No, you don't, you don't know how I feel.

MILT. (*To Val.*) Don't ask him. It'll look like Swiss cheese in here.

MAX. I'm not lying down. I'm not doing nothing. We gotta make some kind of stand, like Spartacus in the war against the Byzanti-mums.

VAL. So what do you suggest we do, Max?

MAX. We quit. We tell them to keep their show and put on shit seven days a week. We walk out of here in single file, our hands up in the air like the heroes of Bataan . . . We're off the air as of today. No show Saturday!! . . . That's what Patrick Henry said.

VAL. He said no show Saturday?

(*MAX glares at him.*)

KENNY. If we walk, Max, they'll sue us.

MAX. Listen, are we together or not? Because if someone here doesn't want to quit, I don't want him here. He can leave.

MILT. That'll show him, Max.

MAX. I'm calling them now. (*HE crosses to phone. HE picks up the phone.*) Helen, get me NBC. (*Hand over the mouthpiece.*)

MILT. Think of it this way, Max. If we go off the air, isn't there a good chance they'll find someone *else* who doesn't mind giving them shit?

MAX. Someone else's shit isn't mine . . . Do you know who said that?

CAROL. Tell us, Max. We'll get it wrong.

MAX. It's in the Bible. You have to look for it.

BRIAN. Someone else's shit isn't mine is in the Bible, Max? Where?

MAX. Bottom of page 162. You think I memorized the whole Bible, for crise sakes?

KENNY. Max, it's a dumb idea. You've worked your whole life for this show. You think ABC or CBS are any different? They have corporate minds, Max. If they could get a TV set to turn out sausages, we'd all be pigs instead of writers. They're not interested in culture. Maybe if Van Gogh and Goya were wrestlers, they'd put them on Friday nights. But if we quit, Max, they win. We give up an hour and a half to *Miss America* and *Beat the Clock* . . . We stay, Max. We do what we've been doing for years. Only we do it better. And we keep doing it. And you know why, Max? Because maybe we'll never have this much fun again in our entire lives.

(Silence. MAX hangs up the phone and sits.)

MAX. I served under General Marshall in the war. We were together in the European front.

MILT. I thought you were in the navy, Max. Playing in a band.

MAX. *(Slowly looks at Milt.)* . . . He came to a dance I played in London. He was fox trotting ten feet away from me. I played a saxophone solo in his honor.

HELEN. *(Comes in.)* He's on the phone, Max. Mr.—you know. NBC. He's waiting.

MAX. *(Rising.)* I'll take it up in my office.

(HELEN leaves, MAX crosses to door.)

MAX. We're not pulling down our flag. I will not break my sword over my knee for anyone. When the Roman legions, led by Augustus the Fourth, fled in defeat, he came back to win on Novembus the Fifth. (*HE thinks about that, wonders if HE got it right, nods and leaves.*)

BRIAN. I think someone's got to get word to President Lincoln.

MILT. Personally, I think we're one phone call away from a career in the garment center.

LUCAS. (*Crossing to buffet.*) Anyone mind if I take some bagels home? Just in case?

KENNY. Why don't we just go back to work and write something?

VAL. What have I been saying all morning?

MILT. Focking pompernickel.

HELEN. (*Enters quickly.*) Listen. Ira is here. He's washing his face. He doesn't look very good to me. (*The PHONE rings Off Right.*) Oooh, I hear my phone ringing. (*SHE rushes Off.*)

KENNY. (*Gets up.*) Alright, listen, everybody. Ira's going to walk in here with his Special Ailment of the day. Pneumonia, phlebitis, cataracts, whatever. No matter what he says, we pay no attention. If he faints at our feet, just let him lay there.

CAROL. That's so cruel, Kenny.

KENNY. As cruel as making us listen to his complaints every day? I don't think so.

LUCAS. (*Who has been near the door.*) Here he comes. (*HE rushes back to others.*)

KENNY. (*Softly.*) Remember. Just stare at him. (*HE sits.*)

(*IRA STONE enters. HE is all energy with a touch of brilliant madness. HE wears a topcoat and scarf.*)

IRA. (*Holds his chest.*) I can't breathe. I can't catch my breath. I think it's a heart attack. It could be a stroke. Don't panic, just do what I tell you. (*HE sits with his coat on. HE talks breathlessly.*) Call Columbia Presbyterian Hospital. Ask for Dr. Milton Bruckman. Tell him I got a sharp stabbing pain down my left arm, across my chest, down my back into my left leg. If he's in surgery, call Dr. Frank Banzerini at St. John's Hospital, sixth floor, cardiology. Tell him I suddenly got this burning sensation in my stomach. At first I thought it was breakfast. I had smoked salmon. It was still smoking. It didn't feel right going down. If his line is busy, call the Clayton and Marcus Pharmacy on 72nd and Madison. Ask for Al. Tell him I need a refill on my prescription from Dr. Schneider. I can't remember the drug. Zodioprotozoc. No. Vasco something. Vasco da Dama, what the hell was it? I can't get air to my brain . . . This scarf is choking me, get it off my neck. (*HE pulls it off, throws it away. NO ONE has moved. THEY've all been through this before.*) Don't call my wife . . . No, maybe you should call her. But don't tell her it's a stroke. If she thinks it's a stroke, she'll call my mother. I have no time to talk to my mother, she drives me crazy. (*HE begins to hyperventilate and wheeze, looking to the others who just stare.*) This could be it, I swear to God. (*HE still wheezes, then looks at Kenny.*) Why are you just sitting there? What the hell are you waiting for?

KENNY. For you to die or finish your instructions, whichever comes first.

IRA. (*He gets up.*) You think this is a joke? You think this is funny? You think I would walk in here with a pain so bad, I—wait a minute! (*HE holds his chest.*) Wait a minute! . . . Hold it! Wait a minute! (*HE doesn't move.*) Ohhh. OHHH . . . I just passed gas! Thank God! I thought it was all over for me. Whoo.

MILT. Gets up, disgusted.) Jee-sus!!

CAROL. (*To Ira.*) I hope you die. I hope you have a stroke right now and die. I hope your mother comes and sees you and *talks to you for* an hour before you die!!!

IRA. You're *angry*? You're upset that I'm still *alive*? What is this, Nazi Germany? Let's kill another Jew?

VAL. Yes. In this case I would make an exception.

IRA. Oh. Okay. fine. Now I know who my friends are.

BRIAN. Friends? What friends? You have no friends. There isn't a puppy in the world who would come out of the *pound* to live with you.

IRA. (*To Brian.*) Hey, wait a minute. From *them* I take. You haven't earned the right. Because of one Goddamn Irish potato famine, I have to put up with you?

BRIAN. You have the nerve to walk in here, telling us you're having a stroke and think you can fart your way out of this?

IRA. (*To others.*) I had a little scare. I didn't know what it was. I'm sorry. I apologize to everyone in this room. (*To Brian.*) Except to him.

(*BRIAN makes a move for him, IRA backs away.*)

KENNY. Hey, come on, guys.

IRA. *(Shrugs to Kenny.)* It's over. Okay? . . . *(HE sits.)* So, read back what we got so far.

VAL. What we got *so far?* You want to know what we got so far? Lucas, read him back what we got so far.

LUCAS. We don't have anything.

VAL. Is what we got so far.

IRA. Eleven o'clock and you've got nothing on paper? What were you people doing in here? Is it always up to *me* to get the show started?

BRIAN. *(Slowly.)* You phony fat faggot-looking egocentric turd. When did you ever come in on time like the rest of us?

IRA. *(Laughs, amused.)* I can't believe my ears. Phony? Fat faggot-looking egocentric turd?—is this what Ireland sent us? We could have had Keats. We could have had O'Casey. We could have had George Bernard Shaw. But no, we get an illiterate anti-Semite immigrant who failed streetcar conductor school. My family, all brilliant Talmudic scholars, almost drowned coming over on the boat to America because your drunken people kept beating the shit out of the captain.

(BRIAN crosses away. HE opens the window and we hear the HUM OF TRAFFIC.)

CAROL. Why do we have to keep making racial jokes? Jewish jokes, Irish jokes, Italian jokes. Hasn't America *progressed* beyond that?

OTHERS. *(Think.)* . . . No. Not really. I don't think so.

VAL. No Let 'em go on. A little aggression is good for writers. All humor is based on hostility, am I right, Kenny?

KENNY. Absolutely. That's why World War II was so funny . . . Schmuck!

VAL. *(To Ira.)* If you didn't go to five doctors every morning, maybe you'd get here by ten o'clock.

IRA. Are you saying I'm a hypochondriac? I've had this throat problem for six months. This thing could be cancer, they don't want to tell me.

BRIAN. Have them call me and *I'll* tell you.

IRA. You goddamn Leprechaun! I've been carrying you on this show for three years . . .

BRIAN. What do you want, a funny contest? You want to take on all of Christianity? Come on. Name your game.

IRA. Funny against funny?

BRIAN. For all you want.

IRA. I'll bet my shoes. My sixty-five-dollar genuine alligator Florsheims against your eight ninety-five Thom McAn cardboard funeral parlor shoes for dead men. (*HE takes off his shoes and throws them into the center of the room.*) There's mine. Ante up, you putz bartender.

BRIAN. You got it. (*HE pulls off his shoes and tosses them next to Ira's.*) Okay. Pick your subject.

IRA. Funny names.

BRIAN. Funny names?

IRA. (*Nods.*) Funny names. Anyone else want in on this? Small bet on the side?

MILT. I'm in for a pair of shoelaces.

VAL. Alright. I give you thirty seconds to play. Then we get back to work. Alright. Are we already?

(*BRIAN and IRA take their places standing face to face, almost nose to nose, glaring at each other.*)

BRIAN. (*Crosses himself.*) Up the Irish!

IRA. Out of Egypt!

VAL. Okay. For the funniest names. Ira first . . . GO!!

IRA. Benjamin Bunjamin.

BRIAN. Angela Jonesela.

IRA. Monsignor Abe Brillstein.

BRIAN. Rabbi John Wayne.

IRA. Monica Hanukkah.

BRIAN. Her Highness Queen Minnie the Moocher.

IRA. President Hi-Dee-Hi-Dee-Ho!

BRIAN. (*Shouts.*) Mr. And Mrs. Jesus H. Christ!

IRA. (*Louder.*) The Earl of Sandwich, Hold the Mayo!

BRIAN. *IRA STONE!!*

IRA. IRA STONE??? What's funny about Ira Stone?

BRIAN. NOTHING! *Nothing* is funny about Ira Stone!

IRA. FOUL!! DEFAULT!! He broke the rules. You can't use names we know. Nobody wins. (*HE picks up all four shoes, crosses quickly and throws them all out the open window.*)

CAROL. Tell me I didn't see that.

(*ALL the others rush and look out open window.*)

LUCAS. (*Looks out window.*) Jeez! It looks like the bombing of London.

BRIAN. (*To Ira, furious.*) Go get my shoes.

IRA. They're not your shoes anymore. They belong to the people of Greater New York now.

LUCAS. Direct hit on man coming out of Bergdorf Goodman's.

BRIAN. (*To Ira.*) Either you get those shoes or you better take some flying lessons real quick, you son of a bitch! You owe me two hundred dollars.

IRA. Two hundred dollars for a pair of gravedigger's camping shoes?

CAROL. (*Out the door.*) Helen, can you come in for a second?

VAL. Alright, we work all night tonight. No one leaves till we finish. And I absolutely forbid any more men's clothing to go out the window.

HELEN. (*Comes in.*) Yes, Carol?

CAROL. Helen, would you please go downstairs and get Ira and Brian's shoes? They're on 57th Street.

HELEN. Are they being repaired?

CAROL. Eventually. Ira threw them out the window.

HELEN. (*To Ira.*) You should have asked me, Ira. I would have taken them down. (*Helen exits.*)

KENNY. (*Looks at Ira.*) This man has a child who actually calls him Daddy.

IRA. Oh. Oh. I see. Have I awakened the sleeping tiger? The California Whiz Kid? The reformed Jew who got Bar Mitzvahed in the Hollywood Bowl where Cantor Solomon Weiss sang the entire score to *Porgy and Bess*.

MILT. (*Throws up his hands.*) He's like a plague. He's like locusts. Billions of locusts. The more you kill him, the more he keeps coming back . . . In ten minutes we'll all be naked.

IRA. *(To Milt.)* I don't have a right to say what I want? When did we lose free speech?

VAL. Okay, that's it. Ira, I'm asking Max to take your name off the credits this week. If you come up with something, you'll get back one letter at a time. Three jokes, you get three letters. If dot's all you come up with, it'll just say "IRA" on the screen, dot's it.

IRA. Oh. Oh. Oh. Okay, what if I wrote the whole show myself? You think I can't do it? Gimme paper. *(HE grabs paper off the writers' table.)* Lots of paper. *(HE grabs paper off the typewriter table.)*

BRIAN. Don't forget to flush.

(IRA turns back and glares at Brian.)

CAROL. You really think you can do it, Ira?

IRA. I think I can win the Emmy Award.

VAL. I think your stroke is coming back.

KENNY. Don't forget to make it funny, Ira.

IRA. Funny? It says funny on my birth certificate.

KENNY. Well, I didn't think it said baby.

IRA. Okay. I'm going. The whole show. Top to bottom. By Ira Stone. *(HE exits.)*

MILT. Are we on a break, because I have to go to the john?

VAL. THERE ARE NO BREAKS!!! We've had our breaks. We've had a bagel break, a Joe McCarthy break, a shotgun break, a hole in the wall break, a Cyclantis break and two pairs of shoes out the window break. We've used op all our breaks!!

MILT. Well, then I'll have to ask Carol to turn around because I'm going to pee in the plant. *(HE starts to unzip his pants.)*

CAROL. *(Screams.)* Don't you dare! *(SHE runs away from table.)*

LUCAS. *(To audience.)* . . . And this was the most respected program in all of television . . . and I knew then and there that if I was going to keep my job, I'd have to become as totally crazy as the rest of them.

*(The second door opens and MAX comes in with his trench coat
   still on, no suit on.)*

MAX. Did Helen come back with my suit yet?

CAROL. No, Max. She's out looking for shoes.

MAX. What was wrong with the shoes she was wearing?

KENNY. How'd the call go with NBC, Max?

MAX. (*Sits.*) The call with NBC? (*HE lights his cigar.*) The call with NBC went fine.

VAL. Everything's alright?

MAX. It's fine.

CAROL. It all got settled?

MAX. It got settled fine.

BRIAN. Was anything decided?

MAX. Fine was decided. We decided fine.

VAL. No problems?

MAX. We had *some* problems but we fined them out.

VAL. That sounds fine to me, Max.

KENNY. You want to give us any details, Max? Any changes?

MAX. Changes? Let me see! . . . Oh, yes. They're cutting us back to an hour. This year is fine, next year is an hour. Next year they cut the budget. Next year they want approval of the sketches. Next year they put an observer on the show. That's all. That's the only changes. Minor stuff. (*HE looks at his cigar. THEY can see HE is controlling an explosion.*)

CAROL. And that's fine with you, Max?

MAX. No. That's fine with *them*. *Them* is fine. We is not so fine yet. But we'll see. We'll wait. We'll think. We'll plan. And then we'll be fine.

LUCAS. What is the observer going to do, Max?

MAX. The observer? He's going to observe. (*HE gets up.*) He'll be around the show observing the coffee, the cream cheese, the potato chips. Maybe he'll come up here and observe us working, observe Ira coming in late. (*HE crosses to the telephone. HE is standing behind sofa.*) Maybe he'll observe me getting upset that he's observing me and then he'll observe me taking the fucking *telephone* and smashing it on the fucking floor. (*In a fury, MAX hurls the phone to the floor. HE grimaces, whimpers softly and then continues. Obviously, HE has hit his foot with the phone.*) Or . . . (*HE steps away, limping on the foot that was hit.*) if the observer is not through observing, maybe he can observe me putting my fist through his *fucking face!* (*MAX punches another hole in the wall, right next to McCarthy's hole.*) And then they'll take him away for surgery and he'll observe the hospital for a while. But right now I'm fine . . .

Lucas, when Helen comes back, tell her to call Tiffany's again . . . Just a simple frame with a gold plaque underneath saying "Fine." (*HE sits.*) So. What have we got for this week's show?

(*The door suddenly opens and IRA comes back with the stack of paper in his hand.*)

IRA. What am I crazy? (*HE throws the entire stack of paper up in the air.*) Write a whole show myself? Get outa here! (*HE looks at Max.*) How you doing, Max?

MAX. Fine. Just fine. (*HE calmly crosses his legs and puffs on his cigar.*)

Curtain

ACT II

Seven months later. Early fall. A little before ten A.M.
LUCAS is sitting with his feet up on the writers' desk writing on a legal pad. HE drinks coffee from a mug. This is a more confident, relaxed LUCAS. The two holes in the wall left by Max are now both framed in silver. There are also two additional holes on another place on the wall. These have simple black frames, no plaques.
LUCAS thinks, then turns and looks at the audience.

LUCAS. (*To audience.*) It was seven months later and as you can see, I made the staff. Mug! . . . (*Holds up a coffee mug.*) I was contributing a lot more to the show but what I think cemented the job for me was the day I poured lighting fluid on the desk and set fire to it . . . I was made an honorary lunatic. (*HE gets up, crosses to buffet to refill his mug.*) The show was cut down to an hour and the budget by a third. There were still bagels and onion rolls but no more Danish, no pound cake, no apple strudel. NBC wasn't paying anymore. Max was. (*HE pours coffee.*) And Max still had his temperamental moments, as you can see from the Wall of Terror . . . Those two new holes with the simple black frames were added when Ethel and Julius Rosenberg were executed . . . And although Max was valiantly trying to cut out the pills and scotch, the pressure from NBC and the sponsors made it a losing battle for him.

(*The door opens and MAX comes in wearing a suit, no trench coat.*)

LUCAS. Oh. Hi, Max . . . This is early for you. Everything alright?

(*MAX stands there, looks around, doesn't answer.*)

LUCAS. . . . Max?
MAX. (*Looks at him.*) What?
LUCAS. How are you?
MAX. No one's in yet?
LUCAS. No. Just me.
MAX. Just you?
LUCAS. Yes, Max.
MAX. So the others aren't here?
LUCAS. No . . . Would you like some coffee?
MAX. Usually they're in early on Tuesday.
LUCAS. I know, but this is Monday, Max.
MAX. (*Looks at Lucas.*) . . . How's your wife?
LUCAS. My wife? She's fine, Max. Thanks for asking.
MAX. Penny, right?
LUCAS. Yes. Penny.
MAX. Yeah. Pretty girl. And smart. I like her.
LUCAS. Thank you, Max. I'll tell her.
MAX. And the kids? How's the kids? Andy and Sue, right?
LUCAS. . . . We don't have kids, Max.
MAX. No kids? . . . Then who's Andy and Sue?
LUCAS. I don't know, Max.
MAX. But you like it here okay?
LUCAS. Working here? Oh, yeah. I love this job, Max.
MAX. Well, we'll see . . . So no one's here, heh?
LUCAS. No, Max. Just us.

(*There is an awkward silence as the TWO stare out. LUCAS soon realizes that MAX is asleep on his feet. HE starts to snore . . . then MAX's head falls back. As LUCAS takes a sip of coffee MAX wakes with a start.*)

MAX. Maybe I'll lie down in my office.
LUCAS. Yeah, that's a good idea.
MAX. Why?
LUCAS. Why? Well, because you look tired.
MAX. Me? Never. Never get tired. I just need a little nap, that's all.
LUCAS. I see.
MAX. So, I'll be up in my office. (*MAX starts off in the wrong direction. HE catches himself and heads toward his office.*) I'm gonna take a little nap.
LUCAS. Oh. Okay, Max.
MAX. (*Starts out, stops.*) I think Andy and Sue are my nephews.

(*LUCAS nods and MAX leaves.*)

LUCAS. (*To audience.*) That was the only time I was ever alone in a room with Max . . . It was hard finding a topic in common with him unless you were up on the Thracian Wars.

(*The first door opens and MILT comes in wearing an all white suit and a white Panama hat, a light blue shirt and tie.*)

MILT. I cannot *believe* I got a ticket for speeding on the Parkway. I was driving so slow, the cop who pulled me over was walking.
LUCAS. What'd you expect? You were asking for it.
MILT. *I* was?
LUCAS. You wear an all white suit and a Panama hat, those guys sit behind a billboard waiting for some schmuck like you.
MILT. I thought I looked like a senator.
LUCAS. No. You look like a Nazi trying to catch a boat to Argentina.
MILT. (*Hangs up his hat.*) I liked you better when you weren't funny.
LUCAS. Ba-dum-bum. Max was just in here.

MILT. This early? (*HE looks at wall.*) No new holes. He must be alright. What'd he say?

LUCAS. Well, he thought it was Tuesday, and he asked me how the kids I don't have were, and then he said he wasn't tired so he was going up to take a nap.

MILT. Well, my suit'll cheer him up. (*HE looks over buffet.*) Are the bagels getting smaller or is this room getting bigger?

LUCAS. Same size. There's just half as many now.

MILT. (*Takes a bagel.*) Well, counting my wife, that's the second thing I lost this week.

LUCAS. Are you serious?

MILT. I'm never serious. But she always is . . . which is why I think she's leaving. (*HE cuts bagel open.*)

LUCAS. I'm sorry about your wife, Milt.

MILT. (*Shrugs it off.*) Don't say anything to the guys, will you? I want to tell Max first.

LUCAS. Yes, sure . . . You okay?

MILT. Oh, yeah. Listen, I should have known it at the wedding. When her father handed me an empty envelope, I knew it wasn't a match made in heaven. (*HE pours himself some coffee.*)

LUCAS. You don't seem too upset about it.

MILT. In this room? I can't afford it. Funny is money. (*Sips coffee.*) I tried to patch it up. I offered to take her on a second honeymoon. She said she didn't like the first one that much . . . Then she said, "ba-dum-bum." That's what really hurt.

LUCAS. Sometimes I think you sell yourself short, Milt.

MILT. Lukie, I'll sell myself in whatever size they'll buy me.

(*HE drinks his coffee. The door opens and VAL enters, excited.*)

VAL. I just heard the news in my car. Did you hear it?

MILT. No. I wasn't *in* your car.

LUCAS. What happened?

(*MILT sits.*)

VAL. Stalin died. Joseph Stalin is dead.

LUCAS. Really?

MILT. (*To Val.*) So I guess you'll be going to the funeral.

VAL. Milt, I want you to hear this because I've been practicing it with a tutor . . . Go *FUCK* yourself!

LUCAS. He said it right. *(To Val.)* You said it right. You actually went to a tutor to learn to say that?

VAL. Obsolutely. Cost me a focking fortune.

MILT. You mean he only taught you to say it *once*?

VAL. No. He only taught me to say it to *you* . . . So wait. There's more news. The U.S. State Department just announced they have positive proof that Russia has the hydrogen bomb.

LUCAS. Jesus! That is scary.

VAL. Tell my children. Because they're the ones who will inherit the devastation the focking politicians left them.

MILT. You know you're saying it worse than ever. You didn't go to a *Russian* tutor, did you?

VAL. This is going to be one hell of a day to write comedy. *(HE looks at Milt.)* What is that, a white suit?

MILT. Oh my God, what did the cleaners do to my blue serge?

VAL. You didn't know Max hates white suits?

LUCAS. Max does?

VAL. Since he was a kid. No one told you about Max and white suits?

MILT. It's a joke, right? Not necessarily the kind you laugh at.

VAL. I swear to God. When Max's father died, they made a mistake and buried him in someone else's white suit. Max had nightmares about it for years. Half his analysis was about white suits.

MILT. I think my wife knew. She was laughing when I left the house this morning.

LUCAS. Take off your jacket. Call wardrobe. Maybe they have a dark suit in your size.

MILT. *(Crossing to phone.)* You're telling me the truth about this, Val? *(HE dials "one.")*

VAL. If Max sees you in that suit, Tiffany's does some business today.

MILT. *(Into phone.)* Helen, could you get me wardrobe, please . . . No, *now.* I need an emergency dark suit. I'll hold.

(The door opens.)

LUCAS. Hi, Momma.

(CAROL enters. SHE is very, very pregnant. About the end of her eighth month. SHE walks with great caution.)

CAROL. Please! Nobody stand between me and that chair.

LUCAS. You need any help?

CAROL. No thanks. I've had enough help from men. *(SHE sees Milt and screams.)* Oh, God! I thought you were a doctor. I was afraid I miscounted my due date.

LUCAS. *(Helping her toward chair.)* When *is* your due date?

CAROL. Whenever my doctor's out of town.

MILT. *(Into phone.)* Come on. Come on. Come on.

CAROL. I'm moving as fast as I can.

LUCAS. *(Still helping her.)* You want to put your feet up?

CAROL. Another gynecologist? *(SHE sits.)*

VAL. Did you hear about Joseph Stalin?

CAROL. Don't tell me. McCarthy put him on the blacklist.

MILT. *(Into phone.)* Hello, wardrobe? Who's this? . . . Hannah? . . . Listen, Hannah. This is Milt Fields, one of the writers. We're working on a sketch here and we need a dark suit, size 40 regular. As soon as possible . . . Yes. Yes, that sounds fine . . . No, I can't come downtown. We need it here in the writers' room . . . Would you, please? Take a taxi. God bless you, Hannah. I love you. *(HE hangs up, then quickly dials "one." Aside to Val.)* Be right with you. *(Into phone.)* Helen? Milt . . . Max is up in his office. I want you to call me in here the *second* he comes down. The exact minute you see his feet, you call me immediately. Someone's life, who we both love very much, depends on this. Okay? *(HE hangs up. Gets up, to Lucas.)* Lucas, when she calls me, I'll rush into the men's room. I'll stay there until Hannah gets here, then you bring the suit to me in the john.

(BRIAN walks in in his drab suit with ash marks on it.)

BRIAN. So the Ruskees got the Big Bazoom. Joe McCarthy is suddenly very popular in America today. *(BRIAN laughs, crosses to food counter.)* Great suit, Milt. You look like the governor of Devil's Island.

MILT. Oh. Mr. Fashion Plate. The man's been wearing a single-breasted ash tray for three years.

BRIAN. *(Wipes ashes off his lapel.)* That's right. And I'll be wearing it opening night of my new play.

ALL. Oooh.

BRIAN. Why don't you wait outside the theater and watch the crowds mob me?

MILT. Oh. His new "play." *A Streetcar Named Failure.*

(KENNY walks in, distressed.)

KENNY. Where's Max?

LUCAS. Up in his office.

KENNY. We have to talk. We got a problem.

CAROL. *(Holds stomach.)* As bad as being kicked in the stomach?

MILT. *(To Kenny.)* No joke about my suit? You're going to deprive me of your wit? You're not going to tell me what I look like?

KENNY. The first rabbi in the Amazon. Come on. This is serious business. I heard from Max again, he got a call yesterday from Aaron, his business manager.

(CAROL starts to sob softly.)

KENNY. The show's been over budget every week this season. According to Max's deal . . . is somebody crying?

CAROL. It's me. I'm sorry, I need a release.

(SHE sobs softly. THEY ALL look at her, like watching a bus accident.)

KENNY. *(To Carol.)* . . . Is this going to take long? We got business here.

CAROL. *(Annoyed.)* Oh. I'm sorry. Is it *annoying* you?

MILT. No! . . . But if you could do it later . . .

KENNY. Leave her alone . . . This is important. Max called me three times last night. Every time he tried to tell me what it was, he broke down. He got a call yesterday from Aaron, his business manager. The show's been over budget every week this season. According to Max's deal, Max is responsible for the overage. He owes the network about a third of his salary so far.

CAROL. Wait a minute! WAIT A MINUTE!! *(Feels stomach.)* . . . The baby's moving!!

MILT. *ARE YOU GIVING BIRTH??*

CAROL. God, I hope not. It's moving up. Toward my head.

MILT. Where the hell is it going?

CAROL. I think it just wants to look out of my eyes.

KENNY. Listen to me, will you? . . . You know Max. He wants the best costumes, the best sets, the best of everything. Only now it's costing him big. So Aaron laid down the law. Cut down on costumes, on sets, on everything.

VAL. I obsolutely agree. There's too much waste around here.

KENNY. Now this comes from Aaron, not Max. He's cutting one person from costumes, one from sets, one from the camera crew, one from the secretaries—and this is where Max broke down in tears—one from the writing staff.

(*There is a numb silence as EVERYONE leans back.*)

MILT. I cannot *fucking believe* I wore a white suit today. (*HE sinks in his chair.*)

KENNY. Somebody has to go, guys. Max is not going to pick him. Aaron is. Aaron, who was once Heinrich Himmler's accountant, is not an easy man to deal with . . . So that's it. One of us is going.

VAL. This is a very bad dilemma.

MILT. Why, you've heard of a good dilemma?

CAROL. Look, in a couple of weeks I'm leaving to have my baby. I'll be out about two months. That buys us some time, doesn't it?

KENNY. Aaron's not looking to buy time. He's looking to get rid of one salary for the entire year.

VAL. But we have contracts, no?

KENNY. No. We have three-month options. In case NBC canceled. Didn't your agent tell you?

VAL. He plays golf a lot. I don't like to bother him.

LUCAS. Who are we kidding? I'm the logical choice. I'm the last one on the staff. You all have seniority. So I go.

VAL. Over my dead body. Obsolutely not. Out of the question. No one has to volunteer for this.

LUCAS. I'm not volunteering. I'm just saying they'll probably pick me because I'm the most expendable.

VAL. Oh. Well, if that's the case, that's different.

KENNY. The irony is Lucas is the safest one here. He makes a third of what most of the staff makes. What Aaron wants is to get rid of one of the top money guys.

BRIAN. Well, I guess I have to be the one to say this. Who's the one on this show who makes *top* money and puts in half the time of anyone else? Pay him by the hour and Max would save almost an entire salary. I'm not naming any names.

KENNY. So Ira goes? Anyone second the betrayal?

VAL. Obsolutely not. We're starting our own blacklist here.

KENNY. Hey, guys. We don't make the choice who goes. Aaron does. And that's it unless someone comes up with an unforeseen miracle.

(The door opens and IRA rushes in with a pained expression.)

IRA. They think I have a brain tumor.

KENNY. *(To others.)* This may be what we're looking for.

CAROL. *(To Ira.)* Who thinks you have a brain tumor?

IRA. I couldn't tie my shoelaces this morning. I forgot how to do it. *Shoelaces!!* . . . My three-year-old kid tied his, I *begged* him to do mine. I poured tomato juice into my coffee. Tomato juice.

BRIAN. Well, it isn't necessarily a brain tumor. Have you ruled out stupidity?

IRA. Remember to say that at my funeral. After you do your little jig on my coffin.

CAROL. Ira, calm down.

IRA. This *is* calm down. This is the best I've been all day.

BRIAN. Listen, there could be a lot of reasons for this, Ira. Maybe you're just underworked.

IRA. *(To Brian.)* You can't wait, can you? You're dying to come to the hospital and sing, "Oh, Danny Boy" at my bedside.

CAROL. *(To Brian.)* Leave him alone, Brian. If he wants a brain tumor, let him have a brain tumor.

IRA. *(Puts his hand over his eyes.)* I have double vision.

LUCAS. You mean right now?

IRA. Right now, all night, all morning. Double vision. Two cabs pulled up in front of my house this morning. I took them both.

VAL. Ira! Since I know you, you've had every disease known to mankind and a few animal diseases. And you're still here.

CAROL. You don't have a brain tumor.

IRA. *(Shouts.)* You want proof? Undeniable, positive, absolute proof? (*HE crosses to desk, picks up a thick pointed black pen and* prints in large bold letters, "I HAVE A BRAIN TUMOR.") There! There it is in black and white! Okay?

CAROL. You actually wrote on the wall with an indelible marker? Children could go to jail for that.

IRA. (Sits, looks at Milt.) I'm seeing double again . . . Milt, will you sit down, please? You look like the entrance to the White House.

KENNY. Ira, we're busy. If you got a brain tumor go down to the shoe maker, he'll take it out.

IRA. Oh, I see. I'm crazy, right? Like Tolstoy was crazy. Like Dostoyevsky was crazy.

KENNY. No. They were crazy in a talented way. You're sort of a fucking waste of time crazy.

VAL. (To Ira.) Either you stay in this room and you write with us together or you go home and have your kid untie your laces and come in tomorrow.

IRA. Did I say no? I'm here. I came to work, didn't I? (HE crosses to desk on other side of room.) I just have to see how my stocks are doing.

CAROL. (To Ira.) Has it ever occurred to you that you monopolize every minute you're in this room?

IRA. Who better than me? What am I, uninteresting?

HELEN. (Rushes into the room.) Milt! Max is coming in.

MILT. NOW? I told you to call me!

(MAX walks into the room. MILT gets down on all fours and hides between Carol and the coffee table. MAX seems very energized.)

MAX. (To Helen.) No calls for anyone. Nobody leaves, nobody moves. We have to talk in here. (HE hangs up his suit jacket.)

HELEN. Yes, Max . . . Sorry, Milt.

(SHE goes, MILT lets out a groan. MAX looks at CAROL who imitates Milt's groan.)

MAX. (Squints over toward Milt.) Who's that? Milt? What's the matter with you?

MILT. (HE gets up.) Don't feel too good. I'll be right back. Have to go to the john. (*HE gets up, grabbing a newspaper and shields his body with it, crossing quickly toward the door.*)

MAX. Save it. We got to talk first. Siddown.

MILT. Two minutes, Max. I'll rush.

MAX. (*Looks at him.*) Are you sick? You look white as a ghost.

MILT. I get that way. I think it's a bladder infection.

MAX. No. Something else. Something different. Why do you look different?

MILT. (*HE's lost.*) I—I don't know, Max. (*HE tries covering himself with the newspaper in an effort to hide some of the white.*)

MAX. (*Suddenly pointing at him.*) Ahh!

MILT. (*Recoils in terror.*) Ahh!

MAX. Ahh!

MILT. Ahh!

MAX. . . . You got a haircut, right?

MILT. Me? Yes. This morning. Just a light trim. Amazing you noticed.

MAX. A man gets a haircut, I notice. Siddown.

(*MILT goes to the waste basket by the bagel table and sits down on the opposite side of room. With hand to his mouth, MAX calls:*)

MAX. Not over there. I'm not talking over there.

MILT. I want to be near the water so I can drink. I can hear you. (*MILT is sitting on the waste basket.*)

MAX. (*Shields his eyes.*) Don't sit in the sun. There's a glare on you. (*HE turns.*) Okay. Where's Carol?

CAROL. Here, Max.

MAX. Anything new with the baby?

CAROL. No. Nothing new. Still in there.

MAX. You got a good doctor?

CAROL. Oh, yeah. Very good. I love my doctor.

MAX. You're in love with your doctor?

CAROL. No. I love that he's a good doctor. I love my husband.

MAX. That's right. You're still with your husband. Good. I'm glad . . . (*VAL is right behind him.*) Where's Val?

VAL. (*HE's never moved.*) Right here, Max.

MAX. (*Yells.*) You keep moving around! Sit on one place!

VAL. Absolutely. Forgive me. My fault. (*HE sits at writers' table.*)

MAX. So, Kenny . . . did you . . . (*Max whispers in Kenny's ear.*)
KENNY. What?
MAX. . . . did you . . . (*MAX whispers again in Kenny's ear.*)
KENNY. What?
MAX. (*Yells.*) *Did you tell them about our phone call?*
KENNY. Yes, Max. I told everyone when I came in.
CAROL. We heard, Max.
MAX. I hope it didn't upset the baby.
CAROL. I don't think so. She's not into show business yet.
MAX. Our children are all we have. They can take everything else away from you. Your dignity, your pride, your set designers, your make-up lady, but they can't take your children. You understand what I'm saying?
CAROL. Yes, Max.
MAX. So far no one's going. So far everyone's still here.
VAL. That's good, Max.
MAX. But so far is only going to last so far. Then so far turns into so long.
KENNY. We understand, Max.
IRA. Understand what? What are you talking about?
MAX. He doesn't know?
KENNY. Ira came in late.
MAX. (*To Ira.*) What'd I tell everybody about coming in late?
IRA. What do I know? I'm never here when you tell them.

(*MAX crosses to Ira when suddenly MAX's eyes go to the wall. HE squints as HE looks at it, then turns to others.*)

MAX. "I Have a Brain Tumor"??? . . . Who wrote that?
IRA. I did.
MAX. Don't lie to me. Who wrote it?
IRA. I just told you. It was me.
MAX. Did someone from NBC do this? Is that what they're trying to tell me? I have a brain tumor? So they can break the contract?
IRA. Max, I swear to God. On my father's grave. On my children's life. I wrote it.
MAX. Why?
IRA. Because I have a brain tumor.

MAX. Is that going to wash off?

IRA. Don't you care what may happen to me?

MAX. First let's take care of what happened to my wall . . . Is that going to wash off?

IRA. No. It's not. It's a permanent marker, okay?

MAX. If this doesn't wash off, you'll definitely have a brain tumor. (*HE crosses back to his chair, sits.*) Alright, Kenny. Tell him about our phone call.

KENNY. (*To Ira.*) You know all about the budget problems the show's been having this year . . . Well, Max has been paying a lot of things out of his own pocket . . .

IRA. Wait a minute! Wait a minute! (*To Max.*) Look at the holes you punched in there. It's a polka dot wall. And I get blamed for a few lousy words scribbled in ink?

MAX. (*Gets up.*) It's my wall. It's my holes. You wanna buy your own wall, this one's for sale. (*HE points to the wall Ira wrote on.*) Take it. For five thousand dollars you can cover it with your entire life's blood pressure . . . Otherwise I want my wall back the way it was. Go on, Kenny. (*HE sits again.*)

KENNY. (*To Ira.*) This is the last time I'm telling you. Aaron won't let Max pay for anything anymore. You hear what I'm telling you? So they're cutting one person from every department on the show? You listening? . . . Which means one writer, one of us, someone in this room, has to go. That's it.

IRA. What are you saying? That one of you guys has to go?

KENNY. I say we hang him out the window. Make him a permanent weather vane.

IRA. Oh, you mean it includes *everybody* . . . Oh, this is funny. This is *The Human Comedy.* This is William Saroyan. This is Reality. I would have come early for this. (*HE sits.*) Okay, so how does it work? How do we pick the one who goes?

MILT. (*On the other side of the room, stands.*) We don't. Aaron is going to pick him.

MAX. (*Stands, looks at him suspiciously.*) What color is that suit?

MILT. (*Backs away nervously.*) This? This is an off-color cream beige, sort of a taupe antique eggshell.

MAX. (*Looks at him.*) You're sure that's not a . . . ?

MILT. No, no, no, no, it isn't.

MAX. Alright. Upstairs I thought it out. There's another way. A better way. We don't need Aaron to pick someone. (HE sits.)

BRIAN. This sounds hopeful, Max. How do we do it?

(MAX motions for them to lean in. THEY ALL lean in.)

MAX. . . . Is Napoleon dead?

VAL. What do you mean?

MAX. I asked a simple question. Is Napoleon dead?

VAL. Yes, Max. He is. Napoleon is dead.

MAX. How do you know? Did you see him dead?

VAL. Not personally, no. But I saw his tomb in Paris.

MAX. Did you open the tomb and look?

VAL. They don't let you do that, Max. And who could lift it? It was just me and my wife.

MAX. So how do you know he's in the tomb?

VAL. It says so. Why would they build Napoleon's tomb if he wasn't in it?

MAX. They built the Eiffel Tower, they didn't put Mr. Eiffel in it.

KENNY. Mr. Kellogg isn't in his box of corn flakes either, Max. What point are you trying to make?

MAX. I just made it. Maybe we can fire a writer, but no one has to go.

BRIAN. How do we do that, Max?

MAX. Easy. I worked it all out. I cut all your salaries down ten percent. Then I fire a writer. Doesn't make any difference who. Then I take all the ten percents and I pay the fired writer. So he stays. And then I pay your ten percents back out of miscellaneous expenses. So the I.R.S. gets paid, all the writers get paid, no one gets fired and it doesn't cost me anything.

KENNY. And when they ask where the miscellaneous expenses are, what do you say?

MAX. *They're in Napoleon's tomb!* WHAT DO I KNOW?? I DON'T WANT TO HEAR ANYMORE. I thought it all out, it works for me. Let Aaron figure out the details. I don't want to fire anyone. My writers are my flesh and blood. There is no miscellaneous in my body, you understand? Now get Helen in here, we got a show to write.

VAL. Lucas, get Helen in here.

MILT. *I'll do it!!* (*HE prances out on tip toes and rushes out of the room.*)

MAX. (*Looks at him go.*) . . . I think he hangs out with ballet dancers.

LUCAS. (*To audience.*) So we finally went to work. We usually based our sketches on what was currently in the news.

(*HELEN comes in quickly, crosses behind Max and hands out paper to all the WRITERS.*)

LUCAS. The movie version of *Julius Caesar* starring Marlon Brando just opened on Broadway.

(*THEY ALL get their scripts.*)

LUCAS. . . . So we worked on it all morning and all afternoon.

MAX. (*To Helen.*) Okay! Read back what we got.

HELEN. From the top?

MAX. From the top.

HELEN. (*Reads.*) Titles . . . High Class Films Present . . . William Shakespeare's *Julius Caesar* . . . Produced by Nigel Bagel . . . Screenplay by Peter Porter and Esther Lester . . . Directed by Sir John Malcolm and his wife, Gloria . . . and starring James Hedgehog, Morris Porridge, Olivia Malaria and Marlon Merlin in his first completely memorized part as Julius Caesar . . . Rome, 44 B.C. . . . Outside the Roman Senate . . .

IRA. Not outside the Roman Senate. Two blocks from the Roman Senate. Two *blocks* is funny.

(*HELEN looks at MAX who nods approval.*)

HELEN. (*Writes, then reads.*) Two blocks from the Roman Senate . . . Brutus speaks.

KENNY. (*Reading.*) Hail, Cassius.

BRIAN. Hail, Brutus.

KENNY. What news from Flavius and Lepidus?

BRIAN. Not well. Flavius has mucus and Lepidus is nauseous.

KENNY. (*Reads.*) Hark! Trebonius approaches . . . Hail, Trebonius. How fare thee?

VAL. (*Reads.*) A slight pain in my kishkas.

CAROL. You think they'll know what kishkas are in Nebraska, Max?

MAX. If you point to it and make a face, they'll know . . . Go on.

BRIAN. What news of the conspiracy?

VAL. Linus told Paulus. Paulus thinks it's much hocus-pocus. Yet Flavius and Lepidus told Marcus that justice must be practiced.

BRIAN. And of the conspiracy. What of it does Caesar know?

VAL. Caesar knows not of that which has yet to become knownst. For if knownst, he becomes of our conspired thoughts then would Caesar not give value to constrain such concerns?

MAX. Am I on?

KENNY. Of that I know not, but that which I do know concerns all conspirators, thus giving recourse to Caesar's compliance to which he has not yet given his dispensation.

MAX. Am I on?

BRIAN. Then it dost fall upon our devoted intentions, that Caesar must not become martyred, for all Rome would give spleen to those that hasten his death which seeks out the profit of this foul and festered—

MAX. (*Stands on chair behind them, yells.*) ALRIGHT!! ENOUGH!! Get me into the Goddamn sketch already. Maybe last year when we had an hour and a half, we could do "what gives spleen to Linus and Paulus upon his martyred kishkas," but this is *this* year, for crise sakes.

HELEN. (*Looking at script.*) I don't have that line here, Max.

CAROL. (*To Helen.*) Try to pay attention, sweetheart.

(*The door opens and MILT comes in. HE tries to be inconspicu- ous. HE is now wearing a dark suit with the cuffs and the pants much too short. HE still has on the white shoes and white socks.*)

MILT. (*Softly.*) Sorry. Just had to go to the john. (*HE crosses to sofa with Carol and looks at pages of the sketch. MAX looks at him in disbelief.*)

MAX. What'd you do, shave? You look different again.

MILT. No. Just washed up.

MAX. I hate your suit. You wear weird things, you know that?

(MILT nods. MAX looks at KENNY, VAL and BRIAN who nod consent. MAX turns to Helen.)

MAX. Okay. Go on.

HELEN. It's Cassius's line.

BRIAN. Caution. Caesar is upon us . . . Hail, Caesar.

KENNY and VAL. Hail, oh mighty Caesar.

HELEN. Max looks up into the sky. They all look up too.

KENNY. What dost thou seekest in the constellations, Caesar?

MAX. *(Reads, doing Brando.)* A clustuh a stahs in da heavens.

BRIAN. And by what name dost this cluster be called, oh, Caesar?

MAX. It is called Stelluh . . . *Stelluh!* . . . Stelluh for Stahlight! *(MAX smiles as MAX.)* That's good. I like that . . . Good joke, Kenny.

IRA. *(Jumps up.)* Kenny? What do you mean, Kenny? That's my joke.

MAX. Who cares?

IRA. I care. I like to be given credit for what I contribute. That's my joke, Max.

KENNY. He's right, Max! It was his.

MAX. It makes no difference . . . I don't want no prima madonnas in here.

IRA. *(Laughs.)* Prima *madonnas?* . . . You know why you're funny, Max? Because you're the only one who doesn't understand what you're saying.

MAX. Really? How about this? . . . You're fired, Ira . . . I understood *that. That* made sense to me. I thought that was *extremely* clear.

IRA. *(Laughs.)* I'm fired?

MAX. Yes. You're Prima Unemployed.

IRA. Max, I know I'm a little nuts. But on the line of crazies, you're a mile and a half ahead of me.

MAX. Oh, I see. You're sane and I'm crazy.

IRA. Don't take my word for it. Ask my shrink. We've been analyzing you for the last ten months.

MAX. You had *me* analyzed?

IRA. Right. We finished me last year, so this year we did you. He thinks you're a comic genius. He worships you, Max. Nobody makes him laugh the way you do. But he thinks you're capable of going to the Bronx Zoo and killing all the gorillas.

MAX. I'll tell you what. I fire you and I fire him. He can't analyze me anymore. And if I see him, he'll be the first gorilla.

IRA. I'm fired.

MAX. Yes.

IRA. Fine. Great . . . I want my Stelluh joke back.

MAX. NO STELLUH!! I paid for Stelluh. I own Stelluh. You can have Linus Paulus Hokus Dokus, you can have "he knows not what he naught knoweth who Pepidus is," but Stelluh is mine!

IRA. I give you Stelluh on one condition.

MAX. No, sir. No conditions.

VAL. Max, hear his condition. What's your condition, Ira?

IRA. I just want you to say you love me.

MAX. (Gets up, fire in his eyes.) Love him?? . . . Love that??? . . . He steals my Stelluh and he wants my love?? (To Ira.) You dreckus schmuckus pyuckiss, toochis! (Jumps on Ira.) I want my salary back. Four years salary. (The GUYS pull MAX off.) And I want my holding tax and my social security and the toy trucks I sent your kid.

IRA. (Crosses to Helen.) Excuse me, sweetheart. (HE takes a page out of her hand, tears out a small piece of the page, then gives her the page back.) Okay. I took Stelluh. I can outcrazy you anytime, Max.

MAX. (Blocks his way.) Paste it back on the page or I'll staple you and your brain tumor to the wall.

IRA. I'm leaving now. And Stelluh's going with me.

MAX. (Holds out his hand.) Give it to me, Ira. Give it to me. Because I'm starting to get one of my Wolf Man headaches.

IRA. You fired me. I gave you your chance. You won't tell me you love me, fine. Say goodbye to Stelluh.

(HE puts it in his mouth and chews it. MAX steams.)

IRA. I'll tell you something. It's a funny joke but it tastes like shit.

(There is a tense moment as MAX just stares at Ira. Slowly at first, MAX begins to laugh. One by one the GUYS join him until finally EVERYONE is laughing. MAX puts his arm around Ira in a friendly fashion, then flings IRA down on the table. The OTHERS try vainly to pull Max off.)

MAX. If you swallow it, I shove my arm down your throat, and pull Stelluh out with your tonsils.

CAROL. Max, it's just a piece of paper. We can write it again.

IRA. *(Gasping.)* Not until he says he loves me.

MILT. Somebody get a torch. Maybe fire will frighten them.

IRA. *(To Max.)* I love *you,* you schmuck. Why don't you love me?

MAX. I *like* you, but I love Stelluh. Spit it out. Spit it out.

IRA. *(Gasping.)* Alright, alright. *(HE spits and the wad of paper sails across the room.)* Jesus! I'm glad I didn't write *War and Peace.*

MAX. *(To Helen.)* Put it back in the script.

HELEN. *(Points to wet paper on floor.)* You mean *that?*

CAROL. No. Just type it back in again. The Smithsonian will pick that up later.

MAX. Okay. I got what I wanted. Now I love you, you bastard.

IRA. Am I still fired?

MAX. No. Val is fired.

VAL. Why me?

MAX. Just for an hour. Everyone has to take his turn.

BRIAN. What about you?

MAX. Absolutely. I'm fired after Lucas. Everyone except Carol. I'm not firing a pregnant woman.

CAROL. Really? Since when did anyone here ever notice I was a woman?

MILT. I knew the first day when you took your coat off. It took me a couple of hours, but I noticed.

CAROL. Well, I don't want to be considered a woman. I want to be considered a writer.

BRIAN. Fine with me, you'll just have to shave like the rest of us.

MAX. What are we talking about here? *(To Carol.)* What's wrong with being a woman? My wife's a woman, she's crazy about it.

CAROL. I like it too, Max, but not in here. I can't survive in here as a woman. But as a writer, I can hold my own with anyone.

MAX. I'm sorry. You *have* to be a woman. The show needs a woman's point of view. Of everybody here, you come the closest.

CAROL. After five years in here, Max, you think I know what a woman's point of view is? I come home at night smelling from cigar smoke, I have to put my dress in a humidor . . . I never said a crude word in my life before I came here. But now I go home to my fucking house and talk to my fucking husband like a fucking sailor . . .

It's okay. I don't mind. If you lived in France for five years, you'd speak French. But I'm not *in* France. I'm here so I speak fuck . . . I don't want to be called a woman writer. I want to be called a *good* writer, and if it means being one of the guys then I'll be one of the guys. I can handle it.

MILT. (*To Carol.*) Well, I agree. And I hope you have a great baby there, fella.

MAX. Okay. Back to work. Where were we?

HELEN. Caesar has the next line.

MAX. (*As Brando.*) Whad is wrong? Whad is dis feeling of doom dat hangs in duh night air? What is dis twelve-inch kitchen knife doing in my back? Oh boy. Dis hoits.

KENNY. Oh, foul deed. Dost thou forgive me, Caesar?

MAX. Oh, Brudus, Brudus, my brudder . . . I depended on thee . . . I counted on thee . . . I coulda been a contender . . .

HELEN. They plunge another dagger in him.

(*MAX does a series of death throes, then falls on his face.*)

MAX. TAXI!!

KENNY. The deed is done. Caesar reigns no more.

MAX. (*Raises head.*) It stopped raining? (*Falls back again.*)

BRIAN. We pray for your soul, Caesar.

BRIAN, KENNY, VAL. Adonday donis latinum moray quantis bellum Nostre Damus losto.

MAX. Nostre Damus lost? Against Southern Calif! ornus?

HELEN. That's where we stopped writing, Max.

MAX. I need a finish. Something to end my speech. Something big.

IRA. I got it, Max. (*HE lies down flat on the floor on his stomach.*) You pull yourself up from the ground (*HE starts to pull himself up.*) . . . then you get on one knee . . . (*HE gets on one knee.*) and you spread your arms out to Rome. (*He spreads his arms out.*) And then you sing . . . (*To the tune of "Swanee."**)

Roma, how I love ya, how I love ya,

My dear old Roma

I'd give the world to be

Among the folks in "Fatza goona poppalini"

* "Swanee" by Irving Caesar and George Gershwin.

Roma, how I love ya, how I love ya
My dear old Roma
The folks at home will see me no more
Till I get to that pasta shore . . .

MAX. Fatz goona poppalini?? . . . The man is crazy . . . but I like it. Put it in the sketch . . .

(THEY join in singing and exit as the LIGHTS come down.)

LUCAS. *(To audience.)* We wrote that week's show and the next week's show and the next two months' shows . . . *(LUCAS is alone onstage and stands in a LIGHT over at the side. The OTHERS have all left.)* The quality was still there but the ratings weren't. America wanted comedy closer to their own lives. Julius Caesar wasn't as familiar to them as kids named Beaver and fathers who knew best. Max never really had to fire anyone because Brian soon left for Hollywood. There was a definite air of gloom around the office because Max was becoming more and more disoriented. He was in constant negotiations with NBC about the future of the show and they took a hard line. It didn't stop Max from throwing his annual, festive Christmas party, but he did, however, punch a large hole in the elevator door . . . Now you didn't have to look up to see what floor you were on . . .

(We hear CHRISTMAS MUSIC coming up softly from the outer offices, and we see a lit Christmas tree in the corner of the room . . . A light SNOWFALL can be seen through the windows.)

LUCAS. . . . To be honest, we were all a little frightened. Because until now, we all had each other to lean on. But like little chicks leaving the nest, we'd soon know the fear, the panic and the courage needed to fly by ourselves.

(The LIGHTS go out on LUCAS.
The LIGHTS come back on in the office. It is night. LUCAS is gone. The CHRISTMAS MUSIC is a little louder and we can hear the chatter from the outside office.

MILT *walks in in a neat double-breasted suit. HE carries a glass and a half-empty bottle of champagne.*)

MILT. . . . So I get the petition for divorce in the mail yesterday, you hear? . . . Two days before Christmas . . . We worked out a nice settlement though. She gave me a beautiful picture of the house . . . (*HE turns around.*) Where are you? . . . Helen? (*HE looks out in the hall.*) Come on in. It's too noisy out there.

(*HELEN comes in cautiously. SHE is wearing a simple black dress, cut revealingly in the front, her hair up. We see for the first time what a handsome woman HELEN is. SHE has a glass of champagne in hand.*)

HELEN. I don't mind the noise. It's a party, isn't it?

MILT. My goodness, Helen, that dress is so becoming to you. Listen, Helen. I'm going to say something now that may shock you. But just hear me out. Because I say it with all sincerity and with my deepest regard and respect for you . . . You're very attracted to me, aren't you?

HELEN. Actually, I'm not.

MILT. But a little, right?

HELEN. No. Not even a little.

MILT. You didn't tell Giselle in the office that you thought I was cute?

HELEN. *Me??* No. Never. Why would I say that? *Cute?* Oh, God, no.

MILT. Maybe it was Giselle who said I was cute.

HELEN. No. Giselle told me she thought *Kenny* was cute.

MILT. Alright. So what are we talking about? Semantics.

HELEN. I think I should be getting back.

MILT. What if I said that I wasn't interested in an affair? What if I said what I really wanted is a deep and lasting relationship?

HELEN. I hope you find it. I really do.

MILT. What if I offered to give you my next year's salary for one night? . . . No, don't believe that. There may not be a show next year.

HELEN. I know.

MILT. I'd be out of a job, out of a wife, out of a family . . . Does pity excite you in any way?

HELEN. I really don't want to miss the party . . .

MILT. What kind of a guy are you looking for?

HELEN. I'm not looking for anyone.

MILT. Then what is it you want?

HELEN. I want to be a writer. I want to write comedy.

MILT. A *comedy* writer?? . . . Oi vey!! . . . Why? You really want to be like me? Like Val? Like Ira? Like any of us?

HELEN. More than anything else in the world.

MILT. Helen! You *know* us. We're disgusting. We're children. We have no life. This room is our life. We curse each other, hate each other. We throw shoes out the window, we set fire to the desk. We've made obscene phone calls to St. Patrick's Cathedral. We'll humiliate and denigrate anyone or anything in the world just to get a laugh.

HELEN. See, that excites me.

MILT. I'll teach you everything I know. (*HE takes her hand and begins to rub it.*)

(*VAL walks in wearing his best suit. HE holds a glass of vodka. HE is drunk.*)

VAL. Max wants all the writers in here. He wants to make a toast.

MILT. First the Danish goes, then the bagels. Now we're down to toast.

HELEN. No, I think he means with champagne.

MILT. (*To Helen.*) Maybe you should rethink this comedy thing.

LUCAS. (*Enters, wearing a suit, carrying a bottle of beer.*) Did you guys hear what McCarthy did? Practically on Christmas Eve?

VAL. He put the Pope on the blacklist. Now the Pope can't get work on TV or in the movies. (*HE laughs.*) Can you imagine how drunk I must be to say that?

(*BRIAN walks in wearing a sprightly houndstooth sports jacket, a hat, tan slacks and loafers, with a cashmere camel's hair coat, with the ever present cigarette in his mouth.*)

BRIAN. Who's got a camera? I want you to see what success looks like.

LUCAS. (HE shakes BRIAN's hand.) I knew you were in town. I heard you coughing.

MILT. Brianchkila! I thought you were going to send for me.

BRIAN. I didn't know you delivered.

MILT. (To Helen.) See. One day you'll say funny things like that.

LUCAS. Jeez, you really went Hollywood. I bet that coat has a little swimming pool in the pocket.

BRIAN. (Snaps fingers.) I sold out like that. I am now not only richer than you guys, I'm also three hours younger.

HELEN. Ba-dum-bum-ba-dum-bum-bum-ba-dum.

MILT. (To Helen.) Later we'll have a little talk about timing.

VAL. (Squints.) Who's that? Is that Brian? Where the hell were you?

BRIAN. You just noticed I've been gone for three months?

VAL. Hey, Brian. Have you heard the news?

BRIAN. What?

VAL. I'm so pissed, I don't give a shit.

MILT. (To Helen.) Russian humor. It's funnier if you're on a mule.

LUCAS. (To Brian.) So where you living out there?

BRIAN. Oh, a little place in the hills overlooking Yvonne De Carlo.

HELEN. God, I'd give *anything* to live in Hollywood.

MILT. Well, that's all it takes, honey.

(CAROL *walks in in a smart suit, her old slim figure is back again.*)

CAROL. Brian! I heard you were in here. Come here. I haven't hugged a Gentile in so long.

(THEY *hug. SHE feels his coat.*)

CAROL. Oh, my God. Is that cashmere?

BRIAN. One hundred percent. (*Removing his hat; HE has a full head of hair.*) My hair is coming in that way too . . . You look terrific, Momma. I heard you had a boy.

CAROL. No. A girl

BRIAN. Well, don't worry. He'll grow out of it.

KENNY. (*Walks in.*) Will someone take my turn with Max while he's throwing up? I pulled his head out of the john so much, I feel like a lifeguard . . . Brian!! How are you?

(*BRIAN starts to answer but coughs and coughs.*)

KENNY. I never heard a pack of Camels talk before.

CAROL. Max looks terrible. What's he been drinking, Kenny?

KENNY. Pina colonics, I don't know . . . The man just ate a roast beef sandwich the size of a Buick.

CAROL. Couldn't you stop him?

KENNY. With what? A harpoon?

(*THEY laugh.*)

MILT. Keep going, Kenny. You're on a roll.

KENNY. If I was on a roll, Max would eat me too.

(*THEY ALL laugh.*)

BRIAN. (*Looks at his watch.*) Listen, I just wanted to say hello. My kids are downstairs. I'm taking them to Mass.

MILT. Mass? Isn't that in Boston?

HELEN. No. They have them in New York too.

MILT. (*To Helen.*) Maybe you should write children's stories.

(*IRA bursts in the room in galoshes and a topcoat over a blue suit.*)

IRA. I was just on my way to St. John's Hospital. I felt a funny feeling in my back, like a broken spine or something . . . So wait'll you hear this . . . About a Chinese-Jew.

BRIAN. Okay. He's setting us up. A Chinese-Jew. Don't tell us his name. Give us one crack at it . . . Seymour Dragon.

MILT. Solomon Take-Out.

KENNY. Charley Chanstein.

CAROL. Pincus Ping Pong.
BRIAN. Pincus Ping Pong is good . . .
HELEN. Can I say one?

(THEY ALL look at her.)

MILT. I don't know if we're all drunk enough to hear this.
BRIAN. *(To Helen.)* You understand the rules? He has to have a Chinese-Jewish name.
HELEN. I know. I get it.
MILT. Listen, who knows? . . . Go ahead, sweetheart. Kill 'em.
HELEN. *(Thinks . . . a long time.)* Let's see . . . er . . . er . . .

(The OTHERS sit down.)

HELEN. Sidney . . . Sidney . . . Can I take back Sidney?
KENNY. Good move, kid.
HELEN. Oh. Oh. I got it . . . Stephen . . . Stephen . . .
CAROL. Helen, can I ask you something? Is Stephen the Jewish name or the Chinese name?
HELEN. No. It's wrong. Let me start again.
MILT. You can't take this long, Helen. Writing a joke isn't a semi-annual event.
HELEN. I'm nervous. I don't know any Chinese-Jews.
IRA. Can I give the girl a name so I can finish this story?
CAROL. Come on, give her a chance, guys.
HELEN. Okay. Alright . . . I got one . . . Vito Tojo.

(THEY ALL look at her.)

LUCAS. Vito Tojo?? . . . Vito is Italian. Tojo is Japanese.
HELEN. Listen, I'm not getting paid to write this stuff.
CAROL. It's alright, Helen. You got the hemispheres right.
KENNY. *(To Ira.)* Alright. We give up. What's his name?
IRA. There's no name. It's a true story. I'm rushing back past Carnegie Hall and there's this filthy-looking bum begging on the street . . . So I give him five bucks and I start to walk away and suddenly I recognize him. It's Velvel, from Brooklyn. I went to high

school with him. So I said, "Velvel, it's me. Ira Stone. Remember?" . . . And he said, "Oh, my God. Ira! How are you? What are you doing, kid?" . . . And I said, "I'm writing a big television show. For Max Prince." . . . He said, "That's great, Ira. Could you use a joke?" . . . I said, "Sure. What's the joke?" . . . He said, "It's about a Jewish girl and a Chinese man on a honeymoon. Have you heard it?" . . . I said, "No." . . . He said, "Too bad. It's a good joke. I can't remember it." . . . I felt so bad for him.

VAL. Ira, with all due respect to Velvel, what was the point in that story?

IRA. The point is, we got the breaks, he didn't. He's waiting downstairs now. I think it would be a nice gesture if we all chipped in fifty bucks a piece for Velvel. I'm giving a hundred myself. (HE points to the window.) Down there, but for the grace of God, go I.

KENNY. Well, but for the grace of God, why don't *you* go down there and send Velvel up here?

CAROL. No. I'm chipping in with Ira.

MILT. Why? You don't even know Velvel.

CAROL. I know. But every once in a while, Ira makes me cry. Go figure.

(*The door opens and MAX walks in with a drink in his hand. HE is drunk.*)

VAL. We were waiting for you, Max. Brian is here. Did you see Brian?

(*MAX looks dazed. Says nothing.*)

BRIAN. Just dropped in from the coast to say hello, Max.

(*MAX blinks. That's all.*)

KENNY. Feeling any better, Max?

LUCAS. You want to sit down, Max? I'll get your chair.

CAROL. I wonder if he hears us?

VAL. (*To Max.*) Max! . . . It's Val . . . Can you hear what I'm saying?

(MAX looks at him.)

VAL. Max, we're worried about you. *(To others.)* I don't think he hears me . . .

(THEY glance at each other.)

MAX. . . . Please forgive me. I'm a little drunk . . . Sometimes I don't know how to say things right . . . Maybe you never noticed . . . But as drunk as I am—I want to tell each and every person here—I love all of you!—Whoo! Boy! Why is that so hard to say? We never said it in my family . . . We said EAT! . . . EAT was love. Potatoes was love. Brisket of beef was a LOT of love . . . But Ira can tell you. I don't say it a lot.

IRA. He doesn't say it a lot.

MAX. Screw it, I'm gonna say it. I love you, I love you, I love you. Wow, does that make me hungry . . . *(HE coughs.)* Can everyone hear me?

LUCAS. Clear as a bell, Max.

MAX. My throat's a little sore. I was in my office and threw *up* out the window. I think I hit a little bum on the street.

IRA. That's Velvel from Brooklyn, Max. It's okay.

MAX. Oh! I have something to tell you. We WON!! . . . You hear? . . . We beat the bastards and we beat them together. *(HE starts to laugh hard, which is mingled with some drunken tears.)*

VAL. We won what, Max? Who did we beat?

MAX. NBC! They surrendered. At five twenty-seven tonight, December 24th, nineteen hundred and—whatever . . . They signed the papers on my desk . . . It should have been on the *U.S.S. Missouri* . . . Or at Appomappo-mappowax! . . . We signed and we exchanged pens . . . Crappy little ballpoints they had . . . But we got what we wanted. Yessir!!

KENNY. That is great news, Max.

(ALL: vocal response.)

VAL. So what was it? A new contract?
MAX. Better.

CAROL. What's better than a new contract, Max?

MAX. *Freedom!* Independence! We're out. On our own . . . From now on we call the shots.

KENNY. You mean we can go to another network? CBS?

MAX. Damn right . . . Except CBS doesn't have any air time next year. They got Walter Cronkite on everything.

BRIAN. I hear ABC is looking for new shows, Max.

MAX. There you are! ABC! . . . But they don't want to do variety. They want sports . . . What am I gonna do, play golf for an hour?

IRA. There's only three networks, Max. There's Channel Five but they've only got one camera.

MAX. Right. So what's the smartest thing we can do?

LUCAS. What?

MAX. We play the waiting game. We wait until the networks are all in trouble . . . Then they line up for us . . . with their tongues hanging out.

(THEY ALL *look at each other.*)

KENNY. How long a wait are you talking about, Max?

MAX. Not long. We don't all have to wait. We break up for a while. You guys take other shows. You got families, you're in big demand, the best writers in the business . . . I'll do a couple of movies, maybe a Broadway show, play Vegas, whatever . . . and then one day the call goes out. They want us back. On our terms. The word spreads everywhere. They're getting together again. They're coming back.

MILT. Sort of like Zorro. We could wear masks and ride white horses . . . No, not white, brown.

MAX. You see? We just gotta wait 'em out . . . Maybe a year, two years, maybe ten years. We're all young. We'll only get better . . . I don't know, maybe it's a crazy idea, but it could happen if we really want it . . . What do you think?

(*Silence.*)

IRA. You love me, I love you, Max. I'm in.

MAX. There you go.

VAL. I have a slight problem with ten years but we'll see what happens.

MAX. That's all I ask. Think about it. Don't rush. I just didn't want to say goodbye tonight . . . We're not ready for it yet . . . No goodbyes, alright?

LUCAS. I just said hello, I don't want to say goodbye.

MAX. (*Nods to Lucas.*) . . . They didn't believe that Hannibal could cross a thousand miles over the Alps on elephants. They said the elephants would all freeze and die. And you know what Hannibal said? . . . He said, "not if they *run* all the way." (*HE breaks up laughing.*) Come on. Let's celebrate. Everybody inside. Helen, go up and get my saxophone.

(*HELEN exits.*)

MAX. I'm going to play "Sleighbells roasting on an open fire."

(*MAX exits. The OTHERS are still stunned.*)

KENNY. I'll give a thousand dollars to the first one who says something intelligent.

CAROL. I think you just won it yourself.

MILT. He doesn't really mean "wait ten years," does he?

KENNY. No. It's just a metaphor.

MILT. For what?

KENNY. For wait ten years.

VAL. I don't know what the hell to think. Somebody tell me what to think.

KENNY. Max knows it's over. And he knows *we* know it's over. But he didn't know how to say it. Not as himself. He had to become somebody else to tell us. The way he hides behind a character on the show.

BRIAN. So who was he just now?

KENNY. Hannibal! Alexander the Great! Maybe Cyclantis, whoever the hell he was.

LUCAS. Am I the only one who thinks that Max was—and don't hit me for this—astoundingly noble?

IRA. Noble??? You think he was noble??? He was Moses, for crise sakes. The man is a giant. He's Goliath. Maybe he's Goliath after

David hit him in the head with a rock, but there's fucking greatness in him, I swear . . . He's got so much anger in him, so much pain, so much strength, so much roast beef and potato salad, that when he goes down, like he did in here tonight, with such a crash, people fell out of their beds in Belgium . . . There'll never be a Max Prince again because he's an original. I'm telling you, guys. We just lived through history. (*IRA goes.*)

KENNY. Let's go in and join Moses before he eats up all the Commandments. (*HE goes.*)

CAROL. I can't believe it, but I think I'm going to miss speaking fuck.

MILT. You're going to miss speaking it? I'm going to miss *doing* it.

BRIAN. I'm telling you guys, Hollywood is great. You'll love it.

VAL. Listen! If you're a Jew, you end up in the desert no matter what.

(*BRIAN laughs and THEY leave.*)

LUCAS. (*To audience.*) I would have followed Max to the ends of the earth . . . But the earth went off the air on June first . . . And we all went our separate ways . . . Some up, some down, some struggled, some had more babies, and one, like Brian, died much too young . . . Helen went to law school and God knows what happened to her . . . But the most wonderful and incredible thing *did* happen . . . On the very last day of the very last show of the season, the newspapers announced that the United States Senate voted sixty-seven to twenty-two to censure Joseph McCarthy for conduct unbecoming a senator. His days were numbered . . . That night Max took us all out to dinner, and he was so unbelievably funny, the tears ran down our faces, and only some of it was from laughter.

(*LUCAS finishes his last line of dialogue to the audience at the end . . . We hear a lone SAXOPHONE playing "Chestnuts Roasting on an Open Fire"* . . . eventually hitting a flat note. It keeps on playing as MILT comes in.*)

* "The Christmas Song" ("Chestnuts Roasting on an Open Fire") by Mel Tormé and Robert Wells.

MILT. Lucas, you have to see this. Max is playing the saxophone . . . and eating a corned beef sandwich at the same time.

(THEY look at each other.)

BOTH. Ba-dum-bum!

(THEY BOTH go off as the SAXOPHONE keeps playing.)
Curtain

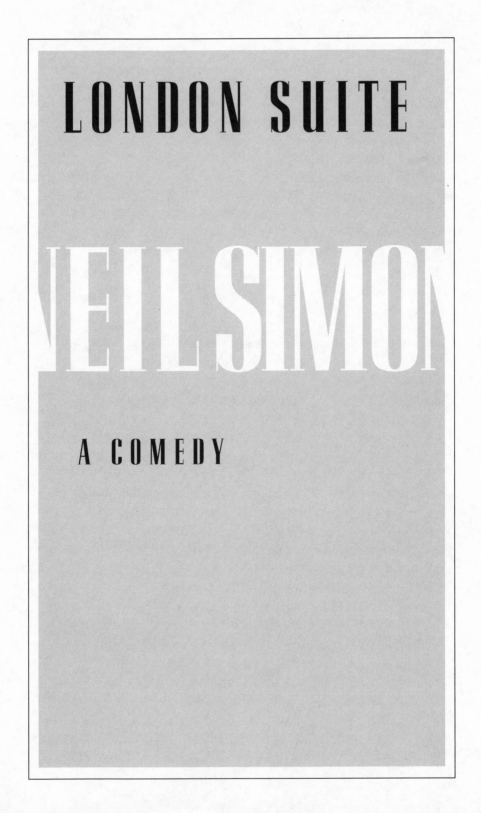

LONDON SUITE

NEIL SIMON

A COMEDY

ACT I

Place: The play takes place in a single suite in a luxury hotel in London, something on the order of the Connaught, for example.
Time: The present.

SCENE ONE
Settling Accounts

(In the dark, we hear the voice of an English airline employee over the public address system.)

WOMAN. Ladies and gentlemen, this is the first call for British Airways Flight 106 to Buenos Aires. All those holding boarding passes will proceed to Gate Number One Seven . . . Thank You.

(We hear the hubbub of noise in the terminal, then the voice of a MAN, Welsh accent.)

BRIAN. *(Cheery but eerie.)* Hello, Billy, fancy meeting you here . . .
BILLY. Brian? Is that you?
BRIAN. Off to Argentina, are you? Beautiful place, I hear. Mind if we have a little chat first, Bill? *(BILL starts to interrupt)* . . . Plenty of time to catch your plane.

(The hubbub slowly diminishes as the lights come up in Suite 402.
About ten o'clock at night.
The lights go on.
BILLY FOX, about fifty, is wearing a dark overcoat over a well-tailored suit. HE is looking frightened. At the side of the sofa,

BRIAN CRONIN, about fifty, in a leather half-jacket, stands holding a gun and a glass of Scotch. The gun is aimed at BILLY.)

BILLY. . . . I've done nothing wrong, Brian, I swear to you. Whatever it is, we can straighten this out, I'm sure.

BRIAN. Oh, don't mind the gun, Billy. It's mostly for effect . . . Bang bang bang! *(HE laughs.)* No, no. I'm just holding it in the unlikely event that I may have to kill you. *(Pause.)* Nice suite, isn't it? Hasn't changed much in what, twenty-two, twenty-three years? Couldn't believe it when you put me up here then . . . Poshest thing I ever saw . . . Who was I? A no one. A young Welsh writer, first time in London, my new book under my arm, wearing the only suit I had. You had a lot of faith in me, Billy, and I'll always be grateful for that.

BILLY. I feel dizzy. I think I'm going to pass out.

BRIAN. Don't try it, Bill. I'll shoot your pecker off, you'll be up in a flash, hoppin' about the room . . .

BILLY. *(HE puts attaché case on his lap, protecting his vitals.)* Do you really hate me that much?

BRIAN. *Hate* you? If anything, Billy, I've always worried about you, about your health and well-being. All of us who depended on you were always concerned. Because if something happened to you, Bill, who would be there to manage our finances?

(HE drinks again.)

BILLY. Brian, this is not the first time I've seen you having delusions. How many other times have I seen you in this state? How much more whiskey do you have to drink before you permanently damage what's left of your brains and your talent?

BRIAN. Seen me like what, Billy? Drunk, mad, whimsical, with a loaded gun in my hand preparing to blow an east to west tunnel through your fucking head? The answer to that is never, Billy . . . How much more whiskey do I have to drink before I permanently damage what's left of my brains and talent? That's easy, Bill. My talent is beyond damage. I didn't destroy it. I used it up. It doesn't keep filling itself over and over again, flooding the banks of your mind like the river Nile every spring. It dries up, Billy. It cracks under the searing pressure of critics and readers who demand art, high standards and enormous popularity all at the same time. I did, however, write eight bloody wonderful books before the drought set in. But those eight books, those eight film sales, those television rights made a packet of money, didn't they, Bill? Prudently salted away to secure the future of myself, my two ex-wives, my children and my grandchildren . . . Until yesterday about noon when I found out quite innocently and by chance, that there *is* no money. That there is nothing left of what I salted away, not even a pinch full of salt . . . In other words, I am fucking *broke*, Billy . . . And in some small measure, it pisses me off.

BILLY. Yes. Well, I can see why you would be . . . But let's just talk some facts here for a moment.

BRIAN. That would be helpful. Shed some light on it, so to speak, eh, Bill? Perhaps you can explain to me how every penny I worked a lifetime for, saved and invested wisely and conservatively by my longtime friend, Billy Fox, adviser and manager, has all suddenly gone. Vanished. Departed to places and pockets unknown. What would cause a strange thing like that to happen, Bill?

BILLY. Well, you must understand, Brian, that these losses are only *paper* losses.

BRIAN. Paper losses, are they? Money is *printed* on paper, isn't it, Bill? And my bank accounts are printed on paper . . . And on that paper, it's printed that my total worth is now eight zeros with no number in front of it . . . Is that what you mean, Bill?

BILLY. May I suggest that if you put down the gun, I think this could be more of a conversation than a life-threatening situation. Don't you think, Brian?

BRIAN. I agree. I see your point. (*HE doesn't put the gun down. BILLY stares at him. Then BRIAN realizes.*) Oh, yes . . . (*HE puts the gun down on the table.*) There. The gun is down. Now it's a conversation. And if it doesn't go well, we can always go back to the life-threatening situation . . . Go on, Bill.

BILLY. Well, in the first place, what makes you think your money is gone?

BRIAN. Now you see, that's a life-threatening question, Bill. (*HE picks up gun again.*) But I'll tell you anyway . . . In my mail yesterday, I noticed a bill from the local butcher. Ordinarily, I send all bills to you and forget about them. But this had "Last Notice" stamped on the envelope. Surprised and curious, I opened it. It was cordial, friendly, said they always enjoyed my patronage and hoped I was satisfied with their service. However, they said you are four months behind in your payments and they were left with the reluctant choice of handing the collection of such debts over to their solicitors.

BILLY. Is that it? Ridiculous. How impertinent of them. All you had to do was ring me direct on my private number.

BRIAN. So I rang you direct on your private number . . . There was no answer.

BILLY. Ahh. Well, then you could have paged me on my pager.

BRIAN. I *paged* you on your pager. But your pager never returned my page.

BILLY. Could be my beeper . . . Did you try my car phone?

BRIAN. Eight times. You were never in your car.

BILLY. Right. Right. The car was in the shop. Repairs, you know.

BRIAN. I was going to send a carrier pigeon but I didn't know your PC number.

BILLY. Now I know. Yesterday I was at Citibank International. They had a proposal for my client on behalf of a large East German Consortium. But you could have asked for Mr. Shepherd at the bank. He handles your daily cash accounts.

BRIAN. So I asked for Mr. Shepherd, who handles my daily cash accounts. "Your account?" said Mr. Shepherd. "That account was closed a week ago by Mr. Fox" . . . "My entire account?" I asked tremulously. "Of course," replied Mr. Shepherd. "Signed by both you and Mr. Fox. That's what you wanted, wasn't it?" he asked. "Oh, yes," I said, with knees buckling and my blood pumping everywhere except to my heart.

BILLY. Yes. I put your money in a foreign investment fund. Explicitly for things like this East German Consortium . . .

BRIAN. So you forged my name.

BILLY. I-have-power-of-attorney. I didn't want you losing out on this incredible opportunity.

BRIAN. So is my money invested with the East German consortium, Bill?

BILLY. Yes . . . It will be.

BRIAN. Will be?

BILLY. It will be as soon as I receive their letter of confirmation.

BRIAN. So is the money here, Bill, or is it there? Or is it, as we speak, flying First Class on Lufthansa Airlines, munching pretzels and nuts?

BILLY. Brian, I think there's a misunderstanding here. If you would just look through your portfolio . . .

BRIAN. Last night, I looked for my portfolio. I never remember where I put it. There are two things in the world I never read, Bill. My old books and my portfolio. I don't read my books because I'm no longer emotionally attached to them. And I don't read my portfolio because I never *had* an emotional attachment to money. I just have no mind for business, you see.

BILLY. That's what you pay me for . . . No one has a mind for business, Brian. It took the ancient Egyptians two hundred years to build the great pyramids but in five thousand years they *still* haven't paid them off.

BRIAN. You haven't put *me* in that one, have you, Bill?

BILLY. All I want is for you to be able to sleep well at night, Brian. That's why we have our quarterly meetings, right?

BRIAN. Four times a year we'd meet in your office, Bill. With charts, graphs, computers, balance sheets, partnership agreements, etc. And you would explain the meaning of all this to me, spewing out all this technical information to me in a fuzzy fucking flurry of financial terminology that not even the bloody Exchequer of England could understand. When you said, "Do you understand what I'm saying?" I said, "Yes," because the only thing I understood was you saying, "Do you understand what I'm saying?" . . . I *never* understand. I never *will* understand. I never *want* to understand. And even if I understood, I would *hate* myself for understanding . . . It's not my bloody business. It's yours. My business is to write books. Your business is to take my business and turn it into things that profit both our businesses . . . My liability is that I have to put all my trust in you. Your responsibility is to honor that trust . . . Somewhere there's been a breach in that trust, Bill. Which is why I'm holding the breach of this gun, drawing closer and closer to the moment of your *DEMISE, EXTINCTION AND EXECUTION* . . .

BILLY. (*HE shields head with attaché case.*) Brian, we've been friends for more than twenty years. Doesn't that mean anything to you?

BRIAN. I cherish those twenty years, Bill. It's only the last day and a half you've turned into a major shit . . . You stole my money, didn't you?

BILLY. No!

BRIAN. Swearzy?

BILLY. May God strike me dead.

BRIAN. That's why he sent me.

BILLY. Oh, Christ, you've taken leave of your senses.

BRIAN. No, *you've* taken leave of my senses, and my pounds sterling and my gold certificates. Tell me, Bill it's a small point but am I still paying for an empty safety deposit box?

BILLY. What's the use? You haven't the slightest intention of letting me explain. Go ahead. Get it over with. Blow my brains out, if it'll make you happy.

BRIAN. I didn't say it would make me happy. It would just make me feel less pent up . . . You did steal my money, didn't you, Billy?

BILLY. No. Absolutely not . . . I borrowed it.

BRIAN. Oh, I *see*!! It's a *loan*! . . . I *loaned* you my life savings. I can't pay my butcher bill because I *loaned* you every cent I have in the world. I didn't know I was that good a friend to you, Bill . . . Well, now since you didn't tell me, technically that could be considered stealing, right?

BILLY. Well, in a semantic sort of way, I suppose yes.

BRIAN. Semantic bullshit!! . . . You stole it!!! Why? . . . I trusted you! Why did you do it?

BILLY. . . . Envy, I suppose . . . Actually, I'm very good at looking after other people's money . . . but not mine, I'm afraid. I make a great deal of money for my clients, you see, but the truth is, it's not quite as difficult as you suppose. It's quite easy to increase the wealth of a man who's worth ten or twenty million pounds. Doors open for him that would otherwise be closed to your ordinary investor. It's a private club, you see. The wealthy, I mean. You don't have to join. You need no references. Your portfolio is your reference and your credit rating gets you into the inner sanctum, where billions of pounds are moving every day like pawns and knights and queens across a sterling silver chess board controlled and managed by the Grand Masters of Finance. And the Grand Masters rarely lose . . . The power of wealth is very seductive. It's not about what you can buy. It's about what you don't *have* to buy. You have nothing to prove, you see. And I was seduced into thinking that some of the power belonged to me. That I'm above the pack by virtue of introducing the wealthy to the Grand Masters. After all, if I increased their wealth, their sense of security, their well-being, their style of living, did I not have a hand in it? And slowly I began to think I was one of them. I felt it was owed to me. I found myself dressing like them, frequenting the same restaurants, inviting them to lunch, picking out their wines, picking up their checks. I started living beyond my means. A house I can't really afford, a few good paintings to show off the house, a wedding for my daughter so costly, it looked like it was mounted by the man who put on *Miss Saigon* . . . For my 25th anniversary, I took sixteen relatives and friends on a private chartered cruise through the Greek islands. I'm still paying that one off. I started mounting debts, and in desperation, I did for myself what I would never do for my clients. I made questionable investments. A play with a big name star that never made it out of Bristol. A film partly financed by two Iranian brothers who withdrew their support in mid-production, leaving myself and another dozen dupes to try to recoup our losses. Instead, they multiplied. If any of this became public, I would lose the faith and trust of my clients. I needed two and a half million pounds, and quickly, without jeopardizing the likely possibility of it becoming public . . . So I borrowed it from my clients, without their knowledge of intention of replacing every pound of it. I will make good on everything, Brian. That I swear to you. It was an unforgivable deceit, I admit to you. But I ask you for only ten days time. If by then, I've not returned every pound you've entrusted to me, you can turn me over to the authorities. I can promise you that public shame will be harsher punishment than any bullet you fire into my head.

(*There is a pause, then BILL looks up to BRIAN for his response.*)

BRIAN. Well . . . Talk about dilemmas . . . But you know what hurts, Billy? . . . Really hurts? . . . That I wasn't invited on the Greek cruise.

BILLY. You would have been bored stiff. They really weren't your sort of people.

BRIAN. No. I was just the sort who would *pay* for their sort of bloody vacation, right, Bill? . . . You know what? I take back cherishing those first twenty years . . . I'm beginning to hate you retroactively, you shit.

BILLY. Brian, my dear friend, Brian. What can I say? I feel so ashamed.

BRIAN. Yes, I can see that. I have just one minor question for you. (*BILL looks up.*) How many of us did you steal from? . . . Half? . . . Ten? . . . Five? . . . How many, Billy?

BILLY. . . . Just you.

BRIAN. Just *me*? . . . Just *me*? . . . Not *them*? Not the *others*? . . . None of your five and ten million pound members of your bloody bleeding Grand Masters sterling silver inner sanctum money movers? Just me! (*Right in BILL's face.*) You whining, worthless piece of treacherous crud! I don't need a gun to kill you. I'll do it with a bloody *fruit fork,* you bastard! (*HE grabs fruit fork from bowl of fruit, grabs BILL by his collar and holds the fork above him.*) Why *me*? . . . Why was *I* the one you picked?

BILLY. Because you were the only one who didn't ask questions! (*BRIAN is stunned; HE releases BILL.*) Do you know why all my other clients are so wealthy, Brian? They pay attention. They ask questions. They could look at their portfolios and know if a digit or a decimal point was in the wrong place. They watched their money like hawks. You never knew where the Goddamn *nest* was. For two months I slipped one egg after another from under your wings. You were *begging* me to rob you, don't you see that? The great writer looking down his nose at the mere mention of money, blinding himself to his responsibility of watching over it . . . It takes two to steal, Brian. One to take and one to give.

BRIAN. (*Looks at him.*) Do I have *anything* left?

BILLY. . . . No.

BRIAN. Not even a little account? One you might have forgotten about?

BILLY. . . . No. I got it all.

BRIAN. All of it? All two million one hundred thousand pounds?

BILLY. Two million six hundred and twelve thousand pounds.

You didn't even know what you had, did you? My four-year-old grandson could steal from you without your knowing.

BRIAN. Started training him already, have you? Well, it's getting past your dead time.

(*HE takes out the gun, grabs BILL by the collar.*)

BILLY. You think you'll get away with this? The bellman saw you. The assistant manager saw you standing behind me when I gave her my credit card.

BRIAN. I'm not trying to get away with anything, Bill. I have no money, no prospect, no talent. I'm as good as dead already

BILLY. If you give me the chance, I can get your money back, I swear. At least hear me out.

BRIAN. And how would you do that, Bill?

BILLY. In Buenos Aires. That's where I was going. I had a deal set up. An enormously wealthy businessman in Argentina wants to buy a fifty-one percent-ownership belonging to one of my clients. But he doesn't want to sell. The members of his board *did* want to sell and asked my help to intercede. I did. I convinced him it was the right move. There are certain problems still to overcome. It would have to be done personally, you see. No conference calls, no faxes. It would have to be the face to face. That's why they're sending me to Buenos Aires. If I can swing this deal, Brian, my compensation would come to almost two million pounds. That's an enormous deal, Brian, the biggest of my life. I can repay a substantial part of my debt to you . . . Give me that chance, Brian. For both of us.

BRIAN. (*Considers this.*) You have this ticket with you?

BILLY. Yes.

BRIAN. Let me see it. (*BILL takes it out of his pocket, gives it to him. BRIAN looks at it.*) This is a one-way ticket to Argentina.

BILLY. Yes. For me that's the most important part. Mr. DeGatto, that's the Argentinean, offered that if we successfully conclude the deal, he would like me to fly back with him to London on his private jet to meet with the board and finalize the agreement. I wasn't being frugal, Brian. I didn't want to buy the return ticket because I wanted to walk into Mr. DeGatto's office with complete confidence, knowing in my heart I was coming back with him. Without that confidence, I could ruin the day. And I refuse to let that happen.

BRIAN. I see . . . Sounds very promising, doesn't it?

BILLY. More than promising, Brian. I know I can deliver.

BRIAN. Hmmm . . . There's only one small point that still bothers me.

BILLY. What's that, Brian?

BRIAN. I don't believe a bloody word of it. Mr. DeGatto is the name of your barber. It was probably the first name you could think of. If they're giving you two million pounds, this deal must be worth hundreds of millions. Why would they send *you*, Billy? In Economy Class? They'd send an entire army of corporate lawyers . . . I may not know a bloody thing about business, Bill, but I know a fucking bad story when I hear it.

(*HE grabs BILLY by this collar.*)

BILLY. (*Drops to knees.*) I swear on the life of my family, the story is true!

BRIAN. I'll tell you why I think it isn't. When Mr. Shepherd told me my entire amount was withdrawn, a little bell went off in my head. So at seven A.M. this morning, I drove to within fifty yards of your elegant home and parked in the shadows. At nine-fifteen you appeared carrying your attaché case. Your wife Margaret came to the door and called out something about not being late for dinner since the Fosters were coming over tonight. Unusual thing for a wife to say to a man who was on his way to Argentina that day . . . unless, of course you never told Margaret . . . I followed you into London. You went into the Bank of Canada coming out twenty minutes later with your attaché case looking a little heavier . . . Then I followed your car out to Heathrow Airport. You checked in at British Airways, Economy Class, and had your bags ticketed, to where they are now, probably halfway across two oceans, headed for the Evita Peron Hotel, I imagine . . . That's when I made my presence known to you with a slight prod in your back with the barrel of my gun . . . So aside from "Don't Cry for Me. Argentina," what do you have to say for yourself, Bill?

(*BILL sits there: HE is visibly shaken. HE's at the end of his wits.*)

BILLY. Nothing . . . I have nothing left to say . . . I'm tired of all this . . . of all the lies . . . of everything . . . I stole from you and that's that . . . you're right about the story, of course. Pure poppycock . . . That's the one area where you *are* supreme, Brian . . . Or were . . . Do what you want, I really don't give a damn.

(*BRIAN sits back and looks at him.*)

BRIAN. What's in the attaché case, Bill?
BILLY. A little money, whatever I could scrape together . . . Sixty-five thousand pounds . . . I'll split it with you.
BRIAN. (*Smiles*) You are a delicious weasel, Billy . . . Hand over the case.

(*BRIAN takes case from BILL.*)

BILLY. It won't open unless I tell you how. (*BRIAN clicks the little locks and they pop open.*) . . . Yes. That's how.

(*BRIAN opens the case and starts to count the money.*)

BRIAN. Seventy, eighty, ninety, a hundred, two hundred . . . Billy, you're not as good with figures as you used to be. There must be almost three hundred thousand pounds here.
BILLY. Closer to five hundred.
BRIAN. Five hundred thousand pounds? You keep sinking deeper and deeper into the slime as we go, don't you? . . . An interesting thing just happened, Billy. As you were telling me your story about Mr. DeGatto, I was amazed to find how quickly I saw through it. That there is still a spark of the writer left in me. Faint embers glowing, I admit, but still a spark. That perhaps my talent isn't quite as dead as I thought. Perhaps it's living in England, writing so much about England, that's dulled the edges of my creative abilities. That perhaps a change of scenery is what I need . . . Billy . . . I'm going to Argentina! With my five hundred thousand pounds. Give me your passport.
BILLY. You can't use my passport.
BRIAN. No, you toad. I'm using my own. (*Takes his passport.*) You're not going anywhere, Bill. You'll be busy here.

BILLY. Doing what?

BRIAN. Working your bloody ass off to return the rest of my money. To be sent in monthly checks to my children and grandchildren . . . If you miss a single payment, a registered letter will be sent to the police and the Inland Revenue Service telling them to examine your books, especially mine. By God, I'm feeling ten years younger, Billy. About the same amount of time you'll be spending at Dartmoor Prison if you skip a single month's check. Actually, I've turned out to be a pretty fair businessman, don't you think? . . . Well, I'm off . . . (*HE looks at his gun.*) Oh, you can have this, Billy. (*HE hands him his gun, starts away. BILLY points the gun at him.*) There's nothing in it but blanks. Pretty much like the expression on your face just now. (*HE crosses to the door.*) . . . You should have taken me on that Greek cruise, Bill.

(*HE leaves quickly. BILLY looks down at the gun, bewildered. BLACKOUT.*)

SCENE TWO

Going Home

(*In the dark we hear the sound of traffic in background.*)

MOTHER. Oh, there it is . . . Driver! We passed it back there. Could you please turn around?

LAUREN. Passed what, Mother?

MOTHER. That shoe store I was telling you about.

LAUREN. Mom, you've hit every shoe store in London.

MOTHER. No. This one just opened. I read about it in today's paper.

LAUREN. We're going to be over our baggage limit on the plane.

MOTHER. Right here, Driver . . .

(*The lights come up. The hotel suite. About five P.M. on a hot, sunny, summer afternoon.*
LAUREN SEMPLE, thirty-one, sits reading a paperback on Shakespeare. A plastic bag of other books just bought are on the table.

The telephone rings. SHE gets up and answers it.)

LAUREN. Hello? . . . Yes . . . My mother *is?* . . . Oh. Okay. Thank you.

*(She hangs up the phone, crosses to the front door and opens it.
Her mother, SHERYL, mid-fifties, comes in loaded with shopping
    bags in both hands, bought in Harrods and other department
    stores. SHE is exhausted and breathing hard.)*

MOTHER. *(As SHE enters.)* I told the concierge to wait three minutes and then call you. Otherwise I'd have to knock on the door with my head. *(SHE sits on the sofa, exhausted, still holding the bags.)* I couldn't get a cab. I walked back fourteen blocks carrying these. Three blocks from the hotel I was going to stop on the street and sell everything I bought at half price. *(SHE is still out of breath.)* Honey, could you do me a favor? *(Holds out one hand, holding some shopping bags.)* Take this bag out of my hand. *(LAUREN helps her.)* My knuckles have locked together. Easy, easy.

LAUREN. Relax, Mother.

(LAUREN puts the bags down.)

MOTHER. *(Indicating her moving fingers.)* Oh, they're alive. That feels good. Thank you. I would have slept with them all night.

LAUREN. I looked all over Harrods for you. Weren't we going to meet upstairs in the restaurant at four?

MOTHER. Yes, but I had to go back to the shoe department. I was missing a pair of shoes. They never found them.

LAUREN. Did you have your receipt?

MOTHER. No. They were the shoes I was wearing when I came in.

LAUREN. You lost your own shoes? Aren't they responsible?

MOTHER. No. Only if they sold them.

LAUREN. Wait a minute. Wait a minute. *(Looks in one of the bags she just put down. Takes out a pair of shoes.)* Aren't these the ones you were wearing?

MOTHER. Oh, my God. I think I bought my own shoes.

LAUREN. How is it I can't get you to work out in a gym for twenty minutes but you'll carry around fifty pounds of shoes all day?

MOTHER. I don't know. Maybe if there was a gym where I could lift shoes, I would go . . . Well, at least we got *you* a beautiful skirt and blouse. Have you tried them on together yet?

LAUREN. No . . . I went back and exchanged them. (*SHE feels guilty about that.*) I'm sorry. I wanted to tell you not to buy them but I didn't want to hurt your feelings. Are your feelings hurt?

MOTHER. No, Honey, it's my fault. I always guess wrong with you. You were *always* so hard to shop for.

LAUREN. (*Crossing to bar.*) Then why do you keep doing it? I'm thirty-one years old and you're *still* trying to dress me.

MOTHER. I stopped trying to dress you in the third grade. You never wanted to look like a little girl.

LAUREN. You never dressed me like a little girl. You dressed me like a three-year-old married woman. (*Pours her coke.*) I swear. One new kid in school thought I was a very short teacher . . . You want something?

MOTHER. What time is it?

LAUREN. (*Looks at her watch.*) Twenty to five.

MOTHER. No. I'll wait for my five o'clock scotch.

LAUREN. Why? It's only twenty more minutes. Is the scotch going to be any better twenty minutes later?

MOTHER. Yes. It'll *age* a little more . . . I don't know. It's a habit. I have habits. Never mind. I'll have my scotch.

LAUREN. Thank you.

(*SHE crosses to the bar, fixes scotch.*)

MOTHER. You seem to have this sudden urge to change my life.

LAUREN. I'm sorry. I didn't mean to. (*Crosses to her.*) Here's your scotch. (*MOTHER takes it.*) You want to hold it for sixteen minutes?

MOTHER. God, you are just like your father was . . . Why do I bother talking to you?

LAUREN. 'Cause you love it.

(*SHE sits in chair opposite.*)

MOTHER. Something's up with you. I can see that mischievous look in your eye

LAUREN. What would I be up to?

MOTHER. I'm not sure. A surprise, maybe . . . Are you and Andy having another baby?

LAUREN. I don't think so. He never tells me things like that.

MOTHER. Do you *want* another baby?

LAUREN. Yes.

MOTHER. Are you trying?

LAUREN. We talked about it on the phone yesterday. Yes. We will when I get home.

MOTHER. Why didn't you tell me? We could have taken an earlier plane.

LAUREN. Would that make you happy? Another grandchild?

MOTHER. Happy isn't the word. It would make my life complete.

LAUREN. Mother, you're forty years away from completion. There's no way my having another baby should make your life complete. What about your *own* life?

MOTHER. Are you suggesting that *I* should have another baby?

LAUREN. Are you sorry you never did?

MOTHER. Honey, bringing you up was like having triplets. No. I love my life the way it is. I don't miss what I don't have.

LAUREN. You miss Dad

MOTHER. Yes. I miss Dad.

LAUREN. It's been six years since he died, Mom. You're too young and attractive to be alone.

MOTHER. I'm never alone. I have my friends. I have my job. I have you. I don't get enough of him. I have my son-in-law, the computer genius. I don't get to see him much but he faxes me every week.

LAUREN. They're stretching the life span every day, Mom. Do you want to be a hundred and ten years old and still be alone?

MOTHER. At a hundred and ten, I think I would prefer it.

LAUREN. I can't budge you a quarter of an inch, can I?

MOTHER. . . . Don't rush me, Laurie. Old habits are hard to break. I'll always be a compulsive shopper, right? (*Reaches down into big bag.*) Can you believe I came to London and bought something at the Gap? (*As SHE pulls Gap bag out of larger one.*) Five thousand Gap stores in America and I come here and pay twice as much . . . When your Dad and I first came here, you could buy things for nothing . . . This suite. We paid one-tenth of what I'm paying now for this suite.

LAUREN. Then why are we staying here?

MOTHER. (*Looks around.*) I wanted to. It's important to me.

LAUREN. I know. But one day you're going to have to let go of the past, aren't you?

MOTHER. I'm working on it.

LAUREN. Good. (*Smiles.*) I'm going to read for a while.

(*SHE crosses into the bedroom.*)

MOTHER. (*Sits on sofa.*) What are you reading, hon?

LAUREN. (*From bedroom.*) "Hathaway and Shakespeare."

MOTHER. Hathaway? . . . Hathaway . . . The Indian?

LAUREN. No. That's Hiawatha, Mom.

MOTHER. I *know* who Hiawatha is . . . Oh, Anne . . . Anne Hathaway. His wife . . . See what happens when I drink too early . . . (*LAUREN is stretched out on the bed.*) Oh God. Shakespeare. My favorite, you know. The plays, the sonnets, the soliloquies . . . I never really understood them but oh, what language . . . I think your father and I saw every Shakespeare play they ever did in London . . . Well, eight or nine, anyway . . . We saw Olivier, of course. Well, there was no one like him. Never will be again . . . You never saw him, did you? On the stage I mean.

LAUREN. (*Lying on bed.*) No. I didn't.

MOTHER. Well, you really missed something. It's a shame . . . No. Wait a minute. You *were* with us. I was pregnant with you. I was in my fifth month the night we saw him in . . . Iago's friend . . .

LAUREN. . . . Othello?

MOTHER. *Othello.* And I said to Daddy, "I hope the baby's listening because she'll remember this her whole life" . . . Well, your Dad just laughed and laughed. That's the night I found out I was funny . . . Anyway, it wasn't just Olivier we saw . . . We saw *all* the great actors then . . . I remember we saw . . . (*She thinks.*) Oh, what's his name? . . . Sounds like that beer.

LAUREN. . . . Alec Guinness?

MOTHER. *(Nods.)* Alec Guinness . . . and we saw . . . er . . . Oh, what is it? . . . Skinny . . . Minny . . . Whinney?

LAUREN. Albert Finney?

MOTHER. Albert Finney. Right . . . and of course there was er . . . oh . . . *her husband.*

LAUREN. Richard Burton?

MOTHER. Richard Burton. Right . . . I'm so bad with names . . . but of course, the one I adored was the good one.

LAUREN. The good one?

MOTHER. Yes, you know him. Famous actor . . . The good one, honey.

LAUREN. They're all good, Mother.

MOTHER. No, it's his name. Good something.

LAUREN. . . . John Gielgud?

MOTHER. Right. John Gielgud. I knew it was good something. *(Looks at watch.)* God, I hate the thought of packing again tonight.

LAUREN. Well, let's do it later. If this is going to be our last night in England, let's make it a good one. *(SHE's crossed into the living room.)* Would you like to go out tonight? Someplace really special?

MOTHER. I wouldn't mind.

LAUREN. Just promise me one thing. Don't say no right away.

MOTHER. Alright. What is it?

LAUREN. There's a rock concert in Wembly Stadium.

MOTHER. *(Looks at her.)* How long do I have to wait before I say no?

LAUREN. Not yet. I could call up the concierge. I bet he could dig up a couple of tickets. It'll be my treat. Think about it.

MOTHER. I thought about it while I was waiting to say no . . . I would feel completely out of place. There's no one my age at rock concerts.

LAUREN. You're wrong. Most rock singers *are* your age.

MOTHER. Anyway, they have riots at those things. I'd be crushed to death. I don't want to die in Wembly Stadium . . . Think of something else.

LAUREN. Okay. Second choice. What about the theater? They have that new David Mamet play at the National.

MOTHER. The National? You think we could get tickets?

LAUREN. I don't think. I *know.* We've got 'em. No charge. They're free. We got an invitation.

MOTHER. From who?

LAUREN. Dennis.

MOTHER. Dennis? Who's Dennis?

LAUREN. Dennis Cummings. The Scotsman we met coming over on the plane. You talked to him for hours.

MOTHER. *(Shocked)* His name is *Dennis*? Oh, God. I kept calling him *Kenneth.* He must think I lisp or something . . . How do you know he invited us?

LAUREN. He's staying here at the hotel. *(SHE takes note out of her pocket.)* He sent a note. *(SHE reads it.)* "Dear Mrs. Semple. I hope this isn't too sudden a notice for you but I just came upon two tickets for the David Mamet play at the National. He's American, you know. Perhaps I'm being too forward but if it interests you at all, please call me in room five sixteen. I'll be there until seven. Hopefully yours, Dennis Cummings."

(SHE looks hopefully at the MOTHER.)

MOTHER. How long have you had that note?

LAUREN. About an hour. Found it when I came in.

MOTHER. You mean you've been setting me up all this time just to get me a *date*???

LAUREN. It's not a date. It's a play.

MOTHER. He's got two tickets. I didn't hear *your* name in there. Or were you going to sit on my lap?

LAUREN. I was going to tell you. I just wanted to get you in the right mood first—

MOTHER. Well, you could have played bagpipes when I came in the door . . . And what about the rock concert at Wembly? What if I had said yes to that?

LAUREN. You would *never* go to a rock concert. I was safe there.

MOTHER. Oh, but you think I'd go to the theater with a man named Dennis that I called *Kenneth* all night.

LAUREN. He probably never noticed . . . or even cared . . . He practically talked to you all night.

MOTHER. I couldn't sleep, he couldn't sleep. So we talked. He told me about Scotland, that he lives on an old estate that's been in his family for two centuries . . . Well, you know me, I'm always interested in old houses. I told him so.

LAUREN. Are you going?

MOTHER. Where?

LAUREN. To see it. I overheard him say, if you're ever up in Scotland, you must drop in.

MOTHER. *When am I ever in Scotland?* . . . I haven't even said yes to the play yet and you have me dropping in on Scotland?

LAUREN. How could you resist a chance to stay in a two-hundred-year-old Scottish estate? As a guest? You could always go home a day later.

MOTHER. You know where it is? Sixteen kilometers from Loch Ness . . . where the monster is . . . I wouldn't even *fly* over that place . . . I want to be back on 84th Street and Third Avenue, thank you very much.

LAUREN. Okay. Forget Scotland. Go to the National. It's only an hour and twenty minutes out of your life. David Mamet writes very short plays.

MOTHER. Why are you doing this?

LAUREN. You *know* why.

MOTHER. Because you think Andy and you and the baby are my whole life. Because you think I'm cheating myself by not looking out there for something else to fulfill me.

LAUREN. I couldn't have said it better.

MOTHER. And you think Mr. Cummings is going to fulfill me?

LAUREN. Not necessarily, but it's a start.

MOTHER. Look, he's a very nice man. A gentleman. But do you actually think I'm going to live out my life three thousand miles away from a good Chinese restaurant?

LAUREN. You didn't think he was attractive?

MOTHER. Very. And very polite. And very shy.

LAUREN. *Shy?* . . . I saw the little Sean Connery move he made on you. (*SHE picks up small pillow from the sofa, holds it up, Scottish accent.*) "Woud ya like a li-il pilla for yer head, Mrs. Sumple?"

MOTHER. You're not going to let up on this, are you?

LAUREN. Why should I? I still have until seven o'clock.

MOTHER. . . . No. I can't do it.

LAUREN. All right . . . I'll tell him.

(*LAUREN crosses to the phone and starts to dial.*)

MOTHER. Wait . . . Let me think about it.

(*LAUREN sits in chair next to phone. The MOTHER, on the sofa, turns her back to LAUREN as SHE thinks.*)

LAUREN. . . . Tick tock, tick tock, tick—(*The MOTHER turns and glares at her.*) Sorry (*The MOTHER turns away again.*) . . . you're going . . . I can tell by the way your shoulder is looking at me. You're going, aren't you?

MOTHER. Yes . . . But not for *your* sake. Not even mine . . . (*SHE is up. Heading for bedroom.*) I'm going because he seems like a decent man and he was nice enough to ask me.

LAUREN. *Great!* . . . What are you going to wear?

MOTHER. What'd you expect? *Kilts?* . . . I'm going casual. I don't want him getting the wrong idea about why I'm going.

(*SHE starts for bathroom.*)

LAUREN. Use your *good perfume.*

MOTHER. Why? I only need to smell good for ninety minutes.

(*Starts to go again.*)

LAUREN. Mother!! (*The MOTHER stops.*) Are you nervous?

MOTHER. No. *You are.* Don't worry. I'll get his name right. Dennis. Dennis. It rhymes with tennis . . . I'll be home about nine thirty. (*As SHE goes.*) Dennis the menace plays tennis in Venice . . .

(*SHE is gone.*)

LAUREN. (*Rushes to the phone and dials, then into the phone.*) Hello? Mr. Kenneth Cummings in five sixteen, ple . . . Dennis! Thank you. (*SHE closes her eyes, to herself.*) Please God, don't let him ask her who her favorite English actors are.

(*We dim out.*)

*(In the dark, we see the glimmer from the TV set above the bar.
We hear the voice of an English commentator giving the latest
football score and the weather.
LAUREN, still dressed, no shoes, is asleep on the sofa, an open
book on the floor just beneath her.
We hear the key in the door, it opens and the MOTHER enters.
SHE closes the door gently. SHE wears the same skirt as in the
first scene, with a smart jacket and the shoes that LAUREN
wore in the first scene. The MOTHER carries a purse and the
program from the National Theater.
SHE walks in on tip toes, sees that LAUREN is asleep, takes the
clicker and turns off the TV.)*

TV ANNOUNCER. *POP!* . . . The sound of cool, tangy mint
exploding in your mouth . . . The *POP* that awakens and refreshes
like an alpine morning . . . for that extra *POP,* try Polar Mints . . .
the mint with that Popular *POP!*

(Music.)

2ND ANNOUNCER. And now for the late night, Sports Wrap Up
with Eric Bruxton . . .

(Music.)

ERIC BRUXTON. And here are yesterday's racing results . . . On
a good track at Doncaster, Achilles Heel left sturdier legs behind as
it came in at twenty to one, with Don't Forget Mikie showing well
but not well enough . . . At Plumpton, Catcha Penny caught the
pack, passing Sticky Money and Blushing Belle for a handsome
eleven to three for its troubles . . . At Wincanton, Ziggy's Dancer
pranced four lengths ahead of Jigsaw Boy but fell behind Indian
Rhapsody at the finish while Two Moves In Front came in six
lengths behind the pack.

*(SHE starts to cross to bedroom when LAUREN speaks without
opening her eyes.)*

LAUREN. Where do you think *you're* going?

MOTHER. Oh. You're up. I was going to get you a blanket.

LAUREN. (*Sits up.*) What time is it?

MOTHER. Twenty to two

LAUREN. Twenty to *TWO*? . . . What happened to nine thirty?

MOTHER. Please! You sound just like my mother. (*SHE takes off jacket.*) Can I get into my pajamas first? I'm exhausted and we have to get up at six thirty.

LAUREN. No, we don't. I packed everything. We can sleep till twenty to seven. What happened?

MOTHER. I'll tell you tomorrow. I'm cold, I'm exhausted and we have to get up at . . . twenty to seven.

LAUREN. Mother! *Come in here and sit down!*

MOTHER. Now you sound like my father.

(*SHE comes into the living room.*)

LAUREN. I've been worried to death all night.

MOTHER. Don't you think I was too?

LAUREN. Please. Just sit there and talk to me . . . Was it terrible?

MOTHER. No.

LAUREN. Was it wonderful?

MOTHER. No.

LAUREN. Then what was it?

MOTHER. Like a curse. You can't wait to go and you can't wait to get back.

LAUREN. All right, I have to hear everything. Where'd you go after the show?

MOTHER. To dinner. It was a Thai restaurant.

LAUREN. What do you mean a Thai restaurant? You *hate* Thai food.

MOTHER. I ordered a lamb chop and asked them to scrape off the Thai stuff.

LAUREN. Did that bother Mr. Cummings?

MOTHER. Why should it? He's not from Thailand.

LAUREN. Okay. So after the scraped off lamb chop, where did you go?

MOTHER. We drove around a bit. We stopped off at an all-night drug store. He had to pick up something.

LAUREN. (*Looks at her*) . . . What?

MOTHER. I was looking at some magazines.

LAUREN. So was he buying . . . you know?

MOTHER. Oh please, it was nose spray. He has bad allergies.

LAUREN. Is that what he told you?

MOTHER. I could see it in the theater. He had trouble breathing. He kept snorting all the time.

LAUREN. What do you mean, snorting?

MOTHER. Snorting. Snorting. (*SHE snorts a couple of times*) Only not that loud . . . It stopped after a while.

LAUREN. Alright. From the beginning. Tell me everything from the minute the night started. (*SHE curls up on the sofa, clutches a pillow to her chest.*) No! Wait! (*SHE jumps up.*) I want a drink to hear this. (*SHE crosses quickly to bar.*) I'm having a brandy . . . Would you like your twenty to two in the morning Scotch?

MOTHER. No. I already had a drink in the restaurant . . . It was like sake or something.

LAUREN. Sake is Japanese. It's a wine made out of rice.

MOTHER. Then that's it. I've been chewing it all night long.

LAUREN. Okay. Start over. We're not in the restaurant yet. We're in the lobby of the hotel. Start from—(*Scottish accent.*)—"Hello, Mrs. Sumple."

MOTHER. Well, let's see . . . He picked me up in his car.

LAUREN. Cool. Very cool. No taxi. I like that . . . Chauffeur?

MOTHER. No, no. He drove himself.

LAUREN. Even cooler. What kind of car? Jaguar?

MOTHER. A silver gray Ferrari sports car.

LAUREN. No-wayy!

MOTHER. It was very low to the ground. We almost drove under a bus.

LAUREN. *I SAW IT!* I was looking out the window. It looked like you but I said, "In your dreams, Laurie" . . . go on.

MOTHER. Then we drove to the National Theater on the other side of the Thames. He said it was normally a fifteen to twenty-minute drive. We made it in six minutes.

LAUREN. The man is definitely hot.

MOTHER. It was a convertible. He had the top down and asked if it was too much air. I wanted to be a good sport, so I said, "No, leave it down" . . . When we got there, my hair looked like "The Bride of Frankenstein."

LAUREN. Perfect! That's how they're wearing it today. (*SHE crawls back on the sofa.*) So you got to the National Theater.

MOTHER. Obviously we were very early so we stopped by a little pub he knew.

LAUREN. So you got out of the car.

MOTHER. Well, first he put the top up. Then when he pulled me out, I hit my head on the metal bar. I think he was apologizing but I couldn't hear it because of the ringing in my ears.

LAUREN. Oh, God. Did it hurt?

MOTHER. No. My hair was so stiff, it took most of the blow . . . We got to the pub and ordered drinks. He had a martini . . .

LAUREN. You had a Perrier with lime. So what'd you talk about?

MOTHER. Nice things. My family. His family.

LAUREN. I know about your family. Tell me about his.

MOTHER. He has a mother, a sister. The sister's name is Glynis. I thought he said Gwyneth. Then he said, "No, no, Glynis." Then I forgot if he was Kenneth or Dennis. Everything he has comes in lots . . . Lots of land, lots of horses, lots of dogs, lots of guns.

LAUREN. Like real estate. That's not bad . . . Does his house have a name? Like Tara. Or Manderly. Or Windsor Castle?

MOTHER. It was a Scottish name. You couldn't say it without hurting your tongue . . . Something like Burn-glo-loch-mon-flay-firth-forth. (*Holds mouth.*) See. It hurts.

LAUREN. Tell me about him. What was he like?

MOTHER. Very neat dresser. Tweedy. Very tweedy. And suedy. Tweedy and suedy.

LAUREN. . . . Tweedy and Suedy? . . . Weren't they in *Bambi*?

MOTHER. Oh, he has deer too . . . *Lots* of deer.

LAUREN. Where? In Burn clog fling flong firth? (*The MOTHER laughs.*) But what was he like as a person?

MOTHER. Considerate. Gentle. A little uncomfortable. Started that snorting thing again. Kept excusing himself and going to the men's room. You could hear him snorting in there . . . I felt badly for him.

LAUREN. Well, you have allergies too.

MOTHER. Yes, but mine are the silent kind.

LAUREN. Okay. So is he divorced or a widower or what?

MOTHER. No. He's a bachelor. Never married. He looked to be in his early sixties . . . Never had the time to marry, he said . . . Anyway, we got up and went to the Mamet play.

LAUREN. How was it?

MOTHER. I couldn't hear the first fifteen minutes because the woman behind me was eating a two-pound bag of sour balls. Every time she took off the wrappers, it sounded like a forest fire. And she didn't suck on the sour balls, she chewed on them, which made it sound like a chain gang breaking up rocks.

LAUREN. Oh, God. And what was the play like?

MOTHER. What I could hear of it, I loved. I think I will have that brandy. *(SHE crosses, gets brandy.)* Dennis had trouble with it. He was embarrassed by the F words. Not at first, but then they started to come like machine gun bullets . . . After the F words came the C words, the P words, the S words, the shove it up your A words.

LAUREN. Maybe he was embarrassed for you.

MOTHER. I thought they were important to the play. Dennis just had a hard time with it.

LAUREN. Dennis, huh?

MOTHER. So he started to cough . . . And cough . . . He coughed on every F word . . . He politely turned away from me so the woman next to him got it . . . So he apologized to her and the man behind him whispered to please be quiet . . . which gave the woman behind me a chance to chew her sour balls again . . . But Dennis couldn't stop coughing so he held his hand over his mouth but that made his face twitch.

LAUREN. What kind of twitch?

MOTHER. You know. Like a tic.

(SHE twitches her face twice.)

LAUREN. Did you say something to him?

MOTHER. Like what? "Don't do that"? . . . Well, we got through the play . . . We walked out, got into the car, he started to wheeze.

LAUREN. Wheeze?

MOTHER. (*SHE wheezes a couple of times.*) He said his allergies weren't from grass or trees or cats. They were mostly from emotional things. Fear, anger, confusion, embarrassment. He was embarrassed to tell me this so he started to twitch again. (*SHE twitches again.*) Isn't there a name for that?

LAUREN. Highly troubled?

MOTHER. So I asked him if he wanted me to drive because every time he twitched, the car swerved.

LAUREN. Maybe this wasn't such a good idea.

MOTHER. Every few blocks he would scrape against a parked car. He had to stop four times to put his personal card in their windshield so he could pay for the damages . . . It must have cost him twelve thousand dollars to get me home . . .

LAUREN. (*Laughs.*) Mother, this is a disaster. It couldn't have been worse.

MOTHER. I know, but it got worse anyway . . . On the way back to the hotel, he turned down a very dark street and slowed down. Then he stopped the car. There was no one around and for the first time I got nervous . . . Then he opened the glove compartment and what do you think he takes out?

LAUREN. Do I want to hear this?

MOTHER. A small tank of oxygen. He said he was having trouble breathing. I helped him strap it around his head but I got the nozzle around his ear instead of his nose . . . Well, he couldn't breathe through his ear, so I let him do it himself . . . So then we sat there for about a half hour. He tried to make conversation with this thing strapped on his face. I couldn't understand a word he was saying. I thought I was in a space ship talking to a Russian astronaut . . .

LAUREN. Why didn't he just go to a hospital?

MOTHER. I finally suggested it and he agreed . . . He drove up and parked in the garage, scraping the fender of a doctor's car. He put another card in the doctor's windshield. They told me Dennis would be all right. It wasn't serious but he'd have to stay the night . . . Dennis apparently gets this fairly often. So I left a note saying I hoped he felt better in the morning and thanked him for a wonderful and memorable evening . . . Then I walked in a light drizzle for twenty minutes until I found a taxi and got rid of all my English coins.

LAUREN. Would you do me a favor? On the plane home, tell me that story again.

MOTHER. I'm sorry I laughed about it . . . But coming home in the taxi, I thought, here's an attractive, intelligent, worldly man who probably wants to get married but found a way to stop himself. By wheezing and snorting and twitching. Like some sort of psychological block that keeps him safe at home in Scotland with his mother, his dogs, his horses and his aunt, never letting himself get involved. Do you know what I mean?

LAUREN. (*Looks straight at her.*) Perfectly.

MOTHER. Oh. I see . . . Thank you for the innuendo. I'm going to bed . . . But thank you for trying, darling . . . Goodnight.

LAUREN. Goodnight. (*The MOTHER crosses into bedroom, takes off her jacket, then sits on the edge of the bed, lost in thought. On sofa, LAUREN calls out.*) You want me to leave a wake-up call? (*A moment.*) Mom?

(*The MOTHER gets up and walks slowly into the living room, stands in the doorway.*)

MOTHER. Laurie . . . can you take a few more minutes?

LAUREN. You mean there's more?

MOTHER. Yes.

LAUREN. Of course.

(*The MOTHER crosses back into living room.*)

MOTHER. You were right about what you said earlier tonight. I do lean a lot on you and Andy and the baby. It's been hard for me without your father, but as you said, it *has* been six years.

LAUREN. Mom, if I pushed you too hard tonight, I am so—

MOTHER. No, no. It's alright. I went out tonight to test the waters. What if it turned out to be wonderful? What if I really ended up in Scotland? Married, living out my life there? How would you feel?

LAUREN. If you were happy, I would be too. I'd miss you but we'd work that out . . . What is it, Mom?

MOTHER. . . . There *is* a man in my life. For about a year and a half now. He lives about an hour from me. I've managed to keep it quiet. You never met him but your Dad knew him. We all used to play golf together. Dad liked him a lot.

LAUREN. And you thought I wouldn't approve? Why couldn't you tell me?

MOTHER. . . . He's married.

LAUREN. Oh . . . Well, that *is* a problem, isn't it? . . . does his wife know?

MOTHER. She had a stroke about three years ago. She's bedridden. The doctors said she'd really never be . . . *never* be there for him anymore, but that she could go on living for years . . .

LAUREN. Oh, God, Mom. I'm so sorry.

MOTHER. For her. For him . . . They can't help it, but I've got a choice . . . Do you think I'm wrong? Seeing him, I mean.

LAUREN. No. How could I?

MOTHER. He's a wonderful man. It's more a friendship than an affair, but it's also more than a friendship . . .

LAUREN. Is it enough for you, Mom? The way it is.

MOTHER. I think so. I don't know how I'd handle a full-out relationship yet. I'd have to build up to it.

LAUREN. You will . . . (*The MOTHER tries to hold back her tears.*) Come on, it's been a long night.

(*LAUREN starts for the bedroom. The MOTHER starts to follow.*)

MOTHER. You know . . .

LAUREN. What?

MOTHER. Somehow . . . I had the feeling you knew about this all along . . . Don't tell me if you did. If you knew, just say, "Let's go to bed, Mom."

LAUREN. If I knew, why wouldn't I have told you?

MOTHER. To protect me. To honor my secret. Because that's what a loving daughter would do.

LAUREN. (*Looks at her, smiles.*) Let's go to bed, Mom.

(*LAUREN crosses into bedroom. MOTHER stands there, then as*
  SHE starts into bedroom . . . WE FADE TO BLACK.)

ACT II

Diana and Sidney

(The lights come up on Suite 402 and 404.
Two of DIANE NICHOLS's suitcases are in the bedroom, one in the living room. Diana is about fifty, still prim and dressed fashionably. SHE is British.
GRACE CHAPMAN, her American secretary, is an attractive, but plainly dressed woman, mid-thirties. SHE is hanging coats up in the hall closet from the open suitcase.
DIANA, in the bedroom, looks out the window.)

GRACE. Well, how does it feel to be back in London, Diana?

DIANA. It's not my London anymore. It's changed. Fifty-story glass and steel high-rises . . . McDonald's on every corner . . . pretty soon they'll tear down Big Ben and put up a giant Swatch watch.

GRACE. Well, eight years is a long time to be away.

DIANA. I don't remember the language anymore . . . Grace, do I still sound British to you?

GRACE. Of course you do.

DIANA. No. I've lost it. I sound like an American tourist . . . Theater brokers will try and sell me tickets to *Cats* . . . I read an article that said that more people have seen *Cats* than there *are* getting cats in America . . . Same thing applies to *Phantom* . . . Are you getting my vodka, Grace?

GRACE. In a minute.

DIANA. No, you're stalling. Trying to dissuade me from my vodka. I respect that you're a member of AA, Grace, but please don't try to convert me. I hate meetings where three hundred people who would kill for a drink get up and say how happy they are . . . Now please get it, there's a good girl. Oooh, that sounded British, didn't it?

(GRACE crosses to bar and puts ice in a glass. SHE eats some nuts from an open tray.)

GRACE. I just wish you wouldn't start drinking so early in the day.

DIANA. I'm not. I'm still on Los Angeles time . . . What is that munching sound? Are you nibbling on nuts again? Don't you dare come in my bedroom with the smell of nibbled nuts on your breath.

GRACE. I'm hungry. I haven't had lunch.

DIANA. Well, be sure you wipe the salt off your lips before Sidney arrives. I don't want you looking like Lawrence of Arabia. (GRACE pours vodka into glass. DIANA looks out the window.) Grace! Hurry! Look out the window. Quickly, hurry up!

GRACE. (Rushes to window, looks out.) What?

DIANA. Is that Sidney coming down the street?·. . . There.

GRACE. I wouldn't know. I've never seen Sidney.

DIANA. My God, he's gotten so old. His hair is all white. And he's walking with a cane . . . And he just got on a bus, thank God, it's not Sidney.

GRACE. Lime or lemon?

DIANA. Neither. Just add more vodka. (SHE looks out the window again.) There are things I do miss about London.

GRACE. (Mixes drink.) Like what?

DIANA. There's a little house in Knightsbridge. I used to walk by it on my way to the theater. Built in 1764. I think Lord Raglan used to live there. Or Lord Cardigan. One of those generals who invented nice clothing . . . I could afford that house now. I could chuck the TV series and spend my last years here. I would age gracefully, away from that Goddamn Malibu sun that turns your skin into crumpled credit cards . . . I might just see if it's for sale.

GRACE. (Comes in with drink.) I think that would be nice.

DIANA. Well, let's see what happens. (SHE drinks.) What time is it?

GRACE. Twelve fifteen.

DIANA. He's in London now. Out there somewhere. Calmly getting dressed, sunburned down to the crotch of his bikini briefs, and not the slightest bit nervous about seeing me, while I'm leaving teeth marks on my glass.

GRACE. (Starts to open another valise on stand in front of bed.) Men usually handle these things better than women.

DIANA. Yes, but he's bisexual. He could at least be half as nervous as me. (*SHE crosses, looks at herself in mirror.*) You were never married, were you Grace?

GRACE. (*Continues unpacking.*) No. But I once lived with someone for six years.

DIANA. Six *years*? That's *longer* than marriage. Why did it fail?

GRACE. It didn't. It ended.

DIANA. Did you ever meet up again?

GRACE. Once. We had lunch together.

DIANA. Was it painfully difficult?

GRACE. Not really. There was nothing at stake. I wasn't in love anymore.

DIANA. Meaning I'm still in love with Sidney?

GRACE. I don't know. Are you?

DIANA. God, no. Too much time has passed. We're divorced. And he's more gay now than bisexual . . . Oh, Christ, yes, of course I still love him . . . But not in a practical sort of way. In a longing sort of way . . . I'd turn gay myself if I thought it would help.

GRACE. Maybe you have to see him again before you can really tell.

DIANA. You're so sensible, Grace. You must always be honest with me, I depend on your reassurance. And your medicine bag. Could I have one of your little stress pills?

GRACE. What stress pills?

DIANA. One of your druggie things, for crise sakes. The special kind that you buy in dangerous neighborhoods through a slit in your car window.

GRACE. I threw those out a long time ago. They were past the expiration date.

DIANA. Grace, I'm not a fool. Pills that come from Bolivia do not have expiration dates.

GRACE. I swore I would never give you another one. You know what I'm talking about.

DIANA. Yes. The dinner party at the Davises'. I thought being carried out to the car in the chair I was sitting in was because of the puddles in their driveway. (*The phone rings. DIANA looks at it, then at GRACE.*) I swear, I knew it was going to ring then. I felt his presence coming into the lobby. After all these years. Isn't that remarkable?

GRACE. (*Looks at her watch.*) Yes. Plus the fact he's exactly on time. (*SHE picks up the phone.*) Hello? . . . No, it's Grace, her assistant . . . Yes, please do. Suite 402 and 404 . . . Thank you.

(*SHE hangs up.*)

DIANA. How did he sound?

GRACE. Pleasant. Brief. "I'm here. Shall I come up?"

DIANA. Cool bastard . . . I'm not going to get through this without one of your pills, Grace. Please. Half a pill. I'll give you half a raise.

GRACE. Diana, you don't need them. Just be yourself. Let him see you at your best.

DIANA. At my best? You think he's coming up here in a time machine?

GRACE. You have no idea what a beautiful woman you still are.

DIANA. What a sweet thing to say. All except the "still are" part. (*SHE looks in the mirror.*) Oh, Christ. I look as though I broke the sound barrier going backwards. (*Looks at mirror again.*) Oh, well, he'll just have to take me as is. (*SHE fixes one earring, then feels the other ear.*) Oh, Christ. I've lost an earring . . . Look on the floor, quickly.

(*THEY both look.*)

GRACE. What did it look like?

DIANA. Like *this* one, you nit. (*The doorbell rings.*) Agghhhh!

GRACE. Shall I get the door?

DIANA. With one earring? He'll think I'm a rap singer . . . Never mind. I'll get another pair. Don't keep him waiting. He'll go away. Entertain him until I can pull myself together.

GRACE. And do what?

DIANA. Sing, "Let Me Entertain You" . . . Grace, I think I'm overpaying you. Just open the fucking door . . . I'll apologize for that later.

(*GRACE crosses to entrance door. DIANA closes bedroom door and starts to primp herself.*

*GRACE opens the door. SIDNEY NICHOLS stands there. In his
mid-fifties, looking fit and tan. HE is dressed smartly in a blue
blazer and gray pants. A light topcoat as well. He is all charm,
warmth and humor, with a twinkle in his eye.)*

GRACE. Hello. I'm Grace.
SIDNEY. *(Smiles.)* Of course you are.

(HE comes into the room.)

GRACE. May I have your coat?
SIDNEY. Yes, but not to keep. I'm short on winter clothes.

(SHE takes it from him, hangs it up.)

GRACE. Diana will be right back with you. Can I get you some-
thing to drink?
SIDNEY. No, but you can lead me to it. *(HE sees bar.)* Ah, there
it is.
GRACE. You have a very nice tan. Have you been on vacation?
SIDNEY. *(At the bar.)* Yes, I have. Going on twelve years now.
GRACE. Oh, yes. You live on an island in Greece, don't you? Is it
true the sun shines three hundred sixty days a year there?
SIDNEY. Absolutely. We import our rain from Spain. *(HE smiles.)*
Is there a Coke here? Found it.

(He starts to open it.)

GRACE. Can I do that for you?
SIDNEY. Oh, no. It's so seldom I do anything physical these days.

*(DIANA, with her new earrings, is putting them on as SHE
creeps to the door and listens.)*

GRACE. *(Looks at her watch.)* Well, I have some errands to do.
SIDNEY. Works you hard, does she?
GRACE. Not at all. I love my job.
SIDNEY. I'm certain of it. It was a pleasure meeting you, Grace.

GRACE. Thank you. She'll be right out. Just finishing up a call.

SIDNEY. Nonsense. She's preparing her entrance.

GRACE. *(Smiles.)* Goodbye then.

SIDNEY. Goodbye. *(SHE leaves. HE crosses to bedroom door with his Coke and puts ear to the door.)* I can hear you breathing against the door, darling.

DIANA. *(Pulls away quickly, shouts.)* I am *talking* to my production manager in Hollywood. *(SIDNEY laughs and walks away. DIANA takes a deep breath, exhales, looks at herself once more in the mirror, then crosses and opens the bedroom door. SIDNEY looks at her. HE smiles. SHE is about to speak but suddenly is overcome with emotion, far more than SHE expected.)* Oh, God, Sidney. I suddenly don't know what to say. Help me.

SIDNEY. *(Simply.)* Hello, Diana.

DIANA. Oh, yes. That's good. I knew you would think of something. Hello, Sidney.

SIDNEY. You look absolutely—

DIANA. *NO!* Not yet! . . . Hug! Hug! *(HE crosses to her and THEY embrace. Not a kiss, but a deep, warm loving hug. SHE turns away and wipes her eye.)* I'm sorry. I won't do that again. I know how you hate sentimentality.

SIDNEY. No, no. We love it in Greece. We sit around and cry buckets and then turn it into soup . . . May I say it now? You look wonderful.

DIANA. You think so?

SIDNEY. Not an unflattering line on your face.

DIANA. I know. They're all tucked behind my ears now. From behind I look eighty-six.

SIDNEY. Well, put a bumper sticker on your back. "If I look old, you're walking too close."

DIANA. But my features have changed, haven't they, Sid? They enlarge with age, you know.

SIDNEY. No, no. You're at least ten years away from enlargement.

DIANA. No, Sid, I can tell. My nose has broadened. I'm breathing in twice as much air as I used to.

SIDNEY. Well, just cut down on your perfume . . . I like your earrings. Aren't those the pearls I bought you in Marakesh?

DIANA. I wore them just for today.

SIDNEY. I have a confession to make to you, Diana. They're paste.

DIANA. I know. They drip in hot weather . . . Oh, God, it's so good to talk to you. Can we spend some time together? When are you going back?

SIDNEY. Tonight. The six twenty plane.

DIANA. You're not.

SIDNEY. I have to. I bought one of those bargain fares. I'm flying cargo class.

DIANA. I am so disappointed, Sid. I've flown halfway around the world to see you.

SIDNEY. I thought it was a twelve-country press tour to plug your TV series.

DIANA. Well, yes. That too . . . Do we have time for lunch?

SIDNEY. I know just the place.

DIANA. Not Greek, I hope. You must be fed up with feta cheese.

SIDNEY. And olive oil. After a while, my shirts start sliding off . . . Where would you like?

DIANA. Here. In the room. There'll be more time for ourselves. And we'll run up an enormous bill and charge it to CBS.

(THEY sit on sofa.)

SIDNEY. It's going very well, isn't it? Your show.

DIANA. Thank God, Sidney. You finally asked. Have you seen it?

SIDNEY. Oh, yes.

DIANA. Amazing how you can encapsulate all the richness of your opinions in two tiny words. Why do you hate it?

SIDNEY. I don't hate it.

DIANA. How many have you seen?

SIDNEY. One.

DIANA. We've been on for eight years.

SIDNEY. I'm sorry. Tell me about the ones I've missed.

DIANA. Not much TV on that island, Sid? What's the name of it again?

SIDNEY. Mykonos.

DIANA. Funny. I keep thinking it's Mickey Mouse.

SIDNEY. Yes, we have TV. Mostly soccer matches and a Saturday morning cartoon based on *Medea*. That's one of the few plays you never got around to doing, isn't it?

DIANA. You're upset because I gave up the theater. You've been in Greece too long, Sid. *Our* theater doesn't exist anymore. They just revive revivals.

SIDNEY. Alright, I admit it. I don't like television. Least of all sitcom shows, the way they make you shout as if sound hadn't been invented yet . . . And I've yet to see one five-year-old child who talks like a five-year-old child. They're all tiny little Clifton Webbs. Jokes and gags instead of behavior. I don't mean to be rude. I'm genuinely glad for your success, Diana. I just hope all the time you're putting into it makes you happy.

DIANA. Meaning, why did I take it?

SIDNEY. Well, aside for the money.

DIANA. For the money. Aside had nothing to do with it . . . The film parts stopped coming, as they usually do for women past 40 . . . Do you know what they pay me now, Sidney? For a one-hour weekly show, which I star in for my own production company, for which I get 40 percent of the gross profits, besides my salary, which doubles every three years, *and* the world syndication rights, eight years on the air going on nine. Guess how much, Sidney?

SIDNEY. More money than I could possibly imagine in my wildest dreams.

DIANA. No. More than that . . . Do you know how many people watch the show, Sidney, each week, worldwide? Guess.

SIDNEY. I don't have to name them, do I?

DIANA. God, why am I trying to impress you? I hate myself for still needing your approval.

SIDNEY. You had it before, you have it now and you will have it forever.

DIANA. But I don't feel it. At your own funeral, Sid, I'll still want your approval. I'd be wondering if you liked the black mourning dress I was wearing, even as they were cremating your ashes.

SIDNEY. You don't exactly cremate ashes, love. Ashes are the residue of a well-executed cremation.

DIANA. I'm a big star, Sidney. Don't correct my syntax . . . God, you're the most irritating man I've ever met . . . Why can't I meet someone like you again?

SIDNEY. Would you want to?

DIANA. Yes. If we could go back to the way it was in the beginning. I thought we were so good together, so right. And I thought the sex was wonderful.

SIDNEY. It was.

DIANA. Then why did you suddenly make a sharp left turn?

SIDNEY. I didn't really. I just took a fork in the road. It wasn't a conscious choice. You find yourself as a boy driving a little blue Volkswagen and suddenly you grow into a flaming red Porsche.

DIANA. I see. And what am I? A run-down Ford station wagon?

SIDNEY. Whatever you are, it's vintage and classic. And I thought we always looked compatible. Being gay doesn't preclude one from loving others who aren't.

DIANA. No. But it precluded me from having a monogamous marriage.

SIDNEY. When did being heterosexual guarantee monogamy?

DIANA. Damn it, why are gays so incessantly honest?

SIDNEY. Perhaps because we've had to lie for so long. But don't give us more virtue than we deserve. Actually the thing we're most honest about is being gay.

DIANA. Things have changed for you since we were together, haven't they, Sid? All the sex barriers are coming down. It's an accepted style of life. Christ, you even have your own parades.

SIDNEY. Well, they're not *all* that popular. They don't exactly close all the schools and the banks just yet.

DIANA. Well, thank God we came out of it still friends . . . And I *am* glad to see you, Sid. And you look very well. I mean that sincerely.

SIDNEY. I feel well.

DIANA. No, you don't look as though you *feel* well. You look as though you look well.

SIDNEY. Really? Well, that Grecian sun does wonders for covering our minor flaws.

DIANA. Yes, I suppose it would. *(SHE drinks.)* And whose Grecian son are you seeing these days? . . . Oh, Sidney. I said something bitchy. That means we're feeling comfortable with each other again.

(SHE refills her vodka.)

SIDNEY. Two vodkas before lunch. That's new, isn't it?

DIANA. They said on the plane to drink plenty of liquids to avoid jet lag . . . Why didn't you write, Sid?

SIDNEY. Sorry. I did write once but your press people must have intervened. I received a nice autographed photo.

DIANA. How can you stay cooped up on that little island? Does anyone know how truly funny you are?

SIDNEY. Oh, I have my moments. Last week in a little coffee shop in the hills of Mykonos, someone asked me who my favorite Greek philosopher was and I said Acidophilus.

DIANA. (Laughs.) There you go. Did they laugh?

SIDNEY. Not boisterously. They were shepherds. But they did knock their poles together quite respectfully.

DIANA. . . . I don't mean to be pushy, Sid, but are you going to be living on Mickey Mouse forever?

SIDNEY. Well . . . that rather depends on the rest of this conversation.

DIANA. I sense something important coming up.

SIDNEY. Yes, I have a favor to ask.

DIANA. Thank God, Sidney. You finally need me for something. What is it?

SIDNEY. There's this—friend in Mykonos.

DIANA. Yes, there would be, wouldn't there? . . . Is he a Toyota or an Infinity?

SIDNEY. He's Swiss, actually.

DIANA. I see. Keeps your watches running on time, does he?

SIDNEY. No. He's an artist. A sculptor, actually.

DIANA. A Swiss sculptor? Doesn't work in chocolate, does he?

SIDNEY. How'd you guess? Does a thriving little business making the Seven Dwarfs, with nuts.

DIANA. I'm sorry, Sidney. I couldn't resist.

SIDNEY. He's a modern abstractionist. Does rather large pieces in stone. Doesn't sell much now but in fifty years they'll be worth a fortune.

DIANA. And you need a favor. Alright, Sidney, I'll buy a dozen large ones. It'll help stabilize my house during earthquakes . . . Are you so strapped for cash? Why didn't you take money from me when I offered it?

SIDNEY. I thought your settlement was generous enough. The television series came after me. That was your doing. I only gave you half a marriage, I admit. I didn't think I was entitled to half your profits.

DIANA. Neither did I . . . Tell me about him.

SIDNEY. We've been living together for about six years.

DIANA. . . . Are you happy?

SIDNEY. Mostly.

DIANA. That's all? Mostly?

SIDNEY. A gay marriage is no more ideal than any other. Even buffalo squabble.

DIANA. Are you saying you're married?

SIDNEY. Well, we didn't go as far as taking vows. But we did have a shower.

DIANA. (*Looks at him in disbelief*) . . . You had a *shower*??

SIDNEY. (*HE laughs.*) No, for crise sakes. But if you're going to tweak me, I'm going to tweak you.

DIANA. . . . But you do care for each other.

SIDNEY. Enormously.

DIANA. I'm glad. No, I really am. Your happiness is important to me. I hope "enormously" continues.

SIDNEY. Yes, well, we've hit a snag.

DIANA. Oh, dear. Trouble in Paradise?

SIDNEY. I'm afraid so.

DIANA. Not the kind of trouble *we* had, I hope. I mean he's not cheating with some woman, is he? That would be pointless. The three of us going around in endless circles chasing the wrong gender . . . Now that's funny, isn't it, Sid? . . . Tell me.

SIDNEY. He's ill.

DIANA. Oh, I see. How ill?

SIDNEY. Very.

DIANA. I'm sorry. It's not that damned plague, is it?

SIDNEY. No. Just your common garden variety of lung cancer. He's been smoking since he was nine.

DIANA. A young man, I suppose.

SIDNEY. Relatively. He's forty-eight . . . you look surprised.

DIANA. I am. I misjudged you . . . You don't know how often I've worried about you. Half of everyone we started working with are gone . . . You're positive it's not *AIDS*?

SIDNEY. The doctor in Athens assured us. Why? Would that make a difference?

DIANA. In terms of *your* health, it might. What's the prognosis?

SIDNEY. He has about six months.

DIANA. How is he taking it?

SIDNEY. Despite his Greek philosophical belief in Gods, he's angry and he's frightened. He wants very much to live but one walnut-shaped tumor stands in his way.

DIANA. I'd like to help, if I can, Sid. I know a genius doctor in L.A. If it's treatable at all, this is the man to see. I can call today.

SIDNEY. Thank you. Unfortunately he's beyond geniuses. The walnut has spread like diseased oak through his body. I need to make him comfortable. I need to do something for him to repay what he's done for *me* these past six years. I need money and I need it now. I'm willing to cut a deal with you, Diana, if that's how they say it today.

DIANA. What kind of deal?

SIDNEY. Whatever shared property we still own, I will sign over to you. The alimony checks, which I greedily but readily accepted, will stop as soon as he's gone. As a Swiss who hasn't been there in thirty years, he doesn't qualify for medical benefits . . . Subsidize the last months of his life, in a way I think he deserves, and I will never ask another thing of you, money or otherwise, for the rest of my life.

DIANA. I see . . . I get to give him a Viking's funeral and in return, we cut off every known contact with each other forever . . . Jesus! Don't you know those checks I send you every month were the last vestige of holding us together? Slim, I admit, but once a month, twelve times a year, I at least had the satisfaction of writing my name on the same piece of paper as yours . . . I will take care of your friend, Sidney. I will send him flying to heaven on first class, if you want, but I'll cut no deals with you. I had half a marriage and a pen pal relationship afterwards, don't offer me goodbye in exchange.

SIDNEY. You're right, of course. I'm not very good at asking for things.

DIANA. I am *angry*, Sidney. And astonished at your insensitivity. The day you left our little flat, you pecked my cheek and smiled fetchingly at the door. You never were overly demonstrative but after sixteen years together, I expected at least a hint of heartbreak from you. And now when you talk about your friend, your lover, your spouse for the past six years, I was touched. I was moved at how much you cared, especially now that he's leaving you. Being left is the only thing you and I have in common now. And if I had gotten one-eighth of the affection you have for him now instead of the half a marriage I got then, I would feel as important to you as your dying Swiss friend on Mykonos. Some people get all the breaks.

SIDNEY. Yes. Well, fairness isn't distributed very well, is it? If it's any consolation, he doesn't think I'm demonstrative enough either. And if he knew I was begging on his behalf now, he would gladly die before I got home.

DIANA. Really? . . . What's his name?

SIDNEY. Maria.

DIANA. (*Looks at him.*) Maria? As in "I just met a girl named Maria"?

SIDNEY. No. As in Erich Maria Remarque. Teutonic bloodline. I call him Max. Except when we argue. Then I call him Maria.

DIANA. Maybe that was our problem, Sid. We never had funny names for each other . . . How did you meet him?

SIDNEY. I was going to Mykonos on a three-day holiday. We met on the boat.

DIANA. And you stayed for six years? You mean you packed that much clothing?

SIDNEY. Greek islands are pretty much informal. Mostly sandals and Tragedy T-shirts . . . I'm sorry. I feel a bit chilled. Do you think I can have a brandy?

DIANA. (*Gets up, crosses to bar.*) This is not Greece, Sidney. It's London in December. If you're going to wear a light linen jacket, at least wear four of them. (*SHE pours the brandy.*) Do you have a photograph of Maria . . . Do you mind if I call him Max?

SIDNEY. Yes, I think I have one here somewhere.

(*He takes out billfold.*)

DIANA. May I see it?

SIDNEY. If you like.

(He takes out a snapshot and hands it to her. SHE hands him the brandy. HE downs the brandy.)

DIANA. *(Looks at it.)* I've underrated you, Sidney. I expected a bronzed Apollo. Instead you've gone for a short, balding gentleman with character in his face. Beautiful smile, though. Warm and intelligent. You're looking a bit grim here, aren't you?

SIDNEY. Yes. I was just getting over the flu.

DIANA. When was this taken?

SIDNEY. About three months ago.

DIANA. Holding up very well, isn't he?

SIDNEY. Yes. Well, you know the Swiss. They sunbathe under avalanches . . . I like your secretary very much. Take good care of you, does she?

DIANA. Grace is indispensable to me.

SIDNEY. *(Putting away billfold.)* Been with you long?

DIANA. Almost four years.

SIDNEY. And devoted, I can tell.

DIANA. Of course. I pay her enough.

SIDNEY. You could pay her less and she would still be as devoted.

DIANA. She's American, darling. She expects raises on every holiday.

SIDNEY. Try her. She would stay if you offered her a bed and watercress sandwiches.

DIANA. *(It dawns on her.)* What are you saying?

SIDNEY. You *know* what I'm saying. I have uncanny instincts about these things.

DIANA. Grace? Don't be ridiculous. She's always looking to fix me up with attractive men.

SIDNEY. She wants you to be happy, love.

DIANA. And wants me as well? Is that what you're saying?

SIDNEY. *(Smiles.)* More or less.

DIANA. Oh, Christ, Sidney. Have I gone and done it again? What is it? Do I attract it?

SIDNEY. I think it's wonderful. Perhaps she's the other half of what I couldn't give you.

DIANA. I'm not interested in two halves of something I don't need . . . Why does everyone in the world come in parts today?

SIDNEY. Easier to ship, I suppose . . . *(HE takes out a hanky and wipes his brow.)* Diana, would you mind awfully if we skipped lunch? I think I've caught a chill.

DIANA. You looked peaked when you came in. I noticed it right off. *(Feels his head.)* Might have a slight temperature as well.

SIDNEY. I'm just queasy. I had fish and chips for dinner last night, for old times sake. The stomach really doesn't care much for nostalgia.

DIANA. Let me get you something, No, I'll call Grace. She's a walking chemist's shop.

SIDNEY. No, I'm fine. I swear. If you want the truth, it's been a strain worrying about Max.

DIANA. You're sweating, Sidney. I'll order you some tea. If I can't be your wife or mistress, at least let me be your mother.

(HE lies back on sofa, head on the arm.)

SIDNEY. If you just let me rest a moment, it'll pass . . . Don't look at me like that. You're over-reacting. A result of being on TV for eight years.

DIANA. . . . Why didn't you bring Max to London with you?

SIDNEY. I came to borrow money, not to spend it on British Airways.

DIANA. Why didn't you have him see a specialist here?

SIDNEY. Because he saw a specialist *there.*

DIANA. No one loved Greece more than Onassis, but when he was ill, he came to England for help.

SIDNEY. Of course he did. He owned the ships, the airlines and probably the hospitals . . . I'm telling you, Diana, Max's case is hopeless.

DIANA. *(Points to phone.)* Call your waterfront cafe and have him come on the next plane. I don't care if he's on a stretcher, I'll pay for everything. You know I will.

SIDNEY. He wants to die in Greece.

DIANA. And where do *you* want to die, Sidney?

SIDNEY. I don't care. I'd rather read a book and have someone tell me when it's over.

DIANA. You said you'd be in London for a few days before I arrived. What did you do here?

SIDNEY. What did I *do?* I bought some new books. Looked up

some old chums. I bought some medicine for Max I couldn't get in Mykonos.

DIANA. You were at the doctors, weren't you? . . . *WEREN'T YOU??* (HE *stares at her blankly.*) Oh Christ, it's you, Sidney, isn't it? Not Max. It's *you*!!

SIDNEY. No. I swear. Of course I saw a few doctors. I talked to them. Whatever I could learn to help Max, that's all.

DIANA. Don't lie to me, Sidney. Please. I don't want to believe it but just tell me the truth. Don't leave me out of this . . . It's you, isn't it?

SIDNEY. What difference does it make? Either way I lose Max, don't I?

DIANA. Oh, God. Oh, God, Sidney . . . Oh God, no, no.

SIDNEY. I'm sorry. If you weren't so stubborn, I would have gotten the money and been out of here in the clear.

DIANA. Why didn't you tell me? When it first appeared, why didn't you call me? I could have helped you. I could have done something.

SIDNEY. I'm not sure. I kept it from Max as long as I could. Even kept it from myself, to tell the truth. As you say, I'm not very demonstrative.

DIANA. Then why all these lies about Max? If you didn't want help, why did you drag yourself all the way to London?

SIDNEY. He's penniless. Whatever you sent me is what we live on . . . The reason I came is because I care so much for Max. And for his kindness and devotion, I was hoping to leave him a modest pension.

DIANA. This is unreal. I don't accept it. Maybe you're not going to fight this, Sidney, but I am. You're coming back to Los Angeles with me.

SIDNEY. No, I can't do that.

DIANA. I'm not asking you. I'm telling you. I'm calling Grace. We'll get the Concorde this afternoon. We can be in Los Angeles tonight.

SIDNEY. I have affairs to settle in Mykonos.

DIANA. You have affairs to settle with me. We're cutting a deal, Sidney. No Los Angeles, no pension for Max.

SIDNEY. Are you telling me I'm your prisoner?

DIANA. We've been prisoners since the day we met. (*Picks up phone, dials.)* Miss Grace Chapman, please. *(To SIDNEY.)* I'm telling you once and for all, Sidney, under no circumstances will you die on me.

SIDNEY. Ever?

DIANA. Ever.

SIDNEY. Sounds tedious, doesn't it?

DIANA. *(Into phone.)* Grace? It's me. I want to book three seats on today's Concorde. Then make direct connections to L.A. . . . No, the press tour is off. My ratings in Bucharest are not a priority just now . . . And call Dr. Leonard Ganz at Cedars-Sinai. I need to speak to him as soon as possible . . . No, I'm fine . . . Grace, I'm fine, stop worrying.

(SHE hangs up.)

SIDNEY. Told you about her, didn't I?

DIANA. I'm not sure I'll get through this, Sidney.

SIDNEY. You'll have to, angel. I'm otherwise occupied.

DIANA. We must do things, Sidney. We have to fill our days with diversions. We'll do giant jigsaw puzzles. The kind that take years to put together. You're so disciplined, you would never die until we finish it.

SIDNEY. You know what I always fancied? To draw, to paint, to sculpt. I'd like to leave something permanent behind besides someone saying, "He dressed well, didn't he?"

DIANA. We have to do normal things. Normal everyday things we never had time for but always promised we'd do together one day. Tell me what you need, Sid, and I'll get it. I promise.

SIDNEY. Max. I need Max. He'll be no bother and he could teach us to sculpt. He does give lessons, you know. We'll pay him, of course. He'll earn his pension. It's not part of the deal. It's a request.

DIANA. *(SHE sits beside him and puts her arms around him.)* Of course. We'll all be together. You, me, Max and Grace. Can't you just see *that* story in *People* magazine? "TV star takes in dying gay ex-husband, his male lover Maria and her devoted female secretary who turns out to be a cowboy."

SIDNEY. And we'll go on those daytime talk shows. And people will call in from Omaha and Memphis and ask questions like, "I know you people are all disgusting but your life seems so interesting."

DIANA. But that's just it, Sidney. We're not disgusting. We're actually quite normal in today's world.

SIDNEY. What will it be like in a hundred years?

DIANA. Ask me then and I'll tell you . . . Sidney, I swear, you're looking better already.

SIDNEY. I *feel* better . . . Aren't we lucky that something like this came along?

(GO TO BLACK.)

SCENE TWO

The Man on the Floor

(In the dark, we hear the drone of a large jet. Then we hear the voice of a British Airways pilot.)

PILOT. . . . Ladies and Gentlemen, we should be landing in Heathrow, London, in about forty minutes . . . If you wish to adjust your watches, the time in London is now nine forty-two A.M. . . . Weather in London will be clear, sunny and cool . . . Thank you.

MARK. You hear that? Clear, sunny and cool. Perfect day for Wimbledon.

ANNIE. Have you got the Wimbledon tickets?

MARK. I've got them.

ANNIE. Are you sure?

MARK. I'm sure.

ANNIE. Don't you want to look?

MARK. I don't have to look. I've got the Wimbledon tickets.

(The hotel suite. About noon on a hot day in July.
The bedroom and living room are in disarray.
Three suitcases are on the floor in the bedroom, one on the bed.
They are all open, most of the clothes have been pulled out,
half in suitcase, half out. A clothes bag hangs from a hook on a
wall. It is unzipped and the clothes pulled half out.

MARK FERRIS is sitting on the edge of the bed, exhausted from looking. HE has a shirt in one hand and four pairs of socks in the other. HE wears a pair of light summer trousers and a sports shirt and loafers. HE is spent, exhausted, defeated and furious.

ANNIE, his wife, is rummaging in a suitcase. SHE is wearing a skirt and a blouse, half hanging out. SHE has no shoes on. SHE too is exhausted from looking everywhere.)

MARK. They're gone, I'm telling you. There's no place left to look.

ANNIE. There is *always* another place to look.

MARK. Like where?

ANNIE. Where? At home. Maybe you left the tickets at home.

MARK. In Los Angeles? . . . Alright. You look there, I'll look in London.

ANNIE. Hey, don't take this out on me, Mark. Every time something like this happens, you take it out on me.

MARK. Do you know how *hard* it was for me to get those tickets? . . . Two seats, six rows behind the Duke and Duchess of Kent . . . and Royalty never stands up. We'd have an unblocked view.

ANNIE. *(Looks at strewn clothes.)* Why did you have to pull everything out of our luggage? Now you mixed up *my* clothes with your clothes.

MARK. *(HE looks at luggage.)* . . . You know something . . . I think maybe this isn't our luggage.

ANNIE. What are you talking about? These are all our clothes, aren't they?

MARK. *Everybody* in Los Angeles dresses like this . . . Last time I fly on *that* Goddamn airline.

ANNIE. You're out of control, Mark.

MARK. I'm supposed to be out of control. Who in their right mind would be in control at a time like this? What am I, a Buddhist?

ANNIE. You screamed at the airlines, at the bellboys, at the closets, at the luggage, at the pockets in your suits and now you're screaming at me. You asked me five times to look in my purse. They're not in my purse. *I WON'T BE SCREAMED AT!!* . . . I'm going down for some tea until you get a hold of yourself.

*(SHE puts on one black shoe and one tan shoe.
Starts for living room, then out the door.)*

MARK. *(Yells after her.)* You're the one who never remembers where you parked your car. Not me. *(SHE slams the door. HE goes back in and looks at the room.)* . . . Alright, we walked in, the bell-boy put our bags in the bedroom. Then I say, better check to see if I have everything . . . I look in my pants pocket. I have my wallet, have my money, I have my keys. I look in my jacket, I have my pass-port, I have our plane tickets, I have my Wimbledon tickets. *(Touches himself where his pocket would be.)* No, don't have my Wimbledon tickets. *(Very calm, very confident.)* Okay. So where would they be? . . . Where would the tickets be? . . . What did I do with the Wimbledon tickets? *(HE stands there calmly, his eyes roam around the room, then HE screams.)* I DON'T KNOW!! THEY'RE NOT HERE! . . . THEY'RE GONE! . . . THEY'RE LOST! *(HE picks up pillow from sofa and punches it.)* God damn you, you stu-pid schmuck!! *(And HE flings the pillow in a fury down on the sofa. As soon as HE does, HE yells in pain and freezes. HE is bent over, unable to move.)* Oh, God! Oh, Jesus! Oh, no . . . Oh, Christ . . . This is a bad one . . . This is a three weeker . . . This is traction . . . this is surgery . . . this is walking with a walker. *(HE tries to kneel down and grab the table for support.)* You had to go for tea, heh? You know how long tea is going to take? I'll be a Goddamn statue by then . . . Annie, I need you. Where are you, Annie? *(HE is near tears. HE lowers himself to his knees. Very carefully and painfully. HE's on his knees now. The telephone rings. The phone is on a table about four feet away from him.)* Jesus. That's twelve miles from here. *(HE starts to edge toward it. The pain is excruciating. The phone rings again.)* Don't hang up. Please don't hang up. *(The phone rings again.)* Don't hang up. Please don't hang up. *(The phone rings again.)* I'm coming. Wait for me. I'm coming. *(HE is now crawling on his hands and knees. It is beyond pain. HE inches closer on all fours. The phone rings again. Now HE reaches up slowly. His hand can reach the table but not quite the phone. His fingers stretch out. It rings again . . . His hand is only an inch away now . . . The phone stops ringing.)* You couldn't wait. It would have killed you to wait one more ring, right? *(Still on his knees, HE holds on to the table with one hand and dials the phone with the other one, dialing 0. HE waits.)* Operator? . . . This is Mr. Ferris in . . . in . . . I don't know where I'm in . . . 402? . . . Right. Thank you . . . I have a problem here. My back just went out . . . I'm going to need a doctor . . . A back doctor . . . A spine doctor . . . A specialist lower spine back doctor . . . And my wife. I need my wife . . . She's somewhere downstairs having tea . . . She's wearing a black shoe and a light tan shoe . . . Would you tell her her husband's on his knees and he can't move . . . She'll know. She's been through it before . . . Thank you. Please hurry. *(HE hangs up just as his strength goes and HE lets go of the table and falls to the floor. HE is on his side, facing the audience. The phone rings. HE looks at the audience for help, then looks at the phone.)* Why are phones in hotels always so high? *(HE starts to pull himself up slowly. The phone rings again. He finally grabs it.)* Hello? . . . No, Mrs. Ferris isn't here. Who's calling . . . *Mr. Ferris is calling?* . . . No, that's me. I said she was downstairs drinking tea . . . *Downstairs!* . . . I'm sorry. I can't hang on anymore. I'm slipping into hell . . . Goodbye. *(He hangs up and slips down into hell. The doorbell rings.)* Annie? Is that you? . . . I'm on the floor. Use your key. *(The doorbell rings again.)* She hasn't got a key . . . She's got a blow dryer and a portable iron but she doesn't have a key. *(The doorbell rings again.)* THE DOORBELL ISN'T GOING TO HELP!! ONLY A KEY WILL HELP!!

    (A key in the door, it opens. MRS. SITGOOD, the associate manager, peers in. SHE doesn't see MARK yet.)

SITGOOD. *(A pleasant Scottish woman with a very Scottish accent.)* Mr. Ferris? It's Mrs. Sitgood, the associate manager. May I come in?

MARK. Down here. On the floor.

SITGOOD. *(Comes in, sees him on the floor.)* Oh, Dear. I'm so sorry. How awful for you. Fortunately, I was on the floor above when the operator called me . . . You look dreadfully uncomfortable. Your back, eh? They say swimming is very good for it.

MARK. Yes. But I forgot to ask for a suite with a pool.

SITGOOD. I can well sympathize with you. We get these fairly often at the hotel. Especially after long flights. Our Doctor McMer-lin is on his way. He's an absolute magician with backs.

MARK. McMerlin the Magician?

SITGOOD. Yes. We had the chief of the Japanese Consulate come in with his back so twisted, he asked to have his trunk put on his back and three of his aides sit on it.

MARK. Did it help his back?

SITGOOD. Yes, but it broke his ribs . . . Well, I know this is an awkward time to be talking about our problem, but we have it straightened away now and I'm sure you're going to be very pleased. It was our mistake and for that, I hold myself personally responsi-ble, Mr. Ferris.

MARK. What mistake?

SITGOOD. The rooms. The mix-up with the rooms.

MARK. What mix-up?

SITGOOD. I thought you were told. Oh, dear. They were sup-posed to phone you. You didn't get a call?

MARK. I got one call that I missed by a quarter of an inch . . . and a second call from myself looking for my wife.

SITGOOD. I see. Well, let me explain. Our Mr. Hobwick, who is new to us, inadvertently gave you this suite. We've been literally swamped with reservations, what with Wimbledon and the Cricket test matches going on, it's a wonder we didn't have more confusion than we did. Your suite is actually 602 and 604, but since that might be a bit of a trek for you in your condition, I did some mas-terful juggling and I've arranged for you to have suite 420 and 422, just down the end of the hall and is actually a larger suite than this. Would that suit you Mr. Ferris?

(HE *looks at her as if* SHE's *mad.*)

MARK. . . . Down the hall? . . . Mrs. Sitgood, as you may have noticed, I'm talking to you from the floor. The floor is the only thing that stopped me from landing in the lobby.

SITGOOD. Oh, we'll cause you no further discomfort. We'll pack up and move your things, of course.

MARK. You mean my things will be in 422 while I'm here in 4-0-2?

SITGOOD. No, no. We're sending up a wheelchair for you.

MARK. Mrs. Sitgood, as you can see, the only things moving now are my lips . . . I don't think I could be lifted into a wheelchair. The only way I could get into a wheelchair is for you to wheel the chair into the room below, raise the chair to the ceiling, then quickly remove the ceiling while I am lowered into the chair.

SITGOOD. Yes, I see. It *is* a problem. And we won't move you until we're sure it's safe . . . The thing is, this suite has been reserved since last March for Mr. Kevin Costner . . . The film star, you know.

MARK. Yes, I know.

SITGOOD. *The Wolf Dancer?* Awfully good.

MARK. *Dances With Wolves.* Yes, very good.

SITGOOD. He's waiting in the lounge now having some tea. I explained matters to him and he's being most patient, I must say.

MARK. . . . Can't you give him another suite?

SITGOOD. Well, we've already booked 602 and 604. There are no other suites.

MARK. Well, build one and he will come . . . Mrs. Sitgood, if you could get velvet covered ball bearings underneath me, I would gladly be rolled into 422. But until I see the doctor, I am part of this room.

SITGOOD. Yes, I understand. Well, let's wait for the doctor's report. I'll speak to Mr. Costner and explain things to him.

MARK. Why don't you give *him* Suite 422?

SITGOOD. Well, because he always stays in this suite. 402 is his favorite.

MARK. You could change the numbers on the door.

SITGOOD. Well, he's very bright. I'm sure he'd notice the difference. (*The doorbell rings.*) Ah. Let's hope that's our Doctor McMerlin.

(SHE *crosses to door, opens it. ANNIE comes in quickly, looks down at MARK.*)

ANNIE. (*To MARK.*) What did I tell you? What did I say to you? You see what happens when you get out of control? *How many times do we have to go through this?*

MARK. Mrs. Sitgood, this is my wife. She's a psychotherapist.

SITGOOD. How do you do. I'm the associate manager. The doctor should be here any moment.

ANNIE. The doctor?

MARK. McMerlin the Magician.

SITGOOD. Is there anything I can get for you?

ANNIE. Wimbledon tickets would be nice. We lost ours.

SITGOOD. Oh, dear. If they're still in the room, I could send our boy up to look. He's very good at finding things. Last year he found twelve pairs of contact lenses. (*The phone rings.*) Shall I get that?

ANNIE. Please. I'll get the pills.

(*SHE crosses into bedroom. SITGOOD crosses to the phone, stepping right next to MARK.*)

MARK. *AAAAAGGGGGHHHHH!!!*

(*HE holds his finger in pain.*)

ANNIE. (*In bedroom.*) God, what a mess.

SITGOOD. (*Into phone.*) Hello? . . . Ah, splendid. Send him up. Oooh. Ooooh. (*SHE hangs up.*) Mr. Costner is getting a wee bit impatient. Doctor's on his way. Don't get your spirits down. Chin up.

MARK. My chin *is* up.

SITGOOD. Ah, so it is . . . Well, I'm away now.

(*Steps on his hand as she crosses.*)

MARK. (*Screams.*) OWWW!!

SITGOOD. Sorry. ·

ANNIE *comes in from bedroom. SHE carries a small leather bag.*)

ANNIE. What was that about Mr. Costner?

SITGOOD. The film star. *The Wolf Dancer.* Awfully good.

(*SHE goes.*)

MARK. Kevin Costner. This is his suite.

ANNIE. What are you saying? We're going to be staying with Kevin Costner?

MARK. Only if his back goes out.

ANNIE. You better take a pill. Which one do you want? *(SHE unzips bag.)* A darvocet, a percocet or a percodan?

MARK. I'll have a darvocet . . . and a percocet and a percodan.

ANNIE. You'll be sleeping here till February. Here's a percocet. Open your mouth. *(HE opens his mouth. SHE puts pill in.)* Don't swallow yet. I'll get some water.

(SHE rushes to bar.)

MARK. You couldn't get the water firtht? *(SHE quickly pours water in glass, rushes back to MARK.)* Hurry up. It'th ditholving. My tongue ith getting paralythed.

(SHE kneels beside him.)

ANNIE. I'll have to raise your head.

(SHE raises it a little.)

MARK. *DON'T RAITHE MY HEAD!!* *(SHE drops his head.)* You never lift a perthonth head with a back injury. Jethuth Chritht!!

ANNIE. I'm sorry, I'll just trickle a few drops in your mouth. Here we go. *(SHE holds plastic bottle above head and pours water in his mouth.)* Did you swallow?

MARK. *(Nods.)* The water went down. The pill is in my wind-pipe.

ANNIE. Drink some more water.

MARK. *No! I'll drown.*

(The doorbell rings.)

ANNIE. Leave it there. It'll dissolve. *(SHE rushes to door, opens it. A BELLMAN stands there in uniform.)* Doctor Magician?

BELLMAN. No, ma'am. I'm the bellman. Mrs. Sitgood sent me up to look for your Wimbledon tickets. *(Looks down at MARK.)* Sorry, didn't mean to wake you, sir.

ANNIE. (*To BELLMAN.*) Just look for the tickets in there, please.

(*The BELLMAN nods, crosses into bedroom and starts to look.
The doorbell rings. ANNIE quickly opens the door. DR McMER-
LIN enters with his little black bag. HE is Irish.*)

DOCTOR. (*A cheerful man.*) Hello. Dr. McMerlin.

ANNIE. I'm Mrs. Ferris. That's my husband down there.

DOCTOR. (*Looks at MARK*) Aha! You're the one with the back trouble, eh?

ANNIE. Yes. He can't move.

DOCTOR. (*Chuckles.*) Can't move, eh? . . . Jest went out, did it?

ANNIE. Yes. It happens when he gets upset.

DOCTOR. I see . . . Can he talk?

ANNIE. Yes, he can . . . Mark, talk for the doctor.

MARK. I was waiting for you to get through.

DOCTOR. Well, that's a start, eh? (*To MARK.*) Know what you're going through. Had it myself many times. Many, many times. Gets so bad, want to put a bullet through your head. (*MARK attempts a weak laugh. DOCTOR, to ANNIE.*) I'm going to need a chair, Mrs. Ferris. Straight back, very *firm* seat.

MARK. I don't think I can sit up.

DOCTOR. It's for me. (*ANNIE looks for a chair, finds one.*) Could be a lot worse. Bloody hot outside, nice and cool in here, eh? (*SHE puts chair down for DOCTOR.*) Ah, thank you. (*HE sits. To MARK.*) Well, let's have a look, shall we? I'm going to lift your leg, Mr. Ferris. I want you to relax and I'll need you to trust me. Will you trust me?

MARK. I'll tell you after you lift my leg.

DOCTOR. Fair enough. Now tell me the *moment* you feel some pain. Here we go. (*HE lifts the leg about three inches before MARK screams in agony. HE drops the leg.*) Well, that's a quick response, wasn't it? How would you describe the pain, Mr. Ferris?

MARK. You mean when you lifted my leg?

DOCTOR. Yes. (*MARK screams the way HE screamed before.*) Very well put . . . Would you say you had a high tolerance for pain or a low tolerance?

MARK. High tolerance for pain. Low tolerance for lifting my leg.

DOCTOR. Very graphically described. I love American humor. Full of gusto and self-deprecation. Laugh in the face of agony and despair. Very Irish that is. Do you have any Irish in you?

MARK. No. Just the percocet.

DOCTOR. Well, we can't leave you down there, can we? Do you think if your wife and I assisted you, we could get you across to the other room and into your bed?

MARK. Couldn't I just have a shot to put me out?

DOCTOR. Yes, but you see if you're unconscious and we try to lift you to the bed, without your vocal capacity to tell us we're exceeding your limits, we could do permanent, irreparable lifetime damage. I don't mean to frighten you.

MARK. And yet somehow you've succeeded.

(BELLMAN looks in from bedroom.)

BELLMAN. Mrs. Ferris! Beg pardon, Mrs. Ferris.

ANNIE. You found the tickets?

BELLMAN. No, but I found a pair of contact lenses.

DOCTOR. Ah, there's our answer. You look to be a strapping fellow. *(To BELLMAN.)* Young man, bring a blanket in here and give us a hand. *(BELLMAN nods and goes to bedroom closet, brings down a blanket.)* Here's what we'll do. We'll put you in the blanket, then pull you gently into the bedroom, then cradle you up to the bed. Does that concern you in any way?

MARK. In *every* way. There is no part in anything you said that doesn't concern me.

ANNIE. He's just trying to help, Mark.

DOCTOR. Come on, let's give it a go. It'll be over before you can say Michael McCarthy. *(To BELLMAN.)* Now spread the blanket out on the floor next to Mr. Ferris. *(DOCTOR and BELLMAN spread blanket on floor.)* This will work, I promise you, Mr. Ferris. *(To BELLMAN.)* Alright, onto the blanket we go.

(DOCTOR and BELLMAN prepare to roll him onto blanket.)

MARK. I can expect this to hurt, right?

DOCTOR. *(Smiles.)* You can bloody well depend on it.

MARK. You've done this before, haven't you?

DOCTOR. I will have after this time. Grab him by the shoulder, boy.

(*THEY roll him onto blanket.*)

MARK. *MICHAEL McCARTHY MICHAEL McCARTHY MICHAEL BLOODY McCARTHY!*

DOCTOR. (*To MARK.*) There you go. Grand job, lad. Now Mrs. Ferris, we'll have to back into the bedroom. You stand behind and give us directions. When you say to go right, we'll go right. When you say go left, we'll go left.

ANNIE. Wait!! When you say go right, doesn't that mean *left* in England?

DOCTOR. (*Thinks about that.*) Yes, but we're not going out into traffic. (*To BELLMAN.*) Grab the blanket, boy. (*HE and the BELLMAN grab the end of the blanket.*) Now don't forget to breathe. Are we ready? One-two-three-*LIFT OFF!!* (*the DOCTOR and BELLMAN pull the blanket. The telephone rings.*) Don't stop now, boy.

ANNIE. I'll get that. (*SHE rushes to phone. DOCTOR and BELL-MAN crash against sofa. Into phone.*) Hello? Yes?

DOCTOR. We lost contact with our control tower.

ANNIE. (*Into phone.*) No, he found his wife. I'm here.

(*SHE hangs up, rushes into bedroom.
DOCTOR and BELLMAN pull him through door.*)

DOCTOR. My God, it's like pulling a month's load of laundry. Stop! All full stop! We made it. (*MARK is on the floor on the audience side of the bed. HE's exhausted.*) Grand job, Mr. Ferris. And you never said Michael McCarthy once.

MARK. No, but I whispered *your* name a few times.

ANNIE. How do we get him up on the bed?

DOCTOR. (*Looks.*) Aye! There's the rub . . . What do you think, Mr. Ferris?

MARK. Forget it. I'll stay here at Camp Three. You and your Sherpas can go on.

DOCTOR. I think the gentleman is right. I think we'll let him rest here and I'll look in tonight . . . Just try this for me, Mr. Ferris. Try to turn your body just a little to the right. Easy now.

MARK. *(Turns to the right.)* Oi-oi-oi-oi-oi-oi-oi . . .

DOCTOR. Good man. Now turn to the left.

MARK. *(Turns to the left.)* Oi-oi-oi-oi-oi-oi-oi . . .

DOCTOR. Well done. Now on your back again.

MARK. *(Turns on his back.)* Oi-oi-oi-oi-oi-oi-oi . . .

ANNIE. That was good, wasn't it?

DOCTOR. Aye. If I could get my dog to do that, I'd be a happy man . . . I just want to feel your lower back once before I go. Don't move. *(HE kneels down.)* I'll just slide my hand under your back. *(HE slides his hand under MARK's back.)* Feels a bit looser to me.

(HE doesn't move.)

ANNIE. I'm so glad.

DOCTOR. The problem is . . . I can't get up.

BELLMAN. Let me help you, sir.

DOCTOR. *DON'T TOUCH ME!!* . . . It's out. My back is out!

MARK. Hurts like hell, doesn't it?

ANNIE. What should we do?

DOCTOR. Don't move me. Don't pick me up. Just lie me back on the floor. *(ANNIE and the BELLMAN start to lay him back slowly on the floor.)* MICHAEL McCARTHY MICHAEL McCARTHY MICHAEL BLOODY McCARTHY!

(He's down.)

MARK. You want a valium? Percocet? Percodan?

DOCTOR. Mrs. Ferris, if you would be good enough to call the concierge and ask him to call for Dr. Stein. He's my colleague. Frank Stein.

ANNIE. *(Picks up phone.)* Hello, concierge? Would you please call Dr. Frankenstein?

DOCTOR. Could you get me some aspirin, Mrs. Ferris? And it's Frank Stein. Not Frankenstein.

(ANNIE hangs up phone and crosses into bathroom. Doorbell rings.)

BELLMAN. I'll get that.

(*HE trips over DOCTOR and MARK, hits head on chair and falls flat. HE is out cold.*
We hear a crash in the bathroom.
Doorbell rings again.)

ANNIE. (*Comes out holding her head.*) I hit my head on the medicine cabinet.
MARK. Are you bleeding?
DOCTOR. Kneel down. Let me look at it.

(*SITGOOD enters.*)

ANNIE. I feel dizzy. Just let me sit a minute.

(*ANNIE falls across the bed.*)

SITGOOD. May I come in? . . . (*SHE goes in. Sees them sprawled out.*) Oh, dear. Am I interrupting? (*Covers eyes with her hand.*) . . . Is the doctor still examining you, Mr. Ferris?
MARK. Well, we're all taking turns.
SITGOOD. Well, I do have the most wonderful news. Mr. Costner saw Suite 422 and he likes it better than this one. So you don't have to bother moving. (*MARK, ANNIE and the DOCTOR nod their heads and moan.*) And I have more wonderful news. As Mrs. Ferris rushed out of the tea room, she dropped something . . . Mr. Costner picked it up. He found your Wimbledon tickets.
ANNIE. They *were* in my purse.
MARK. You wouldn't look in your purse. I *begged* you to look in your purse.

(*HE raises himself, leaning on the DOCTOR.*)

DOCTOR. *Don't lean on me! Don't lean on me!*

(*DOCTOR, MARK and ANNIE moan.*)

SITGOOD. *(To BELLMAN who is out cold.)* Bertram, you don't have to look anymore. We found the tickets.

(SHE slaps him with the tickets.
The lights dim quickly.)

CURTAIN

ABOUT THE AUTHOR

Neil Simon was born on July 4, 1927 in the Bronx, New York. After graduating from DeWitt Clinton High School, Simon managed to find time for writing while serving as a Corporal in the USAAF from 1945–46. Writing soon became his profession without the formalities of college (except for a few courses at NYU and at the University of Denver). His first theater work consisted of sketches for camp shows held in Tamiment, Pennsylvania, in collaboration with his brother, Danny. Simon then became a TV writer for Sid Caesar (*The Sid Caesar Show*) and Phil Silvers (*Sergeant Bilko*), an experience on which *Laughter on the 23rd Floor* is based.

On Broadway, Simon contributed sketches to *Catch a Star* (1955) and *New Faces* of 1956. His first Broadway play was *Come Blow Your Horn* (1961) followed by the book of the musical *Little Me* (1962). His next play, the comedy *Barefoot in the Park,* and *The Odd Couple* were still running when the musical *Sweet Charity* (for which Simon wrote the book) came along early in 1966, and all three of these plays continued their run when Simon's *The Star Spangled Girl* opened the following season in December of 1966— so that Simon had the phenomenal total of four shows running simultaneously on Broadway during the 1966–67 season. When the last of the four closed that summer, there had been a total of 3,367 performances over the four theater seasons.

Simon immediately began stacking another pile of blue chip shows. His *Plaza Suite* (1968) was named a Best Play of its year. His book of the musical *Promises, Promises* (1968) was another smash hit, and his *Last of the Red Hot Lovers* (1969) became his third show in grand simultaneous display on Broadway and his fourth Best Play. *Plaza Suite* closed before *The Gingerbread Lady* (1970, also a Best Play) opened so that Simon's second stack was "only" three plays and 3,084 performances high. There followed *The Prisoner of Second Avenue* (1971, a Best Play), *The Sunshine*

Boys (1972, a Best Play), *The Good Doctor* (1973, a Best Play) and *God's Favorite* (1974). There was not a new Neil Simon play on Broadway the following year because Simon was moving himself and his family from New York to California, partly for personal reasons and partly to base himself closer to his screen activities. By April of 1976, he had *California Suite* ready for production at the Center Theater Group in Los Angeles en route to the Eugene O'Neill Theater (which for a time he owned) in June, 1976 as his fifteenth Broadway script and ninth Best Play.

Simon's tenth Best Play was *Chapter Two*, also produced at the Center Theater Group before it came to New York in December, 1977. He wrote the book for *They're Playing Our Song*, the long-running musical with a Marvin Hamlisch score and Carole Bayer-Sager lyrics. His eleventh Best Play, *I Ought to Be in Pictures*, went the California-to-New York route during 1980. His shortest run New York play, *Fools* (1981), survived for only forty performances; and an attempt to revise and revive *Little Me* in 1982 also fell short of expectations with only thirty-six performances. However, Simon came roaring back in 1983 with the first of three semi-autobiographical works: *Brighton Beach Memoirs* (Critics' Award winner) with the character "Eugene Jerome" portraying Simon as an adolescent growing up in Brooklyn. This popular hit was still running when its sequel, the "Jerome-in-the-Army" Best Play, *Biloxi Blues*, opened in March, 1985, both plays taking the California-to-New York route. The third play in the series, *Broadway Bound*, was about Jerome's efforts at gag writing for radio in collaboration with his brother, which came in from Washington, D.C. tryouts to New York on December 4, 1986 and was Simon's twenty-fourth Broadway script and thirteenth Best Play.

Prior to his third in the Jerome series was a revised version of *The Odd Couple*—changing the two leading characters from men to women—which was produced on Broadway in June, 1985. After *Broadway Bound* came *Rumors* for 531 Broadway performances which began in November, 1988. *Rumors* had tried out at the old Globe Theater in San Diego, as did Simon's next play, *Jake's Women*, but he withdrew the latter in March, 1990, after one week of tryout performances. Yet the beat continued on with *Lost in Yonkers* which arrived on Broadway on February 21, 1991 after tryouts at the North Carolina School of the Arts and the National

Theater in Washington, D.C., Simon's twenty-seventh produced play script, fourteenth Best Play and Pulitzer Prize winner. *Lost in Yonkers* also won Simon the 1991 Tony Award as the season's Best Play. While *Lost in Yonkers* was still in the midst of its 780-performance run, *Jake's Women* began its 245-performance Broadway engagement on March 24, 1992. He adapted his 1977 film, *The Goodbye Girl,* into a musical which opened on Broadway, March 4, 1993 for 188 performances—Simon's twenty-ninth script and fifteenth Best Play. *Laughter on the 23rd Floor* opened on Broadway on November 22, 1993, following original performances at Duke University in Durham, North Carolina.

Simon wrote the screenplays for *Barefoot in the Park* (at that time, the longest runner at Radio City Music Hall), *The Odd Couple* (which broke that record the following year), *Plaza Suite, The Prisoner of Second Avenue, The Sunshine Boys, California Suite, Chapter Two, I Ought to Be in Pictures, Brighton Beach Memoirs, Biloxi Blues* and *Lost in Yonkers* as well as *The Out-of-Towners, The Heartbreak Kid, Murder by Death, The Goodbye Girl, The Cheap Detective, Seems Like Old Times, Only When I Laugh, Max Dugan Returns* and *The Slugger's Wife.*

Simon's many honors include the 1965 Tony Award as author of *The Odd Couple,* a special 1975 Tony for his overall contribution to the theater and the 1985 Tony for Best Play for *Biloxi Blues.* In 1991, he won his third Best Play Tony for *Lost in Yonkers,* and it was in that same year that he won the Pulitzer Prize for the same play. Simon holds Honorary Bachelor of Arts Degrees from both Hofstra University and Williams College. He received the Sam S. Schubert Award in 1968; Writers Guide Motion Pictures Awards in 1968, 1970 and 1975; and numerous Tony, Emmy and Oscar nominations. In 1983, Broadway's Alvin Theater was renamed The Neil Simon theater in his honor. In December of 1995, he received the Kennedy Center Honors in Washington, D.C. and in June of 1996, he received the UCLA Medal, which is the equivalent of an honorary degree. In December of 1996, Simon received the Peggy V. Helmerich Distinguished Author Award and in April of 1997, he received the award for Distinguished Achievement in the American Theater from the William Inge Theater Festival. The first part of Simon's memoirs, *Rewrites,* was published by Simon & Schuster in 1996. Simon is currently working on *The Odd Couple II—Travelin'*

Light, a feature film which is due out in 1998; *Proposals,* a new play due to open on Broadway in November of 1997; and *The Play Goes On,* the second volume of his memoirs. Simon has been thrice married, with two daughters, Ellen and Nancy, by his first wife. He lives in Los Angeles with his wife, Diane Lander-Simon, and daughter, Bryn Lander-Simon.